TM

Names and their Varieties:

a collection of essays
in onomastics

Compiled, with a Preface, by
Kelsie B. Harder

American Name Society

UNIVERSITY
PRESS OF
AMERICA

LANHAM • NEW YORK • LONDON

Copyright © 1986 by

University Press of America,® Inc.

4720 Boston Way
Lanham, MD 20706

3 Henrietta Street
London WC2E 8LU England

Printed in the United States of America

Co-published by arrangement with the
American Name Society

Library of Congress Cataloging in Publication Data
Main entry under title:

Names and their varieties.
  Includes bibliographical references.
  1. Onomastics—Addresses, essays, lectures.
I. Harder, Kelsie B.   II. American Name Society.
P323.N36   1986   412   85-29628
ISBN 0-8191-5232-3 (alk. paper)
ISBN 0-8191-5233-1 (pbk. : alk. paper)

Book Design: Dale Hobson

All University Press of America books are produced on acid-free
paper which exceeds the minimum standards set by the National
Historical Publications and Records Commission.

Preface

P323
N36
1986

Naming began at the dawn of language. Individuals, being separate entities, required labels which can only be communicated through sound — language. The differentiation of persons demanded some kind of fragmenting of sound so that one could be distinguished from another. The process is universal, since everyone has a name, in fact, many names. In earlier cultures, names tended to be occupational, such as Smith, Miller, Baker, Carpenter, or Tanner, many of which survive today with no connotation of the earlier division of labor. Some names described physical features, such as Calvin (bald), Redd (red-haired), Brown (complexion), Crane (long-legged), and many other survivors of the nicknaming custom. The place of habitation often became the personal name, such as Hill (for one who lived near a hill), Grove, Green (from a green place), Brook, Linden (lived at the linden tree), or Head (dweller at the head of a valley). Most of our names have such derivations, although the connotations have generally been lost, except as vocabulary. All help distinguish us from each other.

Place names arose from the need to establish space. Some philosophers claim that a place does not exist until it has a name. A type of measurement, a place name delineates boundaries, albeit somewhat vague ones, that separate places. Earlier places have now become generics, such as Tennessee River, with the specific being *Tennessee* and the generic *river*. Generics now name features, such as hill, mountain, creek, brook, valley, range, mound, reef, or beach. George R. Stewart has made a careful classification of the way the process works. His article, reprinted from an early issue of *Names* has been a strong influence on those who study place names.

Literary onomastics has developed rapidly as a discipline and as a way to decode texts. Usually, such studies become adjuncts to literary criticism, although the imaginative use of names reflects many aspects of a culture within social settings and, therefore, deviates sharply from formalistic criticism, which itself often reflects only the mind of the critic and not the intent of a text. The specificity of names will not allow such flights of fantasy, since names are rooted in the culture, somewhat fixed in connotation and societal restraints. Major writers, such as Shakespeare and Chaucer, as well as others, have been studied through the names they use to name characters and places.

Although much of the energy in the study of names has been expended on personal and place names, at least during the short times of the career of onomastics, lately other areas have been investigated, as the selection of articles reprinted here well indicate. No area is taboo for the study of names, including beer brands, folk names, industrial corporations, or anything else that bears a name. The volumes of the magazine *Names* contain many articles describing such naming processes.

The articles have been selected on the basis of variety so that some intimation of the large scope of the discipline can be shown. Such a selection obviously can only touch on the vast amount available from the pages of *Names*. Some excellent articles were omitted purely on the basis of lack of space, especially the many articles on naming customs in other countries. Some of the major technical articles have been omitted, not only because of space but because of their technical nature. Perhaps future collections will make such articles available to a wider audience.

The authors represent many scholarly fields, although all have in common a desire to further the study of names in all their aspects and categories. Elsdon C. Smith, probably the worlds foremost authority on personal names, is, for instance, a successful attorney. Also, he is a co-founder of the American Name Society. Others are geographers, linguists, teachers in several disciplines, folklorists, sociologists, one a free-lance writer with a speciality in musicology, and one a lexicographer. All have published extensively in onomastics. Indeed, the collection displays the lively interest in a phenomenon that is perhaps the most intimate concerning human beings and the objects and territory that surround them.

Inevitably, many persons become involved in the building of a book, even a collection of essays. First, my wife, Louise, who served as Executive Secretary of the American Name Society, has given continuous support to my study of names and to the many hours devoted to sometimes tedious tasks of simple recording. Next, the authors of the essays themselves are the indispensable contributors and deserve the greatest thanks and my gratitude. Professor L.R.N. Ashley made arrangements with the publisher and, with his boundless energy, continued to support the project to its conclusion. And to my collaborator and former student, Dale Hobson, poet and graphics designer, I owe the debt of the book. Without his guidance and technical knowledge, I could not have finished the compilation.

KH

Potsdam, New York
August 23, 1982

Table of Contents

M.S. Beeler, *America — The Story of a Name* 1

Zoltan J. Farkas, *The Challenge of the Name* **America** 15

George R. Stewart, *A Classification of Place Names* 23

Elsdon C. Smith, *The Name of God in the Revised Standard Version* 36

Allen B. Kellogg, *Nicknames and Nonce-names in Shakespeare's
Comedies* 41

O. Paul Straubinger, *Names in Popular Sayings* 45

Kemp Malone, *Meaningful Fictive Names in English Literature* 53

C.W. Wrenn, *The Name Bristol* 66

Thomas Pyles, *Bible Belt Onomastics or Some Curiosities of
Anti-Pedobaptist Nomenclature* 72

G. Thomas Fairclough, *New Light on Old Zion* 89

John Rydjord, *Falkland Islands: Nationalism and Names* 100

T.M. Pearce, *The Names of Objects in Aerospace* 114

Myron Brender, *Some Hypotheses About the Psychodynamic Significance
of Infant Name Selection* 124

John R. Krueger, *Beer Brand Names in the United States* 133

Hamill Kenny, *Place-Names on the Moon: A Report* 137

J. Boddewyn, *The Names of U.S. Industrial Corporations:
A Study in Change* 146

L.B. Salomon, *Lucifer's Landholdings in America* 160

Robert M. Rennick, *Obscene Names and Naming in Folk Tradition* 166

P. Burwell Rogers, *The Names of the Canterbury Pilgrims* 189

Peter Tamony, *Coca-Cola: The Most-Lawed Name* 197

Larry S. Champion, *Shakespeare's "Nell"* 203

William Green, *Humorous Characters and Attributive Names in
Shakespeare's Plays* 208

J. L. Dillard, *Afro-American, Spanglish, and Something Else:
St. Cruzan Naming Patterns* 217

Robert F. Fleissner, *Anent J. Alfred Prufrock* 223

John Algeo, *From Classic to Classy: Changing Fashions in
Street Names* 230

W.F.H. Nicolaisen, *Names as Verbal Icons* 246

Patricia Anne Davis, *Soviet Russian Given Names* 253

Allen Walker Read, *Is the Name* **United States** *Singular or Plural?* ... 263

Francis Lee Utley, *Onomastic Variety in the High Sierra* 271

Eugene B. Vest, *Names on the Ocean Bottom, or Some Observations
on the Invisible Landscape* 281

John Leighly, *Biblical Place-Names in the United States* 291

Clarence L. Barnhart, *The Selection of Proper Names in
English Dictionaries* 305

J. L. Dillard, *On the Grammar of Afro-American Naming Practices* 310

America—The Story of a Name

M. S. BEELER

IT IS APPROPRIATE that our journal open with a consideration of the name "America." Not only does this word appear in the name of our society, but its history is well suited to illustrate the problems which arise in the study of all place names. These problems are both of a historical and of a linguistic character, and a satisfactory and complete story of any place name needs both the historian and the linguist. What is here presented is a review of the many discussions which have been devoted to the history of "America."

There are many questions that arise when we come to consider any place name. Who proposed it? When and where was it first suggested? Why was this particular name given? Why does it have the form which it does, and has this form been modified in the course of its history? Has the extent of territory which it names varied, and has the name moved from one place to another? Why has the use of this name persisted, when so many names that have been proposed have not been accepted or have not endured? What etymologies have been suggested for the word, and why is any one of these to be preferred to the others? It will usually be difficult to find adequate answers to all these questions about any specific name, and these difficulties will increase the older the name is. For the name with which we are concerned here, however, a long series of scholars have succeeded in supplying for most of these questions solutions which seem to me, and I think to most others, to be, if not the whole truth, at least very close to it. For the importance and significance of the New World is such as to have attracted to the study of its name a very great many diligent workers; as a consequence of this, and of the fact that the story of this name is well documented, there will be little more to be done in ferreting out its secrets.[1]

Many Americans, if asked why America is so called, will say that

it was named for Amerigo Vespucci, or Americus Vespuccius. But
further questioning will elicit very little or no more information:
about such questions as who Vespucci was and what he did, and
why America was named for him rather than for its discoverer one
generally will find much curiosity but little knowledge.

The nature of the character and achievements of the Florentine
Amerigo Vespucci constitute one of the great puzzles of history.
Diligent research in the libraries and archives of Italy, Spain, and
Portugal has unearthed for us a large number of facts about his life,
his career, his activities. He was born in Florence in March, 1454,
the son of a cultured and aristocratic family. He received enough
education to be able to write both Latin and Italian with tolerable
accuracy. He was trained as a merchant and a banker, and in 1483
he was chosen to be *maestro di casa,* or manager, of the banking firm
of the Medici, the chief family of the city. At the end of 1491 or the
beginning of 1492 he was sent to Spain to represent the Medici
house in the branch offices they maintained there. In January of
1492 he was in Barcelona, in March in Cadiz, and in December in
Seville, which remained his chief residence for the rest of his life.
In 1503 or 1504 there appeared in various European cities[2] a pamphlet of from eight to sixteen pages in Latin, with the title of
Mundus Novus and in the form of a letter from *Albericus Vesputius*
(or *Vespucius*) to *Laurentius Petri Francisci de Medicis;* a voyage
of discovery in the service of the king of Portugal is described, and
the idea put forth that the newly found lands in the west were not
a part of Asia but constituted a new world. In 1505 or 1506 there
appeared in Italian, probably at Florence, a second pamphlet of
thirty-two pages, also in the form of a letter, this time to Piero
Soderini, the *gonfaloniere* or chief magistrate of the city, and describing four voyages of discovery and exploration in the west
undertaken by *Amerigo Vespucci.* In 1505 he became, by royal
decree, a naturalized citizen of Castille and Leon. In 1508 he was
named *piloto mayor* (chief pilot) of Spain, an office created for him
and which carried the duties of examining, classifying, and pre-
paring all the pilots of the country; of teaching them piloting,
navigation, and cosmography; and of constructing and keeping up
to date hydrographic charts. He died at Seville on February 22,
1512. In the eighteenth and nineteenth centuries there were published from manuscript copies in Florentine archives three further

letters from Amerigo Vespucci to Lorenzo de' Medici,[2] containing accounts of two voyages undertaken by him across the Atlantic, one for Spain and one for Portugal; these accounts differ in a great many respects from those published during Amerigo's lifetime, although both sets of them refer in part at least to the same data. It is generally agreed that the differences between them are so great that both of them cannot be regarded as coming from the same man: no more than one set can be accepted as genuine.

Was this Amerigo a great cartographer, cosmographer, navigator, and explorer, a man with ideas in advance of his time and as such worthy of having his name applied to the New World? This is a thesis maintained by many who have studied the problem constituted by the fragmentary character of the evidence for the personality and accomplishments of the man. Others just as vehemently have asserted that he was ambitious, unscrupulous, envious of Columbus and eager to supersede him in popular esteem, that he stooped to intentional forgery, and that he was no more than "an obscure ship chandler," "the pickle-dealer at Seville," a "beef-contractor," a "boatswain's mate," or a "thief." This debate was commenced in 1559 by the great Spanish bishop and historian Fray Bartolomé de Las Casas, and has continued for a full four centuries. Italians have been his warmest defenders, Spaniards and Mexicans among his sharpest critics. It may be pertinent here to note that all statements made about Vespucci during his lifetime confirm what we should surmise about his character and abilities from the employments we know to have been given him. What we want to know is why his name was chosen for the new hemisphere of land in the west of which he may have been one of many discoverers and explorers.

This is a question to which we know the answer. Columbus in his famous letter of 1493 claimed that he had entered the sea of India, and to the end of his life believed that the islands and the mainland upon which he set foot were parts of Asia. The map of 1503 constructed by his brother Bartolommeo, and the map by Juan de la Cosa of 1500 show Hispaniola, Jamaica, and others of the West Indies as islands off the coast of China; that is, nothing hitherto unheard-of or unknown was thought to have been found. To be sure, the Italian Peter Martyr had surmised in a letter of 1493 that an entirely new world had been discovered, but this

guess was not widely known. Then in 1503 (or 1504) appeared the
Mundus Novus under the name of *Albericus Vesputius* describing
a voyage to lands which may be identified as the coasts of Venezuela,
Guiana, and northern Brazil, and on the first page of this account
there is the following passage:

Superioribus diebus satis ample tibi scripsi de reditu meo ab novis illis regionibus
quas et classe et impensis et mandato istius serenissimi Portugalie Regis perquisivimus
et invenimus. Quasque Novum Mundum appelare licet. Quando apud maiores nostros
nulla de ipsis fuerit habita cognitio et audientibus omnibus sit novissima res.[4] [Some
days ago I wrote to you at some length concerning my return from those new regions
which we searched for and found, with the fleet and at the expense and command of
His Most Serene Highness the King of Portugal. They may be called a New World.
For there was no knowledge about them among our ancestors, and it is a most new
thing to all who hear of it.]

By 1506 this thin brochure had appeared, according to Vignaud,
in at least thirteen separate editions in Latin and nine editions in
German; this large number of printings illustrates the intense and
widespread interest of the Europeans of that day in the new discoveries, and also served to make the name of Vespucci familiar to
the Latin-reading and German-reading public. This fame was increased by the publication in 1505 or 1506 of the letter to Soderini,
which appeared, as we have seen, at Florence in Italian, and which
describes four voyages of discovery made between 1497 and 1504.
The third voyage here described is regarded as being identical with
that presented in the *Mundus Novus*.

The scene now shifts to a small princely seat on the western
slopes of the Vosges mountains in Lorraine, on the frontier between
Germany and France. In this town of St.-Dié there had been as-
sembled, under the patronage of the reigning duke, René II, who
bore the grandiloquent title of king of Jerusalem and of Sicily, a
small group of scholars and humanists, calling themselves the *Gymnasium 'Vosagense*. It is not unimportant that one of the members
of the group, Walter Lud, owned and operated a printing press.
We are in the period of the Renaissance and of the great discoveries,
of enthusiasm for the revival of classical antiquity and for the increase of geographical knowledge. And so the members of this
college projected one more new edition of Ptolemy, the chief of
ancient geographers. This edition was to be provided with an introduction dealing with the principles of cosmography, the composition of which was entrusted to a member of the group who calls

himself *Martinus Hylacomylus.* The diligent researches of Alexander von Humboldt[5] in the nineteenth century succeeded in identifying this individual with the Martin Waldseemüller who was matriculated as a student in the University of Freiburg im Breisgau in 1490, and who, like many of the humanists of the age, had translated his name into Greek, this time rather unsuccessfully. The proposed edition of Ptolemy came to naught for the present, but the published works of Vespucci had made such a vast impression on the learned world that it was decided to republish the letter to Soderini, translated into Latin, as an appendix to the introduction written by Waldseemüller.[6] A certain amount of courage was required to think of the classical authority Ptolemy as no longer supplying the complete truth about the geography of the world: maps published more than forty years later still represent the land masses of the globe according to the Ptolemaic system. Some liberties were taken in the translation: the letter was now stated to have been written not to Lorenzo de' Medici but to Duke René, favorable references in the Italian version to Columbus were deleted, and a continental area called *Lariab* had its name changed to Parias, a name already known from Columbus' account of his third voyage. Although the intent to glorify Vespucci at the expense of Columbus is evident, one need not attribute this action to deliberate malice; the members of the *Gymnasium Vosagense* were simply persuaded in 1507 that Amerigo was the more worthy of the two men.

In the cosmographical introduction appears the following famous paragraph, which gives the name of "America" to the new world and tells us why that name was chosen.

Nunc vero et hec partes sunt latius lustratæ et alia quarta pars per Americum Vesputium (ut in sequentibus audietur) inventa est: quam non video cur quis iure vetet ab Americo inventore sagacis ingenij viro Amerigen quasi Americi terram / sive Americam dicendam: cum et Europa et Asia a mulieribus sua sortita sint nomina. Eius situm et gentis mores ex bis binis Americi navigationibus quae sequuntur liquide intelligi datur. (But now these parts [i.e. Europe, Asia, and Africa, the three continents of the Ptolemaic geography] have been extensively explored and a fourth part has been discovered by Americus Vesputius, as will be seen in the appendix: I do not see what right any one would have to object to calling this part after Americus, who discovered it and who is a man of intelligence, [and so to name it] *Amerige,* i.e. the land of Americus, or *America:* since both Europe and Asia got their names from women. Its situation and the manners and customs of its people may be clearly understood from the twice two voyages of Americus which follow.)[7]

Some comment on this passage is appropriate. First, the description of Amerigo as a man *sagacis ingenii* may be an invidious reference to Columbus, who persisted in regarding the lands he had discovered as part of Asia and who had been returned to Spain in 1500 in disgrace and in chains: if Amerigo is a man of intelligence and learning and Columbus is not, and if further he is the discoverer of the fourth part of the world, as the passage claims, it is fitting that *his* name rather than that of Columbus be given to this fourth part.

The coinage *Amerige*, which is defined as *Americi terra* "the land of Americus," consists of course of the truncated *Ameri(ci)* combined with the Greek for "earth," γή(gē). This creation, illustrating its maker's love of the use of Greek in names, may have been influenced by the Italian form of the name: *Amerig(o)* > *Amerig(e)*. But the name Waldseemüller first proposed was never repeated, and we pass immediately to "America." The statement that both Europe and Asia took their names from women seems to be the justification for proposing the form with feminine ending, since the names of both those continents were of feminine gender in Latin and Greek (so also was the Latin *Africa*, but no classical myth connected that name with a woman). *America* is then the feminine of *Americus*, and the latter is Waldseemüller's Latinization of *Amerigo*. As we shall see, Vespucci's Christian name was frequently spelled with two *r*'s; that, however, was not known to Waldseemüller, and to his lack of this information is undoubtedly due the subsequent spelling with a single *r*. For his mode of turning the name into Latin consisted simply of replacing the *g* of the Italian form by *c*, and then supplying the common Latin ending. The substitution of *c* for *g* fitted into a familiar pattern; the Italian names *Federigo* and *Arrigo* were known to correspond to the Latin *Fredericus* and *Henricus*, and the connection of such Italian words as *bottega*, *pagare*, and *lactuga* with the Latin *apotheca*, *pacare*, and *lactuca* was perspicuous. But *Amerigo* was not at all a common name, and consequently there existed no standard equivalent for it; Waldseemüller's Latinization as *Americus*, which he seems to have been the first to use, was but one of several. Of these the best known is the *Albericus* of the *Mundus Novus;* it was surely devised because *Albericus*, in its various forms, was a far commoner name in medieval Europe than was *Amerigo*, and because it had some similarity with the latter. There is no warrant whatsoever for taking *Amerigo* to be the result of phonetic alteration of an antecedent **Albericu:* the cluster *-lb-* does not yield *-m-* in Italian.[8]

There is another point to be considered in determining why the name of our hemisphere has the shape that it does. In Italian *Amerigo* is stressed on the penultimate syllable, a fact which Hylacomylus may or may not have known. Our stress on the antepenult is certainly the result of an association of this newly coined word with the well-known *Africa*, which is the name of another principal part of the world and which may seem to be formed with the same suffix.

Why did Waldseemüller choose *Amerigo* and not *Vespucci* as the prototype for his name? Surely for the same reason that the South American country is called *Colombia* and not **Christophoria: America* is a more euphonious word than **Vesputia* or **Vespuccia* would be. In addition, men were in the fifteenth and sixteenth centuries much more frequently referred to by their baptismal than by their family names. Further, Humboldt[9] thinks it probable that the geographer of St.-Dié would not have considered proposing the Christian name of Vespucci had it been, as were those of many of his ancestors, *Michele, Romulo,* or *Biagio;* his father was called *Nastagio,* the Florentine form of Latin *Anastasius.* And so America owes its name to the chance that the presumed author of the *Mundus Novus* and of the *Letter* to Soderini had been baptised with the name of his grandfather, a name that was uncommon enough to be distinctive and at the same time most euphonious, consisting as it does primarily of vowels, nasals, and liquids.

In the title of the *Cosmographiae Introductio* there is the statement that the book was to be accompanied by both a globe and a map, illustrating the distribution of the lands of the earth. The map here mentioned was long unknown, but turned up in a castle in Austria in 1901. Presumably made at the same time—1507— that the book was published, it exhibits Waldseemüller's prejudice in favor of Vespucci by putting an imaginary portrait of him in a position of honor equal to that accorded Ptolemy, the classical authority; and on it there appears, for the first time on any map anywhere, the name *America*, applied however only to the southern continent. Thus the new name was launched. The *Introductio* was reprinted several times, in Strassburg in 1509, in 1510 at Lyon, in

1532 at Basel and Paris, and in 1555 at Basel, and with each reprinting there increased the fame of the man and the familiarity with
his name used as that of the New World. In 1538 we find it for the
first time applied to the whole of the western hemisphere on a map
drawn by the famous cartographer Mercator.

But this fame of his began to decline in the middle of the sixteenth century, and that of Columbus to rise. Bishop Las Casas, who
had himself come to America in 1502 and had spent most of his
long life there, accuses Vespucci in his *Historia general de las Indias*
(written after 1559) of malicious intent to make himself famous by
usurping to himself the discovery of the mainland. The attack was
continued by Herrera in 1601 and the repute of Vespucci de-
scends to its nadir in 1627 when Fray Pedro Simon proposed "the
suppression of all geographical works and maps containing the
name America."

From this low point the esteem in which Amerigo was held
began in the eighteenth century to recover slowly. The biography
by the Italian Bandini contributed to this result, and the long
critical study devoted to Vespucci and his writings by Alexander
von Humboldt in the fourth volume of his *Examen critique* did
much to place the Florentine in a more favorable light. The debate, however, continued to be lively throughout the nineteenth
century and into the twentieth, until the appearance of the crucial
study of Alberto Magnaghi in 1926.[10] The thesis of this book has
been accepted by almost all subsequent writers on Vespucci whose
work has come to my attention.[11] It is that the *Mundus Novus* and
the *Letter* to Soderini, the two pamphlets which led to the giving
of the name *America*, are not, in their published form, from Vespucci's pen; the only genuine accounts of his that have survived
are the three letters published from manuscript copies in the
eighteenth and nineteenth centuries. This conclusion was based
upon a painstaking examination of both sets of documents, and
the two publications that appeared during Vespucci's lifetime are
branded forgeries because of internal contradictions, the sus-
piciously schematic arrangement of dates, and for other reasons.
The unknown editor or compiler is thought to have had access, in
Florence, to genuine letters of Amerigo, both those that have survived and perhaps others that have since disappeared, and because
of motives no longer ascertainable to have treated this material in

a most cavalier fashion, without the knowledge or consent of their declared author. And so we reach the bizarre conclusion that the name of our new world was based upon forged documents, that the apparently honest and capable merchant and traveler and amateur geographer whose name it bears had nothing to do with its naming and may well have died without any knowledge of the immortality which the obscure German professor in distant Lorraine was to confer upon him.

Although this evaluation of Vespucci now prevails, one may still encounter derogatory judgments about him, which seem to derive from the long period of more than three hundred years when his repute was at low ebb. Thus we read in a standard work on American history[12] that Amerigo's account (the Soderini letter, now considered a forgery) was "inflated and pre-dated." And the editor of a new printing of this letter issued in Mexico in 1941[13] speaks— surely mistakenly—of the propaganda in favor of Vespucci made by his friends and by himself, and calls the naming of the new continents the first instance of a perfectly organized publicity campaign.

The one question that remains to be discussed is that of the etymology of *Amerigo*. This question was not asked until the age of Romanticism, which was distinguished among other things for its interest in antiquity and in the ancient origins of institutions and of language. Characteristically the question was first asked in Germany, and characteristically a Germanic origin was found for the name. One day in Berlin about one hundred and twenty years ago the philologist Friedrich Heinrich von der Hagen, noted for his edition of the Nibelungenlied (1816), suggested, in conversation with Alexander von Humboldt, at that time engaged in the writing of his *Examen critique,* that the name Amerigo was Germanic. Asked by von Humboldt to give substance to this suggestion, he wrote an article called "America, an originally Germanic Name,"[14] in which he proposed a connection of *Amerigo* with a Germanic name appearing in Old High and Middle High German and in medieval Latin documents. The name is found in a variety of forms, among which the most common are *Amalrih, Amelrich, Amalaric. Amelrich* occurs in the Nibelungenlied[15] as the name of the brother of the Danube ferryman, and he is there described as *"ein helt guot."* The name is common in south German documents of the sixth to the ninth centuries. Von der Hagen shows by numerous examples that it, like many other Germanic names, such as the Italian *Federigo, Arrigo, Corrado,* was borrowed into lands of Romance speech: he cites an *Amelrico* who was bishop of Como in 865 and another *Amelrico* who was viscount of Milan in 870; the name *Amalricus* was borne by a bishop of Tours in the ninth century and an archbishop of Narbonne in the thirteenth.

The use of this name in the Middle Ages in southern Germany and in Italy and France represents simply a repetition of an older prototype: we all know that personal names may be repeated from generation to generation. As far as is known the first man who bore this name was a son of the Visigothic king Alaric the younger and a grandson, in the maternal line, of the famous Theodoric, king of the Ostrogoths. Born in 507, he was the last Visigothic king to reign in France, and lost his life and his kingdom to the Franks at the battle of Veuillé in 531. His name appears in Latin as *Amalaricus*[16] and in Greek as Ἀμαλάριχος.[17] These transliterations into the classical tongues certainly reflect a native Gothic **Amalarīk-*, which would have been spelt **Amalareik-* in the orthographical system employed by Wulfila, the translator of the Bible into Gothic. **Amalarīk-* is an example of the standard type of the ancient Germanic personal name, which consisted, as personal names did in Indo-European times, of two elements.[18] At an earlier period the name formed by the compounding of these two elements, usually both nouns, no doubt constituted a meaningful whole, but in the fifth and sixth centuries that was no longer true. At that time a limited number of word-stems were employed in the formation of personal names, some of which could appear either in first or second position, and others of which were limited either to the first or to the second position. The meaning of the resultant compound was not a product of its constituent elements. The use of some of these constituent word stems was often characteristic of, or limited to the members of one family. In naming a child the parent frequently took one part of his own name and combined it with another element to form a new compound name. The system prevailing in the fifth century is well illustrated by the names of members of the East Gothic ruling house: a sister of Theodoricus (Gothic *þiuda-reiks*) was Amalafrida (*amala-friþa); her son was Theodahadus (*þiuda-haþus) and her daughter was Amalaberga (*amala-bairga.) One of the daughters of Theodoricus was Amalasuentha (**amala-swinþa*), and she was the mother of Athalaricus (**aþala-reiks*) and of Mathesuentha (**mata-swinþa* ?). Another daughter of Theodoric, Thiudigoto (**þiuda-guta* ?), was married to the West Gothic king Alaricus (**ala-reiks*) and became the mother of Amalaricus.

The meaning of most of these name elements is certain: *þiuda* is "nation, people," *friþa* is "peace," *haþus* "war, battle," *swinþa* "strong," *guta* "Goth"?, and *ala-* "all." *Amala-* (Go. **amals*) was the source of the Latin *Amalus, Amali*, a sort of appellative which is applied in Jordanes' Gothic history to all members of the Ostrogothic royal house; it was derived from the name of a shadowy ancestor *Amal*.[19] A derivative in *-unga-* "man of, subject of, descendant of" yielded the Middle High German *Amelunc, Amelunge*, which is the only name for the Goths in the Nibelungenlied. Much ink has flowed in attempts to determine the original meaning of *amala-*, but its etymology is uncertain and will not be pursued here. *Reiks*, a prehistoric loan from Celtic (cf. Irish *rí, ríg* "king") into Germanic, is used in the Gothic Bible in the rather vague sense of "an official, an authority"; in other Germanic languages it occurs only in personal names.

Now *Amerigo* might be derived from *Amalaricus*, but there is a difficulty. Syncopation of the third *a* did yield the attested *Amalrico*, of which *Amelrico*—likewise citable—is a variant; for in the dialects of north and central Italy *a* is frequently palatalized to *e* before *l* plus consonant: cf. the widely diffused *elto* from Latin *altus*.[20] In the same areas the normal reflex of intervocalic *k* is *g*;[21] and the pretonic cluster *-lr-* is assimilated to *-rr-* in *vorrei* "I should wish," from **vol(e)r-ái*.[22] These changes would produce *Amerrigo*, a spelling of the name occasionally employed by Vespucci himself[23] and one which was for long regarded as confirming the etymology proposed by von der Hagen. The difficulty is this: in Tuscan the cluster [-rr-] is perfectly stable, from the earliest times to the present; but the name *Amerigo* is in Italy always written with a single *r*, from the Middle Ages on, and is today pronounced [ame′rigo], not [ame′rrigo]. We therefore must consider a different Germanic etymon.

The Old High German *Haimirich*, derived from Germanic **haimi-* "dwelling-place, village, house, home" and Germanic **rīk-*, is found in documents from 728 A.D. on in the variants *Haimerich*,

Heinirih, Aymerich, Aimirich, etc.[34] According to Dauzat[35] this German personal name developed in northern France into Henri
(> Eng. Henry), and in Provence yielded *Aimeric* or *Aymeric.* The
cultural influence of the Midi in the twelfth and thirteenth centuries upon Italy was pervasive, and it cannot be doubted that the
name *Aimeric* could have been borrowed. Now it happens that precisely in the Tuscan area immediately contiguous to Florence there
is adequate evidence for a change of *ai* to *a:*[36] Lat. *placitus* >
piaito (Lucca) > *piato;* Old French *laid* "ugly" (< OHG *laid;* cf.
German *Leid,* English *loath*) > Old Italian *lado* (literary Italian
laido) ; Latin *aiutat* "he helps, aids" > Old Italian *aita* and *ata.*
Hence it is quite possible that *Amerigo,* the use of which appears
to be confined to Florence and to its immediate environs, and which
always shows only intervocalic *-r-,* may come from the Provençal
name. Or the Romance forms of Germanic **Haimi-rīk-* and
*Amala-rīk- may have converged, and *Amerigo* may owe its shape
to a blend of the two; it is a question impossible to decide, although
at present it appears that the major influence in the formation of
the name ought to be attributed to the first.[37]

Further search in the archives of Florence for the period of the
twelfth to the fifteenth centuries would probably yield more information on earlier forms of the name, and might therefore enable
us to determine definitely the source of Vespucci's Christian name.
And a painstaking examination of historical records might make
possible a more thorough documentation of cultural interchange
between the Provence and Florence, and so render much more
probable what must here remain a guess. As in so many name-
studies, we find here that more than one etymology is plausible,
and that complete certainty—at least in the present state of our
knowledge—is unobtainable. The preceding discussion will serve
to emphasize the wisdom of not accepting too readily the first
etymology of a name that may be proposed and the necessity for
subjecting all such etymologies to as rigorous an analysis as the
character of the available evidence will permit.

The Germanic etymology of "America" is universally accepted,
because the evidence in favor of it is overwhelmingly convincing. It
is to be expected, however, that some scholars will have had other
ideas, and will have sought an American origin for the name of the
new world. Strangely enough, the most ardent supporters of such

a thesis were themselves Europeans. Between 1875 and 1895 some five or six theories were set forth by writers claiming to have discovered Indian prototypes for "America." Jules Marcou in 1875 printed, for the first time anywhere, the name of an Indian tribe and of a district in Nicaragua called indifferently *Amerrisque* or *Amerrique,* and asserted that this district—rich in gold—had been visited both by Columbus and by Vespucci, who then made this name known in Europe. Thomas Lambert de Saint-Bris in 1888 saw the source of "America" in a native empire called *Amaraca* which, he thought, stretched in pre-Columbian times from Peru to the mouths of the Orinoco in Venezuela and north to Yucatan. E. N. Horsford, an American manufacturing chemist, argued in 1892 that "America" came from the native name of the island of Jamaica, which appears in early accounts in the variants *Jamaiqua, Tamarique, Ymaiqua,* and *Riqua;* but *Jamaica* itself is a word, according to him, that had been carried to the West Indies from New England, where the Algonquin tribes had altered the name *Eirikr* of the Icelandic settler of Greenland into *Em-i-ca!* This brief sampling will show the character of the efforts of those who approached the problem of a name etymology not in order to search for the truth but in order to plead a case.

All the great nations of western Europe but one had a part in this name giving: it was a German living in France who suggested the name of an Italian in the service of the kings of Spain and Portugal. The destiny of America as the land of the melting pot for the peoples of Europe was foreshadowed in the very act of its naming.

NOTES

[1] A detailed bibliography of writings on Vespucci and on the naming of America is contained in the book of Henry Vignaud: *Améric Vespuce, 1451–1512. Sa Biographie. Sa Vie. Ses Voyages. Ses Découvertes. L'Attribution de son Nom à l'Amérique. Ses Relations Authentiques et Contestées* (Paris, 1917). Later publications are listed in the bibliography of Frederick J. Pohl, *Amerigo Vespucci, Pilot Major* (New York, 1944).

[2] Florence, Paris? The first edition mentioning place and date of publication is that of Augsburg, August, 1504.

[3] A convenient reprinting of these letters will be found in Magnaghi's work (pp. 235–272) referred to in note 10, below.

[4] Cited from Vignaud, p. 305.

[5] *Examen Critique de l'Histoire du Nouveau Continent,* 5 vols. (Paris, 1836–1839), IV (1837), 105–106.

[6] *Cosmographiae Introductio. Cum quibusdam geometriæ ac astronomiæ principiis ad eam rem necessariis. Insuper quatuor Americi Vespucci navigationes. Universalis cosmographiæ descriptio tam in solido quam plano eis etiam insertis quæ in Ptholomeo ignota a nuperis reperta sunt* (St.-Die in Lorraine, 25 April 1507).

[7] This translation of mine is freely adapted from that of John Fiske.

[8] I have heard the suggestion that *America* is related to the name of Oberon, king of

the fairies, in Shakespeare's *Midsummer Night's Dream*. The Germanic *Alberik-* would yield in French *Aubéry*, in which the *y* could have been replaced by the suffix *-on*, thus giving *Aubéron*. But *America* is not from *Alberik-*.

[9] Humboldt, *op. cit.*, IV, 48–49.

[10] *Amerigo Vespucci. Studio critico, con speciale riguardo ad una nuova valutazione delle fonti, accompagnato dai documenti non ancora pubblicati del codice Vaglienti* (Rome, 1926).

[11] Gutierre Tibón, *America, Setenta Siglos de la Historia de un Nombre* (Mexico, 1945). Stefan Zweig, *Amerigo, A Comedy of Errors in History* (New York, 1942). Pohl, *op. cit.* Julio Montebruno Lopez, *Vespucio, el Personaje más Calumniado de la Historia* (Santiago de Chile, 1944).

[12] Samuel Eliot Morison and Henry Steele Commager, *The Growth of the American Republic* (New York, 1942). I, 21.

[13] Manuel Toussaint, ed., *Carta de Americo Vespucio de las Islas Nuevamente Descubiertas en Cuatro de sus Viajes* (Mexico, 1941), p. x.

[14] Fr. Hein. von der Hagen, "Amerika ein Ursprünglich Deutscher Name," *Neues Jahrbuch der Berlinischen Gesellschaft für Deutsche Sprache und Alterthumskunde*, I (1836), 13–17. The word *deutsch* is, of course, used here in the sense of "Germanic," not "German," in conformity with the practice of the brothers Grimm. Von der Hagen's etymology became widely known because his article was reprinted *in extenso* by Humboldt, *op. cit.*, IV, 53–57.

[15] Strophes 1548, 1552, and 1556.

[16] Jordanes, *De Origine Actibusque Getarum*, ed., Th. Mommsen (Berlin, 1882), p. 134.

[17] Cf. e.g., Procopius of Caesarea, *History of the Wars*, Loeb Classical Library (London and New York, 1919), III, 128, 130.

[18] For a complete treatment of the system of early Germanic name giving, see Adolf Bach, *Die Deutschen Personennamen* (1st ed.; Berlin, 1943), pp. 69 ff.

[19] Jordanes, *op. cit.*, p. 76: "Augis genuit eum, qui dictus est Amal, a quo et origo Amalorum decurrit."

[20] Gerhard Rohlfs, *Historische Grammatik der Italienischen Sprache und ihrer Mundarten* (Bern, 1949), I, 92–93.

[21] *Ibid.*, pp. 325–326.

[22] *Ibid.*, II, 395.

[23] Humboldt, *op. cit.*, IV, 48. Cf. also Juan Bautista Muñoz, *Historia del Nuevo-Mundo* (Madrid, 1793), p. x: "El [i.e., Vespucci] firmaba Amerrigo."

[24] (Cf. Bach, *op. cit.*, 204; and E. Förstemann, *Altdeutsches Namenbuch*, Nordhausen, 1856, s.v.).

[25] A. Dauzat, *Dictionnaire étymologique des noms de famille et prénoms de France*, Paris, 1951, ss.vv. *Aimery* and *Henri*.

[26] Rohlfs, *op. cit.*, I, 75 ff.

[27] I am indebted for some of these ideas to my colleague Prof. Bruno Migliorini, of Florence; but the responsibility for the final formulation is my own. I am also indebted to the thorough treatise of Gutierre Tibón, cited in footnote 11, who has gathered a wealth of information on the subject.

Madison S. Beeler, Ph.D., Harvard, is associate professor of German at the University of California and author of *The Venetic Language*.

The Challenge of the Name *America*

ZOLTAN J. FARKAS

THE NAME *AMERICA* was a challenge for historians and linguists maybe from the moment of its birth, in Europe as well as here in America. It is well known that our continent was named after Amerigo Vespucci. It is also known that the historians still question the importance of Vespucci's role in America's discovery or even exploration.

Martin Waldseemüller (1470 or 1475–1512), however, is credited with being the godfather of America. He was a German clergyman and professor of geography at the University of Strassburg. He wrote his "Cosmographiae Introductio" in Latin and published it in 1507. The only existing copy of it is located today in the University Library in Strassburg. Dedicated to the "Divine Maximilian, Caesar Augustus," it contains nine chapters of geography and maps. On page 18 he says that the world's fourth part is "America" (= South America). On page 25 he is more specific: "The fourth part of the world, since Americus discovered it, "Amerigen" (Greek: *-gen* = land) i.e., Americus' land as well America could be called." He explains on page 30 his suggestion: "The fourth part of the world was discovered by Americus Vespucius – as it will be learned in the following letters – therefore I do not see for what reason should be objected, that this land after Americus – the discoverer and a man of sagacious mind – Americus' Land or America should be called, since Europa and Asia are also named in feminine form."

The *United States Catholic Historical Society Monograph*,[1] which consists of four parts, contains Waldseemüller's *Cosmographiae Introductio* in facsimile of the 1507 edition and its English translation by Edward Gaylord Bourne. It also contains Vespucci's letters about his four voyages and their translation into English by Dr. Mario E. Cosenza. The third part is Waldseemüller's map. The 8' by 4½' original is reduced here to 14' by 26" in facsimile. Ac-

---

[1] New York 1907 (on the 400th. anniversary of the original's publication).

cording to Waldseemüller about a thousand copies of this map were
sold in a short month after it was published. Today, however, only
one copy is known to exist – in the castle of Wolfegg in Württem-
berg, Germany. The fourth part is a facsimile of Waldseemüller's
globe. The original globe is today in the Hauslab-Lichtenstein Collection in Vienna.

The Cosmographiae Introductio is actually a handbook and explains why he had used the name "America" on the maps. Six years
later in 1513 on another map, however, Waldseemüller again calls
America "Terra Incognita" (the unknown land).[2] He also gives
the following explanation: "This land with adjacent islands was
discovered by Columbus, a Genoese, under the authority of the king
of Castile."

Vespucci's nephew Giovanni published a map in 1523 and did not
use the name America. In Spain the name "The Indies" was used;
the French Postel used the name "Atlantis" in 1561, and Michael
Servetus called the name "America" a mistake in his Ptolemy in
1535. On Mercator's Globe of 1541, however, South and North
America is named "America"; the German Oertel called North
America "Columbana" and South America "America." Only in
the seventeenth century did the names "South America" and "North
America" become popular.

Bourne gives an interesting explanation why Waldseemüller himself abandoned the name "America" and why Servetus called this
name a mistake. According to Vespucci's letters to several person-
alities of his time, he made four voyages: in 1497, 1500, 1501, and
1503. According to Bourne, the year of his first departure was
actually 1499, and not he but a man named Hojeda was the head
of the expedition. This time, however, Vespucci explored the northern coasts of South America. Already his departure was inspired by
Columbus' successful trip in 1497, and maybe for the same reason he
has dated his departure two years earlier. I think, however, the
main reason of his popularity could be that he wrote very interesting
descriptions of his. He pointed out that the natives had no rulers,
no money, and no clothing; their love life was free, and nature
provided their living; they had no agriculture, but had tall buildings; and that their women were brave – that once when the timid

<hr />

[2] Edward Gaylord Bourne, "The Naming of America," American Historical
Review, Volume 10, October-July 1904-1905.

men sent their women to deal with a young Spaniard the women simply ate him.

Another important reason could be the fact that at first neither the world nor Columbus thought that he had discovered a new continent. Everybody believed that Vespucci was the first to explore the "Terra Incognita."

Today Columbus is unquestionably acknowledged as America's discoverer. Vespucci, however, is called sometimes an explorer, sometimes just an adventurer; but our continent is named in his honor.

While Bourne answered the challenge entirely as a historian, Heinrich Charles[3] approached the name *America* from a very different point of view. He sees poetic and euphonic value in this name and regards it as "the shortest, the most popular, and the most enduring poem ever composed."[4] He thinks that our continent is the only one that has not just a birthday, the day of Columbus' landing (October 12, 1492), but a name day, too, the day Waldseemüller's book was published (April 25, 1507). Therefore it is not surprising that Charles is the most devoted defender of Vespucci against his most fanatic critic Ralph Waldo Emerson,[5] who calls Vespucci not only a pickledealer but a thief, too. He (Emerson) devotes almost half of his book (83 pages) to proving that Vespucci was rather a scholar than an adventurer and that neither he nor Waldseemüller knew that the name *America* was given to the same territory where Columbus landed first.

Although *Charles* discusses briefly the origin of the name "Amerigo," too, he is more interested in the history of persons and places involved. He begins with the name *Amal* the Asa god of creative labor in the Mythological or Saga period, and mentions many important people who had a similar name over the Heroic, Romantic, and Chivalrous periods. He enjoys giving an elaborate historical background and therefore devotes a whole chapter of his book to the history of the city *St. Die'* where Waldseemüller's book was published.

It is also interesting to read his "fantastic stories and theories" about the name *America* "as long as the facts of the naming of the

---

[3] *The Romance of The Name America.* Published by the author in New York, New York, 1926.   [4] *Ibid.*, p. 4.

[5] *English Traits*, Boston 1856, p. 148.

New World were unknown."[6] He even knows of two namesakes of America, two towns: "Ammerschweier" in Alsac and "Monfort l'Amaury" in the Department Seine-et-Oise (Chapter 15).

It is not surprising that the name "America" challenged the *American Name Society*, too. The first article of the first issue of *Names*, the official journal, is devoted to the name of our country. Madison S. Beeler[7] gave here the best summary of the history and etymology of this name so far.

The challenge of the name America made Joy Rea[8] a challenger himself, but he – mainly following the French Jules Marcou (1875) – singled out Beeler to argue with his statements about Waldsee-müller's and Vespucci's role in creating the name "America." His basic statement is that Beeler "gives Waldseemüller credit for having named the new continent in honor of Vespucci."[9] He thinks that Waldseemüller's statement on page 30 of his *Cosmographiae* ... "could also be read as explanation in which Waldseemüller stated that the had *heard* that this land was called America..."[9]. I cannot see it in this way, but he gives a lengthy explanation that Columbus could have brought back the name *Amerigue* from his fourth expedition in 1502. This was the name of an Indian tribe, a district, and a mountain in Nicaragua. He also mentions the English explorers and buccaneers who used the name "America." They *could have* heard the word and *could have* made it into a "culture word."[10]

Rea's arguments are emotionally appealing but not convincing. He neglects the fact that the English explorers at the end of the XVI century could also have learned the word from Waldseemüller's maps. Maybe this is the explanation why about a thousand copies of this map were sold in a month after it was published in 1507.

Another argument of Rea is that Beeler "does not explain why Waldseemüller did not employ the Latinization that had already been used – *Albericus Vesputius*."[9] He could have found a depend-

---

[6] *Ibid.*, pp 168, 169.

[7] "America – The Story of a Name." *Names*, 1.1, March, 1953.

[8] "On the Naming of America." *American Speech*, 39:42–50, Feb. 1964.

[9] *Ibid.*, p. 42.   [10] *Ibid.*, p. 50.

[11] *The Romance of the Name America.* Published by the author in New York, New York, 1926, p. 44. – In chapter 13 ("Fantastic Stories of the Naming America"), Charles writes about Marcou and others: "These notions, however, are in so far interesting as they show to what aberrations of the mind speculation can lead to if not supported by the actual facts" (p. 173).

able explanation to that in Charles' book[11] that this was a misprint. The basic mistake of Rea was, however, that he ignores the fact that our Vespucci was named "Amerigo" after his grandfather who had the same name.[12]

It is hard to understand why he singled out Beeler and disregarded all other historians who discussed this name. Many of them questioned Vespucci's right to give his name in naming "America" but not the fact that it happened. But it is even harder to understand why he ignored the second part of Beeler's article, in which the latter gives a very elaborate etymology of the name. This etymology alone excludes the theory that Vespucci's Latinized name was only an accidental choice between "Albericus" and "Americus."

Beeler follows the linguistic history of the name, taking *Friedrich Heinrich von der Hagen*[13] as his guide, who thinks that the name *Amerigo* has a Germanic origin, and *Amalrih, Amalrich*, was its first form in the Old High German. von der Hagen shows several variants of this name and mentions its latest appearances in the ninth century: *Amelrico*, the bishop of Como; *Amelrico*, the viscount of Milan, and *Amelricus*, the bishop of Tours. The first person known by this name was the son of the Visigothic King Alaric, *Amalaricus*.[14]

In Italian "Amerigo" and "Americo" were used in Vespucci's time. The name in Tuscan, however, was neither popular nor unknown. The Italian linguists trace the name back to German in two lines: one to *Heinrich* (Amerigo, Americo, Emerico, Enrico, Henrico, Heinrich); the other to *Amalarich*. *Fumagalli*[15] says that "Amerigo, Americo, Emerico, sono forme toscane dell' antico nome tedesco' Amalarico' da cui i francesi hanno fatto' Amaury'." ("Amerigo," "Americo," and "Emerico" are the Tuscan forms of an old German name "Amalarico," which the French changed to "Amaury.")

---

[12] Giuseppe Fumagalli: *Piccolo dizionario dei nomi propri italiani di persone*, Genova, 1901.

[13] "Amerika ein Ursprünglich Deutscher Name." *Neues Jahrbuch der Berlinischen Gesellschaft für Deutsche Sprache und Altertumskunde.* 1.13–17 (1836).

[14] Jordanes: *De Origine Actibusque Getarum*, Th. Momsen, Berlin, 1882, p. 134.

[15] Giuseppe Fumagalli, *Piccolo dizionario dei nomi propri italiani di persone*, Genova, 1901.

In the *Encyclopedia Americana*, representing the popular theory here in America, *Marion Wilcox*[16] says that the Old High German *Amalrich* originated among the Goths and was carried into all western European countries. *Amal* was an East Gothic hero; after him a dynasty was named "Amala" or "Amelungen." We find the name among the West Goths, too; a grandson of Theodorich the Great was called "Amalarich." Here the first part of the name, which means "labor, effort" has a *rich* suffix. This suffix can be found in the Old English of "Beowulf," where *ric* means "power-full" as an adjective and, "domain" or "empire" as a substantive. The whole name means therefore "rich in efforts" or "powerful in efforts." It is easy to follow the linguistic development from "Amel-rico" to "Amerrico," to "Americo," and to "Amerigo," Vespucci's first name. It is not unusual that the *l* assimilates to *r* in front of another *r*, and that the voiceless *c* [k] becomes a voiced *g* between two vowels.

That the names Amerigo-Americo and Emerico are the same is not Fumagalli's opinion only. *Carl Egger*[17] says that "Americus" (Latin), "Amerigo" (Italian), "Americo" (Spanish), "Americk" (Old English), "Almarich" (German), is composed of the Germanic *amal* (labor) and *rihhi-* (ruler). He makes here two other statements too: 1) This name was given to Vespucci after whom the continent was named, but which was discovered by Columbus. 2) This name is regarded according to its origin the same as "Henricus" (Haim-rich, Heinrich). He repeats his last statement when he says that though "Emericus" is regarded as a separate name, "Emerico" (Italian), "Emery" (Gallic), "Emerico" (Spanish), "Emmery," "Emry" (Old English), "Emmerich" (German), "Emericus" (Latin) have the same origin as "Americus" (Latin) and "Amerigo" (Italian).[18]

The Brazilian, *Rosario Farani Mansur Guerios*,[19] says also that "Americo" has the same origin as the German "Emmerich" which he derives from "Heinrich," *haims* meaning "home country" and *rik* meaning "ruler." He has an entry for "Amalrico" also, deriving

---

[16] Marion Wilcox, "America," *Encyclopedia Americana*, New York: Americana Company, 1956, 1:478–79.

[17] Carl Egger, *Lexicon Nominum Virorum et Mulierum*, Romae, Studium 1957.

[18] *Ibid.*, p. 61.

[19] *Dicionário Etimológico de Nomes e Sobrenomes*. Curitiba, 1949.

it from the German "Amalrich," in which *rich* means again "ruler," but *amal* means "war."

Ernst Förstemann[20] lists the personal names grouped under the root syllables from which they are derived. He says that the Old High German root "*Haimi*" comes from the Gothic *Haims* (home), and we find listed here a score of names derived from this root with the date of their earliest written record. "Haimirich," "Haimrich," and "Heimrich," for example, are found in documents from 728 A.D.

Summarizing *Fumagalli, Guerios, Egger,* and *Förstemann's* conclusions we may presume that the Italian "Amerigo" can be derived either from "Amalrich" or from "Heinrich." Although Beeler, modestly claimes that he presented only "a review of the many discussions which have been devoted to the history of "America," he makes a very interesting remark.[21] If (Beeler says) *Amalrico* were the ancestor of the name *Amerigo*, the palatalization of the *a* to *e* in *front* of an *l* plus consonant, as well as the change of the intervocalic *k* to a voiced *g*, can be considered as a normal phonetical development. So is the assimilation of the pretonic cluster -*lr*- to -*rr*-. But this -*rr*- cluster is stable in Tuscan. This means that if really *Amalrich* were the original form, *Amerrigo* would be the prevailing spelling of Vespucci's name. And Beeler comes to the conclusion that the Old High German name *Haimirich* alone should be considered as the ancestor of the name *Amerigo*.

This theory seems to be supported by the fact that *Amalrich* can be found mostly in Western Europe and *Haimirich, Heinrich* in Central and Eastern Europe.

von der Hagen mentions that variants of *Amalarich* were popular in the ninth century, but I think that it is questionable that this name survived the following six centuries while the East Goths became extinct, and the power of Germanic stems shrank in Europe after Charlemagne, in the ninth century. His two sons encouraged the separation of the Germanic and Romance people in Europe, and Italy was definitely not a Germanic territory.

The Hungarian linguists seem to have an answer to this question. Dr. János Karácsonyi[22] writes about the first Hungarian king, the

---

[20] *Altdeutsches Namenbuch.* Vol. II, Second Ed. Published by P. Hanstein's Verlag at Bonn, 1900–1916.   [21] *Names*, I:11.

[22] "Az Arpád-ház Szentjei" on pp. 305–321 of *Arpád és as Arpádok Történelmi Emlékmü*, edited by Dezsö Csánki, Budapest, Franklin Translat., 1910.

later *St. Stephen*, that he named his son – the later *St. Emeric* –
after the queen's uncle, the ruling German emperor and the later
St. Heinrich II. In naming his son after the German emperor he
intended to strenghten not only the family ties but also the political
situation of the new Hungary. Hungarians were good riders and
fighters, but it became evident that they could establish and maintain a permanent country between the Germanic and Slavic blocks
only if they turned to Christianity and made peace with their neighbors. *Stephen* converted the Hungarians to christianity and married
a German princess, Gisella.

Emeric is *Imre* in Hungarian. Gergely Czuczor and János For-
garasi[23] analyzed this name and identified it with the German
Heinrich, too, but they think that the Hungarian form is influenced
by the Arabic word *imre* which means "man."

St. Stephen's son Emeric had already become a saint of the
Catholic church in 1083.[24] He is the only saint with this name.
Amerigo Vespucci must have been baptized after him because in the
Catholic church generally a name with a patron saint can be given
in the baptismal.[25]

Carlo Tagliavini[26] seems also to confirm this theory. He discusses
one name each day for the Italian radio according to the calendar
of the Roman Catholic Church. He knows that *Imre* is very popular
in Hungary and identifies it and its variants *Imbreh, Imreh* with
the Latin *Emericus, Hemericus*, which comes from the Germanic
Haimirich.

This way the Germanic *Amalrich* or *Haimric* had to be accepted
by the Hungarians first, who gave the name a patron saint so that
it could be given in the baptismal to a man after whom our continent was named. The name *America* has a colorful European
history, but it became genuinely American.

Georgia Southern College

---

[23] *A Magyar Nyelv Szótára I–VI*, edited by G. Emich, Pest. 1862–74.

[24] *The Catholic Encyclopedia*, 14:287.

[25] *The Catholic Encyclopedia*, 10:674–75.

[26] *Un Nome al Giormo: Origine e Storia di Nomi di Persona Italiani I–II*,
Torino, Edizioni Radio Italiana, 1955–57, 1:29, 2.234–36.

A Classification of Place Names

GEORGE R. STEWART

IN WRITINGS ON PLACE NAMES various categories of names are generally assumed, e.g., descriptive names, incident names, etc. This present study attempts to set forth the matter systematically, and thus to present, with an attempt at consistency and completeness, the classes into which place names may be divided according to their manner of origin, which is in general the matter of primary interest and importance to the onomatologist.

The classification might also be said to be with respect to the means or mechanisms by which places are named. These means or mechanisms have, furthermore, a relationship to the psychological processes (i.e., the motives) of the original namers in distinguishing one place from another by various methods, but any adequate study of the psychological processes of naming would have to be conducted at a much deeper level than is here proposed.

In brief, however, we may attempt to distinguish between mechanism and motive in naming. . . . All naming of places stems from one basic motive, that is, the desire to identify a place and thus distinguish it from others. In order to do so, the namer makes use of one of several different mechanisms, e.g., description. (A desire to describe can scarcely be called his motive, unless the namer happens to be a self-conscious artist.) At the same time, however, other motives may be present in his mind, even consciously. He may be thinking, for instance, "I want to distinguish this place, and have some fun too." In such a case we may say that humor is a secondary motive, as it often is. But by setting up a category of humorous names we would only be heading for confusion. We should have to go on to establish such categories as patriotic names, obscene names, sentimental names, *ad infinitum*.

Nevertheless, two of the common classes of names (commemorative and euphemistic) seem to require for their definition some consideration of the secondary motive.

The essential field of the onomatologist seems, however, to be the mechanisms of naming, rather than the motivations of the namers, except in so far as the former at times reflect the latter. Study of names will probably progress better if this distinction is kept clear. Humor, for instance, cannot be called a mechanism of naming in the same way that description is. In fact, most of our humorous namings will be found to use a descriptive mechanism, that is, they name the place by means of one of its characteristics that seems ridiculous, as when an out-of-the-way community is called Seldom Seen.

Since almost any conceivable stimulus, conscious or unconscious, may be working on the namer at the time of naming, a study of the motivations of naming would scarcely be able to stop short of a whole treatise on human psychology. On the other hand, the mechanisms of naming are comparatively few, and at the same time yield a useful classification of the names themselves.

Nine classes of names are here postulated, viz., 1) Descriptive names, 2) Possessive names, 3) Incident names, 4) Commemorative names, 5) Euphemistic names, 6) Manufactured names, 7) Shift names, 8) Folk etymologies, 9) Mistake names. In addition it is recognized that border-line cases may occur.

I have some confidence that this classification is practical and is as nearly all-inclusive as can be expected. I worked it out some years ago, and have tested it pretty thoroughly since that time.

1) DESCRIPTIVE NAMES. A descriptive name is one that originates from some permanent or semi-permanent quality of the place itself. The practical test of a descriptive name may be said to be that a traveler coming to the place of naming should be able to recognize the reason for the naming.

The majority of descriptive names perpetuate a quality of the place that can be appreciated by one of the senses, most commonly sight. Hearing, smell, and other senses may serve. More intellectualized or fanciful descriptions are possible, as in Pliocene Ridge, and Matrimony Creek—so named because it was hard to get out of.

It should be remembered that description may apply only to the particular place picked upon by the namer. Thus Roaring Creek may roar only at one point in its whole twenty-mile course. Streams, in particular, are very likely to be named by their characteristics at one point, that is, at the place where the first trail crossed them. Obviously, a stream is usually named before anyone has a chance to explore all along it and decide upon what would be the best descriptive name for the whole.

Actual *false description* is rare. Most of its examples would be better classified under euphemistic names. Others are to be explained as incident names, that is, the original namers observed the place under unusual circumstances and their name perpetuates these circumstances, and does not describe the ordinary nature of the place.

Negative description is also so rare as to be of little importance, but may be found in such a name as Nowood River.

Since descriptive names constitute a very large class, a breakdown into the three chief sub-divisions is offered.

1a) *Pure description.* This specifies a quality genuinely and inalienably connected with the thing named, e.g., Black Butte, Long Island, Crescent Lake, Granite Mountain, Roaring Run, Echo Rock, Stinking Spring, Bayport, Horse Heaven.

1b) *Associative description.* This specifies a trait rather loosely connected with the thing named. It might be said not so much to describe the thing itself as to identify it by means of something associated with it. Thus a stream may be identified merely by the fact that certain plants or trees happen to be growing near-by (Pine Creek, Onion Creek). It may be called Boundary Creek, because it happens to run close to some boundary. Or it may be identified by some work of man (Mill Creek, Bridge Creek). Being less a part of the thing itself, these names are also less likely to be permanently appropriate. Mill Creek will become a misnomer if the mill falls into decay and disappears. Although there would be grounds for setting up associative names as a separate class, such names are usually considered descriptive, and I think that they are better made a sub-division.

1c) *Relative description.* This specifies a relationship of the place to something else, e.g., Fourth Crossing, Lake Superior. Here also may be included *compass-point names* (North River, South Island), and *mile-post names* (Ten Mile Creek). Although, in a sense, relative description may be said not to describe at all, yet it cannot be surely distinguished from other descriptive names. In fact, rather few descriptions can be called absolute. Thus there is no absolute standard of bigness, and Big River may get its name only because it happens to be bigger than the streams near it. Many *counterpart names* display this tendency toward relative description. Thus Red Butte may scarcely be red in any absolute sense, but may be called so because it is relatively red as compared with near-by Black Butte.

2) Possessive names. Many names have been applied because of the feeling that some person or group of persons owned that particular place. The ownership, of course, need not have been legal, because the mere residence of a squatter would supply an equally good title for this end. In fact, the "ownership" might rest upon mere right of discovery. In English, these names are generally marked, in their original forms, by the use of the possessive case.

These names resemble associative-descriptive names so closely that they could well be classified with them on purely theoretical grounds. For practical purposes, however, they seem to be better distinguished.

Three sub-divisions are of value.

2a) *Personal names.* These are very common, and most parts of the habitable world are studded with such names as Culp's Hill, and Smith Creek.

2b) *Ethnic names.* These names merely do for a group what the personal names do for an individual, e.g., Mohawk River, Chinese Camp, American Fork. The term *ethnic* has not been much used by American scholars, but seems better than the more common *tribal*, which is hardly fitting for such names as Chinese and American. *Gentile* has also been used as a technical term in this sense, but it is likely to cause even more confusion.

2c) *Mythological names.* Names are sometimes given to places under the belief that they are "possessed" or haunted by some supernatural being or beings. The occurrence in Siouan place names of the element *-wacan,* meaning *spirit,* is an example.

3) Incident names. These identify the place by means of some incident which has occurred at or near it. As opposed to descriptive names, incident names record only a temporary characteristic or association of the place. This is a very important distinction. For instance, most *animal names* (Wolf Creek, Antelope Spring) fall into this category. They do not mean that the animal was unusually plentiful at that spot or especially characteristic of it, but merely record a particular occasion upon which the animal was encoun-

tered. Many names of people as applied to places record merely some momentary incident which caused that particular name to be associated with the place in the minds of an early traveler.

Incident names have seldom received their due, and the whole class seems to be in bad odor with some scholars. This is unfortunate, but the reason for it is obvious. Incident names, by their very nature, suggest stories, and so people tend to tell tall tales to explain them. These later-made-up stories are unauthentic, and many of them are ridiculous. An investigator thus tends to become disgusted, forgetting that the falsity of one story does not prove that the place was not named for an incident of which the true story may be still to be discovered. Anyone who has studied the actual records of explorers is struck by the many names given as the result of incidents. (See, for instance, the narratives of the expeditions of Portolá and of Lewis and Clark.)

Many of the most colorful place names are derived from incidents. These names may generally be distinguished from descriptive and possessive names by their being, superficially, inappropriate. A certain Mad River, for instance, is a comparatively gentle stream; it was so named because a man once lost his temper there.

Some names, by their very nature, suggest incidents—Hat Creek, Murder Creek, Earthquake Creek, Moonlight Ridge, Lightning Peak.

Calendar names generally record the incident that someone was at this particular place on a particular day. Thus Independence Rock was named because some early travelers celebrated the Fourth of July there. Even the common use of saints' names among the Spanish explorers, although it is usually attributed to piety and thus considered commemorative, could just as well be considered a mere attempt to record a particular day.

Many names may arise from either description or incident. Thus Horseshoe Creek might come from a bend in the stream or from the finding or loss of that important bit of pioneer equipment. Even Blue Lake should not be written off thoughtlessly as only another commonplace description; it might have arisen because someone happened to feel "blue." Occurrence from an incident is often difficult to prove, but this should not mean that names should therefore be classified as descriptive until shown to be something else.

4) COMMEMORATIVE NAMES. These arise by the process of taking an already established name and giving it a new application, for honorific ends. In this instance the secondary motive, i.e., commemoration, or at least a desire to perpetuate the old name for some reason, may be considered essential.

The mere application of an old name to a new place does not suffice to make the name commemorative. A body of water in Vermont, for instance, is called Caspian Lake because its outline resembles that of the Caspian Sea. This should, it would seem, be classed as a descriptive name. The namer presumably had no interest in re-applying the old name, but was merely noting that the lake in question was "like the Caspian Sea."

In the same way a California town is named Sebastopol, not—it is believed—from any interest in the Russian city, but because of a local squabble that was humorously compared to the famous siege of the Crimean War. Sebastopol has here become really a symbol or a common noun, as if we should speak of "a sebastopol." The name, therefore, would be classed as an incident name.

The situation is also complicated by the current use of the term *transfer name*. This refers to a place name that has been "transferred" from an older place to a newer one. Thus Cambridge, England, was transferred to Cambridge, Maryland, and then to Cambridge, Ohio. *Transfer name* is not, however, synonymous with *commemorative name*. Most transfer names are commemorative, but not all of them, e.g., Caspian and Sebastopol, in the examples given above, would seem to be transfers but not commemoratives. Moreover, many commemoratives, especially those honoring people, are not transfers. I therefore consider *transfer name* to be a useful special term, but not a primary one in my classification.

The term *commemorative* itself, though it is well enough established and seems to cover the situation fairly well, is not altogether a happy one. Sometimes the actual idea of commemoration is scarcely apparent. Along early western railroads, for instance, the stations were often given old-world names merely because they had to be named in some way, and such names were conveniently available to anyone consulting a gazetteer. Nevertheless, it would be rash to say that some conventionalized idea of homage to the already established names was not present even here.

In spite of these difficulties, the commemoratives form a well-established and useful group, as clearly distinguishable as any of the others.

Frequently thus honored are famous men. The common use in the United States, for instance, of the name Washington rarely indicates that any Washington owned the place or lived there, or was ever connected with it by an incident, but usually that George Washington is honored.

Saints' names should doubtless be separated from those of famous men, especially since they include St. Michael and certain others who presumably never were men. As noted under incident names, the application of a saint's name on the calendar-day of that saint can possibly be included under the head of incident.

A notable usage of commemorative naming occurs when colonists, whether ancient Greek or modern European or American, name their newly founded town after some town of the mother-country. (See also, however, under *Euphemistic Names*.)

Many other names are also applied to places commemoratively. Returned soldiers have frequently used the names of their victories, and thus Cerro Gordo and other Mexican names were multiplied across the United States. Any famous name, whether actual or legendary or mythological, is likely to be used. Thus in the United States, as the result of our admiration for classical Greece, we have place names for actual people and places (Lysander, Solon, Athens, Corinth), and also for legendary characters (Hector, Ulysses), for mythological places (Hesperia, Elysian Fields), and for gods (Apollo).

5) EUPHEMISTIC NAMES. These are names, comparatively few in number, given with reference to the future, rather than with reference to the past or present. They picture the place by means of an idealization, and are therefore to be distinguished from descriptives, which picture the place, in essence, realistically. The name Greenland—given by Eric the Red, "because men would the more readily go there if the county had a good name"—may serve as a type-example.

As with commemoratives, the secondary motive must be considered with euphemistic names. On the whole, this is the most uncertain and probably is one of the smallest of the classes. On the grounds of pure logic the objection can be raised that euphemistic names always display some other mechanism, and so can better be grouped as descriptives, or commemoratives, or in some other class.

Yet the term is established and is a useful one. If a promoter names his "development" Eden or Paradise, one can hardly maintain in a serious way that this is a descriptive name. Moreover, though Eden and Paradise are old names, one can scarcely maintain that they were re-bestowed for commemorative purposes—unless indeed the namer had come from a place already so named.

The point at which description becomes euphemy is, in fact, often doubtful. Downright *false description* is comparatively rare. The matter of looking toward the future, of an expression of an ideal to be attained rather than of a present reality, is probably the best test of a euphemistic name. Thus Homeland may be named before anyone has established a home there; Wheatland, when the country is still unplowed prairie.

The line between euphemistic and commemorative names is also difficult to establish, and probably a great many names will always be classed as commemorative which might equally well or better be classed as euphemistic. For instance, the replacement of Indian names by the names of English towns for early colonial settlements is generally considered commemorative. But in some instances it might certainly be considered euphemistic—that is, the namers were trying to make the new settlement seem more attractive to settlers by getting rid of what they sometimes termed "the savage name" and substituting the safe-sounding name of a well-known English town.

Not a few places in the United States have been named Athens in the hope that they would become educational centers, as at least two of them now actually are. In such instances, one can note again the idealistic or symbolic quality that is usually associated with euphemistic naming. In the early nineteenth century the name Athens was scarcely so much the name of a city as a symbol of education and culture. The naming of a town after a man may mingle commemoration with euphemy. The giving of the name Lincoln, for instance, honors the hero but it also is a "good" name and may be thought attractive to settlers. In the same way, this name and others like it have been given to commercial products.

6) MANUFACTURED NAMES. These are names constructed, to form new words, from recombined sounds or letters, out of fragments of

old words, from initials, by backward spellings, by reversal of syllables, and so forth. Saybrook, Connecticut, formed in 1635 from the titles of Lord Say and Sele and Lord Brook, is probably the earliest example of such a name in the United States. As typical examples we may note Tesnus (from Sunset), Romley (from Morley), Somerange (from Summer Range), Alicel (from Alice L.), Ti (from the reversed initials of Indian Territory), and Michillinda (from the abbreviations of three state names, with an added *a*.) *Boundary names* (Calexico, Texarkana) form a sub-division.

7) SHIFT NAMES. These are names that are placed upon places by the mere shift of the specific from one generic to another in the vicinity. Thus from White Mountain may spring White Lake, White River, and Whiteville, although none of these may be white. The resulting group of names is often called a *name-cluster*.

I have been forced to coin the term shift-name. *Transfer name* has sometimes been used. This term, however, more commonly indicates a name transferred from one place to another, not merely from one generic to another in the same region. I am unable to find that any other term has been used for what I here call *shift name*.

By a very broad interpretation shift-names might be classed with associative—descriptive names, but they are better, I think, kept distinct. Shift names differ in that they are really not descriptive at all, and are often actually misleading.

The possibility, however, cannot be ruled out that a shift name may *also* be descriptive. Thus, White Lake might actually have a whitish tinge to its water.

8) FOLK ETYMOLOGIES. A well-recognized process is that of folk etymology, e.g., *Purgatoire* to Picketwire, *Cayo Hueso* to Key West, *Chemin Couvert* to Smackover. Objection may be raised that this does not originate a new name but merely results in the transformation of an old one, and that it therefore cannot be considered basic. Although this may be granted theoretically, the transformation is often so great as to result in what is something wholly new, and for practical purposes the onomatologist will do well, I think, to recognize it as independent.

Some may prefer the term *false etymology* to that of folk etymology, since the process does not always occur at what they consider the folk level. Thus Seneca Lake (or originally, the Seneca tribe)

left its Indian original and assumed the form of the name of the
Roman philosopher and dramatist presumably by the error of
someone who possessed some Latinity. The term folk-etymology,
however, seems well enough established to be left in possession. It
certainly covers the vast majority of cases. And are not even men of
learning also of the folk in the larger sense?

A difficult but fascinating problem is, sometimes, to determine
the point at which folk etymologies have gone far enough to be
considered to have produced new names and not merely transformations of old names. In some cases only a part of the name
may be affected; in others, the result may merely resemble new
words or word-elements. As examples of names in which the process
seems to have stopped half-way, we may list: Kingsessing, Walpack,
Westkeag, Aughwick, Octorara, Quisquamego. All of these go back
to originals in some Indian language, but have assumed a partial
or nonsensical English or Latin form.

In connection with folk etymology one should also not forget
that it represents, in a special way, its own mechanism for the
forming of new names, i.e., a kind of punning or verbal play. In
many instances the process was undoubtedly wholly conscious and
had a humorous motive. We can hardly think, for instance, that
the British soldiers of 1914 really were confused to the point of
thinking that Ypres was the equivalent of *Wipers*. In fact, we
should note that this is actually what may be called an eye-pun
and can have nothing to do with speech in its origin. In the same
way the unknown Arkansan who made *L'eau Froide* into Low
Freight may well have been a wholly conscious humorist.

9) MISTAKE NAMES. These result from a mere mistake. In some
instances, the mistake may result only in a somewhat changed
name, e.g., in a variation of spelling. In many instances, however,
the mistake means that the name shifts from one word to another
having a different meaning, or else to a linguistic combination
having no meaning at all. A mistake may also be said to be involved
in folk etymology, but folk etymology always rests upon some kind
of logic, even if false logic. Mistake names, however, arise from
what might be called the operations of chance and mis-chance, e.g.,
typographical errors, illegible handwriting, careless copying, faulty
enunciation, faulty hearing. An example of a mistake name is
Lamoille River (Vermont), originating from *La Mouette*, which

first became *La Mouelle,* supposedly by failure of a map-engraver to cross his *t*'s. Oregon is another name believed to have originated from a mistake on a map. Other examples of mistake names, originating in various ways, are: Tolo (Oregon) from Yolo; Darrington (Washington) from Barrington; Plaski (Texas) from Pulaski.

A question arises whether mistranslations should be classed as mistake names. If the mistranslation is complete, the result would have to be considered an entirely new name, and might therefore be called a mistake name. More commonly mistranslations are mere inaccuracies, and lead back to the original. A famous example is the Staked Plains. Several explanations have been offered as to what the stakes were, but actually the Spanish *estacado* would apparently have been more properly translated as *palisaded,* and refers to the cliffs or palisades that bound certain parts of the plain.[1]

Although the great majority of names will be found, if their manner of origin can be determined, to fall clearly into one or other of these nine classes, there also exist a certain number of border-line instances. Some of these—such as descriptive-euphemistic and commemorative-euphemistic have already been discussed. A few others may also be illustrated.

a) *Descriptive-incident.* An incident, if recurring, may become characteristic and therefore descriptive. Roaring Creek, for instance, might have been named at a time of an exceptional flood (incident); Rattlesnake Lake, because a man came upon a single rattlesnake there. Yet the creek may roar for enough of the time to make the name properly descriptive, and the lake may be the location of a den of rattlesnakes, and therefore have many rattlesnakes at the end of every hibernation-period.

b) *Incident-possessive.* Since possessive names are so closely connected with associate-descriptive, they also are naturally connected with incident names. The test is chiefly the length of time involved in the connection of the man and the thing named for him. A typical incident-naming was the result, in frontier times, of some man being killed by Indians near a nameless stream, which was thereafter either formally named after him by his comrades or merely remembered for the incident and thus called by his name. On the other hand, if a man lives on a stream for a week and starts to build a cabin there and then is killed—is this a possessive or an

incident name that results? Obviously we pass from one to the
other at some point.

c) *Euphemistic-manufactured.* Although names may be manufactured in different ways, the product is usually submitted to a
euphemistic test before finally being adopted. Obviously, if a certain scrambling of syllables or a certain chance combination of
vowels and consonants should yield an obscene or ridiculous result,
it would probably not be used. Experimenters with combinations
of sounds generally have two interests—to avoid association with
the past, and to attain euphony. Both of these have euphemistic
suggestions.

Border-line cases can, in fact, be probably found lying between
most of the classes. Descriptive-commemorative and incident-
commemorative are certainly of some importance, but need not
be separately discussed.

Since a discussion of the ways of naming, however, cannot entirely escape a consideration of motive, one can also point out that
mixed motives naturally result in mixed mechanisms. Theoretically, one might assume that a single motive and therefore a single
mechanism is always predominating, but even when a namer gives
us two reasons for the naming, he does not always state, and doubtless he cannot always know, which was the predominating one.
Thus Herrera declares that Ponce named Florida because of its
flowers (descriptive) *and* because he discovered it at the season of
Pascua Florida (incident). Although he necessarily states one before
the other, he gives no indication as to which was the more important.[2] Actually, statements by namers that they gave a name for two
reasons are rare. This must be attributed partly to the mere trouble
of writing both reasons down. Even the recording of a single reason
is by no means common. Yet we cannot doubt but that the namer
was often conscious of more than one reason.

A special case occurs when names are given communally, e.g.,
by the vote of a group of settlers. In such a situation, one motive
may dominate in one mind; another, in another.

Finally, it should be stated, as a special warning, that this classification does not mean that any particular word used as a name
falls always under one heading. It would be incorrect, for instance,

to say that *red* is a descriptive adjective and that therefore all features so named have been descriptively named. Obviously the scholar should recognize that Red Creek might originate as a shift name, a folk etymology, and a mistake name. But it can also be a possessive name, for a man nicknamed Red, and having doubtless passed through the intermediary Red's Creek. It can also be an incident name, being perhaps named from blood, just as we have Bloody Creek. It might, conceivably, be a commemorative name, named after some stream that a man had known in the region from which he had come. Doubtless a considerable majority of names using this adjective will be found to be descriptive, but this is no excuse for throwing all such names into that omnibus classification.

NOTES

[1] An occasional namer has called upon chance. Yet I have difficulty in seeing how a name could originate entirely from chance. If so, it would doubtless be a manufactured name. A man may close his eyes, put his finger on a map of South America, and thus get Callao. But the mere fact that he uses a map of that continent shows that he has determined to use a transfer name and that his motives must be much the same as those of anyone who transfers a name for commemorative reasons. Moreover, how do we know that he would not reject any chance-given name if he did not like it? The Russians in 1812 chose the name of their fort in California by drawing names from a vessel, but someone had previously written various names on slips of paper and placed them in the vessel, so that chance was confined to narrow bounds. The name thus selected would have to be classified as a commemorative one.

[2] Herrera did not name Florida and was not present at the naming, and so the case is not altogether certain. Yet Herrera was a careful historian, and he seems to be paraphrasing Ponce's own report, now lost. Incidentally, the name is an interesting one for another reason, that it seems to be an indubitable example of a name transferred from one language to another by means of the written or printed form. Otherwise we should expect it to be accented on the second syllable, as it actually is in the local pronunciation of the Florida Mountains in New Mexico. Englishmen, we may believe, first seeing Florida as a printed word, took to pronouncing it as if it were the Latin adjective, not the Spanish one.

The Name of God
in the Revised Standard Version

ELSDON C. SMITH

IN THE Hebrew Old Testament the principal names used for God
are three: *Elohim, El* and *Yahveh. Jah,* an abbreviation of *Yahveh,*
is also occasionally found. There is much to be learned from a
serious study of these names and the way in which they are used.

Elohim is the plural form of the name *Eloah.* By using the plural
form the Jews did not mean to imply that there were many gods.
Some have suggested that *Elohim* referred to the Trinity, Father,
Son and Holy Spirit, but the Jews used this form in the first chapter
of *Genesis* and throughout the entire Old Testament. That by
Elohim was meant one God is evidenced by the fact that it is used
with a singular verb and with singular pronouns. Among the early
Hebrews the plural form was used to indicate intensity of some
kind, and thus the name in this form denotes extreme reverence.
Eloah means 'the worshipped'; *Elohim* means 'the most worshipped.' *Eloah* is found only a few times in the Old Testament
and then chiefly in the poetical and later books.

El, as a name for God, is not an abbreviation or shortened form
of *Eloah;* its plural is *Elim.* Among the Semitic peoples *El* is found
as a common term for God, although it occurs in the Old Testament only 217 times compared to the 2570 times that *Elohim* is
found. As a common noun it is analogous to our term *God,* but the
two words differ in meaning. *El* signifies 'the might, or power,'
while the Anglo-Saxon word *God* means 'one who is invoked, or to
whom sacrifice is offered.'

While both *Elohim* and *El* are used as common nouns for God,
and also for pagan gods, the real, personal name of God is the four-
lettered *Yod He Vav He,* the Tetragrammaton of the Hebrews,
which is most accurately transliterated to *Yahveh.* It is found more

than six thousand times in the Old Testament, not once in the New Testament. This is the name God gave in answer to Moses' request for God's name when He talked with Moses out of the burning bush (*Exodus* iii, 15). The King James version does not make it very clear.

When God first revealed His sacred name to Moses, He used the form *Ehyeh,* which is translated to 'I AM.' With the Hebrews the meaning of a name was more important than its form. When God pronounces His name, it is 'I AM'; when others enunciate it, the form is 'He is,' which is *Yahveh,* although God also used that form later. When God gave His name to Moses, He probably meant it as a symbol that His great promises would be kept, similar to the way we sign our name to a contract to indicate our assent to be bound.

Jehovah is strictly a Christian form of *Yahveh,* never having been used by the Jews. It was originated in 1270 by mistakenly giving the Tetragrammaton the vowels of *Edonai* or *Adonai,* meaning 'Lord.'

The Pentateuch uses both *Elohim* and *Yahveh,* while the strong theocratic and historical books relating to Israel, such as *Joshua, Judges, Samuel* and *Kings,* use chiefly *Yahveh.* The *Psalms* (except *Psalms* 42 to 84) usually employ the name, *Yahveh.*

To the Jews during the Christian era, *Yahveh* was such a sacred name that they refrained from pronouncing it except in the Temple. When reading the Old Testament they substituted another word, such as *Elohim, Adonai, Tetragrammaton* and *Lord.* Even some of the substituted names, such as *Elohim* and *Adonai,* later became so sacred that they ceased using them, or substituted incorrect spellings. In writing they used various symbols in place of the Holy Name, usually one to four yods.

After the captivity the Jews pronounced the Name only once a year, and even then it was pronounced only by the High Priest in the Temple at Jerusalem on Yom Kippur, or Day of Atonement. It was given in a low voice during the chant so that the people listening could not hear it. In the provinces they always used a substituted word. After the destruction of the Temple the "great and terrible name" was never pronounced. Thus the pronunciation was wholly lost, and scholars today can only conjecture as to the correct sound. Most scholars are agreed that *Yahveh* represents very closely the original sound of the Name.

The superstitious heathen, always ready to employ the name of any god as a magic name, quickly seized upon the four-lettered name revealed to the Jews. The careful and reverent use of the Name by the Jews, and particularly their refusal to pronounce the Name, convinced the pagans that it was indeed a most potent, magical name. *Yahveh* became the greatest magical name in the world. A thousand failures to invoke magic by the use of the Name would be ascribed to the inability to pronounce it correctly, while one apparent success would serve to convince them that the Name, exactly pronounced, was the key to godly power.

Ancient peoples among almost all nations firmly believed that there was magic in the names people bore. While the medieval Jews and pagans recognized that gods had power, they also thought that there was creative power in their god's names separate and apart from the powers wielded by the god. Gods were thought, in Egypt and elsewhere, to have created themselves originally by the act of pronouncing their names.

It is unfortunate that the translators of the Revised Standard Version decided to eliminate *Yahveh* entirely and to use *LORD* instead. It would seem that a name revealed by God Himself would be of such importance that translators would try to include it in as accurate a form as possible. The translators of the Revised Standard Version did affirm that the Bible was more than a historical document—more than a classic of English literature; they recognized it as a record of God's dealing with men, of God's revelation of Himself and His will. As it is a revelation of God, the revelation of His Name is important.

Those working on the Revised Standard Version announced their decision not to use "Jehovah" as far back as 1938. At that time Dr. Luther A. Weigle was quoted in the newspapers as saying that the change was made because, "Jehovah is not a functioning religious term." He further contended that people never think of praying to Jehovah.

Just what Dr. Weigle meant by saying that Jehovah was not a "functioning religious term," is not clear. If he meant that people did not fully understand the Name, this would scarcely be a reason for not retaining it. If we were to retain in the Bible only that part that was fully understood, we would lose much of that sacred book.

Perhaps Dr. Weigle meant by "functioning religious term" that

the Name was not used or understood in modern religious worship. Many lay people do understand it, though. And if the Name
given directly by God Himself is not a "functioning 'religious
term," it should be. That would be a further reason for retaining
the Name and making it crystal clear to students of the Bible. The
exact words of God, when we know them, should not be lightly
discarded.

That the members of the Committee were not fully satisfied with
their decision to discard the name *Jehovah,* although their decision was unanimous, is, perhaps, emphasized by their full discussion of the problem three different times—in 1930, 1937 and 1951,
as reported by Professor George Dahl in the portion he wrote of
the Introduction to the Revised Standard Version of the Old
Testament.

The Committee recognized the fact that *Jehovah* was not a correct rendering of the Tetragrammaton. Why didn't they adopt the
term *Yahveh* then? It is not suggested that the form *Jehovah* should
have been retained, although that would be better than dropping
the sacred name entirely; *Yahveh* should have been adopted.
Merely because that form was unfamiliar to many lay readers was
not a valid reason for discarding it. They altered words in the
twenty-third Psalm which many people can recite from memory,
and changed many other well-known words in many familiar verses
because they regarded the changes as a more accurate translation
of the original Scriptures.

Professor Millar Burrows wrote that the Committee accepted
seriously the fact that "the belief in divine revelation makes it
obligatory to seek only the real meaning of every word and sentence in the Scriptures, and to express just that meaning as exactly
and adequately as it can be done in English." *LORD* is not an
English translation of the divine Name; it is merely a word used
instead of the sacred term. No attempt was made to translate other
personal names in the Old Testament.

Even if it were decided to follow the King James version and
substitute the term *LORD* in most places, the correct name might
well have been retained in enough passages to bring it to the attention of serious readers. A footnote is not sufficient.

In many places in the Old Testament the rendering *LORD* is
awkward and unsatisfactory. When God replied to Moses' inquiry

as to His name, saying, "Say this to the people of Israel, 'The LORD, the God of your fathers, the God of Abraham, the God of Isaac, and the God of Jacob, has sent me to you'; this is my name for ever, and thus I am to be remembered throughout all generations," (*Exodus* iii, 15), the statement of the Name is far from clear. The full implications of God's words from the burning bush are difficult enough to comprehend without the concealment of His name. When the Revised Standard Version records Moses and the people of Israel singing, "The LORD is a man of war; the LORD is his name" (*Exodus* xv, 3), the rendering is unnecessarily awkward. In *Psalm* lxxxiii, 18, the song ends, "Let them know that thou alone, whose name is the LORD, art the Most High over all the earth," the revealed Name should appear to avoid confusion. Again in *Isaiah* xlii, 8, the Revised Standard Version has it as "I am the LORD, that is my name"; the reader must stop and remember that *LORD,* written all in capitals, refers to the sacred Name.

Is it clear to the Bible student when he reads in *Exodus* vi, 2, 3: "And God said to Moses, 'I am the LORD. I appeared to Abraham, to Isaac, and to Jacob, as God Almighty, but by my name the LORD I did not make myself known to them.' "?

That God regarded His name as an important revelation of Himself to man is clear from the many times he enunciated it. In *Exodus* xxxiii, 19, God told Moses, "I will make all my goodness pass before you, and will proclaim before you my name 'The LORD'; and I will be gracious to whom I will be gracious, and will show mercy on whom I will show mercy." In *Exodus* ix, 16, God directed that His name be declared throughout all the earth.

God regarded the proper use of His name as so important that He made it a part of His ten commandments, when He ordered, "You shall not take the name of the LORD your God in vain; for the LORD will not hold him guiltless who takes his name in vain." God did not say that His name was not to be used, only that it was not to be used, "in vain."

That the Name of *Yahveh* is important in the worship of God is further emphasized by the many times it is mentioned in the *Psalms.* Indeed, no Biblical scholar will deny the importance of the form *Yahveh.* To see at a glance the attention the term "name" has been given in the Bible just turn to that word in a concordance.

Nicknames and Nonce-names
in Shakespeare's Comedies

ALLEN B. KELLOGG

Nicknames, in the modern sense of substitute, gratuitous, and more or less leechlike forenames, are by no means abundant in Shakespeare's comedies. We certainly appear to have a genuine nickname, though, in Sugarsop, i.e. 'sugarplum' (in *The Taming of the Shrew,* IV.i.91), the concluding name in a series of first names spoken by Grumio as he directs Curtis to call forth the servants to greet Petruchio and his bride.[1] Likewise in *Pericles* (II.i.12–14) two of the fishermen address each other as Pilch 'leather jacket' (?) and Patch-breech. Possibly *these* should be termed quasi nicknames.

Under this designation we could include the names of several of the more or less clownish characters in the comedies: Speed, Moth (pronounced like *mote,* either word being admirable to suggest diminutiveness), Costard (a kind of large apple—applied humorously to the head), Elbow, Froth, Touchstone, and Verges ('verjuice'—with dialectal pronunciation). Verges, however, may have been a surname; Dogberry pretty clearly was.

As students of names are well aware, nicknames are a fertile source of surnames. *Shakespeare* itself is an example and gives us the pattern for *Falstaff* and *Martext.* The appropriateness of the name is, in this last instance, surely meant to be relished, as is true of such names as Aguecheek, Belch, Shallow, Slender, Mistress Quickly (quick + lie), Mistress Overdone, Alice Shortcake, and Kate Keepdown. Often the surnames, as in the cases of Anthony Dull and Peter Simple, are so patly descriptive as to be nicknames in effect. And the effect is heightened when, as is usually true, the surname is used throughout the play to the virtual exclusion of the forename. In the case of one clownish character, though, Pompey (in *Measure for Measure*), we learn his surname (Bum 'bottom') only when he is brought before an examining magistrate.[1]

Names like Shylock strike us as surnames. However, it has recently been suggested that Shylock is a (contemptuous) descriptive term rather than a true name. Norman Nathan points out that Tubal never calls Shylock by name—also that neither Lorenzo nor his friends use the word Shylock in Jessica's presence.[2]

Assumed names are sometimes descriptive in the manner of nicknames; note Imogen's *Fidele* (in *Cymbeline*). In *As You Like It* Celia, choosing a name for herself in her self-imposed exile, decides upon *Aliena* as "Something that hath a reference to my state."

Nicknames include familiar forms of Christian, or given, names. More than a dozen different pet forms and diminutives are to be found in Shakespeare's comedies. Kate, a diminutive of Katherina, comes to mind at once, as does Meg, derived from Margaret. The pet form Nell, in *The Comedy of Errors,* might come from Ellen, Eleanor, or Helen;[3] but in *Troilus and Cressida* when Paris speaks of "my Nell" he is of course referring to Helen. Nan is a pet form of Ann, and Maud (coming through French) of Matilda. Maudlin is from the French Madeleine, which goes back to Magdalen. Nick (Bottom) is a pet form of Nicholas, and Robin (Starveling) is a diminutive of Rob, a pet form of Robert. Dick (in Sir Toby's "Dick surgeon") is a nickname for Richard, as Tom is an abbreviation of Thomas. Ed, an abbreviation of Edward, appears in *The Merry Wives of Windsor* in the dialect form Yead. Malkin, a diminutive of Moll, a pet form of Mary, had, before Shakespeare's time, become a common noun with the meaning 'kitchen-maid' (*Pericles,* IV.iii.34). Likewise Tib, from Isabel, had taken on the meaning 'a low woman,' as in Marina's lines (*Pericles,* IV.vi.175–76):

> ". . . doorkeeper to every
> Coistrel that comes inquiring for his Tib."

Jack, a pet form of John, is used in at least four ways: (1) as a forename (Jack Rugby in *The Merry Wives of Windsor);* (2) as a general term for *man* (always coupled with Jill—as in the final scene of *Love's Labour's Lost);* (3) in the compound Jack-a-Lent 'puppet,' found twice in *The Merry Wives of Windsor;* (4) as a term of contempt (= 'knave') in such phrases as these:

> "play the flouting Jack" (*Much Ado About Nothing*)
> "these bragging Jacks" (*The Merchant of Venice*)
> "Jack priest" (*The Merry Wives of Windsor*)
> "Every Jack-slave" (*Cymbeline*)
> "play'd the Jack with us" (*The Tempest*)

Similar to the nicknames, except in the quality of permanence, are the nonce-names—ranging from slightly disrespectful to openly scornful—which various characters fling at one another or apply to someone not present. As might be expected, *Much Ado About Nothing* provides several examples. Beatrice, at the very outset, refers to Benedick with a fencing term, *Signior Mountanto* (he pays her back shortly with *Lady Disdain* and *my Lady Tongue*), and later speaks of Claudio as Count Comfect ('comfit'). The nonce-names Monsieur Love (in Act II) and Lord Lackbeard (in Act V) reflect the changing attitude of Benedick toward Claudio. The scorn in *Pedascule* ('little pedant'), which Hortensio hurls at Lucentio in *The Taming of the Shrew,* is as obvious as the expression is amusing. In *As You Like It* Jaques and Orlando close a diverting bout at repartee, during which they have desired to be better strangers, with:

> "I'll tarry no longer with you. Farewell, good Signior Love."
> "I am glad of your departure. Adieu, good Monsieur Melancholy."

In *Pericles* Helicanus characterizes a flattering lord with *Signior Sooth here;* in *The Tempest* Stephano calls Caliban *Mooncalf,* and Antonio speaks of Gonzalo as *this Sir Prudence.* Ulysees' reference, in *Troilus and Cressida,* to Achilles as *Sir Valour* contains more than a grain of irony, whereas the context in *The Comedy of Errors* makes it quite clear that Dromio of Syracuse's name for the greasy kitchen-wench Nell, Dowsabel (*'douce et belle'*), is ironically applied.

The nonce-name shades off almost imperceptibly into the abusive epithet. In *Measure for Measure* (III.ii.52) Lucio addresses Pompey as *Trot* (literally 'old woman'); in about half the editions which I have consulted the initial *t* of *Trot* is not capitalized. So far as I have observed, no editor capitalizes the initial *c* of *crack-hemp* ('gallows-bird'), a name which the outraged Vincentio in *The Taming of the Shrew* hurls at his dissembling servant Biondello.

From the rich store of nounce-names in Shakespeare's comedies a few more examples will suffice. In the concluding scene of *All's Well That Ends Well* Helena addresses Parolles as *Good Tom Drum*. In *Measure for Measure* Mistress Overdone is announced by Lucio, a fantastic, as *Madam Mitigation*. The Host, in *The Merry Wives of Windsor*, taking advantage of the French physician's limited knowledge of the ways of English, addresses him as *Mounseur Mockwater*. Benedick speaks of the conscience as *Don Worm*, thus reminding us of the medieval practice of representing the conscience under the symbol of a serpent. And when, in *The Winter's Tale* (II.iii.74–75), the incensed king upbraids Antigonus with

> "Thou dotard! thou art woman-tir'd, unroosted
> By thy dame Partlet here"

our minds flash back to happier scenes in an incomparable tale told by a certain nun's priest.

NOTES

[1] The numeration of acts, scenes, and lines is that of the New Cambridge Edition, *The Complete Plays and Poems of William Shakespeare,* edited by William Allan Neilson and Charles Jarvis Hill and published in 1942 by the Houghton Mifflin Company.

[2] Norman Nathan, "Three Notes on *The Merchant of Venice,*" *The Shakespeare Association Bulletin,* Vol. 23, pp. 152–173.

[3] See E. G. Withycombe, *The Oxford Dictionary of English Christian Names* (New York, 1947) under the entry *Nell(y)*.

Names in Popular Sayings

O. PAUL STRAUBINGER

THE ACTIVE INTEREST in human nomenclature, its origin, meaning and history has been reflected in an evergrowing store of popular writings. Considering the wealth and scope of this literature, we must wonder why only scant attention has been paid to the many relevant insights that may be gained from an investigation of the widely current use of personal names in proverbs and popular sayings. The patent disregard for this interesting field of investigation cannot be attributed to a paucity of source material but rather to a neglect of proper collecting. The most cursory perusal of any proverb collection will yield a ready and bountiful harvest of pertinent sayings, containing personal names in a great variety of pattern and meaning. However, such random samplings are of no great value to the study of names. Only methodic compilation, based on a diligent search through the tomes of proverb collections, will provide a reliable foundation for an authoritative discussion of the wealth of proverb lore that has been linked to many names.

Depending on emphasis and method, an examination of sayings relating to personal names will prove productive from several points of view. The analysis of their content will throw new light on the diverse and interesting connotations with which the common man has invested so many names. The study of their style will demonstrate a correlation between certain proverb patterns and the proverbial use of names. The evaluation of the quantitative yield with regard to specific names will provide valid evidence of their regional popularity in a historical perspective, evidence which in turn may be related to specific causative factors. The impact of history, of human fame or infamy, is found in the curious and often quite unexpected manner in which names from history or legend have caught popular fancy and persist in proverbial allusion. Occasionally the reference to a name may prove to be our only clue to the meaning of an obsolete proverb and enable us to establish its place and time of origin.

The assiduous collector of pertinent sayings may wisely choose to limit his collection to proverbial references to a single name. Professor Wayland D. Hand has given us an excellent example of the fruitfulness of such a highly selective approach in his comprehensive investigation of words and idioms which are traditionally associated with Judas Iscariot. Analogous limitations to instances of the use of personal names in such specific proverb patterns, as rhymes or puns on names, or alliterative formations should prove equally rewarding. Any collector who attempts to gain a wider perspective and who embarks on an all-inclusive compilation will soon find himself confronted with the difficult problem of finding a feasible arrangement for the analysis of countless sayings that differ widely in content and style.

To list all pertinent sayings alphabetically by name is one practical solution which has the obvious advantage of being very convenient for ready reference. However, this conventional arrangement fails to bring into focus one of the most important distinctions in the discussion of the proverbial use of names, i.e. the essential difference between proverb lore that alludes either directly or indirectly to the name of a specific character from history or legend and, on the other hand, the anomalous multitude of sayings in which personal names appear in a non-allusive sense to represent the concept of man or woman in general. The expediency of limiting one's collection to a single language is equally inadequate because it does not account for numerous instances of international currency. In view of these difficulties it seems advisable to limit comparative studies in this field to groups of sayings which can be clearly defined and circumscribed by some common characteristic.

The investigation of proverbs which pertain to names of individuals is particularly rewarding. Proverbs of this type are manifestly of earlier origin and of a wider regional distribution than the non-allusive sayings and lend themselves quite readily to meaningful groupings. There is, for instance, an abundance of allusions to Biblical characters. These allusions reveal or confirm many of the traditional beliefs which have been associated with some of the popular figures from both the New and the Old Testament. In a broader sense they also delineate some of the sources and the general scope of the common man's familiarity with the Scriptures. We may note, for example, the early origin and widespread currency of numerous proverbs that refer to Adam and Eve to attest that the dramatic narrative of the creation of man, of his temptation and fateful punishment, has never lost its deep symbolic meaning to mankind. The connotation of moral frailty which has been linked to the appellation *the old Adam* lends a deeper meaning to the widely current proverb *We are all Adam's children* as well as to its recent satiric expansion *We are all Adam's children, but silk makes the difference.* Similar allusions to the same connotation may be found in German, e.g. *Der alte Adam lebt noch* (Old Adam is still alive); *Der alte Adam guckt heraus* (Old Adam peeks out); *Nach dem alten Adam schmeckt jeder* (Every one has a touch of old Adam). Another German proverb *Alle Frauen sind Evastöchter* (All women are daughters of Eve) shows that analogous allusions to Eve are marked by similar innuendoes.

Proverbs linking Adam's name to that of Eve lend themselves readily to the creation of types employing the rhetorical device of parallelism or contrast. An early and widely known example of this type is the English rhyme *When Adam delved and Eve span, where was then the gentleman?* This extremely popular proverb was originally a part of a defiant revolutionary song. We know that it was used as early as 1381 by John Ball as the theme for his famous sermon on the equality of man and we can trace its rapid spread across the sea into Holland, Germany and the Scandinavian countries in the course of the following century. One of the reasons for its widespread currency in the Germanic languages lies without doubt in the ease with which the rhymed pattern of the English prototype could be imitated in these related tongues, e.g. in Dutch *Wie was die edelman, doe Adam groef ende Eve span* (ca. 1460); in Swedish *Ho was tha een ädela man, tha Adam groff ok eua span* (1476); in Early New High German *Da Adam reütet vnd Eva span, wer was die Zeit da ein Edelman* (1493). Closely related variants in the Romance and Slavic languages show, however, that linguistic bar-

riers were no obstacles to the expression of the ideal of human
equality in the simple words of this old adage.

Numerous allusions to Biblical characters in the form of proverbial comparison illustrate another type of popular saying which
becomes meaningful only through a common cognizance of the
Biblical connotations of the names involved. Sayings like *As wise
as Solomon* and *As old as Methuselah* have been current since the
Middle Ages. Biblical accounts of exemplary virtue inspired com-
parisons like *As modest as Judith; As obedient as Rebecca* and *As
chaste as Susanna.* The concepts of misery and patient suffering
have long been linked to the names of Job and Lazarus in *As
patient as Job* and *As poor as Lazarus.*

An interesting transposition of reference appears in the well-
known saying *To rob Peter to pay Paul.* In England this phrase is
commonly regarded as a historical allusion to the repair of St.
Paul's Cathedral done at the expense of St. Peter's at Westminster
during the reign of Edward VI. However, the assumption of this
particular reference becomes quite untenable in the light of much
earlier documentations of a medieval Latin equivalent *Non est
spoliandus Petrus, ut vestiatur Paulus* as well as in view of widely
current vernacular parallels on the Continent where any allusion
to a local English event would have been completely meaningless.
A German variant *Man muss nicht St. Peters Altar berauben, um
St. Paulus zu bedecken* (One must not rob St. Peter's altar to cover
St. Paul's) offers a clue to a more likely explanation which links
our saying to the religious custom of decorating the respective altar
of every saint on his special day. Normally this was done by trans-
ferring a special set of decorations from altar to altar. Since the
Saint's day of St. Peter coincided with that of St. Paul, it often was
impossible to grace the altar of one without baring the other.

The fervent cult of the saints during the late Middle Ages proved
extremely productive of sayings that base their metaphoric content
on a general knowledge of the lives of these venerated men and
women. Legendary accounts of their miraculous deeds and harsh
tribulations were familiar to the common people, who in proverbial allusion paid unwitting tribute to their saintly virtues.
Almost all the extant sayings of this type prove to be mere con-
tinuations or variations of the great wealth of proverb lore relating

to saints that was current in the sixteenth and seventeenth centuries. In Catholic countries we may still note an unmistakable correlation between the popularity of a particular cult and the yield and dissemination of relevant allusions. This explains, for instance, the abundance of French sayings which refer to the colorful legends about St. Martin, bishop of Tours and patron saint of France.

The dearth of similar sayings in Protestant regions is quite noticeable. We may safely charge it to the iconoclastic zeal of the early days of the Reformation, which apparently discouraged even the most innocuous expressions of apostasy. Among the few surviving English allusions to the name of a saint, we find some curious references to St. Anthony, as patron saint of the swineherds, in the sayings *As fat as St. Anthony's pig* and *He will follow him like St. Anthony's pig.* The latter is still used to scorn obsequious behavior. Both sayings were originally inspired by the familiar sight of "St. Anthony's pigs" in the streets of Old London, where the proctors of St. Anthony's Hospital had been granted the privilege of letting their swine feed on public land. Homage to St. George, the patron saint of England, is paid in the expressions *As bright as St. George* and *St. George to boot.* The facetious simile *Like St. George who is always on horseback and never rides* was obviously inspired by the familiar sight of countless statues and pictures of St. George as a heroic warrior.

The number of proverbial allusions to historical characters other than saints is surprisingly small. Apparently the great of the past were so quickly forgotten by burgher and peasant that any reference to them soon lost its meaning. Popular ascriptions that assign many sayings to definite characters are therefore frequently open to question. The seeming reference to Alexander the Great in *If Alexander were a cook, all the world would know it* becomes somewhat questionable when we note that this is evidently a less suggestive variant of a proverb which is widely current in German and Spanish and reads in literal translation "If Alexander were a cuckold, God and all the world would know it" (*Wenn Alexander ein Hahnreih ist, so weiss es Gott und alle Welt; Si Alejandro es cornudo, sepalo Dios y todo el mundo*). The more specific allusion of the continental version lends some weight to a conjecture that relates this proverb to a certain Alexander Pheseo, governor of Thessaly, who according to long forgotten accounts was murdered by his own wife when he took extreme measures to curb her notorious infidelity. Allusions to characters from English history are equally uncertain. The proverb *King Harry loved a man* is supposed to derive its ironic connotation from the reputation of Henry VIII for wanton greed and selfishness. We have yet to find a plausible explanation for the jocular use of *This was a hill in King Harry's day* or for the old Sussex saying *My Lord Baldwin is dead,* which was used in an ironic sense to let people know that their news was already commonplace knowledge. The early currency of the proverbial comparison *As bold as Beauchamp* suggests that it may have been prompted by the numerous accounts of the chivalrous pursuits of Richard de Beauchamp, Earl of Warwick (1382–1439), yet later periods were prone to regard it as an allusion to the fame of other, contemporary bearers of this illustrious name.

A typical example of a proverbial allusion which is no longer linked to any specific character is our well-known expression *Let George do it.* In American usage it is commonly associated with the appellative use of this name for a Pullman porter. Yet we are told that Louis XII used to express his confidence in George d'Amboise, his minister of state, by saying: "Laissez faire à Georges, il est homme d'âge." In spite of the striking sameness of expression, we find ourselves hard pressed to explain why the French phrase was allegedly translated and so widely adopted by the American people.

These instances are but a few of many that could be cited to illustrate the difficulties in the search for the origin and meaning of proverb in which the allusion to a name is no longer understood. Our success in tracing these references to definite historical or legendary characters depends not only on the patient search through authoritative works on history, legend, or superstition but also to a large degree on the grace of fortuitous discovery.

The proverbial use of personal names in a general, non-allusive sense, as in *All work and no play makes Jack a dull boy* is of comparatively recent origin. First documented at the close of the fifteenth century, these sayings about Dick, Tom, and Harry have become increasingly popular and in the case of names like Jack or

John extremely productive. Instances of international currency are rare and invariably limited to closely related language groups. The popular character of these sayings accounts for a general tendency to use abbreviated forms like Dick, Tom, or Bess in preference to the full name. The brevity of these pet forms also conforms with a natural inclination to make proverbs short and concise. The use of these names in the generic sense of man or woman is, on the whole, much less common than their endowment with specific connotative values.

The historic development of the proverbial use of names in a general, non-allusive sense clearly reflects the relative popularity of the names involved. Ultimately we must attribute the vogue of certain names to explicit factors like the missionary zeal with which the Medieval Church promoted the use of names from the Calendar of Saints or the ancient custom of naming children after the ruler of the land. To illustrate the correlation between the vogue of a name and its proverbial use we only need to point to the abundance of proverbs in every Western tongue which contain the name of John in one of its many variant forms. Being not only the name of the Baptist and of Christ's favorite disciple, but also that of 23 popes and of no less than 994 saints, this name has outranked all other Christian names for more than half a millennium.

The connotations, that are attached to names, generally strike a disparaging note. In English we may note this early instance of the use of Jack, the curious English pet for John, in sayings like *Jack would be a gentleman if he had money* or *Jack would be a gentleman if he could speak French,* dating from the close of the fifteenth century. Another early example of more pronounced disparagement may be found in the use of Malkin, an obsolete diminutive form of Maud, in the sixteenth-century proverb *You cannot love both at once the mistress and Malkin, her maid.* Being used at this stage as a stock name for a servant girl, Malkin subsequently deteriorated in meaning to the point where it became a synonym for harlot.

Popular delight in rhyme and alliteration inspired the creation of sayings like *Jack shall have his Gill; If Jack's in love, he is no judge of Jill's beauty; There is a silly Jock for every silly Jenny;*

There is not so bad a Gill, but there is a bad Will. Such juxtaposi-
tions of the names of the opposite sexes permit many variations of
parallelism or of contrast in thought and stylistic structure.

Within the narrow compass of this brief discussion, the few examples cited can offer merely a glimpse of an abundance of chal-
lenging materials for fruitful investigation. In addition to the use
of names in proverbial sayings, one should also mention their use
in mocking rhymes, in weather rules and in magic formulae, i.e. in
curses or invocations. There can be no question that the methodic
search and the critical analysis of these neglected fields of research
will yield some notable contributions to name research.

◇   ◇   ◇

Meaningful Fictive Names in English Literature

Kemp Malone

Fictitious characters with characterizing names are to be found in all literatures known to me. A good Greek example is the Mentor of the Odyssey, whose name means 'counselor' and whose function is that of giving counsel to young Telemachus. In this paper, however, I am restricting myself to names of this kind found in English literature. And because of the great number of such names I shall have to rest content with a mere sampling of the English material. I will give my examples in chronological order, beginning with our oldest English poem, *Widsith*, composed in the seventh century.

Widsith took name from its chief character, a minstrel who in the exercise of his profession had traveled far and wide. The name means 'long journey' and serves to characterize the minstrel as a great traveler. Other characters in the poem have meaningful names; thus, King Wald of the Woings (line 30), whose name means 'ruler.' But since it is possible, though most unlikely, that a king so named actually lived, I do not include the name *Wald* in my survey, which is restricted to the names of fictitious persons. For the same reason, I leave out some very striking names found in the English epic poem *Beowulf*. Thus, the would-be trouble-maker who engages in a fliting with the hero early in the poem has a name, *Unferth*, that means 'disturbing the peace, dissension, trouble-making' or the like. He may well be fictitious, but since there is some reason to think that he goes back to a historical character I am not putting him in. The Danish king Scyld, however, who figures in the introductory part of the poem, is undoubtedly fictitious and his name therefore comes within the scope of this paper. It means 'shield,' that is, 'protector,' and denotes an important function, if not indeed the chief function of a king, that of protecting his people against invasion, crime, and other troubles, including a failure of the crops, something that the right kind of

king in olden times was supposed to keep from happening. I might
add that even in our own enlightened day bad economic weather
makes trouble for rulers and political parties in power, though it is
no longer the custom to try to improve the weather by putting the
king or president to death.

A familiar kind of meaningful name is that of the personified
abstraction. English literature swarms with fictitious characters
that represent abstractions and are named accordingly. The
beginnings of such personification may be found as early as *Beowulf*.
The author of this poem speaks both of death and of wyrd (i. e.
fate) in such a way that we may well suspect him of having personified these abstractions. Thus, in line 1205 we are told that Wyrd
carried King Hygelac off. Later on, under the influence of classical
mythology, Wyrd was made into three sisters, and by Shakespeare's
day the Weird sisters had become mere witches, a degradation
which their Greek counterparts were spared.

Many personified abstractions appear as characters in Chaucer,
but in nearly every case they were taken from the poet's sources
and he usually plays them down rather than up. Thus, in the
Parlement of Fowles a large number of male and female characters
of this kind are to be found: e. g. Delight, Gentleness, Beauty,
Youth, Flattery, Desire, Peace, Patience, Jealousy, and Riches.
But these are disposed of with a mere mention. Love and his
daughter Will get more space, but the only personified abstraction
who plays an important part in the poem is Nature. When we turn
to *Piers Plowman*, a poem of the same century, we find a very
different state of things: nearly all the characters are personified
abstractions and the characterization of most of them is worked
out vividly and at length. Typical of this difference in treatment
is the character Mede (i. e. bribery); both poets have her but Chaucer
merely mentions her whereas in *Piers Plowman* she plays a leading
part.

In the medieval drama personified abstractions belong especially
to the morality plays. In the *Castle of Perseverance*, for instance,
the characters are nearly all personifications: e. g. Meekness,
Charity, Abstinence, Chastity, Industry, Generosity, Patience;
Lechery, Sloth, Gluttony; Lust, Folly, Covetousness; Confession,
Penance; Mercy, Peace, Truth, Righteousness; Death. The main
character, Mankind, personifies human nature besides representing

the human species and goes back to an abstraction on both counts. The moralities were serious plays to start with, but a comic element got into them by way of the wicked or evil characters, who tended to degenerate into mere mischief-makers, practical jokers, or wise-crackers as the medieval drama developed. In this way the per-sonified abstraction Vice (i. e. depravity) came to be little more than a stage jester or buffoon. In later times we find personified abstractions in a great variety of literary compositions; they are especially common in lyric poetry. I illustrate with the first sonnet of Rossetti's *House of Life*:

> I marked all kindred Powers the heart finds fair: —
> Truth, with awed lips; and Hope, with eyes upcast;
> And Fame, whose loud wings fan the ashen Past
> To signal-fires, Oblivion's flight to scare;
> And Youth, with still some single golden hair
> Unto his shoulder clinging, since the last
> Embrace wherein two sweet arms held him fast;
> And Life, still wreathing flowers for Death to wear.
> Love's throne was not with these; but far above
> All passionate wind of welcome and farewell
> He sat in breathless bowers they dream not of;
> Though Truth foreknow Love's heart, and Hope foretell,
> And Fame be for Love's sake desirable,
> And Youth be dear, and Life be sweet to Love.

Here truth, hope, fame, oblivion, youth, life, death, and love are personified. One may compare another passage from the same sonnet-sequence, in which today, yesterday, and tomorrow are personified:

> "Thou Ghost," I said, "and is thy name Today? —
> Yesterday's son, with such an abject brow? —
> And can Tomorrow be more pale than thou?"

Another very old kind of fictitious character, the representative of some occupation, type of person, social class, or the like, may either go nameless or be given a name that brings out his re-presentative function. He goes nameless in the *Wanderer*, an Old English poem which has for chief character an old retainer whose lord has died and who in consequence has become a lordless man, a wanderer on the face of the earth. In another poem, *Eadwacer*, which has come down to us in the same MS, we find a character

named Wulf (i. e. outlaw), but unhappily the poem is very obscure
and we cannot be certain that Wulf was really an outlaw, though
this is the usual interpretation. As everybody knows, most of
Chaucer's pilgrims in the *Canterbury Tales* have no names: thus,
the knight, the squire, the yeoman, and many others. Some of the
pilgrims do have names, but these are almost never used in the
narrative. Thus, in one line of the poem we are told that the host
was named Harry Bailly, but everywhere else he is called simply
the host (i. e. the innkeeper).

By way of contrast, let us look at the sixteenth-century play
Roister Doister. The play begins with a speech by Mathew Merry-
greek, whose surname means 'merry fellow, roisterer' and who
behaves accordingly, as he himself tells us. More particularly, he
explains that he keeps body and soul together by dining now with
one friend, now with another, and these friends all have names
indicative of their way of life. To quote,

> My living lieth here and there, of God's grace:
> Sometime with this good man, sometime in that place;
> Sometime Lewis Loiterer biddeth me come near;
> Somewhiles Watkin Waster maketh me good cheer;
> Sometime Davy Diceplayer, when he hath well cast,
> Keepeth revel-rout as long as it will last;
> Sometime Tom Titivil maketh us a feast;
> Sometime with Sir Hugh Pye I am a bidden guest;
> Sometime at Nichol Neverthrives I get a sop;
> Sometime I am feasted with Bryan Blinkinsop;
> Sometime I hang on Hankin Hoddydoddy's sleeve,
> But this day on Ralph Roister Doister's, by his leave.

Of the surnames in this passage, *Loiterer, Waster, Diceplayer,*
and *Neverthrives* need no comment. *Titivil* is a word of doubtful
etymology but it was current in fifteenth and sixteenth century
English in the sense 'scoundrel,' with particular application to a
mischiefmaking tell-tale, and Tom Titivil is to be taken as such a
character. *Pie* (i. e., magpie), applied to a man, may mean either
'chatterer' or 'wily, cunning person.' One cannot tell which of these
two senses is meant here. *Blinkinsop* may be compared to our modern
phrase *blinkin' idiot,* though the element *sop* means not 'idiot' but
'worthless person.' *Hoddydoddy* means 'blockhead, dolt, fool.'
Compare the obsolete words *hoddypeak* and *doddypoll,* both of

which have this meaning. The last surname in the passage, *Roister Doister*, is obviously a riming compound. Its first element *Roister* is a well known sixteenth-century word with the sense 'swaggering, blustering bully.' The second element *Doister* may be the same as the modern dialectal *doister* 'tempest' (compare Scottish *dois* in the same sense); if so, it serves to mark the character wild in behavior.

Other characters in this play that have meaningful names are: Gawin Goodluck, Tristram Trusty, Dobinet Doughtie, Tom Trupenie, Sym Suresby, Harpax, Christian Custance, Madge Mumblecrust, and Tibet Talkapace. Of these, Goodluck is truly well named, since he has won the heart of a rich widow. His friend Trusty in the course of the action shows himself indeed one to be trusted, and the servants Trupenie and Suresby live up to their names by their conduct. Of Roister's two servants, Doughtie has a name that means 'capable' and he serves his master accordingly; at any rate, he obeys orders. Harpax, whose name means 'robber,' is a proper servant for a man who tries to rob Goodluck of his betrothed. The widow Custance (i. e. constancy) is so named to emphasize her faithfulness to the absent Goodluck. Of her servants, the old woman Madge Mumblecrust is named in terms of a physical disability that goes with old age: she has no teeth and must mumble the crusts that she eats. The verb *mumble* used to mean 'chew with toothless gums.' Tibet Talkapace is a great talker, as her name indicates. The only character in the play with a name that makes trouble is Annot Alyface, the housemaid. Here the element *-face* is clear enough but what does *Aly-* mean? Various guesses might be made but I find none of them satisfactory.

Roister Doister, though a school play, has only one character with a name drawn from a classical tongue: *Harpax*, which is Greek for robber. A later play of the same century, Lyly's Endymion, is classical throughout in its name-giving, and the author presumably took for granted that his audience would know enough Latin and Greek to tell what the names of the characters meant. It must be added, however, that only a few of the names can reasonably be taken for characterizations. Endymion's friend Eumenides has a name that means 'the wellmeaning or well-minded one' and the name fits his character beautifully; he is indeed a true friend. His adviser, the old man at the fountain, is called Geron, the Greek word for old man. Other characters with obviously meaningful names are Tellus (the earth), her friend Floscula (little flower), the court ladies Scintilla (spark) and Favilla (glowing ashes of the dead), the old witch Dipsas (snake), and her servant Bagoa (poisoner).

The name *Bagoa* is of special interest. It is the feminine of *Bagoas*, a Persian name borne, among others, by a notorious poisoner who was put to death by King Darius III, the opponent of Alexander the Great. It was this historical character who gave the name *Bagoas* the association with poisoning which Lyly made use of in naming the servant of Dipsas. Yet though Bagoa poisons Endymion by fanning him with a hemlock leaf, she does this unwillingly, obeying the orders of her mistress, and the poison merely puts Endymion to sleep; it does not kill him. In other words, Lyly made Bagoa a character reminiscent of the historical Bagoas yet different from him not only in sex but also in spirit. In the same way, Lyly's Dipsas has remarkable powers but does not use them to give her victims a raging thirst, as the snake Dipsas does in Greek story. At any rate she put Endymion to sleep instead.

The ladies-in-waiting Scintilla and Favilla were so named in order to make possible the action with which the second scene of the second act begins. Favilla has called Endymion's page a silly boy. The page retorts: "Alas, good old gentlewoman, how it becometh you to be grave." And Scintilla adds: "Favilla, though she be but a spark, yet is she fire." The two speeches, taken together, give us the meaning of the Latin word *favilla* if we take into account the pun on *grave*. As everybody knows, the Romans practised cremation of the dead. The body was burned and the ashes, so long as they still glowed, had the special name *favilla*, a name no longer applicable after they had lost their glow. It befits our character Favilla, then, to be grave (i. e. seriousminded), since by virtue of her name she is dead and in her grave; yet not quite, for there is fire in her ashes still. One is reminded of Chaucer's reeve in the Canterbury Tales, who in his prolog speaks for old people as such, saying

> Yet in our asshen olde is fyr yreke.

But Favilla can play the etymological game herself. She responds: "And you, Scintilla, be not much more than a spark, though you would be esteemed a flame." The give and take goes on for a number of lines more, but I have said enough to show that the meaning of these names is functional in the play.

The queen in the play is called Cynthia; that is, she goes by the same name that the English poets of the day gave to Queen Elizabeth. Since *Cynthia* had long been familiar as a name for the moon-goddess, the author could use it with perfect propriety in his play about Endymion's love-affair with the moon. But in so doing he made the name doubly meaningful: in many passages it applies to the moon and to Elizabeth at the same time. This feature of the play has led scholars to seek hidden meanings throughout and to connect characters other than Cynthia with historical persons. But it would take me too far afield to go into these matters here.

Italian as well as Latin and Greek was fashionable in the England of Queen Elizabeth and King James, witness the many characters with Italian names in Shakespeare's plays, names found even when the setting is not Italian, as the Horatio of Hamlet. Most such names are not meaningful, though they give a certain flavor that the public of that day evidently liked. Sometimes, however, they serve to characterize their bearers. In Ben Jonson's play Volpone (i. e. the fox), named after its chief character, most of the names have a characterizing function. Besides Volpone himself we have Mosca (fly), Voltore (vulture), Corbaccio (raven), Corvino (crow), Bonario (good-natured, credulous), Nano (dwarf), Castrone (eunuch) and Androgyno (hermaphrodite). The English audience was expected to know enough Italian to understand the meaning of these names.

The scene of the play is laid in Venice and the characters with Italian names are Italians, but Jonson adds three English characters, tourists who turn up in Venice and play a part in the action. These are Peregrine (traveler or falcon), Sir Politic Would-be, and Lady Would-be. Both meanings of the word *peregrine* fit the character so named: he is a traveler and he plays the falcon when he pounces on Sir Politic in the fifth act. The surname Would-be is most appropriate both for Sir Politic and for his lady, but in the dialog the knight is often called Sir Pol (i. e. parrot), and his flow of words makes this name very apt. It will be seen that the characterization in terms of birds, so conspicuous in the Italian names, extends to the English names as well.

In Jonson's play characterizing names are the rule. In some plays of the period, however, only comic characters are given such names. A good example is Shakespeare's Twelfth Night. The scene of this play is laid in Illyria, but two of the characters, Sir Toby Belch and Sir Anthony Aguecheek, have English names nevertheless, names with a characterizing function. The verb *belch*, alongside its literal meaning, has had since Old English times the figurative sense 'utter, speak with vehemence or violence.' Compare Latin *eructare*. In Shakespeare's day *belch* in this figurative sense was restricted to "the utterance of offensive things, or to furious vociferation" (NED). Now as a character Sir Toby behaved in just this way, especially when he was in his cups. Shakespeare's name for him is therefore obviously meaningful. With him goes Sir Andrew Aguecheek (i. e., shivering or shaking cheek), whose name is indicative of his cowardice, a characteristic made much of in the play. A third comic character is Malvolio (i. e. ill will). He is a straitlaced spoilsport who takes himself so seriously that he becomes a figure of fun; his very lack of humor makes him comic. Finally, we have Feste, the clown, whose name means 'the festive one, the gay one,' and who lives up to the name beautifully. The serious characters of the play do not have meaningful names.

In the course of the seventeenth century French replaced Italian as the fashionable tongue of western Europe and fictive name-giving changed accordingly. Thus, the two main characters in Congreve's play The Way of the World have characterizing names French in form and meaning. The heroine, Millamant, (i. e. *mille amants* '1000 lovers') seems to have been so called because all the gallants in town paid court to her. Her suitor Mirabell (i. e. Latin *mirabilis* 'wonderful') bears a name that was actually current in Middle English; Congreve used it in its older French form, equivalent to modern French *Mirabeau*. The meaning of the name fits the character perfectly; certainly all the ladies of fashion thought he was wonderful and envied Millamant her suitor. One of the minor characters, too, has a French name: the maidservant Foible (i. e. feeble, weak). Her weakness was that of disloyalty to her mistress. But most of the characters in the play have English names, names that serve to characterize them neatly enough. Lady Wishfort, for example, plays the coquette in spite of her age; she wishes she were a fort to be besieged and stormed by some man or other;

almost any man would do. Fainall, her son-in-law, would fain have all and in the end lost all. Squire Witwoud is a would-be wit, and his half brother Sir Wilful has a name that sums up his character if we take *wilful* in the old sense 'willing; consenting; ready to comply with a request, desire or requirement' (NED): first Lady Wishfort persuades him to marry Millamant and then Mirabell persuades him not to marry her. Squire Witwoud's companion Petulant owes his name to his insolent, rude ways; *petulant* meant 'rude, insolent' in Congreve's day, though this meaning is now rare if not obsolete. Finally, Mrs. Marwood is indeed well named; she mars the hero's plans one after the other almost to the end.

To illustrate our theme in the eighteenth century I have chosen the personal names in Sheridan's play The School for Scandal. I include not only the names of the characters but also the names of persons mentioned in the speeches of the characters. We begin with Lady Wormwood, mentioned in the Prolog:

"Lord!" cries my Lady Wormwood (who loves tattle,
And puts much salt and pepper in her prattle) ...

The lady is smacking her lips over the scandalous items of news she finds in the morning paper but changes her tune when she finds an item about herself:

"A certain lord had best beware
Who lives not twenty miles from Grosvenor Square;
For should he Lady W. find willing
Wormwood is bitter" — Oh! that's me! the villain!
Throw it behind the fire, and never more
Let that vile paper come within my door.

Next comes Lady Sneerwell, who throughout the play shows how good she is at sneering. Her confederate Mr. Snake has the bad qualities associated with that reptile. The next three names, Lady Brittle, Capt. Boastall, and Mrs. Clackitt, hardly need any comments, but I will quote a bit from the dialog:

Lady Sneerwell: Did you circulate the report of Lady Brittle's intrigue with Capt. Boastall?

Snake: That's in as fine a train as your ladyship could wish. In the common course of things, I think it must reach Mrs. Clackitt's ears within four-and-twenty hours; and then, you know, the business is as good as done.

Lady Sneerwell: Why, truly, Mrs. Clackitt has a very pretty talent, and a great deal of industry.

Snake: True, madam, and has been tolerably successful in her day. To my knowledge, she has been the cause of six matches being broken off and three sons disinherited, of four forced elopements and as many close confinements, nine separate maintenances and two divorces.

Evidently Mrs. Clackitt was a scandal-monger indeed, and fully deserved the name Clackitt (that is, blab it, spread it far and wide).

Sir Peter Teazle, who plays a more important part than the characters just mentioned, has a name that befits him well enough. The teazle is a plant "the heads of which have hooked prickles between the flowers and are used for teasing cloth" (NED); that is, for combing its surface so as to make a nap. The word is derived from the verb *tease*, which originally meant 'shred' or the like but is now chiefly used in the figurative sense "worry or irritate by persistent action which vexes or annoys" (NED). Sir Peter is well equipped with verbal hooked prickles and is fond of using them. As he tells us in the first scene of Act II, with reference to his wife, "though I can't make her love me, there is great satisfaction in quarreling with her," and in Act III he says, "How happy I should be if I could tease her into loving me." Lady Teazle was anything but a tease before her marriage, but with the new name she took the behavior proper to one so called, and in the play she shows herself fully her husband's match.

Three characters in the play have Surface for surname: the rich old bachelor Sir Oliver Surface and his young nephews Charles and Joseph. All three play a surface part that differs greatly from the reality beneath. To begin with, the uncle has just come back from the East Indies, where he had lived for fifteen years. In consequence, he does not know his nephews by sight nor they him, and on both sides any identification must depend on surface appearances. Sir Oliver takes advantage of this fact to visit Joseph in the character of an impecunious relative begging for a loan, and to visit Charles in the opposite character of a professional money-lender. In each case the false surface deceives the nephew but enables the uncle to penetrate beneath the surface: Joseph, who in the eyes of the world is a model of manly virtue, shows himself to be a scoundrel, whereas Charles, who by all surface indications is a hopeless profligate, shows himself to be a man of good heart. Be it added that Joseph Surface's given name has its significance too: unlike the son of Jacob in the Bible, our Joseph has a clandestine affair with another man's wife, thus proving that he is a Joseph only on the surface.

Our next group of characters comprises Sir Benjamin Backbite, Mr. Crabtree, Mrs. Candour, Miss Gadabout, Sir Filigree Flirt, and Miss Prim. Of these, only Mrs. Candour has a name that needs comment. The word *candour* here means 'friendliness, freedom from malice' and Lady Sneerwell duly gives Mrs. Candour a character to correspond, saying that though she is "a little talkative, everybody allows her to be the best-natured and best sort of woman." The dialog continues thus:

Maria: Yes, with a very gross affectation of good nature and benevolence, she does more mischief than the direct malice of old Crabtree.

Joseph: I'faith, that's true, Lady Sneerwell; whenever I hear the current against the characters of my friends, I never think them in such danger as when Candour undertakes their defense.

Two characters with Italian names follow: Mrs. Festino (i. e. entertainment) and Colonel Cassino (i. e. casino, used in eighteenth century England in two senses: 'public hall for dancing etc.' and 'kind of card game'). These characters, and many others in the play, are obviously personifications. With them go Mr. and Mrs. Honeymoon, Miss Tattle, Lord Buffalo, Sir H. Bouquet, and Mr. Tom Saunter. I have no information about Lord Buffalo, but Sir H. Bouquet is presumably Henry Bouquet, famous for his successes against the Indians in the American colonies. One wonders what he is doing in this galley.

Our next is a group of four: Lord Spindle, Sir Thomas Splint, Captain Quinze, and Mr. Nickitt, all of whom, according to Mrs. Candour, are facing financial ruin. *Spindle* and *splint* seem to be derogatory epithets. Quinze got his name from the gambling game, and presumably he lost his money at cards. As for Mr. Nickitt, his name means 'cheater' and perhaps he is to be thought of as having cheated once too often.

This group is followed by a group of women: Lady Frizzle, named in terms of her hair; Mrs. Drowzie, one who puts others to sleep; Miss Nicely, so called because she is so careful, prudent, and cautious; Miss Piper, the shepherdess; Mrs. Ponto, whose name, if it is Latin, means 'bridge of boats' and whose assembly certainly made slanderous communications easier; and Lady Dundizzy, the *dizzy* of whose name means 'foolish' (compare Lord Dundreary of

a later day). In the next Act we get another such group: Lady Betty
Curricle, whose name reflects her fondness for driving in Hyde
Park; Miss Vermilion, who uses the rouge-pot freely; Mrs. Ever-
green, who tries hard to look young in spite of her age; the widow
Ochre, who paints her face with the pigment so called; Miss Simper,
who smirks all the time, to show off her pretty teeth; Mrs. Prim,
who keeps her lips primly closed to conceal the fact that she has
lost her teeth; Mrs. Pursy, the fat dowager (*pursy* means 'fat');
Mrs. Quadrille, who may personify either the card game or the
square dance; Miss Sallow, presumably so named to describe her
complexion; Lady Stucco (i. e. imitation; plaster made to look like
stone); and Mrs. Ogle, an eyeful of ugliness, a freak to be stared at.
Truly an unsavory lot, if one listens to the scandal-mongers.

In Act III a Jewish moneylender, appropriately named Moses,
is introduced, and he in turn introduces a Gentile moneylender,
with equal appropriateness named Premium. We also learn that
Lady Teazle had had a suitor named Sir Tivy Terrier (i. e. Sir
Tory rent-roll) but had refused him to accept Sir Peter. In the next
scene Charles Surface's servant Trip takes the stage, and plays a
part lively enough to befit his name. In one of his speeches he
mentions a friend of his named Brush. This name is suitable enough
for a servant, who among other things has the duty of brushing
his master's clothes. In addition, Brush may be there to remind
learned playgoers of the Peniculus of Plautus's Menaechmi.

I conclude my look at the personal names in Sheridan's play
with Mr. Careless, Sir Harry Bumper (i. e. one given to drinking
bumpers), Sir Richard Raveline (i. e. outwork; Sir Richard is a
military man), and William and Walter Blunt, plain-spoken
members of parliament. The only characters in the play whose
names are not meaningful are Rowley and Maria.

We come now to the nineteenth century. I illustrate with Bernard
Shaw's play Candida, named after its chief character. The Latin
adj. *candidus* properly means 'shining white' but it may have
figurative senses, as 'clear, lucid' and 'honest, straightforward.'
Both these figurative senses fit the Candida of the play, who has
a clear, lucid mind and is honest, straightforward in her dealings.
Her husband Morell[1] is described as a moralist by Marchbanks in

---

[1] The spelling *Morell* (instead of *Morel*) indicates that the stress falls on the
first syllable and that the *e* has its obscure value. Here British differs from American
pronunciation (compare *Purcell* etc.).

one of his speeches and the description fits the man: Morell lives by the conventional morality of his group, the Christian Socialists, and he thinks accordingly.

Candida's father has *Burgess* for surname. The word is the English counterpart of French *bourgeois*. It denotes an inhabitant of a borough (i. e. town) and applies in particular to a member of what used to be called the lower middle classes. In the play Burgess typifies one kind of *bourgeois*: a crude business man, lacking in cultivation and interested only in his business activities, which are not always strictly honorable. Candida's would-be lover, Eugene Marchbanks, has a given name that means 'well born,' and in fact he is a member of the British aristocracy. Morell's secretary, Miss Proserpine Garnett, is a jewel of a secretary but not one of great price. Her tragedy is that of unrequited love, and the Greek goddess's residence in Hades makes the secretary's given name not inappropriate.

I end with a twentieth-century play: Elmer Rice's Adding Machine. The leading character is Mr. Zero, whose name needs no explaining. His office mate, Daisy Diana Dorothea Devore, has a name indicative of the love stories and movie romances that she lives by. In one passage Zero comments on Daisy's name "Daisy. That's a pretty name. It's a flower, ain't it ? Well – that's what you are – just a flower." But Zero is too colorless and conventional to have a real love affair, even if the woman gives him every encouragement. His friends Mr. One, Mr. Two, Mr. Three, Mr. Four, Mr. Five, and Mr. Six, with their wives, are as empty-minded as he is. They are all no more than animated adding-machines. The only characters in the play who have normal names are the prostitute Judy O'Grady and the cosmic policeman Charles with his assistant Joe.

Our survey of the centuries has yielded an abundant supply of meaningful fictive names. As I pointed out in the beginning, I have made no effort to give you more than a sampling of the material. English literature swarms with names of this kind, so much so that a complete list would make a book. Here it will be enough to show by examples that such name-giving has always played an important part in our imaginative literature and is worth studying for its own sake.

The Name Bristol

C. L. WRENN

T HE NAME BRISTOL is both frequent and widespread in the United States of America. Besides many lesser places, there are well known examples of the name as that of a town in at least six states: Connecticut, Pennsylvania, Rhode Island, Tennessee, Virginia and Florida. The older English form of the name, which is BRISTOW, on the other hand, is far less frequent: the only relatively well known instance is in Oklahoma.

Both BRISTOL and its older form BRISTOW clearly belong to that vast group of English names which have at various times been carried to the United States by English settlers and completely transplanted there. It follows, therefore, that its origin and history are to be looked for primarily in England.

It is perhaps worth noticing, however, that BRISTOL as the name of a hotel or bar has had, and continues to have, a very wide currency in the capitals and tourist centres of most of Europe and of Latin America. But this use of the name owes its existence historically to that once famous English traveller and epicure the Marquis of Bristol, England: and honour has thus, in an indirect sense, continued to be paid to this great patron of the very best hotels and bars long after the Marquis himself was almost forgotten. The origin of the vast number of "Bristol Bars" and "Hotels Bristol", then, will scarcely present any problem to the student of place names, though probably of very considerable interest to the social historican.

In what follows, therefore, I shall confine myself strictly to England.

The original form of the name BRISTOL is commonly assumed to be the Old English or Anglo-Saxon BRYCG STOW recorded in MS. D of the Anglo-Saxon Chronicle under the year 1063. This meant "the place (or possibly shrine) near the bridge"; and this explanation seems to fit very well into the geographical situation, since there has been an important bridge from time immemorial over the Bristol Avon river, and since it was apparently around this bridge that the town of Bristol grew up. The scribe of the Norman Domesday Book recorded the name as BRISTOU, which seems clearly to represent the naturally reduced colloquial form of the name. Both the forms BRISTOW (corresponding to the Domesday Book's form) and BRISTOL (recorded as BRISTOLIA in Latin charters purporting to date from the mid eleventh century but probably actually *inspeximus* of the late thirteenth) survived side by side until comparatively recent times when BRISTOL ousted its rival except for the still fairly frequent use of BRISTOW as a surname.

At first sight then, the problem would seem to be the origin of the -L in BRISTOL. Yet there is some evidence that the form of the name ending in -L may be a good deal earlier than its first recorded appearance in English documents, which is found in the Curia Regis Rolls of the year 1200. Here occurs the first -L form as BRISTOLL. For, as indicated above, Latin charters of the reign of St. Edward the Confessor, though only apparently surviving in late thirteenth-century copies in the form of *inspeximus*, regularly record only BRISTOLIA. Now if the Latinizing clerks had intended to record a form of BRISTOW (for the fuller form BRYCG STOW), one would have expected them to write forms of the type BRISTOUIA or BRISTOVIA. But this in fact seems never to occur.

For the addition or substitution of the -L which turned BRISTOW into BRISTOL(L), comparison has rightly been suggested with the name PLEMSTALL (or PLEMONSTALL) in Cheshire.[1] This place must clearly have got its name from an unrecorded Old English PLEGMUNDES STOW, which first appears in the Taxatio Ecclesiastica under the year 1291 as PLEYMUNDESTOWE. Plemstall is traditionally the place where the famous Plegmund, Archbishop of Canterbury under King Alfred and Edward the Elder, had a cell or hermitage at some time earlier in his career; and the meaning of PLEGMUNDES STOW is clearly "Plegmund's cell (or hermit-

---

[1] For this and for references to all documentary evidence, see E. Ekwall's *The Concise Oxford Dictionary of English Place-names*, 3rd ed. corrected, Oxford 1951.

age)." It has been suggested that PLEMSTALL got its second element -STALL in substitution for -STOW in a manner parallel to that of -STOL for -STOW in BRISTOL as against BRISTOW. In view, however, of the early occurrence of the form BRISTOLIA in Latin charters, such a substitution would have to be assumed to have been an early phenomenon.

Another apparent example of the substitution of an -L ending for one that was originally vocalic is the name of the town WALSALL in Staffordshire. But here the original ending or second element was not -STOW but -HOH, the Old English word for "heel," surviving in the modern HOUGH, and meaning in toponymy "a headland," "point of land," "piece of rapidly rising ground," etc. An Anglo-Saxon will of the year 1002 in Miss Dorothy Whitelock's collection[2] has the earliest recorded form of WALSALL as (AET) WALES HO, in which the final syllable must be the dative case of HOH (though otherwise unrecorded). The meaning of this name must therefore have been something like "a piece of sharply rising ground belonging to a Briton (or serf)." The first element of the compound is the Old English W(E)ALH "Briton" or "(foreign) serf" in its genitive singular case W(E)ALES. This word W(E)ALH is most familiar in place-names in those beginning with WAL-, such as WALTON (OE WALA TUN), where the WAL- represents the genitive plural WALA. Now the replacement of the Old English HO by a form ending in -L in the current WALSALL is recorded as early as the year 1169. The Pipe Rolls of that year have WALESHALE; and the Curia Regis Rolls for 1201 have WALESHAL. By an old apparent slip, the *Oxford Dictionary of English Place-names* derives the second element in the modern WALSALL from Old English HALH "valley," though it correctly cites the above-quoted form WALES HO as the earliest recorded form. If WALSALL is thus to be derived from Old English WALES HALH as against the recorded WALESHO, it would still have been a case of the substitution of a word with -L in its second element for one with the original vocalic ending; but such replacement would have had to have occurred already in late Old English. But if -HALE (dative of HALH) did replace HO in the early middle English period, the difference in meaning between HŌH and HALH would be strik-

---

[2] *Anglo-Saxon Wills* edited by Dorothy Whitelock: Cambridge (England), 1930.

ing and odd, unless we could suppose a change in the conformation of the land had made HALH more appropriate than HŌH by then.[3]

Probably the least unacceptable explanation of BRISTOW becoming BRISTOL so far offered by scholars would be, as Zachrisson has shown,[4] to connect the substitution of the -L ending in BRISTOL with a sort of popular tendency in some local pronunciations to reverse that type of phonetic process by which Old French -AL became -AU as in GENERALS becoming GÉNERAUX, or Picard -OL developing into -OU as in Latin SOLIDUM giving French SOU. But such a view could only rest upon unverifiable conjecture; and the phonetic processes and chronologies of mediaeval French dialects and of those of Middle English are anything like clear or agreed.

A second and somewhat plausible explanation of BRISTOL might be to regard the change from BRISTOW as not phonological at all in its origin, but more simply as the substitution for the second element of the word of another form meaning "place" for the earlier -STOW. That is, to assume the replacement of the original -STOW by the Old English -STAELL (found also as STEALL and STALL) meaning "place." For the Old English STAELL STALL is fairly common as a second element in place-names; as in TUN-STALL (Durham), DUNSTALL (Lincoln), both of which originated in Old English TUN STAELL or TUN STALL, the "place or site of a TUN or farm." One might compare BIRSTAL in Yorkshire and BURSTALL in Staffordshire, both derived from Old English BURG STALL "fortified place" or BYRIG STALL of the same meaning. Similarly is developed the Kentish place-name BORSTAL, from Old English BORG STAELL "protecting place." But in fact the substitution of BRI-STAELL or BRI-STALL for BRI-STOW (the colloquial form of the original BRYCG STOW) would not be so good an explanation as it seemed at first sight. For whereas all the other place-names containing the element OE -STAELL -STEALL or -STALL show *only* later forms in -STALL, BRISTOL never had such a form as BRI-STALL or BRISTALL as far as known records go. The earliest known forms of BRISTOL termi-

---

[3] See the *Place-name Dictionary*, op. cit., under WALSALL.

[4] See R. E. Zachrisson, *Anglo-Norman Influence on English Place-names*, Lund 1907, and his *Two Instances of French Influence on English Place-names*, Stockholm 1914.

nating in an -L are the Latin charter type BRISTOLIA and the
Curia Regis Rolls form BRISTOLL of the year 1200.

It seems clear, therefore, that the development of BRISTOW to
BRISTOL was *direct*, and that it was not by way of the rounding
of the vowel in -STAL(L) to that seen in the -STOL of BRISTOL.
Moreover, while PLEMSTALL seems quite certainly to show the
substitution of -STOW by -STALL, since the original Old English
name must have been PLEGMUNDES STOW as already explained,
such a substitution cannot possibly lie behind WALSALL developing from its origin as Old English WALES HO. Furthermore, it
appears that there is not a single instance of any of the place-names
with -STAL(L) as second element having at any time been recorded
with the change of -STAL(L) to -STOL, which could parallel the
hypothetical *BRISTAL(L) becoming BRISTOL(L).

In view of the unsatisfying nature of the above-mentioned two
hypothetical explanations, I myself would, very tentatively, offer
yet a third. Put quite simply, this explanation would rest on the
known fact of a popular pronunciation in the speech of some speakers
from parts of the West of England which adds an -L to the final
syllable of words ending normally in a vowel. During the period
1940 to 1944, while living in Bristol, I encountered several native
Bristolians who, in their natural speech habitually added an -L to
certain words ending in a vowel. I heard, for instance, INDIA
pronounced as INDIAL [INDIəL], and VICTORIA as VICTORIAL
[VIKTəRIəL]. Similarly I have been informed, though I have not
myself heard it, that there are speakers in more than one Southern
area of the United States of America who pronounce WHEEL-
BARROW as WHEEL-BARROL [HWI:L-BARL]. We have no
means of knowing how early or in how wide areas this phenomenon
appeared in Western English dialects and regions. But it may be
worth noting that both WALSALL and BRISTOL belong to the
Western half of England. Now if this speech-tendency could be shown
to have arisen very early and over a wide area, it would account for
WALSALL arising from Old English WALES HO (cf. the thirteenth-
century forms of the type WALESHAL), as well as for BRISTOW
becoming BRISTOL. It might even explain the development of
PLEGMUNDES STOW to PLEMSTALL, though this latter may be
more plausibly accounted for by the assumed substitution of -STALL
for -STOW, both meaning "place," as the second element of the

place name. The Latin Charter form BRISTOLIA would of course be covered by the same hypothesis as BRISTOL.

I cannot pretend to have made anything like a thorough examination of place names of the types involved in the foregoing discussion; still less have I systematically studied the phonology of the dialect-types mentioned. But, since BRISTOL has not, so far as I know, yet been satisfactorily explained, it seemed worth while to put forward the above hypothesis. This latter is at least supported by the ascertained fact of the addition of an -L to the final vocalic syllable of certain words in actually heard pronunciations. Others more appropriately qualified, I venture to hope, may think it worth while to explore further this intriguing problem in place name history along the lines indicated in this paper.

Bible Belt Onomastics or Some Curiosities
of Anti-Pedobaptist Nomenclature

THOMAS PYLES

In 1947 Mrs. Hoyette White, a former teacher and the mother of five fair daughters, graduated from Oklahoma City University. At the same time one of the aforesaid daughters, Norvetta, graduated from Oklahoma A. and M. University with a fine arts degree in piano and voice; a second daughter, Yerdith, graduated from Classen High School in Oklahoma City, where she distinguished herself as a clarinet player in the school band and as a member of the swimming team; a third, Arthetta, finished her work at Wilson grade school; and a fourth, Marlynne, did not graduate from anywhere, but got into the newspaper anyway. Mother Hoyette's fifth daughter, Wilbarine, had already graduated in 1943 from Oklahoma City University and married a man prosaically named John.

Even in Oklahoma such a clutch of euphoniously named females as Hoyette, Norvetta, Yerdith, Arthetta, Marlynne, and Wilbarine seems to have been noteworthy, if not the actual occasion for the newsworthiness of the White family, for the feature writer in the Oklahoma City *Daily Oklahoman* (May 19, 1947, p. 1) asks, "Wondering where they got those names?" and goes on to give Mrs. White's explanation:

> When my mother saw I looked so much like my father, she made a girl's name out of the family name Hoyt and called me Hoyette. That started the names.

> When I named my own girls, I wanted names no one had ever had and names nobody would ever want. So I made them up.

On St. Valentine's Day, 1948, Mr. and Mrs. Finis Finch of Oklahoma City had been married almost sixty-eight years. It was evidently the opinion of the feature editor of the same newspaper cited above that this almost incredibly prolonged Darby-and-Joan existence qualified them as authorities on romantic love, and they were accordingly the subjects of an interview by one of the paper's feature writers. The entire family of the Finches at that time included five children, twenty-two grandchildren, thirty-seven great-grandchildren, and four great-great-grandchildren. It is not surprising that the Reverend Mrs. Finch, a preacher in the Holiness Church, had difficulty in remembering some of the children's names. She complained as follows: "They don't use old-fashioned names that are easy to remember. They name them things like Linda and Treva, Mickey Gail and Suevella and —" turning to her husband — "What is Eddie Sue's boy's name ?" (Feb. 14, 1948, p.1.)

One more illustrative quotation, and then to my muttons. The speaker this time is the eminent Senator Rayburn of Texas, as reported by Mr. Drew Pearson: "I was named Sam, not Samuel. We don't believe in putting on airs in our family." (Jacksonville *Florida Times-Union*, April 16, 1955. p. 11.)

Here we may see three leading factors in American name-giving: the desire to be unique, to be fashionable, and to be folksily democratic. We shall encounter yet others as we proceed.

In a youth agreeably misspent *in partibus infidelium*, I was little conscious of the tendencies in name-giving with which I am here concerned. It is true that names which were thought strange or amusing did in those days occasionally come to one's attention, but they were almost invariably cited as curiosa and equated with naïveté, inferior social standing, and ignorance. They were more or less sporadic even on the social level at which they were believed most likely to occur and were regarded as the creations of those who led drab and lowly lives — the onomastic *bijouterie* of the underprivileged.

It was not indeed until my translation, fairly late in life, first to the southwestern and later to the southeastern sector of the Bible Belt — in Mencken's classic definition, as utilized by M. M. Mathews in the *Dictionary of Americanisms*, "those parts of the country in which the literal accuracy of the Bible is credited and clergymen who preach it have public influence" — that I first became aware of such names in high places. To what extent the onomastic mores with which I am here concerned have become nationwide I do not really know. Mr. Thomas L. Crowell in *American Speech* (XXIII [1948], 265—272) contributes some very fruity specimens from

Washington, a city which has a more or less transient population, and has collected similar examples in New York City. Menken also cites a good many from outside the Bible Belt. It is likely that the isoglosses demarcating the Fancy Names Belt have by now spread considerably beyond the limits of the Bible Belt. Two World Wars have brought hosts of anti-pedobaptists from the hills to the towns and cities, where their fecundity has shown no signs of abating. Their places of worship have moved from deserted stores to gaudy, neon-illuminated erections and, among the more sophisticated, to tabernacles of neo-Gothic and colonial meeting-house architecture. But the moral, social, and ecclesiastical customs of the rural Bethels linger on, as do also the naming habits of the remoter areas, despite increasing prosperity, superficial sophistication, and considerable distinction in business, politics, and the professions on the part of many. In the towns of the inland South and even to a large extent in the cities, the pastors of these formerly more or less obscure religious bodies[1] have retained much of the public influence which they and their predecessors had in the hill country, but unlike the pedobaptist men of God whom they have displaced in prestige, they exert no influence over the name-giving habits of those committed to their charge. The naming of Christians is no part of their ghostly office.

According to the 1958 *World Almanac*, the total Christian church membership in this country is 98,014,954 (excluding the Christian Scientists, who release no figures.) Of these, 26,011,499, or considerably more than a fourth, do not practice infant baptism. These have their greatest strength in the inland South. The effect of these circumstances peculiar to our American religious life in the matter of name-giving is obvious. Where name-giving is no part of the sacrament of baptism, and where consequently a clergyman with some sense of traditional onomastic decorum has no say, individual taste and fancy may run riot — and usually do. It is highly unlikely

---

[1] The Baptists were of course never obscure in American life. But there are now, according to my friend and former student, the Reverend James Sims, himself a Baptist pastor, at least 117 other anti-pedobaptist denominations among the 272 listed in the 1956 *World Almanac*. (Of still others he was not sure.) The groups most prominent in the inland South, in addition to the various Baptist bodies, are the Assemblies of God, the Churches of Christ, the Disciples of Christ, Jehovah's Witnesses, the Churches of God, the Pentecostal Assemblies, and the Church of the Nazarene.

that any man of God, even though the canons of his church were not explicit in the matter, would consent in the course of his sacerdotal duties to confer upon hapless infants such names as Buzz Buzz, Coeta, Merdine, Aslean, La Void, Arsie, Phalla, and Raz — all legal names borne by Bible Belters of repute. And it is certain that Ima Hogg, the *grande dame* of Houston society, whose father was once governor of Texas, was so named without the connivance of any anointed priest.

One result of the increasing numbers and prestige of anti-pedo-baptists has thus been, ironically enough, the decline of the Christian name in what is certainly the most self-consciously and vocally Christian of all lands, where God's name is minted into the very currency and He runs on all sides of every political campaign. It has also, incidentally, given rise to a new type of urban Christianity, quite unlike anything ever known in Europe and probably never before known even in this nation under God.

The proud bearers of the names which I shall shortly begin to cite are all, unless otherwise specified, Christian Caucasians of good standing in their communities — people of sufficient importance that their engagements, their marriages, their parturitions, and, alas, their deaths are recounted fairly fully on "society" pages and in full-length obituaries in the newspapers,[2] which are a veritable onomastic treasure-trove. Other important sources have been class lists, yearbooks, official lists of voters and of property owners, telephone directories, and commencement programs. These last have provided entertainment and instruction during many commencement addresses by atomic physicists, business executives, industrialists, generals, and presidents of neighboring colleges and universities panting after yet another honorary doctorate to add to their string. Many of my handsomest specimens were collected under such otherwise depressing circumstances. It should be obvious that the names culled from these sources are not those of the underprivileged, the economically depressed, or whatever the current term for "poor and lowly" happens to be. Nor are such names to be regarded as nicknames, since they appear in formal and digni-

---

[2] Among my richest sources are the Oklahoma City *Daily Oklahoman,* the Norman (Okla.) *Transcript,* the Jacksonville *Florida Times-Union,* and the Gainesville (Fla.) *Sun.*

fied surroundings — those in the commencement programs being obviously the same as those which appear in Old English calligraphy on diplomas.

The formal and official use of diminutives by adults is quite common in the Belt. The most popular of these diminutives is Billy (with "clear" l), usually masculine, though considered perfectly appropriate for women also, with Bobby, Johnny, and Jimmy — also bisexual — running slightly behind. In a single year (1950), no fewer than eighteen Billys, including two Billy Joes, two Billy Genes, and one feminine Billye, received degrees from the University of Oklahoma. In addition, there were four Willies.[3] At the University of Florida in the same year, three Billys graduated from a single college, Business Administration.

So prestigious is Billy, in fact, that one of Florida's representatives in Congress, Hon. Donald Ray Matthews, has adopted the name, using the official style D.R. (Billy) Matthews. It is unlikely that many of his constituents are even aware that *Billy* is merely a *nom de guerre*. For similar reasons, doubtless, Rev. Dr. Billy Graham long ago abandoned the full form of his name, which happens really to be William. ("We don't put on airs in God's family.") Diminutive forms occur frequently in combination with clipped forms, as in the previously mentioned Billy Joe and Billy Gene, and with non-hypocoristic forms, as in Billy Donald, Larry Leroy, and Jerry Roscoe.

I have collected scores of printed instances of diminutives and apparent diminutives used as legal names by adults, some of them adults of advanced years, some recently gone to their Great Reward. Most of these are commonplace enough (like Dannie, Davie, and Maxie), most are bisexual, and some are diminutives by virtue of their endings, without being necessarily derivative. Only Zippie (Mrs. Billy), Sippie, Vandie, Watie, Beadie, Lamie, Collie, Cossie, Ossie, Carlie (Mrs. Bobby), Omie (f.), Fonzy, Lonzie, Lokie, Mammie, Toppy, Schiley, Mealy, Bussie, Jadie Obie (m.), Nicy, Dicey, Ledgie, Raffie, Dilly, Coarsey, Sugie, Urksey, Skeety, and Ripsie seem to me particularly noteworthy, though I confess to a personal fondess for the comparatively conventional Early Bill and Jody Elijah.

---

[3] The preferred spelling of the *W*-form seems to be *Willie* rather than *Willy*.

Inasmuch as these diminutive forms occur in the most formal
and dignified contexts, usually preceded by honorific, often with no
front or middle initial, and sometimes with second name in full
form, it is generally safe to assume that they are legal names. Occasionally, however, a newspaper item like "Mr. and Mrs. Bobby
_____ are announcing the arrival of a son, Robert Craig" (*Sun*,
Sept. 13, 1951, p. 4) leads to a somewhat different conclusion. Perhaps we may infer that the right to use the seemingly less dignified
and presumably more "democratic" diminutive form is the father's
prerogative. We can hope that, reversing what used to be the normal
procedure, young Robert Craig will wax in folksy virtues to such
an extent that he too may in time merit the juvenile form of his
name which apparently symbolizes complete acceptance by one's
fellows. Then he will really "belong."

Nor does the Bible Belt perceive any incongruity in the prefixing
of professional, ecclesiastical, or political honorifics to diminutives
and apparent diminutives. Dr. Billy and Dr. Lonnie are respected
physicians in northern Florida. Dr. J. Ollie,[4] a native of Georgia,
is president of a well-heeled anti-pedobaptist university in southern
Florida. Hon. Toby, formerly a judge, is now one of Oklahoma's
representatives in Washington. Hon. Jimmie is State Auditor for
Arkansas. Hon. Eddie became a member of the Oklahoma State
Legislature in an election in which Hon. Billy Joe was defeated
despite his onomastic advantage. Hon. Zollie is Texas' Secretary
of State. Hon. Charley is a member of the Florida State Senate and
a former governor of the state. Hon. Jodie was re-elected chairman
of Florida's Jackson County Commission in 1956. The full name of
the mayor of Pine Bluff, Arkansas, is Hon. Offie Lites. Rev. Dr.
Billy Graham, the most glamorous of the anti-pedobaptist theologians, has already been alluded to. My collectanea include such
lesser luminaries as Rev. Ikie, Rev. Willie Lee, Rev. Woody, Rev.
Jimmy, Rev. Tommy, Rev. Johnny, and Rev. Sister Lessie, all
entrusted with the cure of souls in northern Florida and southern
Georgia, of which northern Florida is, because of its settlement
history, a cultural as well as a linguistic extension.

---

[4] The *J* stands for John. The preference for the style *J. Ollie* to *John O.* may
indicate the superior standing of the diminutive, the feeling that *John* is lacking
in distinction, or the prestige in America of an initial letter, preferably *J*, at the
beginning of a name.

Clipped forms, although lacking the connotations of eternal juvenility possessed by the diminutive forms, are perhaps even more redolent of bonhomie and camaraderie — qualities highly regarded in our democracy. Judging from the contexts in which they occur, these also must be regarded as legal names. The assumption is strengthened by the fact that they are sometimes used in combination with a more formal designation, as in John Bob, Leslie Ike, and Guss [sic] Herbert. I have already cited Congressman Rayburn's statement that in his family to name a child Samuel rather Sam would have been regarded as putting on airs. Many of Hon. Sam's contrymen would seem to be at one with the Rayburn family. Oklahoma used to be represented in the U.S. Senate by Hon. Josh Lee, who in 1942 failed of re-election. He was opposed in the primary by two other Josh Lees, one a furniture dealer and the other a farmer. The state is now represented in the Senate by Hon. Mike Monroney,[5] and in the House by Hon. Ed and Hon. Tom, along with the aforementioned Hon. Toby. In the same legislative body Texas has, in addition to Hon. Sam Rayburn, Hon. Jim, Hon. Jack, and Hon. Joe. Representing Tennessee are Hon. Joe and Hon. Tom. Georgia, whose Secretary of State is Hon. Zack, is represented in Congress by Hon. Phil. Similarly with the hieratic title. There is no need to multiply examples; I shall content myself with citing the (doubtless inadvertently) alcoholically named Rev. Dr. Tom Collins (his full name), who is Moderator of the Jacksonville Baptist Association.

The extent to which this ordinary use of what were formerly considered nicknames has gone is indicated by the fact that 190, or more than 10 percent, of the 1,517 June graduates of the University of Oklahoma in 1950 bore names which were diminutives or clipped forms. This figure does not include hypocorisms unconnected etymologically with traditional names, coinages — the sort of "fancy" names to be discussed later — and names which were once regarded as nicknames but have long been commonly used as ordinary legal names, such as Ray, Betty, Harry, Frank, Don, and Bert.

Often a hypocoristic name becomes so closely identified with a person that it is customarily inserted in parentheses after his legal

---

[5] Originally Aylmer Stillwell Monroney and no anti-pedobaptist, he now uses the style A. S. Mike Monroney.

given names or initials. This retention of what in some instances must be by-names acquired in school is by no means confined to the Bible Belt though it is probably of more frequent occurrence in anti-pedobaptist civilization than in the Sodoms and Gomorrahs of the Atlantic Coast. I must confess that I was brought up suddenly by the following item from the Gainesville *Sun* (Oct. 1, 1952, p. 5): "Friends of Mr. A. W. (Poopy) Roundtree, Sr., will be interested to know that he is recuperating following an operation in Lake City." Similar, if less colorful, specimens, all taken from printed sources, are Tootie, Tucky, Bus, Tiny (male principal of an elementary school), and Lefty. Hon. Juanita (Skeet), a former mayor of High Springs, Florida, is now languishing in durance vile at the State Penitentiary for moonshining activities. Hon. E. L. (Tic) Forester is a representative of Georgia in the U.S. Congress. Rev. Charles E. (Stoney) Jackson came into national prominence some time back as a participant in one of the TV quiz shows. Hon. J. Emory (Red) Cross represents his home county in the Florida State Legislature; his hair is not red.

The use of a parenthetical *derivative* nickname in one's formal style is of course not unusual among popular men, e.g., Hon. W. A. (Bill), the style of a Florida State Senator whose name is actually William. Sometimes, however, a popular man may use a nickname which is derivative from some name other than his own, for example, Hon. Harold L. (Tom) (former Chief Justice of the Florida Supreme Court), Rev. A. A. (Bob), who is pastor of the Ramona Boulevard Baptist Church, Jacksonville, and Rev. H. G. (Pat), who is pastor of a drive-in church, succeeding Rev. Jimmy. Judging by the frequency of their occurrence in such contexts, Pete and Pat seem to be overwhelming favorites. That the style is not limited to the Bible Belt is indicated by its adoption by the Governor of California, Edmund G. (Pat) Brown.

I am convinced that such forms as Buddy, Bubba, Bud, Buck, Sonny, Bunnie, and Buster, which occur with an almost nauseating frequency, are legal names, not merely alternate names like those cited just previously, since they appear alone in formal connotations without quotation marks. They are frequently preceded by honorifics, as in an account of a reception following a large church wedding at which Mrs. Buddy was "floor hostess" — whatever that is — and Mrs. Buster greeted guests. (*Times-Union*, Feb. 20, 1949,

p. 11.) The ceremony might have been performed either by Rev.
Buck or by Rev. Buddy, both of whom are in my files, but I regret
to say that it was not. A third-generation Buddy is indicated in
"A.O.M. 2-c. Buddy E. C. Kelly III, son of Mrs. Clara Kelly and
the late Mr. Buddy E. C. Kelly, Jr."[6] A new trend may be indicated
by the fact that a Mr. and Mrs. Buddy named their son Ronald
Eugene (*Times-Union*, Aug. 18, 1958, p. 22) and a Mr. and Mrs.
Sonny named theirs Randy Allen (*loc. cit.*).

Because they share a certain indefinable folksy quality which
is highly regarded in the inland South, I have grouped the following
names, some of them derivative forms, together; all are borne by
substantial citizens: Lum, Dub, Teet, Quince, Zack, Zeph, Zeb,
Clem, Wash, and Sim. Had I never been privileged to live in the
Bible Belt, I should have thought to this day that their only existence was in the literature of backhouse humor. *Ish*, though it had
no previous associations for me, seems to me nevertheless to have
the same homely, down-to-earth flavor. It is borne by Hon. Ish
W. Brant, Superintendent of Public Instruction of Duval County,
Florida (the county seat of which is Jacksonville), who has the
additional distinction of being governor of the Florida District of
Kiwanis International. When Hon. Ish was merely a candidate for
the political office which he now holds with grace and distinction,
his campaign slogan was "Ish Is Everybody's Wish." His opponents
were Mr. Coke L. Barr and Mrs. Iva Sprinkle.

Many a Bible Belter who is a democrat by conviction boasts a
title as given name. Etymologically Leroy, with principal stress on
the first syllable in Bible Belt pronunciation, belongs here, but it
is doubtful that parents who so name their male offspring are aware
of its dynastic meaning. I have collected a Leroy King, and so has
Mr. Crowell (*Am. Sp.*, XXIII, 272), along with Roy King and
Leroy Prince. From royalty and the peerage come Hon. Czar D.
Langston, a high-ranking official of the State of Oklahoma, listed
in the current *Who's Who in the South and Southwest*; King Pharaoh
(d. *aet.* 65, *Times-Union*, Sept. 22, 1951, p. 3), Queen Adina (d.
aet. 81, *ibid.*, Aug. 21, 1951, p. 10), and Queen Victoria, whose surname is Cambridge (*Sun*, July 2, 1958, p. 8); three Princesses;
Hon. Prince Preston, U.S. Congressman from Georgia, and Prince

---

[6] This gem appeared in the Gainesville *Sun*. The cutting is in my possession,
but I carelessly neglected to take down the date.

Albert, a Floridian whose only distinction known to me other than his name was his involvement in a minor automobile accident (*Sun*, Oct. 4, 1953, p. 12); Regent Gaskin, who is a Master of Education; Rev. Dr. Duke McCall, who is President of the Southern Baptist Theological Seminary; Baron Darvis, a Bachelor of Arts in Education; three Ladies — Lady Grace, Lady Jane, and Lady Percy; and one baronet — or perhaps he is only a knight — Sir Maud. More democratically inclined were the parents of the gentlemen named President (*Sun*, April 15, 1956, p. 26), Electer (*Sun*, May 6. 1958, p. 1), and Chancellor Irving (M.S. in Agriculture, Univ. of Florida, 1951). The family doctor has perhaps been honored in the names of four Docs, one of them a Dr. Doc, whose dissertation subject was "Refinement of an Instrument to Determine Certain of the Working Patterns of School Principals" (Gainesville, Fla., 1956).

The armed services have been a prolific source of names. My collections include General Phillips and Lieutenant Tisdale, who were inducted into the army as privates at Knoxville, Tennessee (*Times-Union*, March 11, 1952, p. 5); Major General Williams, who at the age of 17 enlisted in Birmingham, Alabama, as a member of the Marine Corps, explaining to reporters that his parents decided to name him something "everybody else wasn't" (*Times-Union*, Jan. 11, 1958, p. 17); and General Morgan, who died in Waycross, Georgia, in 1952, survived by a son named Colonel. But it is unnecessary to multiply examples of generals who have never heard the roar of cannon fire; I have many more. I consider General Salor [*sic*] (*Sun*, Sept. 24, 1954, p. 8) and General Ulysses Grant (his full name) who graduated from the University of Florida in 1956 with a B.S. in Education, to be my prize specimens. I pray that General Grant does not encounter discrimination if he is now practicing his chosen profession in the Confederacy. Colonel and Major are also popular, but I have only a single Cap, a single Ensign, a single (aforementioned) Lieutenant, and, it is perhaps needless to say, no Sergeants, Corporals, or Privates. Bishop and Judge occur a number of times, but these are probably family names, particularly the first when borne by anti-episcopalians. Missie Frankie was a first-year student in the University of Florida in 1957–58, and may well now be a sophomore for all I know.

When one has the same surname as a great man or woman, the temptation to confer his or her given name (or names) upon one's

offspring — and in the case of the aforementioned General Ulysses
Grant, a title as well — is for many Bible Belters practically ir-
resistible. (In the examples which follow I shall of course be required to give surnames.) Enrollment records at the University of
Florida since 1900 disclose the fact that its student body has included, as is to be expected, a good many Robert E. Lees, along
with a number of Andrew Jacksons and Benjamin Franklins. My
researches in the newspapers and telephone directories have brought
to light Lon Chaney, Gloria Swanson, Jefferson Davis, Woodrow
Wilson, George K. Washington and his daughter Martha, William
H. Taft, Dick Whittington, and Josh Billings. When Abe Lincoln
of Oklahoma City made a contribution to that city's United Fund,
the fact was considered newsworthy by the Associated Press (*Sun*,
Dec. 4, 1958, p. 7), but no Oklahoman would consider it anything
out of the ordinary, for in that state alone Daniel Boone, Oliver
Cromwell, Joe E. Brown, Mae West, Joan Crawford, Brigham
Young, Al Jennings, Will Rogers, Huey Long, Jack Dempsey,
William Cullen Bryant, and Robert Burns have all aspired to, and
some have held, political office. As Secretary of the American
Dialect Society, I was always delighted to receive a cheque for the
subscription of the University of Texas signed by, of all people,
Jesse James, Texas State Treasurer. Bryan Jennings, of Norman,
Oklahoma, Lee Grant, formerly of the University of Florida, and
De Leon Ponce, late of Jacksonville, Florida, present interesting
anomalies.

The practice of naming children from celebrities is of course
universal, only the choice of celebrity having any sociological
interest. The classical influence is strong in the Bible Belt, e.g.,
Euclid, Orion, Marcus Tony, Plato, Corydon, Amazon (m.) Hana-
bal [*sic*], Julius Cicero, Virgil Q., Ovid, Solon, and Leda. The French
ending *-ous* in Latin names (and Hebrew names which have come
to us via Latin) is found in Arelious, Olynthous, Romulous, Julious,
Lucious, and the like. Omer and Ector, the French forms used in
Middle English times and later replaced in educated usage by the
classical forms with *h*, survive in the Southern hills and their settlement areas. Omar, as in the name of General Omar Bradley (b. in
Missouri), is no Mahometan name, but merely a spelling of Omer
and usually so pronounced. The Book of Books holds its own with
Amanuel [*sic*], Jacob, the aforementioned King Pharaoh. John the

Baptist, Dorcas, Nazarine [*sic*], Hezikiah [*sic*], Zadok, Hosea, Malachi, Juda, and Lazarous [*sic*]. An Onan who graduated from the University of Oklahoma in 1950 and another of the same name who died in Florida in 1954, aged 74 (*Times-Union*, Jan. 23, 1954, p. 7) were apparently not named from the ungallant gentleman in the 38th chapter of *Genesis* — at least it is to be hoped not; I think it more likely that the name in question is an independent creation of parental fancy.

Belles lettres, the drama, and music are represented in my files by Casanova (b. 1950), Amber Marteen, two Romeos, Trilby, two Ouidas, Thais, Melba, Orlando, Tiny Tim, Oberon (f.), two Annie Lauries, Ivanhoe Elizabeth, St. Elmo, Kathleen Mavourneen, Tom Mix, Rob Roy, and, strange as its occurrence in a Deep-South Caucasian may seem, Othello. Tommy Tucker, Tom Sawyer, and Buster Brown are the full names of adults. Geographical names include Cuba (and Cubie, which may represent an old-fashioned pronunciation), which I should have supposed to be bisexual, though the two specimens which I have are male; Persia (f.) Savanah [*sic*] (f.), Utah (m.), Arizona (m.), Missoura [*sic*] (f.), and Venice (m.).[7] Botavia [*sic*] and Odessa are probably to be explained as fanciful creations rather than place names.

A number of bisexual names have already been cited. Lee, Pat, Jo(e), Robin, and Lynn are doubtless given to boys and girls indiscriminately all over the country nowadays, and can hardly be considered Bible Belt names. The following names, which are usually feminine or which one would expect to be feminine, are borne by males in the inland South: Paulyne, Pearlie, Delories, Fay, Adell, Ardelle, Ellie, Bonnie, June, Junell, Merrilett Jessie, Loice, Jewell, Bernice (also Burnice), Ivy, Buna Joe, Pink, Jonice, Dixie, Beryl, Nance, Bronzell, Alvine, Nolia, Cledith, Dee, Elizie, Gayle, Rae, Ovida, Jackie Jo, Sam Ella, Laurie, Carman, Verdell, Juadean, Lorraine, Sharon Lee, Amander, Berta, and Euzema, Jr. Conversely, the following apparently masculine names are borne by females: Terry (also -ie, -i), Gil, Stacy, Tracy, Bobbie, Laddie, Mick, Mickie, Ira, Bennie, Benjie, Mackie, Willie, Jimmie, Tommy, Kimberly Ann, Kelley, Nigel, Vincent, Juan, Billie Joe, Danny, Deane,

---

[7] Crowell, *Am. Sp.*, XXIII, 270, has many more specimens of geographical names used as given names.

Don, Page, Toni, Maxie, Montez, Nathan, Sandy, Glen, Sammie, and Henri.[8] The popularity of LaVoid and LaVerne, both bisexual, I am totally at a loss to explain. It may be that some of these onomastic reversals of sex may be due to the desire to name a male child after his mother, or a female child after her father. A number of names borne by females are somehow formed from the given name of a male relative, usually the father, e.g., Julie Anne (dau. of Julian), Philelle, Lloydene, Gina (dau. of Gene), Basilene (dau. of Alfred Basil), Charlsie, Dennisteen, Donita (dau. of J. Don), Elmerine, Johnita (dau. of Johnny), Orvillyne, Harolyn (dau. of Harold), and Methadene (dau. of Metha).

When, like Mrs. Hoyette White, quoted at the beginning of this paper, people set out to make up names, they tend to follow certain well-established principles. Pure root creations, some of which will be cited later, are somewhat less common than creations with conventional affixes. Blends and compounds occur fairly often, such as Sherliana, Jamesvee (f., perhaps from James V., father's name?), Beneva (Ben + Eva?), Neldagae, Bettijane, Joashley (m.), Texanna, Charlouise, Vickianne, Loiciebelle, Kalynn, Annijane, Alimae, Jimton (f., civil defense chairman for the Arlington Woman's Club of Jacksonville, *Times-Union*, Nov. 24, 1957, p. 49), Marijac, Marynelle, Marytom, Suellen, JoNez (Joe – Inez?), and Joella. The highly ingenious ChaRu (*Sun*, Nov. 16, 1952, p. 14) is probably a combination of Charles with Ruth or Ruby; in any case, the father's name is Charles. When bisexual Lugene (or Lougene) is a girl's name it is probably a blend of Lou and Gene, both of which are also bisexual. As a boy's name it may possibly be a riming form of Eugene, which is very popular in the South. The opposite tendency occurs in Joe Cephus, Emma Lena, Fitch Gerald, Cad Walder, Do Remus, Cull Pepper, Shir Lee, and Hezzie Kiye.

The riming principle just alluded to doubtless accounts for such curiosities as Jenneth, Jarold, Flemuel, Arlysle (f.), Veryl (m., suggested by Beryl, common among Bible Belt males?), Vernice (bisexual), Rinda, Valcom, Dolive, Taura (f.), Burtis, Lurtis, Hertis, Burnest, Bernon, Harl, Bloria, Glennard, Verton, Floyce, Dorma, Derl, Verl, Flarain (m., suggested by bisexual Lorraine?), Lomer,

---

[8] This last is also cited by Crowell, *loc. cit.*, p. 271, along with other bisexual names which I have not encountered.

Mevelin, and Delain. Occasionally there may be internal instead of initial change, as in Zenokia, which was almost certainly suggested by Zenobia.

I hasten to cite a few miscellaneous whimsicalities, all full names, which have appealed to me for one reason or another: Oleander Lafayette Fitzgerald III, Ed Ek, Shellie Swilley, Early Hawaiian McKinnon, Sandy Gandy, Earl Curl, Jr., Percy Nursey, Rev. Fay de Sha (m.), Lovie Slappey, Esperanza Le Socke, Pamela Gay Day, Staff-Sgt. Mehogany Brewer, Girlie Burns, Fawn Grey Trawick Dunkle, Alure Sweat (f., sister of Alfa, Alta, Sabry, and the late Cleveland Sweat [*Times-Union*, Feb. 12, 1958, p. 22]), Bloomer Bedenbaugh, Martha Magdalene Toot, Okla Bobo, and Melody Clinkenbeard. The last-cited given name may be bisexual, for a fellow townsman of Miss Clinkenbeard's is Hon. Melody Reynolds, an officer of the Veterans of Foreign Wars in Norman, Oklahoma. The same bisexuality seems to be characteristic of Memory: Hon. Memory Martin is lieutenant governor of division 6, Florida Kiwanis district, as well as a former school teacher and principal; my files also disclose Memorie Frances Griner, whom I take to be female from the spelling of the second name. Hon. Cowboy Pink Williams, former Lieutenant Governor of Oklahoma, was defeated to succeed himself in 1958 despite a style which should have endeared him to all Southwesterners. It is possible that Cowboy Pink is merely a *nom de guerre*, but the hon. gentleman is so listed in the 1958 *World Almanac* and in the *Britannica* Yearbook.

In the whimsies which follow I omit surnames: Dawn Robin, Kitty Bit, Lance Amorus, Lovely, Charme, Greek (f.), Pearl Garnet, Dimple, Dixie, Pixianne, Cherry, Orchid Favia (f.), Rose Bud, Satire, Fairy (a missionary of the Church of the Nazarene to Africa, *Times-Union*, Jan. 26, 1952, p. 6), Acid, Buzz Buzz, Tyty, Hubert Herbert, Kae Rae, Mary Sunshine, Boysy, Madonna Ruth, Delyte, Doe, Dovey, Echo, Edelweiss, and Brunette (who turned out to be a blonde). The children of Mr. Stanford Bardwell, a realtor and a graduate of Louisiana State University, and his wife Loyola, are Stanford, Jr., Harvard, Princeton, Cornell, Auburn, and the twins Duke and T'lane. When the Bardwells go on holiday they travel in a specially equipped school bus called the "Collegiate Caravan." (*Times-Union*, Aug. 29, 1954, p. 13.)

The following combinations of given name and surname represent the conscious, if misguided, humor of parents with no priestly hand to guide or restrain them, though some are doubtless to be attributed simply to parental naïveté: Pleasant Weathers, Honey Combs, French Crown, Golden Gamble, Royal Child, Goode Carr, Early Priest, Robin Starling, Paris Singer, Paris Miracle, Etta Turnipseed, Summer Robbins, Shari Glass, Fannie Bottom, Love Snow (f.), Rocky Mountain, Alto Hooten, Early Wages, Drew Swords, English Piper, Candy Barr, and Minor Peeples. Everyone has by now doubtless heard of Dill L. Pickle, of Rolling Fork, Mississippi, who grew up to be a pickle salesman for Paramount Foods, a Louisville concern. Less widely publicized are Never Fail of Oklahoma City, who did fail to graduate from Harding Junior High School in that city (*Sun*, May 26, 1950, p. 7) and Dr. Safety First of Tulsa, Oklahoma. I have elsewhere recorded Bunker Hill, Charming Fox, Ima Fox, Diamond Queen, France Paris, Jack Frost, Winter Frost, Merry English, Erie Lake, Pinky Bottom, Virgin Muse, and Fairy Guy, among a good many other such jocular and would-be jocular names (*American Speech*, XXIII [1947], 263). It seems to me unlikely that any of these names — and they are legal names, not nicknames — were conferred in the course of administering the sacrament of baptism.

The bulk of my collection comprises what for want of a better term we may call made-up names — many of them root creations, some with prefixes like *Le*, *La*, *De*, and *Du* (used without the slightest reference to gender, as in La Don [m.] and Le Vaughn [f.], and suffixes like *elda*, *etta*, *eta*, *dean*, *ine*, *ena*, *elle*, and others, which usually designate females, though I have some in *ell(e)* which are borne by males.

So that the full beauty of these manifestation of the linguistic fancy of a people unhampered by ecclesiastical or civil authority or by onomastic traditions may be savored, I have arranged a few from my collection in octosyllabics. When I began to do this, I expected very little, but what has emerged has, it seems to me, a certain poetic quality, along with a certain power of allusiveness in its *Klang*-associations. *Metris causa* — i.e., because I needed a few monosyllables — I have had to include some names which more properly belong in other categories.

1

Yerdith, Virtus, Frow, LaDonna,
Nishie, Alderine, Zollie, Conna;
Garalene, Methalene, Ethelyne, Fal,
Bennilene, Gatsey, Ripsie, Ral.

2

Dolliree, Jetteree, Mauderie, Flem,
Nubit, Wogan, Omria, Kem;
Pheriba, Yuba, Twylah Jo,
Ovidetta, Zava Roe.

3

Leos, Cubie, Dicie, Metha,
Shi, Revonie, Sag, Uretha;
Arsie, Kissie, Bussie, Missie,
Yada, Telka, Clell, Elissie.

4

Ozena, Madula, Oleta, Zippie,
Ozella, Schiley, Florine, Rippie;
Amorus, Onan, Coeta, Pasco,
Reion, Merkin, Jeline, Vasco.

5

Incia, Phenis, Phalla, Icy,
Idlene, Birdene, Ala, Nicy.
Rectus, Dilly, Dally, Nil;
Mosco, Oco, Rumbo, Zill.

6

Stobo, Chlorine, Bamma, Floyce,
Willamane, Voncile, Thair, La Voice;
O'Leita, La Gita, Ludille, La Coy,
Arnetta, Loonis, Fanida, Hoy.

7

Shira, Reva, Terrayne, Aslean,
Etrelle, Mardelle, La Nan, Rudine.
Zazzelle, Glathu, Lavora, Troy,
Colonys, Wylodean, Cy, La Joy.

8

Alfa, Alto, Shyne, Arveta,
Pledger, Mortis, Cance, La Nita;
Anys, Cyrese, Bink, Eloyde,
Verdine, Merdine, Pink, La Void.

9

Raÿsal, Quintelle, Raz, Zerene,
Estyl, Bytha, Bevelene;
Boysy, Lugen, Lavator, Lake,
Eskaleen, Lueverine, Voline, Flake.

10

La Vada, La Voime, Donrue, La Nelle,
Kartaleen, Avalene, Zan, Jamelle;
Ronalene, Darlene, Denna Fo,
Japnel, Oynel, Wynell, Bo.

11

Vivett, La Carl, La Bruce, La Don,
La Vondus, Burtis, Joette, Lavon;
Zedro, Velpo, Bryna Lee,
Zefferine, Windell, Zim, La Mee.

University of Florida

"New Light" on "Old Zion"

A Study of the Names of White and Negro Baptist Churches
in New Orleans

G. THOMAS FAIRCLOUGH

Among the least explored regions which lie open to students of American names is that of organized religion. Research in the names of American churches has been limited to one anonymous pamphlet published in the nineteenth century and a few remarks in Mencken's monumental study of American English.[1] This paper makes no claim to cover any great extent of this onomastic *terra incognita*. It is an examination of the names of congregations belonging to a single Protestant group and located in a small geographical area. Yet within this restricted compass may be found some interesting indications of the part which ethnic factors play in the naming of churches, as well as a picture, in miniature and with local variations, of trends in church naming which operate throughout American Protestantism.

New Orleans was selected as the locale for this study because it is the largest American city to list white and Negro churches under separate headings in its telephone directory. The principal reference work used was the New Orleans Telephone Directory for 1959, published in January of that year by the Southern Bell Telephone Company. Occasionally during the investigation it was helpful and interesting to check the naming pattern of New Orleans Baptist churches prior to World War II. For this purpose a 1941 publication

---

[1] The pamphlet, published in Cambridge in 1891, dealt only with Protestant Episcopal churches and bore this imposing title: "On the Dedications of American Churches: An Enquiry into the Naming of Churches in the United States, Some Account of English Dedications, and Suggestions for Future Dedications in the American Church." Mencken summarized its findings and remarked on naming tendencies of other groups in *The American Language, Supplement Two* (New York: Alfred A. Knopf, 1936), pp. 589–591.

of the Work Projects Administration's Historical Records Survey, entitled *Directory of Churches and Religious Organizations in New Orleans*, was used.

The Baptist denominations belong to the great group of "free churches," Protestant sects without a tradition of state support or strong centralized authority. Baptists in the South are especially proud of the degree of autonomy which their local congregations enjoy. Among the many activities in which the individual church is subject to little or no regulation or supervision is the choice of a congregational name. The presence of this liberty of choice, assuring a variety of names for study, was the reason why I chose to investigate Baptist names.

In New Orleans this right of free choice has certainly been exercised. The common reader of telephone directories might well be content, after reading more than five columns of Baptist church names, merely to borrow Dryden's phrase and say, "Here is God's plenty." However, a closer consideration reveals an abundance of naming pattern: the pattern followed by each of the two races, and the Baptist pattern of the city as a whole and its relation to a nation-wide Protestant system of name categories.

All names borne by Christian churches in the United States can be placed in one of three classes: religious, secular, and a combination of the first two.[2] Among Protestants, the greatest number of religious church names are taken from the Bible. Most of these are personal or place names, with the word *Saint* prefixed to many New Testament personal names. A special subclass of personal names comprises those dedicated to an aspect of the Deity — *Christ, Our Saviour's, Messiah, Trinity, Divine Paternity* (this last is a

---

[2] The conclusions about a national pattern of Protestant church naming which are stated in this and several succeeding paragraphs were formulated after a study of about two dozen W. P. A. publications and current telephone directories, as well as some fairly extensive personal reconnaissance. The W. P. A. directories included *Directory of Churches and Religious Organizations of Rhode Island* (1939); *Directory of Churches in New Jersey*, vol. 16, "Passaic County" (1941); *Directory of Churches and Religious Organizations: Greater Detroit* (1941); *Directory of Churches, Missions, and Religious Institutions of Tennessee*, no. 33, "Hamilton County," and no. 79, "Shelby County" (1941). Some of the current classified telephone directories checked were those for New York (Manhattan), Chicago, Los Angeles, Baltimore, St. Louis, Nashville, Scranton, Duluth, Lincoln (Nebr.), and Waterloo (Iowa). I attempted to examine cities of various sizes, in as many sections of the country as possible.

historic Universalist congregation in Manhattan). Also used are the names of Biblical events (*Transfiguration*), Biblical edifices (*Temple*), and spiritual characteristics emphasized by Biblical writers (*Grace*). Occasionally, and almost always as the designation of a group proud of its fundamentalist approach to doctrine, the word *Bible* itself is used as a congregational name.

The names of saints who are of later than Scriptural date are used frequently by Episcopal churches but are otherwise quite uncommon. Protestants other than Episcopalians sometimes name their churches for what might be called their own saints, persons prominent in the history of the denomination. Detroit and West Lincoln, Nebraska, are two of many American communities containing Methodist churches named *Asbury*, after Francis Asbury, the first American Methodist bishop. Occasionally churches will be named for places connected with the lives of denominational saints. Examples are *City Road Methodist Chapel* (Madison, Tennessee), commemorating a London thoroughfare where John Wesley lived in his later years and whose Methodist graveyard is the place of his burial, and *Epworth Methodist Church* (Lincoln, Nebraska, and several other cities), named for the English village where John and Charles Wesley were born. Such non-Biblical but clearly religious place names do not seem to be used by other than Methodist congregations.

Purely secular names, understandably, manifest a greater variety. One large category, used by most American denominations but virtually unknown among Protestants in other countries, is that of numerical designations (*First, Second*, etc.). Place names bulk even larger and are of several kinds. Sometimes the name of the town will serve as the church's name; this usage is confined to small towns and villages where each denomination is represented by only one church,[3] and in larger cities to the one congregation of a particular faith to be found there. A church located in the central business area of a city may be called *Downtown, Central*, or *Mid-City* (e.g., the *Central Methodist Church* in the heart of Detroit). Outlying neighborhoods which, although part of a larger city, are cohesive enough

---

[3] In recent years, some congregations in this situation have experimented with numerical designations. The chief deterrent to this practice is that members of other sects usually regard the *First Methodist Church*, in a community of 500 people, as a manifestation of the sin of pride.

to have a local identity and a name, usually give that name to at
least one of the Protestant churches in the area. The Havelock
section of northeast Lincoln, Nebraska, has a *Havelock Methodist
Church*, a *Havelock Church of the Christian and Missionary Alliance*,
and a *Havelock Assembly of God*.[4] Most particularized of all the
locality names are the street names which many Protestant churches
bear. Usually they are the names of the streets on which the
churches front; rarely, they are taken from nearby streets of more
importance. The *Fifth Avenue-State Street Methodist Church* of
Troy, New York, uses the names of both the streets which form its
intersection, but in speech it is universally referred to as the "State
Street Methodist Church."

Some secular place names are more general than those in the
last two subclasses, yet somewhat more imaginative than the *Central* or *Downtown* group. These names have as their referent a nearby
landmark of some kind, natural or man-made, and they usually
allude to it with a kind of elegant vagueness. An example is the
Lake Shore Presbyterian Church of St. Clair Shores, Michigan, which
is located within a few blocks of Lake St. Clair.

A final subclass of secular place names for churches, though comparatively small, deserves mention for its miscellaneous nature. This
is the group of place names without any local reference. A number
of American congregations seem to have been guided in their choice
of name by no more precise criteria than euphony and pictorial
connotation. The *Belle Vista Methodist Church* of Clifton, New
Jersey, and the *Pleasant Green Baptist Church* of St. Louis are examples.

Secular personal names are not so frequently used as secular place
names, but in some localities they form a fairly sizable group. They
are almost always the names of deceased persons who have been

---

[4] Before 1930 this section of Lincoln was an independent village. The *Havelock
Methodist Church* was founded prior to Lincoln's annexation of Havelock, and might
consequently be considered (historically, at least) as the bearer of a town rather
than a neighborhood name, and as originally belonging to the first rather
than the second subclass of secular place names. The other two congregations,
established since Havelock lost its municipal identity, ought clearly to be considered
as bearers of a neighborhood name; and in the interest of simplicity I have so
classified *Havelock Methodist Church* as well. When Havelock ceased to be a city
and became a neighborhood, the church's name, in my opinion, became a neighborhood name also.

prominent in the affairs of the local congregation. Churches named for local people usually add the word *Memorial* to their names. Scranton, Pennsylvania, furnishes a good example of such commemoration in the *Dr. Jones Memorial Congregational Church.*

Nationality designations, such as *Filipino Methodist Church* (Oakland, California), require little explanation. Most Protestant churches so named are missions which direct a special evangelistic effort at the group specified.

A last category, which tends to blend into one of religious churchnaming, consists of what I call "secular grace names." These are names of mental or spiritual characteristics and other abstractions whose source, or at any rate whose principal source, is not the Bible. Such a name as *Liberty Baptist Church* is more apt to be assumed from a vague patriotic sentiment than from a desire to allude to "the perfect law of liberty" (James 1: 25).[5] *Union* is a similar secular grace name (*Unity* is its rather rare religious equivalent);[6] it is particularly useful to designate a congregation formed by the amalgamation of two or more others, and perhaps to indicate the presence of spiritual oneness among the members of the merged groups. The most charming name that I know of in this classification is the *Amicable Congregational Church* of North Tiverton, Rhode Island.

The third main category of church names, composed of religious and secular elements combined, is noticeably the smallest. It is also the most marked by efflorescent and untrammeled fancy. In New Orleans, names of this third category are borne by an unusually large percentage of the total number of Baptist churches, and are entirely the property of the Negro Baptists.

White Baptist congregations in New Orleans are distinguished today, as they were in 1941, by a definite predilection for secular names, and particularly for secular place names. In 1941 there

---

[5] The *Liberty Presbyterian Church* of Troy, New York, is a case apart. Originally it was located at First and Liberty Streets and was called *Liberty Street Presbyterian Church*. It is now on State Street near Sixth Avenue, almost half a mile from Liberty Street. When the move was made, the word *Street* was dropped, and a place name became a grace name.

[6] Non-Trinitarian denominations can find in *Unity* an adequate Deific name to substitute for *Trinity*. A combined Unitarian-Universalist congregation in Springfield, Massachusetts, is called the *Church of the Unity*.

were twenty-one white Baptist churches in New Orleans; sixteen bore secular names, and twelve of those were place names. Today the number of white churches is thirty-one; twenty-one have secular names, of which seventeen are the names of places. Street names are the most popular; there are churches named *Canal Boulevard, Carrollton Avenue, Coliseum Place, Franklin Avenue, Napoleon Avenue, St. Charles Avenue, Third Street,* and *Valence Street.* With these should be included the *Elysian Fields Baptist Church,* for although the complete thoroughfare name is not used, the church is located on Elysian Fields Avenue. Six congregations have neighborhood names: *Central, Mid-City, Gentilly, Lakeview, French Quarter Chapel,* and *Oak Park.* Three have numerical designations; one has a combined numerical and nationality designation — *First Spanish-American Baptist Church.* *Edgewater Baptist Church,* although honoring no specific neighborhood, bears witness to its location near Lake Pontchartrain. One name, *Golden Gate,* belongs to the class of place names without local reference.

The ten white churches which bear religious names all commemorate Biblical persons, places, and things. In only one, *St. Paul,* does the word *Saint* appear. Two congregations, *Trinity* and *Emmanuel,* bear names which express certain aspects of the nature of the Christian Deity; another, *Grace,* is named for an attribute which is both God-possessed and God-bestowed. Biblical places contribute *Bethany* and *Calvary;* Biblical edifices provide *Tabernacle* and *Temple.* One group commemorates an important event chronicled in the second chapter of Acts by calling itself *Pentecostal;* this name may also indicate participation in or approval of the "pentecostal" techniques of worship which characterize a fairly large segment of American Protestantism. And one congregation calls itself the *Bible Baptist Church,* to make known its more than ordinary fidelity to the precepts of that Book.

The names of most white Baptist churches in New Orleans follow a quite conservative secular pattern. They are oriented to specific realities in the here-and-now world rather than to emblems of a religious past. The minority of churches which bear religious names is equally conservative; all names are taken from the Bible, all are simple in form (one or two words), most commemorate *things* as do the secular names, and only one refers to a Biblical personage

other than God. The avoidance of all but the most common and
well-known religious names probably signifies, in a city so heavily
Roman Catholic in population, a desire to appear as unlike the
Catholics as possible.

Such a desire does not seem to affect the Negro Baptists of the
city much, if at all. The 1959 telephone directory lists 131 Negro
Baptist congregations, and purely secular names are borne by only
twelve of them — less than ten per cent. Six are numerical designations combined with some other term; in three of the names, the
second half is the nationality term *African*. Two combine numerals
with a geographical location which is itself numbered: *First African
Baptist Church of the Sixth District* and *Second Baptist Church of the
Sixth District*. One joins a numeral to a secular grace name — *Sixth
Union Baptist Church*; and one prefixes its numeral with a somewhat pretentious adjective — *Historic Second Baptist Church*. Of
the six remaining secular names, three are street names and three
refer to non-local places: *Law Street* is a representative example of
the former, *Plymouth Rock* of the latter. (This last is almost certainly intended to allude to the faith and virtue of the Pilgrim
Fathers, even more than to the mere geographic locality.)

Negro churches with religious names number 52, slightly more
than a third of the total. Neither the name nor the idea of sainthood
is avoided; ten of these churches commemorate saints. Nine saints
are New Testament personages, but one, *Saint Rose*, is post-Biblical.
In 1941 there were two Negro Baptist churches named *Saint
Mary's*, a name which, although Scriptural, is rarely used by American Protestants because of their abhorrence of anything like Mari-
olatry.

Biblical place names total nineteen, most of which are taken
from the Old Testament. The names of physical eminences are
apparently considered peculiarly appropriate to churches, which
represent human attempts to reach spiritual heights. Seven congregations are named for Biblical mountains: *Mount Ararat, Mount
Carmel, Mount Hermon, Mount Moriah, Mount Zion, Olivet*, and
Zion Hill.[7] Biblical nations are another popular source, providing

[7] The 1941 list contains interesting variant spellings for two of these names
(Mount Herman, Mount Mariah), as well as a *Mount Parin* (properly Paran—Deu-
teronomy 33:2) and a *Mount Corinth*. This last shows a certain unfamiliarity with
Scriptural record, as does a present-day Mount Salem, since Corinth and Salem
(Jerusalem) are Biblical cities.

Galatia, Israel,[8] and *Macedonia,* as well as *Beulah* and *Beulah Land*
on a more spiritual plane. ("Thou shalt be called Hephzi-bah, and
thy land Beulah: for the Lord delighteth in thee, and thy land shall
be married." — Isa. 62: 4.) Biblical cities supply *Antioch* and *Beth-
saida.* Ebenezer is the name of a stone set up by the prophet Samuel
to commemorate an Israelite victory (I Sam. 7: 12), and as such
carries a symbolic significance far greater than its importance as a
geographical name. Perhaps the most obscure Biblical place to be
adopted in the designation of a church is *Stone Ezal (sic).* Its source
is I Samuel 20: 19, in Jonathan's speech to David: "thou shalt go
down quickly, . . . and shalt remain by the stone Ezel." A marginal
gloss translates Ezel as "that sheweth the way."

Several names contain the word *Star;* several others come only
indirectly from the Bible. Two churches are named *Morning Star*
and *Bright Morning Star;* these are Scriptural enough, being used
to describe Jesus in Revelation 22: 16. By analogy with these, two
other churches have been named *Evening Star* and *Rising Star.*
There is also a *Star Bethel,* an interesting compound. Bethel was the
place where Jacob dreamed, as recounted in Genesis 28: 10–19;
there is, however, no star involved in the episode. It seems probable
that the name was originally conceived as a parallel to the familiar
phrase "star of Bethlehem," which is itself not found in the Bible.
Even further from specific Biblical language, although clearly religious in connotation, are such names as *New Birth, New Hope,*
and *New Light.* The first, although not a Biblical term, expresses
one of the most fundamental ideas of New Testament Christianity
(cf. John 3: 3, I Peter 1: 23). The second has no such evident source,
but a glance at Hebrews 6: 18–20 shows its fitness for use as the
name of a Christian church. *New Light* has been a fairly common
term among Protestants since the days of the Old Light and New
Light Burghers in eighteenth century Scotland. Light is throughout
the Bible and in all later Christian literature a symbol of spiritual
understanding; when it is prefixed by *New* it generally indicates the
possession, by those who use it, of a special illumination which outsiders have not yet achieved. Finally, a religious tract and a hymn

---

[8] This might be regarded as a personal name, for such it originally was (cf.
Genesis 32 : 28); however, the great majority of Biblical references to Israel are to
the nation.

which have been Protestant favorites for more than two centuries are honored by churches named *Pilgrim Progress* (*sic*) and *Rock of Ages*.

The remaining 67 Negro Baptist congregations have names of the mixed type. Here are most of the seemingly extravagant coinages, such as the *Greater King Solomon Baptist Church*, the *Mount Pilgrim Fourth Baptist Church*, and the *Second Zion Baptist Church No. 1*. Even here, however, some elements of pattern may be isolated and described. The usual sequence of terms in mixed names consists of a numeral followed by a religious name, preceded by an adjective of size (*Greater*, *Lesser*) or of age (*Old*, *New*). Occasionally, as in the second example in this paragraph, the order is reversed.

In considering the elaborateness of such names and the large number of Negro groups which bear them, it is important to keep in mind the manner in which Negro free churches proliferate. Many are "store-front" congregations, with little formality in their services or in their organizations. Secessions are frequent. A splinter group may pay its respects to the parent congregation by adopting its name with a qualifying word (*New*, *Second*, *Greater*) added. These qualifying words may also be added simply to distinguish a new church from a totally unrelated older one which happens to bear a popular name. A large number of post office names in the United States have undergone a similar alteration. Among the Negro Baptists of New Orleans, *Zion* is the basic element in no fewer than eleven names of the mixed type: *First Zion*, *Greater Mount Zion*, *Little Zion* (two of these), *Little Zion No. 2*, *New Zion*, *Old Zion*, *Pleasant Zion*, *Second New Pleasant Zion*, *Second Zion*, *Second Zion No. 1*, and *Zion Travelers First*. *Pilgrim* has bred *First Pilgrim*, *Pilgrim Rest*, and *Mount Pilgrim Fourth*.

A few churches have names, compound and otherwise, which are the products of such elaborate or arcane mental processes that it is difficult to deal with them unaided. Attempts at correspondence with the clergymen in charge were fruitless. I can offer only conjectures regarding such names as *Amozion Baptist Church* and *Gloryland Mount Gillion Baptist Church*. In the 1941 directory an *Amazon Baptist Church* was listed, with the same street address as the present *Amozion*. During the intervening years the process of verbal corruption has evidently been at work, changing a non-local place name to a nonce name with Biblical connotations (note the last four letters of the new version). The reason for the choice of the original name remains unknown to me. *Gloryland Mount Gillion* is the result of the merger of two congregations. *Gloryland* is clearly a non-Biblical religious place name, a common synonym for "Heaven"; *Mount Gillion*, however, is impossible to locate in either sacred or secular geography. It has been suggested to me that the name may be a portmanteau term. "Mount Gilead" appears in the seventh chapter of the book of Judges, which recounts the story of Gideon's battle with the Midianites. The first syllable of *Gilead* and the last two of *Gideon*, combined, result in the blend *Gillion*. This remains no more than a possibility. On the other hand, such a name as *Crescent Straight Life Missionary Baptist Church* may be analyzed with comparative ease, despite its unusual length and complexity. *Crescent* is a secular place name, referring to the bend in the Mississippi River at New Orleans and to that part of the city adjacent to it; *Straight Life*, for all its echoes of the insurance policy, is here evidently a secular grace name suggestive of a morally upright existence; *Missionary*, found as an element of many Baptist church names in the South, shows approval and support of evangelistic activities, as opposed to "Hard Shell" or anti-missionary congregations.

Although a number of sociological treatises deal with the Christian religion as practiced by American Negroes,[9] the manner in which church naming reflects differences between white and Negro religion has been discussed only incidentally. The names which have been studied are those of independent and "cult" congregations, rather than those found in denominations to which a great number of Negroes belong, and are consequently not truly representative.

The differences between white and Negro Baptists in New Orleans — between their attitudes toward the religion they practice and the world they live in — are probably mirrored quite accurately in the striking divergences of their church-naming patterns. The white congregations take their names primarily from "this present world,"

---

[9] Most important of these is Benjamin E. Mays and Joseph W. Nicholson, *The Negro's Church* (New York: Institute of Social and Religious Research, 1933). Other accounts include Carter G. Woodson, *The History of the Negro Church* (Washington: Associated Publishers, Inc., 1921) and Maurice R. Davis, *Negroes in American Society* (New York: McGraw-Hill, 1949), ch. 7, "The Negro and Religion."

and particularly from their own immediate neighborhoods. This would seem to indicate a primary concern with what religion can do in this world and for its people, rather than with the best way to prepare men for another world. In contrast, the names of almost all the Negro churches contain some religious element, although by no means all are strictly religious, and several have no direct Biblical derivation. The great popularity of definitely religious words and phrases in church names indicates that the religious life of New Orleans Negro Baptists is otherworldly in its orientation, directed toward a consideration of a better life which is not here but to come. The individual names which are most used, singly and in compounds, go far toward substantiating this contention. *Morning Star* is not only an Apocalyptic name for Jesus; it is, even within its Biblical context, a term of hope and aspiration. The star, indeed, is a symbol of aspiration in our most common proverbs. *Pilgrim* is no less a term of search and spiritual desire. "These all...confessed that they were strangers and pilgrims on the earth. For they say that such things declare plainly that they seek a country" (Hebr. 11: 13, 14). *Zion* has become, in Christian history, a synonym for the Christian church and the New Jerusalem as well as the Old Testament mountain of God. Such hymns as John Newton's "Glorious things of thee are spoken, Zion, city of our God," and Thomas Kelly's "Zion stands with hills surrounded" extol the wonders of the heavenly city and its colony upon earth. The Negro Baptists of New Orleans, if the names of their churches are any criterion, still think of themselves as seekers after a more desirable habitation, as did those other temporally handicapped people, the early Christians. Their extensive use of elaborate mixed names shows a willingness to use not only faith, but imagination and inventiveness, in the search.[10]

University of Nebraska

---

[10] As a sort of check upon the study described in this paper, I classified the white and Negro Baptist congregations of two medium-sized Midwest cities which I know well — Lincoln, Nebraska, and Waterloo, Iowa. These cities have far fewer Baptist churches than New Orleans (eight in Lincoln, seven in Waterloo); but both provide confirmation, on a smaller scale, of the basic trend noted in the Southern city: whites favoring secular names, Negroes preferring religious.

Falkland Islands: Nationalism and Names

JOHN RYDJORD

THE FALKLAND ISLANDS OR MALVINAS, located some three hundred miles east of the Strait of Magellan, have been the center of controversial claims since their discovery. Much of their history is associated with their names which have changed with the nationality of their explorers and with the claims and controversies of rival nations. As one author says: "Today the name of every bluff, and reef, and smallest channel of them — though many names are changed and lost — writes out the islands' history."[1]

The Spaniards and the Portuguese, with crews of mixed nationalities, were the first to enter the South Atlantic area of the New World, exploring the *Terra Australis Incognita*. Later the *Incognita* was dropped but *Terra Australis* was occasionally used. Vicente Saenz, a strong advocate of Spanish claims, attributed the discovery of the Falkland Islands to Magellan, who was not Spanish but a Portuguese in the Spanish service, and whose name was Magallanes or Magalhães. Spain was too busy colonizing her large New World empire to devote her efforts to distant and desolate areas "like those of the ardhipelago, . . . which were known under the general name of Magallanes Islands."[2] Magellan's name was not at first applied to the Strait which now bears his name; it was applied to the land in this whole southern area. The Strait was called the *Strait of Martin Behaim* in honor of that great map-maker, and the surrounding coast "became known as Magalhães."[3] It is unlikely that Magellan ever saw the islands which briefly bore his name, although one of his men, Estevão Gomes or Esteban Gómez, a deserter, may have seen them.[4]

---

[1] V. F. Boyson, *The Falkland Islands* (Oxford, 1924), pp. 13–14.

[2] Vicente Saenz, *Latin America Against the Colonial System* (Mexico, 1949), pp. 97–104.

[3] Boyson, *op.cit.*, pp. 15–17.

[4] Paul Groussac, *Las Islas Malvinas* (Spanish ed., Buenos Aires, 1936), p. 69, n. 87. See also "Falkland," *Encyclopedia Americana*.

The claim has been made that the islands had been seen by Amerigo Vespucci; but Amerigo, whose name spread from the land of the *Papagayos*, which became Brazil, to the whole New World, left no name for the Falklands. The supposition that he saw them is mere "conjecture."[5] On the issue of nationality and names it may be of interest to note that Amerigo was an Italian; he was in the service of the Spaniards; he gave his name to a Portuguese colony; his name then spread to all the nationalities of the New World; and yet the name *American* has been largely monopolized by the Anglo-Americans of the United States.

There are many who have attributed the discovery of the Falklands to John Davis, the English explorer who saw the islands in 1592, but the islands were already on the map by 1529. Ribera's map of that year showed them as *Ya de Sanson*, the *Ya* for *Ysla*, and it could mean the Island of Sampson. Sebastian Cabot, an Italian in the Spanish service and the brother of John in the English service, knew them as "Islands of Sanson and they bene 8."[6] Actually, they "bene" over a hundred.

Early explorers also called the islands *Islas de Patos* because they found there "Many very fat penguins, so fat that they were scarcely able to walk, and only half feathered." The name *Patos* might better have been applied to ducks and drakes. The large size of these strange penguins may have suggested the name of *Sanson* or Sampson to the sailors. The *Patos* or penguins must have been moulting since they were described as "only half feathered," *media pelados*, thus reminding the sailors of the shorn Sampson of Biblical times.[7] Alonso de Santa Cruz, cosmographer to Charles V of Spain, used both names, *Ysla de Sanson Y de Patos*. Diego Gutierez's map of America in 1592, when Davis was "discovering" the islands, labeled them as *Insule de Sanson*.[8]

Ascension Islands, located vaguely at that time between South America and Africa, seem to have floated freely in the minds of visionary explorers all the way to the Falklands. However, *Ascension* may have been applied independently to the Falklands. There was no consistency in the spelling of the name; it was written

---

[5] Julius Goebel, *The Struggle for the Falkland Islands* (New Haven, 1927), p. 15.

[6] Boyson, *op.cit.*, p. 18.

[7] Goebel, *op.cit.*, p. 15, n. 40 and p. 17.

[8] *Ibid.*, p. 19.

Ascension, Isla d'Ascension, Asençao, I de Acenca, Asenca, and *ace-cam.*[9] It was also suggested that *Sanson* was a corruption of *Ascension*. This, says Goebel, is "philologically absurd," and shows "a lamentable ignorance of the rough humor of seamen."[10] Seamen have certainly left names with a seaman's sense of humor, but one should not dismiss the evolution of the spelling or the sound of a name because it is "philologically absurd." Whatever the source, sailor's humor or philological evolution, *Patos Islands* and *Sanson Islands* were both used, singly or jointly, in the sixteenth century, as were the various forms of *Ascension*. The latter name was revived in 1708 when Captain Alain Parée sailed along the northern shores of the islands which he named *Côtes de l'Assomption*. This was not, however, for the elusive *Ascension Islands* of the South Atlantic but for his ship *Nôtre Dame de l'Assomption.*[11]

Before the end of the sixteenth century, British explorers, privateers, and pirates were penetrating the New World empire of Spain. Trailing Columbus by a century, John Davis, in the Cavendish expedition, from which he had been separated, said he had been driven among some islands, as Dampier quotes him, "never before discovered by any known relation, lying fifty leagues or better off the shore, east and northerly from the straits." Dampier adds without hesitation: "These were the Falkland Islands, of which Captain Davis certainly has the honour of being the original discoverer, . . ." Captain Davis left without claiming them or naming them. But Admiral Burney, possibly more aware of British ambitions, christened them "Davis's Southern Islands." Dampier said of Davis that this was "a distinction to which that celebrated navigator is fully entitled."[12]

Two years after the "discovery" by Davis came Richard Hawkins in the service of Queen Elizabeth of England. His naming of the islands is best told in his own delightful language:

> The land for that it was discovered in the raigne of Queen Elizabeth, my sovereigne lady and mistress, and a Maiden Queene, and at my cost and adventure, in perpetuall memory of her

---

[9] *Ibid.*, pp. 31–33; and Groussac, *op. cit.*, p. 90.

[10] Goebel, *op. cit.*, pp. 31 *et seq.*

[11] *Ibid.*, pp. 13–16.

[12] *Lives and voyages of Drake, Cavendish, and Dampier* (New York, 1832), p. 154; and Boyson, *op. cit.*, p. 22.

chastitie. and remembrance of my endeavours, I gave it the name HAWKINS maiden-land.[13]

A more fulsome and frank naming of a place name one may seldom find. Although these islands were named in honor of the Queen "in perpetuall memory of her chastitie," perpetuity is a long time, and *Hawkins' Maiden Land* was the accepted name for about a century and only intermittently after that until it was replaced and forgotten.

Hawkins' description of the islands is so unrealistic that there are those who say that he never saw them. Promoter that he was, he named one island the *Fayre Iland*, since it was, as he says, "all over as greene and smooth as any meddow in the spring of the yeare."[14] His descriptions were written long after his expeditions and after many years in a Spanish prison which might have made the free world look greener, but the grass was green in the Falklands. Groussac says of Davis and Hawkins that they may have discovered the "Malvinas" but at a place where they do not exist.[15] Nevertheless, their names were applied to the islands.

Next came Sebald de Weert, Dutch captain of the *Geloof*, who left Rotterdam in 1598 and, after a peek at the Pacific, returned through the Strait of Magellan and "discovered" some islands "hitherto neither noted nor drawn on any map."[16] He may have seen only a few of the islands of Hawkins' Maiden Land, but they had been both "noted" and named. However, the expedition of Sebald de Weert became well known and his name was given to the islands in many variations, such as *Iles de Sebald de Weert, Sebaldine Islands, Sebaldinas, Sebaldes, Sebaldines*, and, in Dutch, *Sebald van Weert*.[17] William Dampier, British buccaneer, sailed the southern seas and said he had seen three islands which he called "Sibbel de Wards," an interesting example of a phonetic transition from one language to another. This name, used loosely for the archipelago at first, was soon restricted to a cluster of smaller isles northwest of the main group, known later as the *Jasons*.

---

[13] *Lives . . .of Drake, Cavendish, and Dampier*, p. 154; and Boyson, *op. cit.*, p. 22.

[14] Boyson, *op. cit.*, p. 24, n. 1; see also Robert Fitz-Roy, *Narrative of the Surveying Voyages of H. M. Ships Adventure and Beagle* (3 vols., London, 1939), 2. 232.

[15] *Las Malvinas*, pp. 85–90.

[16] Boyson, *op. cit.*, p. 25.

[17] Goebel, *op. cit.*, p. 45.

William Dampier and Ambrose Cowley, his companion, entered
the South Atlantic in 1684 in a fine Danish ship which they had
captured and renamed *The Batchelor's Delight*. They knew about
the Sebald de Weert islands and yet they spoke of having "discovered" them. William Hacke, the editor of Cowley's journal, mis-
judged their location but, as "a compliment to the then secretary
of the admiralty," he named them *Pepys Islands*. John Harris, a
contemporary writer, says that Cowley "bestowed the name of Pepys
Island on it in honor of that great Patron of Seamen Samuel Pepys,
Esquire Secretary to his Royal Highness James, Duke of York,
when Lord High Admiral of England."[18] *Secretary's Point* and
Admiralty Bay may also have been named to honor him. It has
been said that Cowley and his corsairs "invented the Pepys Islands," but the name remained for some time;[19] and, as late as 1771,
Dr. Samuel Johnson referred to the islands as "Pepys or Falkland
Islands."[20]

In 1689–1690 Captain John Strong, with letters of marque, was
searching for commerce or conquest along the Argentinian coast
when strong winds drove him from *Puerto Deseado* to the shores of
"Hawkins' Land." Strong sailed the nameless channel between the
two larger islands which he named *Fawkland Sound* and which,
with a change of spelling, introduced the name of *Falkland*, not for
the island but for the channel.[21]

During the War of the Spanish Succession, Captain Woodes
Rogers, in command of the *Duke* and the *Duchess*, English privateers, encountered a French expedition under Captain Alain Parée
which he drove away. Rogers is quoted as having said: "This is
Falkland's Land," using the possessive which would help to make it
British. He is said to have been "the first to call the islands by their
present name Falkland, giving to the islands the name Strong gave
to the Sound between them."[22]

For whom or for what the Falkland Islands were named is still
debatable. It may have been for Lucius Cary, the Viscount of Falkland. One author said that Falkland Sound was named for Anthony,

---

[18] Boyson, *op. cit.*, p. 29.

[19] Groussac, *op. cit.*, p. 98; Fitz-Roy, *op. cit.*, 2. 230.

[20] *Thoughts on the Late Transactions Respecting the Falkland Islands* (Reprint
London, 1948), pp. 10, 12; Groussac, *op. cit.*, p. 97.

[21] Boyson, *op. cit.*, p. 34; Fitz-Roy, *op. cit.*, 2. 231.   [22] Boyson, *op. cit.*, p. 33.

Viscount Falkland, who was then supposedly commissioner of Admiralty and later First Lord of Admiralty, and at one time treasurer of the navy.[23] This assumption is questionable, and it has been questioned, since there seems to be no record of a Viscount of Falkland after the death of Lucius Cary, Second Viscount of Falkland, in 1643. Falkland Castle, once the happy home of Mary Queen of Scots, may also have been the source for the name. Near Falkland Castel, James II built a "Royal Burgh," also named Falkland, in the County of Fife.[24] Groussac suggests that Falkland Sound was not named for the Viscount, who had long been dead, but for the little burg of Falkland which was near the birthplace of John Strong.[25] But the name of Falkland was not adopted by the rivals of the British.

French sailors from St. Malo found the islands open for occupation and for a host of new French names. Jacques Beauchêsne Gouin left St. Malo in 1698 and entered the Pacific through the Strait of Magellan. On his return he found an "unknown" island which he thought was near the Sebaldine Islands. This island was then, "according to custom," named for the "discoverer" and became known as *Ile Beauchêsne*.[26]

Members of an expedition in 1711 saw what they considered to be "new islands" which they named *Isle de Danycan*, as they said, in honor of Noel Danycan de Lepine, the owner of their ship.[27] According to one report the ship's commander, M. Fouquet, "named the cluster of islets near which he anchored, the Anican Isles." They were also called *Isles d'Anican*.[28] Captain Bernard, an American, later identified the Anican Islands which "lie low and dark and desolate at the S. E. entrance to Falkland Strait."[29] A French map of 1724 combined the French names and called them the *Nouvelles Isles d'Anycan et de Beauchêsne*.[30]

---

[23] Goebel, *op.cit.*, p. 136, n. 44. See also "Lucius Cary," *Dictionary of National Biography*.

[24] Iain Moncreiffe, *The Royal Palace of Falkland* (Edinburgh, n.d.), *passim*.

[25] *Las Malvinas*, p. 101, n. 129.

[26] Goebel, *op.cit.*, p. 145.

[27] Boyson, *op.cit.*, p. 34; Groussac, *op.cit.*, p. 107.

[28] Fitz-Roy, *op.cit.*, 2. 232: E. W. Dahlgren, *Les Relations Commerciales et Maritimes entre La France et Les Côtes de L'Océan Pacifique* (Paris, 1909), p. 385.

[29] Boyson, *op.cit.*, p. 84.

[30] *Ibid.*, p. 34; Groussac, *op.cit.*, p. 107.

Many of the early explorers used the term "new islands" to make them appear to be new discoveries. Amedée Francois Frézier, one of France's foremost geographers, headed his own expedition to the South Atlantic in 1712–1714. He had been stationed at St. Malo and was quite familiar with the explorations of the St. Malo sailors. In his report, published in 1716, Frézier used the name *Isle Nouvelle* or *Isle Neuves*. He placed *I. Sebald* on a northwestern group; and farther south he located *I. Beauchésne*.[31] Lord Byron referred to some islands south of the Sebald de Weert as the *New Islands*.[32] In the nineteenth century North American whalers frequently found refuge on *New Island*; today one little island, privately owned, still bears that name.[33] In this manner the name *Isle Neuve* has been preserved.

In 1721 Jacob Reggeween, heading a Dutch expedition, explored the islands and he named one point *Cape Rosenthal* for a sea-captain, and another, *New Year Cape* for the day on which it was discovered. The archipelago was called *Belgia Australis* because, "when inhabited, those who dwelt on it would be at the antipodes of the Low Countries."[34] It was no longer *Terra Australis Incognita*, nor did it remain *Belgia Australis*, but it could still be *Terra Australis*.

The French were to supply the name which would rival the English name of Falkland. Having come from the port of St. Malo, the French sailors were known as *Les Malouines*, and it was only a step to transfer the name of the sailors of St. Malo to the islands which they explored, and so the islands became *Les Isles Malouines*. Frézier used this name and *Les Malouines* may also be found on Delisle's map of 1722. In fact Delisle takes credit for the name when he says: "La terre que j'appelle l'archipel Malouin, parce qu'il a été découverte par les vaissaux de Saint Malo, . . ."[35] After referring to Frézier's use of the name, Samuel Johnson said in 1771 that *Malouines* was "the denomination now used by the Spaniards."

---

[31] Boyson, *op. cit.*, p. 36.

[32] Saenz, *op. cit.*, p. 99.

[33] Boyson, *op. cit.*, p. 84; Olin S. Pettingill, "People and Penguins of the Faraway Falklands, "*National Geographic Magazine*, 109. 406.

[34] Boyson, *op. cit.*, p. 84.

[35] "The land which I call the archipelago of Malouin, because it was discovered by the ships of Saint Malo." Quoted by Dahlgren, *op. cit.*, p. 381, n. 4. Cf. Boyson, *op. cit.*, pp. 33–36.

The Spaniards, he added, "seem not till very lately to have thought them important enough to deserve a name."[36]

Before the middle of the eighteenth century, Lord Anson suggested that the British seek a foothold in "either Pepys Island or the Falklands." Anson seemed to distinguish the areas for which the names were applied but Samuel Johnson used both names as if they were interchangeable.[37] The British government accepted Lord Anson's suggestion to investigate and, with unusual courtesy, asked Spain for permission to explore the islands. The Spaniards protested and, with imagination and some exaggeration, said that they had "long since discovered and inhabited" these islands which they called *Islas de Leones*. They were named for the sea lions because of "the quantities of these amphibious animals to be met upon their coasts."[38] The Spaniards may have intended to use the name for all of the islands in order to enhance their claims but the name was later relegated to only a small group in the southeastern part of the archipelago. The British and the French ignored both the name and the claim and Spain had no colony there to defend.

As a result of the Seven Years' War, France suffered serious losses in North America and efforts were made to care for colonials from the Evangeline country. Prompted by the Duke de Choiseul, premier of France, Louis Antoine de Bougainville, a brilliant French navigator and explorer, decided to use Les Malouines as a colonial sanctuary for dispossessed Acadians.[39] The main inlet along East Falkland, Bougainville named *Choiseul* in honor of the minister, and the site for the settlement he named *St. Louis* for his ship. Incidentally, Bougainville's first name was Louis and it has therefore been assumed that this was the source for the name.[40] Having named places, Bougainville then took possession of all the islands "under the name of Les Malouines," after which the French held a celebration with a *Te Deum* and a *Vive le Roi*! Two hundred penguins perished in a fire which Bougainville set on one island and so it was

---

[36] Johnson, *op. cit.*, p. 10. See also Fitz-Roy, *op. cit.*, 2. 232.

[37] Johnson, *op. cit.*, pp. 10, 12.

[38] Quoted from Benjamin Keene by Goebel, *op. cit.*, pp. 195–199.

[39] *Ibid.*, pp. 225–226; and *Cambridge History of the British Empire* (New York, 8 vols., 1929), 1. 698.

[40] G. M. Coombs, "The Antarctic Claims," *The Contemporary Review*, 163. 216–220.

named *Burnt Island*. Finally, *Cape Bougainville*[41] was named in honor of the French explorer, whose name is, however, better known in the South Pacific.

The British also busied themselves with projects for colonization. Commodore John Byron, grandfather of the poet and a contemporary of Bougainville, was instructed in 1764 to call at "His Majesty's Islands call'd Falklands and Pepys' Islands situate in the Atlantick Ocean near the Streights of Magellan" to make some surveys and to select a site for settlements.[42] According to Groussac, Byron was searching for Pepys Island without being concerned about the Falklands, expressing a Spanish view which might restrict the British interests.[43] Byron seems to have sailed between *Saunders* and *Keppel* islands. *Saunders Island* was likely named for Charles Saunders, a captain in Anson's famous expedition against the Spaniards. Viscount I. Augustus Keppel was a second generation Englishman of Dutch origin who had joined Anson in 1740 and participated in his expedition around the world. Lord Byron had served as midshipman on the same voyage and his name was left on *Byron Sound*.[44] So three of Anson's men — Saunders, Keppel, and Byron — left their names on the Falklands. A century later an effort was made to change the name of *Port Louis* to *Anson*, but this was not a lasting change.[45]

Commodore Byron added several place names as he continued his explorations. *Port Egmont*, on Saunders Island and not on West Falkland as some have supposed, was named for John Perceval, second Count Egmont and First Lord of the Admiralty, one of the most ardent promoters of the colonization of the Falklands.[46] After leaving Port Egmont, Byron sailed north of Pebble Island and named *Cape Tamar* and *Cape Dolphin* for two ships in his fleet. He even tried to change the name of Falkland Sound to *Carlisle* but in

---

[41] Boyson, *op. cit.*, pp. 40–43, and map opposite p. 414.

[42] Conway to the Lords of Admiralty, July 20, 1765, Goebel, *op. cit.*, p. 231.

[43] *Las Malvinas*, p. 121.

[44] *Ibid.*, pp. 120–121; Fitz-Roy, *op. cit.*, 2. 232. For Saunders and Keppel see *Dictionary of National Biography*.

[45] Boyson, *op. cit.*, p. 117. Both Anson County, North Carolina, and Ansonburgh which he founded are named in his honor. *American Cyclopedia* (New York, 1874), 1. 538.

[46] Boyson, *op. cit.*, p. 54; Groussac, *op. cit.*, 121, n. 165.

this attempt he failed. Byron then took possession for his king, George III, of the whole archipelago "by the name of Falkland's Islands."[47]

Admiral John McBride followed Byron in 1766 in H. M. ship *Jason*. He saw Sebald de Weert's Islands, ignored their accepted Dutch name, and renamed them *Jason's Islands* for the name of his ship. The Jasons were later distinguished by individual names: *Great* or *Gran Jason, Steeple Jason, Elephant Jason, Flat Jason,* and *South Jason*.[48] One author added a third name to the group and called them the *Sebaldines, Jasons,* or *Salvages*.[49] They first had a Dutch name, then an English name from Greek mythology, and they now received a Spanish descriptive name. *Salvages*, which could mean savage, may mean rough or wild and is appropriate for the inhospitable isles.

McBride whose name is found on *McBride Head*, later ran into the French colony and demanded to know by what right it was there. The French were equally curious and critical about McBride and the British. The Spaniards in turn questioned the right of either to be there. They first challenged the French. Spain and France, with Bourbons on both thrones, were supposed to be on friendly terms, and Bougainville, in recognition of the Spanish claims' agreed, for a price, to withdraw the French colony. Consequently the Spanish flag replaced the French flag on April 1, 1767, and the hapless Acadians were again dispossessed.[50] The British were challenged three years later.

The Spaniards had not previously been much concerned about the names of the Falklands but, having taken possession, it was now their turn. In the words of Boyson: "Awed by its stern aloofness and far-flung solitude they gave it no name, as English and French had done, of friend, or sovereign, or loved place of home;" but being "visionary, lofty, impersonal," they "bestowed on the islands the most beautiful, they called it Isla Nuestra Señora de la Soledad."[51] *Baie St. Louis* of the French, *Berkeley Sound* of the British, now became *Bahia de Soledad* for the Spaniards. As the settlers gradually

---

[47] Boyson, *op.cit.*, pp. 44–50; Goebel, *op.cit.*, 232, 273–274.

[48] Groussac, *op.cit.*, map opposite p. 200; Boyson, *op.cit.*, pp. 46–47.

[49] Fitz-Roy, *op.cit.*, 2. 232.

[50] Boyson, *op.cit.*, p. 50; Goebel, *op.cit.*, p. 228, n. 19.

[51] Boyson, *op.cit.*, p. 54.

deserted the desolate isle, it finally and fittingly became in its solitude just *Soledad*.[52]

Now all of the islands were in need of a Spanish name in order to
support the Spanish claims. The Spaniards had been for some time
content to use the French name of *Les Malouines* but this they now
modified to make it look like Spanish and sound like Spanish even
though it might lose its meaning in the transition. First they
changed *Malouines* to *Maluines*, and occasionally *Maluynas*, leaving out the "o," in accordance with Spanish orthography. Then they
changed the "u" to a "v," an easy transition, and there they had
a new name, *Las Malvinas*, a name which persisted to the present
as a rival of the English name Falkland. After the Spanish government adopted the name Las Malvinas, Groussac adds in parentheses,
but with doubtful accuracy: *tal fue desde entonces su unico nombre
reconocido*.[53]

Anglo-Americans and the English also had trouble with the
French name *Malouines* and, by ignoring the French pronunciation
of the "i," they called the islands the "Maloons."[54] The Germans
merely put a German ending on the French name which changed it
to *Malouinische Inseln*. With their meticulous care for detail and
with great impartiality, they referred to the islands as *Hawkins
Maiden oder Jungfern-Land von Johann Hawkins 1593 entdeckt sonst
Falklands oder Malouinische Inseln*. They combined both the Dutch
and the English for the Sebald Islands as *Sebald Inseln, 1598 von
Sebald de Weert entdeckt itzt Jasons Eilande* in German; in English:
Sebald Islands, now Jasons Islands, discovered by Sebald von
Weert in 1598. Those called *Islas de Leones* by the Spaniards were
naturally *Seewölffelsen* in German. While using the English name
Falkland for the whole group, East Falkland was labeled *Franzo-
sen I.*, giving the French preference even in German.[55]

Only determined diplomacy or the resort to war could untangle
the title to the islands and the linguistic confusion. If the Spaniards

---

[52] Forrest McWhan, *Falkland Islands Today* (Sterling, Scotland, 1952), p. 16;
Goebel, *op. cit.*, p. 273.

[53] "Such was from then on its only recognized name." *Las Malvinas*, p. 141,
n. 198.

[54] Boyson, *op. cit.*, p. 33; Fitz-Roy, *op. cit.*, 2. 232.

[55] See map in Goebel, *op. cit.*, p. 360. One may note that the Germans mistakenly
gave credit for Hawkins's expedition to "Johann" rather than to his son Richard.

could rid the islands of foreign intruders, the name could remain *Las Malvinas*, the "only recognized" one, as Groussac suggested. The Spaniards from *Isla Soledad* demanded that the British leave West Falkland; the British were equally ardent in demanding that the Spaniards depart. Spain had bought off the French and were determined to drive out the British. On June 10, 1770, with warships and troops from Buenos Aires, the Spaniards took possession of the British colony at Port Egmont. The British became belligerent when the news of the loss of Port Egmont reached England in September.[56] With French support, by means of the Family Compact, Spain might fight over the Falklands or Malvinas with some hope of success; without it, she might better seek a settlement and peace.

The personal and political battle between Madame du Barry, the French king's mistress, and Choiseul, the king's minister, decided the issue and determined the name. Choiseul recommended that France support Spain, even though it meant war with Britain. Madame du Barry objected, for personal reasons — it seems — rather than for reasons of state. The king listened to the mollifying voice of Madame du Barry rather than to the belligerent and anti-British voice of Choiseul, and Choiseul was dismissed. Where the minister had lost, the mistress had won, and therefore Spain sought peace with Britain.[57]

The king of Spain ordered the restitution of the British colony at Port Egmont, without, however, in any way affecting his "prior Right of Sovereignty of the Malouines Islands, otherwise called the Falklands."[58] Lord Chatham complained fruitlessly to the House of Lords that Port Egmont alone had been restored and not Falkland. Samuel Johnson, using the name of *Junius*, ridiculed the idea of going to war over what he called a "Magellanick rock," reviving the neglected name of Magellan. Had the Bourbons combined against the British the latter might have suffered serious losses. The British were happy for the "miraculous interposition of Providence"[60] which brought them peace, and they should also have been thankful

[56] *Cambridge History of the British Empire*, 1. 701–703.

[57] Boyson, *op.cit.*, pp. 58–64; Groussac, *op.cit.*, 317, n. 4.

[58] Boyson, *op.cit.*, p. 68; Groussac, *op.cit.*, 134–136.

[59] Boyson, *op.cit.*, p. 69.

[60] *Ibid.*, pp. 69–70; and *Cambridge History of the British Empire*, 1. 703.

for the interposition of Madame du Barry who had prevented
French support for Bourbon Spain without supporting Britain.

The return of Port Egmont to Britain strengthened her claim to
the Falklands. But the period of British occupation was brief. In
1774 the colonists were happy to abandon these desolate and distant
islands. While deserting them, however, the governor put up a
notice, engraved oñ lead, claiming the Falklands.[61]

During the Spanish American wars for independence the islands
were generally neglected and ignored. The Spaniards had deserted
Soledad by 1811. Having won their independence from Spain, the
United Provinces of La Plata, as Argentina was then called, assumed
that they had inherited the Falklands. Not until 1829, however, did
they take possession by establishing a colony at Soledad.[62] The
British protested but they had no colony there to support their
claims, and to defend.

During the years of neglect, North American sealers and whalers
found refuge in the bays and inlets of unoccupied islands. Even the
Americans left place names. *Bernard Harbor* was named for Charles
H. Bernard, an American sea captain; *Smylie Channel* was named
for William H. Smyley, with a change in spelling.[63] When Louis
Vernet, the Argentinian governor, arrested Americans for "vio-
lating Argentine fishing laws," Silas Duncan, commanding an American naval expedition, captured the Argentinian garrison, arrested
the governor, and destroyed the settlement, making Soledad once
again a place of solitude whose sovereignty as well as its name was
at stake. Argentina and the United States then started a heated
debate over their respective rights in the Falklands, which even the
North Americans called "Las Malvinas."[64]

While the two argued, in 1833 Britain moved back into the Falklands with colonists and a colonial garrison, insisting that she had
never abandoned her claims. The Argentinians protested vehemently but they have been unable to budge the British to this day.
Each gives preference to its own nomenclature. A map made by the

---

[61] The Spanish governor took the name-plate and stored it in the archives of
Buenos Aires; but when General Beresford captured Buenos Aires in 1806 he
brought the plaque to Britain. Boyson, *op.cit.*, p. 82.

[62] Saenz, *op.cit.*, pp. 101–103; Boyson, *op.cit.*, pp. 94–98.

[63] Boyson, *op.cit.*, pp. 84 *et seq.*

[64] *Ibid.*, p. 94.

Argentinian Military Geographical Institute refers to the two large Falklands as *Malvina Oeste* and *Malvina Este,* and the name Falkland is restricted to the channel where it was originally applied. A typical Argentinian title for the archipelago is *Islas Malvinas (o Falkland) poseidos actualmente por Inglaterra,* giving preference to the Spanish name and using the English name only parenthetically.[65] A book by Juan Carlos Moreno, an Argentinian, with the title *Nuestras Malvinas,* was so popular that it went through six editions between 1938 and 1950.[66] To the Argentinians the islands are not only *Nuestras Malvinas* but also the *Terra Irredenta.* Yet English names are now scattered all over the islands with an occasional foreign name to give them an international flavor. During World War I the British won a great victory over the German navy in the Battle of the Falklands, bringing those remote and murky islands into the limelight and stimulating the pride of possession. Yet the dual claims and the dual names persist.

University of Wichita

---

[65] See map in Groussac, *op. cit.,* opposite p. 200.
[66] (6th ed., Buenos Aires, 1950).

The Names of Objects in Aerospace[1]

T. M. PEARCE

THERE IS, PERHAPS, NO VOCABULARY in contemporary use more significant than the terms for objects in aerospace. The word *aerospace*, in itself, is a coinage and of recent invention. It is carefully defined by Woodford Agee Heflin, in his *Aerospace Glossary*, as "the earth's envelope of air and the space above it; the two considered as a single realm of activity in the flight of air vehicles and in the launching, guidance, and control of ballistic missiles, earth satellites, dirigible space vehicles, and the like."[2] The noun can also be used in the attributive sense, as an adjective, in *aerospace activity*, *aerospace medicine*, *aerospace power*, *aerospace vehicle*, etc. Dr. Heflin, under the term *aerospace*, writes:

The upper limits of the aerospace recede upward as technology and science bring it under greater control. Three kinds of flying vehicles are adapted to its exploitation — the aircraft that flies within the atmosphere, the space-air vehicle, such as Dyna-Soar, that flies both within and above the sensible atmosphere, and the true spacecraft that flies principally in space either in orbit or under directional control.[3]

Aerospace, then, consists of three great zones in which flying objects may navigate, both under human controls and independent of them. These zones are the atmospheric space-bands encircling the earth; the non-atmospheric areas between the earth and the solar systems; and the marginal areas between the two. This paper is concerned with the nomenclature of objects designed by man to move in these zones. The title of this paper, however, is broader than its contents. The classifications presented here exclude natural objects moving in aerospace. They also exclude the designations for airplanes and gliders piloted by human beings in the earth space

---

[1] Presidential Address delivered at the 9th Annual Meeting of the American Name Society in Philadelphia, Pa., December 27th, 1960.

[2] Research Studies Institute, Maxwell Air Force Base (Alabama, September, 1959), p. 3.

[3] *Loc. cit.*

zones, but they include manned satellites and space platforms, those space ships of the astronauts, 'star navigators,' earthlings who are gradually gaining mastery over the earth's envelope of air and the space above it. The main vocabulary discussed here is devoted to rockets, rocket ballistic missiles, and satellites, both those that are destructive and those that are non-destructive. All the names are proper nouns. Common nouns and general type nouns are excluded, that is, such terms as *aerial torpedo, aeroballistic missile, rocket vehicle*, etc. Such generic words are descriptive of the broad areas in which the specific object-names fall. This paper is devoted to the object-names themselves, as they fill in the broader classes or categories. Many of these names are to be found in Dr. Heflin's *Aerospace Glossary*, but some have appeared since his collection was printed in September, 1959.

Before presenting the tables of names, some distinction must be made between the general categories. We have divided aerospace into three zones: the outer, inner, and transitional bands between atmospheric and non-atmospheric space. Into these zones, objects are projected from the earth. They may return to earth or they may remain in space. According to *The Oxford English Dictionary*, the term *missile*, for an object thrown to a target, appeared first in English in the year 1606, using the Latin form *res missiles*, for 'largess or gifts of perfumes and sweets reported thrown by the Roman emperors to the people.' In 1611, the word appears in a phrase *missile weapon*, describing an object thrown by hand or machine to injure or destroy a target. The term *rocket*, from French *roquet* or Italian *rocchetta*, apparently is a diminutive of Italian *rocca*, 'rock,' and it became an English word in the year 1611, when it was used to describe a cylinder of paper or metal containing a combustible substance which, if ignited, could be projected into space.

Today the term *rocket* can be applied to any projectile that is self-propelled in flight, such as the Army *Dart*, the Air Force *Atlas* and *Thor*, the Navy *Rat*, and the Navy-Air Force *Sidewinder*. It can also be applied to a self-propelled vehicle that lifts another object, perhaps a destructive missile, i.e., nuclear warhead, research cone, or space satellite. When the rocket vehicle lifts another object with intent to hurl it free at a target or into space, it becomes part of a ballistic missile. Both rockets and rocket ballistic missiles may be either destructive or non-destructive. Non-destructive rockets are referred to as "sounding rockets," and are sent into space to obtain research data. Rocket ballistic missiles may consist of multiple-stage vehicles, as is the case of those which launch a satellite or a space platform.

The solid rocket projectile was the first stage for aerospace vehicles, and it was limited in range, speed, and both destructive and research possibilities. The ballistic missile developed a much greater potential in all these respects, and made possible the space projects in the two outer zones, those beyond the earth's atmosphere. In the development of nomenclature, both the intellectual scope and the imagination have grown as scientific progress has opened up these broader areas of exploration and conquest.

Exploration in the twentieth century Space Age has something in common with exploration in the sixteenth century New World period. The discovery of America, a new land mass on the earth, was dependent upon improved carrier vehicles and new instruments of navigation. Discovery proceeded from the areas known to men to those unknown. New types of apparel, new ways of living, and new tools to sustain life were developed by adaptation to a new environment. The whole world stands on the threshold of a vast new experience which will come through space travel. The changes in the language may be revolutionary. The naming of space objects is simply the early step across this threshold of a new language horizon.

As the *Susan Constant*, the *Discovery*, and the *Godspeed* were the three small ships which carried the first English colonists to Jamestown, Virginia, in 1607, so *Bold Orion*, *Project Mercury*, and the *Dyna-Soar* may be the type of vehicle which will cross air-space to put latter-day English explorers on some unknown planet in the year 1967. Both the older names and the new ones fall into definable categories. The *Susan Constant* would seem to have carried a personal name into the New World. The name of the *Discovery* is an abstract concept presupposing the search for something in existence but not previously known. *Godspeed*, the third ship, was also named for an abstract concept, based upon the contraction of "God speed you" or "God give you success," a phrase based upon religious faith. Thus, one may safely assume that the modern categories of names in aerospace will include personal names and abstract concepts based upon hope or faith. Furthermore, the investigator will find that a large group of space vehicles derive their names from the stories and figures of Classic myths, a lost area of religious faith. Scientific theories, poetic imagination, historical tradition, classes of birds, beasts, and animals contribute to the naming groups. Finally, verbal ingenuity using the letters of the Greek alphabet or combining modern letters and syllables will be used to produce acronyms and blends. Wit and humor will play their part in the naming patterns. A great variety of sources,[4] then, are to be found, but they may be classified into such large groups as are discussed in the following pages.

I said, previously, that in the development of nomenclature for aerospace objects the first single-stage rockets were given less imaginative names than were the later ballistic missiles or the satellites and space-platform projects. Nevertheless, the names of the early rockets are instructive and interesting. They fall chiefly into the categories of description, personal commemoration, or bird and animal names.

Of descriptive identification some representative names are the *Dart*, a U.S. Army low-altitude missile, wire-guided, and directed at enemy tanks; or the *Pencil*, a Japanese test rocket only nine inches long. Descriptive, too, would be designations like *Redeye*, an Army bazooka-type projectile with infrared guidance for use against aircraft; *Wagtail*, an Air Force missile launched from airplanes at surface targets; the *Sidewinder*, a Navy and Air Force anti-aircraft rocket; and the *White Lance*, an Air Force missile to serve fighter bombers.

Rockets named for personal commemoration are found in several countries. In the United States, there is the *Davy Crockett*, a light battle rocket with nuclear capability, assigned to artillery groups and, presumably, performing for the modern Army what the Davy Crockett long rifle did for the frontiersman more than a century

---

[4] The United States Navy was instructed by Act of Congress, March 3, 1819, to name "all ships of the first class... after the States of the Union, those of the second after rivers and those of the third after the principal cities and towns." This act was amended subsequently to schedule battleships for States; cruisers for cities; destroyers for "deceased persons" in various categories; submarines after "fish and denizens of the deep;" minesweepers after birds. H. L. Mencken, *The American Language, Supplement Two* (New York, 1948), pp. 584–85.

ago. The *Bomarc* is an Air Force interceptor missile named for Boeing, maker of the frame, and for Marquardt, manufacturer of the ramjet engine. The Swedish *Bo 4* rocket is named for the Bofors Company which made it; the German glide bomb, the *Henschel 293*, was named for the Henschel und Sohn Company of Kassel, Germany, which converted its plant in 1933 from the manufacture of railroad locomotives and trucks to the production of airplanes and rocket-propelled bombs. The Russian *Golem* is an underwater rocket named for a sixteenth-century Jewish rabbi, reputed to have created a mechanical man. And finally, in the personal category, the American *Kettering*, an aerial torpedo in World War I, was named for the designer C. F. Kettering. This airborne missile was also called the *Liberty Eagle*, and thus became an early representative of a rather sizable group of rockets named for bird genera, such as the *Falcon*, a radar guided missile; the *Goose*, a diversionary missile decoy; the *Quail* or *Green Quail*, another diversionary missile; the *Hawk*, a missile designed to hit aircraft; the *Petrel*, a Navy missile launched from the air as an underwater torpedo; and the *Sparrow*, a Navy rocket guided by the launching aircraft's radar.

In the overlapping category, combining description, personal association and humor, belong such names for rockets as *High Card*, *Honest John*, *Little John*, *Little Joe*, *Shillelagh*, and *Holy Moses*, the latter term being applied to a World War II aircraft rocket that is no longer in production.

There are many rockets which are non-destructive and destined for research. In this group one is named *Marco Polo*, for the thirteenth century Venetian explorer whose trips into Asia and the Near East charted much of that terrain for European travel. This rocket is also known as the *Viking*, another type of explorer. Research missiles called drones have been named *Kingfisher*, *Spaerobee*, and *Teal*, bird designations appropriate to target objects. Some of the rocket names, however, are whimsical, such as *Baby Bobbin*, *Bumper*, and *Snooper*.

We turn from the rocket missile group to the rocket ballistic missiles, which are more complicated mechanisms, involving rocket vehicles plus projectiles, or multiple-stage rocket vehicles plus missile projectiles. Here the name categories draw upon the history of combat and of fighting men. The names even enter the world of myth and legend, indicating that as the range and potential for the

destruction or salvation of mankind grew, human imagination became correspondingly stirred. A glance at the classification of destructive ballistic missiles will show that several of the machines
bear the names of combat men, such as the *Black Knight*, the *Corpo-
ral*, the *Sergeant*, the *Matador*, and the *Minuteman*. Moving into the
sphere of mythology, ballistic rockets assume such names as *Atlas*,
Jupiter, *Thor*, and *Titan*. *Atlas*, of course, is the Greek demigod
who, after revolting against the heavenly powers, was condemned
to hold the earth upon his shoulders, a more stable attitude than
a ballistic missile aims to produce. The Roman *Jupiter* and the
Scandinavian *Thor* are both associated with natural power, as
expressed in thunderbolts and lightning. *Atlas*, however, as a name
for an object in aerospace, may not have resulted from memory of
the Classics at all. There is an aircraft company which owned that
name before it manufactured a rocket capable of launching a satellite. Still, aircraft or rocket engine, the name associates with Classic
myth. Some of the ballistic missiles bear the names of historic
weapons used by fighting men and gods, such as the *Mace*, the spiked
club used by medieval warriors for breaking armor, and the *Trident*,
a three-pronged spear carried by Neptune to show his authority
over the sea.

The best known of all ballistic missiles were also the first, that
is, the famed *V-1* and *V-2* German robot bombs of World War II.
The initial *V* is said to have been the German answer to Winston
Churchill's two-fingered *V-for-Victory* sign, but the *V* in German
stood not for 'victory' but for 'vengeance,' as in the German phrase
Vergeltungswaffe Eins, 'Vengeance Weapon One.' These terrible
objects were first launched on June 13, 1944, and can be said to
have introduced the present epoch of missiles space-borne by
rockets. Although they entailed great destruction of life and property, a variety of popular names were coined to identify them, such
as 'buzz bomb,' 'doodle bug,' 'robot bomb,' 'comet bomb,' and
'whirley.' The name 'Vengeance' was sufficiently unpleasant to
suggest that the *V* stood for something else, as for the initial letter
of German *Versuchsmuster*, 'experimental type,' but this has not
been supported by evidence.[5]

Illustrating some of the categories previously alluded to which
also appear in the naming of ballistic missiles are the descriptive

---

[5] *Aerospace Glossary*, p. 110.

Blue Streak; the bird name *Loon*; the personal commemorative
Pershing; and the humorous blend *Snark*, a name coined by Lewis
Carroll, from *snake* and *shark*.[6] But the most important contribution
of the name categories for ballistic missiles is their identification
with the realms of mythology. Some of the rockets were given
classic names, such as the *Nike-Ajax* and its two brothers, *Nike-
Hercules* and *Nike-Zeus*. Nike as the Greek Goddess of Victory,
becomes a worthy companion to the great warrior Ajax, and to
Hercules and his father Zeus in undertaking labors greater than the
twelve feats Hercules accomplished in former days.

One of the ambitious projects for the defense of the United States
in case of an attack by intercontinental ballistic missiles has been
named the *Argus* project, for the Greek monster who was equipped
with one hundred eyes. Only two of these eyes were said to sleep at
any one time. What better symbol of watchfulness could have been
bestowed upon a defense project ? One trusts that the designer who
named the project recalls what happened to Argus. Jupiter was in
love with Io, the sister of Argus, and he transformed her into a heifer
to avoid detection by his wife, Juno. The latter placed Argus as a
guard, but Jupiter sent Mercury in the guise of a shepherd, and Mercury played upon his reed so sweetly and told stories at such length
that all the eyes of Argus were closed when the former ceased. Then
Mercury slew Argus and released Io from her captive form.[7] There
is an obvious moral here, which is that any defense will collapse if
the owner is lulled to sleep by music and stories. The *Argus* project
calls for the discharge of radioactive particles to burn up incoming
missiles, and thus provide a protective shield for the country. But
ninety-eight of the eyes of Argus must ever be kept open.

On the 12th of August, 1960, a communications satellite balloon
was launched from Cape Canaveral, Florida. This balloon was
enclosed in the nose-cone of a missile, but once in orbit the balloon
inflated to the height of a ten-story building. Then the inflated surface acted as a sounding board for voices or signals broadcast from
the earth. As everyone knows, the name chosen for this satellite was
Echo, who in story-lore was a beautiful mountain nymph chattering
so constantly that the goddess, Juno, condemned her to the loss

---

[6] "The Hunting of the Snark."

[7] Greek and Roman mythological accounts in this paper are drawn from C. M.
Gayley, *The Classic Myths in English Literature and Art*, (Boston, 1893, 1911).

of her voice except for purpose of reply. Spurned by the handsome youth Narcissus, the nymph fled to the caves and hills where nothing remained but her voice. In the instance of the communications satellite *Echo I*, the voices being heard may even become full-bodied, for it is said to be possible to relay television images along with the sounds through the balloon satellite, resulting in a world-wide communication system.

King Midas, of the fabled golden touch, was not a god, though bequeathed certain godlike powers, such as turning everything he touched into gold. None of this, however, seems to be involved in the naming of a project of the Advanced Research Projects Agency, which orbited a *Midas* satellite on May 24, 1960, aimed to detect the launching of other satellites. The name is an acronym developed from the initial letters of *Mi*ssile *De*fense *A*larm *S*atellite. The acronym process can produce provocative combinations, as in the case of *Tiros*, a camera-eye satellite orbited on April 1, 1960, when it began immediately to send back space-pictures showing the boot of Italy, the Straits of Gibraltar, the Suez area, the eastern Mediterranean, and the southwest coast of Europe. Thousands of pictures have been sent by this television satellite, many of which have helped to improve weather forecasting, as they show cloud cover over various portions of the earth. Such satellites as *Tiros* will also help to remove the curtains from all national borders, for they will be all-seeing eyes. But does the name signify omniscient over-sight ? One thinks of Latin *tiro*, 'a recruit or a beginner,' and concludes that this satellite was the beginner or novice of a series planned to provide continual inspection of aerospace. But then he learns that the name is devised from the initial letters of "*T*elevision *I*nfrared *O*bservation *S*atellite." One wonders, however, if the phrase was not designed to make the name, because the words could be arranged just as easily in a way that spelled something else.

Another satellite which is in the planning stage will be called *Samos*. This is related to the project *Sentry*, which launched the *Discoverer I* satellite or February 28, 1959. Samos is an island in the Aegean, and was once famed for a great temple to the goddess Venus. However, I cannot find that the first *Discoverer* satellite in orbit was directed to the planet Venus. Yet space reconnaissance could come from this direction as well as from any other.

The United States had thrown forty-eight satellites into orbit by January 2, 1962. Russia had put up sixteen. Of the American satellites, the names were *Discoverer*, *Explorer*, *Vanguard*, *Atlas*, *Courier*, *Echo*, *Lambda*, *Midas*, *Pioneer*, *Samos*, *Transit*, *Greb*, *Tiros*, and *Oscar*. On January 2, 1962, thirty-four American satellites were still in orbit, and three Russian. This did not include the so-called space debris, i.e., parts of rocket machines, of which some fifty objects were also whirling around the earth.

But satellites alone do not tell the story of mythology worked into the naming of space objects. An instrumented vehicle called the *Jovian* probe, manned or unmanned, is designed to approach close enough to the planet Jupiter to discover and report new data upon this planet. Although the *Jovian* probe is still to come, a *Jupiter* rocket vehicle has been the booster in the *Explorer* satellite series, and the *Jupiter C* rocket is also called the *Juno I* rocket research engine, and both have been joined, or will be, by such other members of the Classic Olympian household as the *Apollo* spacecraft, launched by a *Saturn* engine; the *Mercury* man-in-space program; and the *Venus* probe.

So, in a measure, the Age of Greece has returned to rule the space age. One of the early projects at Cape Canaveral was called *Hermes*. An antimissile once under development was named *Plato*, though why the greatest of the Greek philosophers should be called upon to designate an *anti*-something-or-other produces surprise. Even the Greek alphabet has been called significantly into play, for in numbering and dating the satellites in each year, the first satellite is called *Alpha*, with the year date prefixed; the second is called *Beta*, with the year date prefixed, and so on. *Sputnik I*, for instance, which the Russians tossed into orbit on October 4, 1957, was also called "1957 Alpha" by the International Geophysical Year scientists. *Sputnik II*, which followed on November 3, then became "1957 Beta." The first American satellite in orbit on January 31, 1958, became "1958 Alpha." *Explorer III* and *Explorer IV*, orbiting in 1958 were "1958 Gamma" and "1958 Epsilon," respectively.

One could conclude with a miscellany, pointing to the two rockets named for American Indian tribes, the *Navajo* and the *Zuñi*; the two named for magicians, the *Genie* and the *Wizard*; the four named for dogs, the *Bulldog*, *Bullpup*, *Hound Dog*, and *Terrier*. One would like to know more about all the various "godfathers" of these objects. When and by whom were they named ? Was there a little ceremony and a formal christening, or did the name just come as a signature off the drawing board ? Whatever the origins, the names of objects in aerospace are varied and appropriate. They express the intent, the aspiration, the will of modern science. Let us hope that the positive and the good are written into them in greater degree than the negative and the malevolent.

University of New Mexico

Some Hypotheses About the Psychodynamic Significance of Infant Name Selection

MYRON BRENDER

T HE IMPORTANCE that the human mind attaches to the name is amply attested to by the antiquity of documented interest in names and the naming process. According to Garnot's[1] examination of the ancient *Texts of the Pyramids*, even before 2000 B.C. belief in the power of the proper name to determine the behavior and the destiny of its possessor was commonly held. Smith[2] cites a quotation from Antisthenes, c. 400 B.C., which states, "The beginning of all instruction is the study of names." Even the more recent pioneering essays in English onomastics — Patton's *The Calendar of Scripture*, Warren's *The Nurcerie of Names*, and Camden's monumental *Remaines*[3] — which also illustrate a serious interest in the subject, belong to past centuries.

Apart from the testimony of history, the universal importance of the name in human society is also reflected by the fact that anthropologists have been able to discover only a few primitive groups, notably certain aboriginal Australian tribes, that fail to endow their members with personal names. The Astantes in Africa were reported by Herodotus and Pliny to have exhibited this curious characteristic.[4]

An examination of the literature on the topic suggests that the formal study of names usually is approached from one of three directions: the etymological, the socio-anthropological, or the psychological.

The etymological orientation, exemplified by the bulk of the contributions appearing in the pages of *Names*, seems to be the one most commonly adopted.

---

[1] Garnot, Jean Sainte Fare, "Les fonctions, les pouvoirs, et la nature du nom propre dans l'ancienne Egypte d'apres les Textes des Pyramides." *Journal de Psychologie Normale et Pathologique*, 1948, 41, pp. 463—472 (abstract in English appearing in *Psychological Abstracts*, 1949, 23, p. 599, abstract no. 4750).

[2] Smith, Elsdon C., *The Story of Our Names*. New York: Harper & Bros., 1950, p. 277.   [3] Smith, *op. cit.*, pp. 277—278.   [4] Smith, *op. cit.*, p. 178.

The socio-anthropological approach, as represented in part by the work of Miller[5] and, more recently, that of Loseff,[6] concerns itself primarily with the social, or group, determinants of naming practice as manifested principally in primitive, preliterate, or alien cultures. "The folkways built about the name . . . the customs of naming and the form of the name" as they reflect "the evolution of social institutions and the nature of social forces" are investigated intensively in the belief that they can serve to "give significant insight into the organization, history, and ways of thought of these peoples."[7] Social custom, tradition and heritage, and their rational and irrational underpinnings occupy the central focus in this point of view, and, presumably, are regarded as the salient, if not indeed the exclusive, causal agents responsible for determining the choice of names in common currency within a particular society.

The psychological approach, in contrast, typically limits itself to matters pertaining to the individual rather than to group phenomena. Furthermore, the preponderance of the material published to date in the general area of the psychology of names has tended to deal mainly with reactions of the individual to his own name or to the names of others in terms of aesthetic preference, and with those factors that may be related to this individual preference. This restriction in research interest characterizes both the methodologically naive early studies issuing from the renowned psychological laboratories of Titchener at Cornell[8,9] and more sophisticated later studies.[10] Even in those instances where the attack employed has

[5] Miller, Nathan, "Some Aspects of the Name in Culture History." *American Journal of Sociology*, 1927, 32, pp. 585–600.

[6] Loseff, E. D., "Comparative Study of Names and Naming Patterns in Selected Cultures." Unpublished M.A. thesis, University of Southern California, 1951.

[7] Miller, *op. cit.*

[8] English, G., "On Psychological Responses to Unknown Proper Names." *American Journal of Psychology*, 1916, 27, pp. 430–434.

[9] Alspach, E. M., "On Psychological Responses to Unknown Proper Names." *American Journal of Psychology*, 1917, 28, pp. 436–443.

[10] Walton, W. E., "Affective Value of First Names." *Journal of Applied Psychology*, 1937, 21, pp. 396–409.

Allen, L., Brown, V., Dickinson, L., and Pratt, K. C., "The Relation of First Name Preferences to Their Frequency in the Culture." *Journal of Social Psychology*, 1941, 14, pp. 279–293.

Finch, M., Kilgren, H., and Pratt, K. C., "The Relation of First Name Preferences to Age of Judges or to Different Although Overlapping Generations." *Journal of Social Psychology*, 1944, 20, pp. 249–264.

been dynamic and speculative[11] rather than purely descriptive and empirical, the focus has been upon reactions to the name rather than upon the naming process or the process of name selection and be-stowal *per se*. The present paper is intended to bridge the gap be-tween the socio-anthropological and the psychological approaches to the study of names by applying a speculative, psychodynamic mode of conceptualization — borrowed from motivational psycho-logy — to the analysis of the naming process. The position taken here is that such an attempt is both feasible and worthwhile because in a small, simple and relatively homogeneous cultural group, as is typified by most primitive, preliterate societies, social custom and tradition is the most potent, and perhaps the only, determinant of naming practice; whereas in a complex, heterogeneous culture, such as ours, idiosyncratic factors are at least of equal and quite often of greater importance in determining the choice of name. In keeping with this view, an effort will be made here to elucidate the psycho-logical significance of the personal determinants that operate in the naming process as it occurs in American society. In the interests of scientific rigor, however, it should be noted that the subsequent dis-cussion is intended to be suggestive and heuristic rather than defini-tive and conclusive. All propositions and statements are to be re-garded as hypotheses subject to future verification by controlled empirical research.

The present writer's system for classifying the principal determi-nants of name selection coincidentally parallels and duplicates in

Eagleson, Oran W., "Students' Reactions to Their Given-Names." *Journal of Social Psychology*, 1946, 23, pp. 187—195.

Arthaud, R. L., Hohneck, A. N., Ramsey, C. H., and Pratt, K. C., "The Relation of Family Name Preferences to Their Frequency in the Culture." *Journal of Social Psychology*, 1948, 28, pp. 19—37.

Savage, B. M., and Wells, F. L., "A Note on Singularity in Given Names." *Journal of Social Psychology*, 1948, 27, pp. 271—272.

Houston, T. J., and Summer, F. C., "Measurement of Neurotic Latency in Women with Uncommon Given Names." *Journal of General Psychology*, 1948, 39, pp. 289—292.

Dexter, Emily S., "Three Items Related to Personality: Popularity, Nicknames, and Homesickness." *Journal of Social Psychology*, 1949, 30, pp. 155—158.

[11] Plottke, Paul, "On the Psychology of Proper Names." *Individual Psychology Bulletin*, 1946, 5, pp. 106—111.

Murphy, W. F., "A Note on the Significance of Names." *Psychoanalytic Quarterly*, 1957, 26, pp. 91—106.

Drake, David, "On Pet Names." *American Imago*, 1957, 14, pp. 41—43.

many respects the classificatory method devised by Smith.[12] While the author arrived at his system independently and previous to his reading of Smith's work, the priority and exhaustiveness of Smith's contribution is appreciatively acknowledged.

For the purposes of this study, it is postulated that various psychological or, more broadly, psycho-social motives, needs, or values underlie the choce of a name for an infant in our culture. An *a priori* analysis of the infant-name-selection process suggests that any of the following factors may serve to influence the final choice.

Family Tradition: In family-oriented parental units where familial tradition carries inordinate weight, the choice of a name for an offspring may be decided by family custom. Thus, it may be the usual family practice to restrict the selection of an infant name to a relatively narrow predetermined range of choices traditionally in use in the family. The order of birth of the newborn child within its immediate family unit, as well as its sex, may determine the choice of name that is finally made from the traditional set of family names. The conscious or unconscious parental attitude underlying conformity to this practice at least implies a need on the part of the parents to defer to family expectation in this matter; possibly it is also a reflection of a more general attitude of compliance with regard to family claims, demands, and expectations. The basis for such acquiescence to familial wish may be a sense of psychological, or emotional, dependence experienced by one or both parents of the infant, or it may be a maneuver prompted by an anticipation or a hope of material (perhaps monetary) gain. Where the motivation is solely or principally that of emotional need, the emotion involved may be that of guilt or an unsatisfied wish to gain approval or love or to avoid disapproval, rejection, or figurative punishment. Again, it should be stressed that any one or any combination of these emotional needs may characterize one or both parents where the choice of name is made solely in accordance with family tradition. Likewise, the hope or expectation of material gain for self and for the child can co-exist with a sense of emotional dependency and can act as an equipotent determinant of name-choice. An illustration of this mixture of motives might be the case in which an infant is named Stacey, Beaumont, Dalton, or O'Neill both because it is traditional in his

---

[12] Smith, *op. cit.*

family for the first-born male child to be given this particular name and because wealthy great-aunt Stacey, Beaumont, Dalton or O'Neill might be more favorably disposed in her will toward a youngster bearing the appropriate name.

Religious or Ethnic Custom: (E.g., the custom among Jewish people of bestowing upon the new-born a Hebrew name in addition to the Christian name, where a Christian name is also given, and of choosing the Hebrew name in commemoration of a deceased relative. Thus, an infant whose name is Malcolm, Mark, Maurice, or Morris, as entered on his birth certificate, may, at the traditional Hebrew circumcision ritual, also be given the Hebrew name of Moshe in commemoration of a deceased grandfather Moshe.) This practice carries with it the implied attitude of willingness to conform to religious or ethnic requirements as well as to family expectations. The latent psychodynamics probably are essentially the same as those described under the preceding rubric.

Current Fashion or Fad: Here the infant's name is chosen in accordance with the dictates of current fashion in name selection. This phenomenon points to a tendency on the part of the parents to defer to the subtle pressures of prevailing social taste and preference, a wish or a need to move with the crowd, at least in this matter. To the extent that this piece of behavior mirrors a general attitude of social compliance, an issue which must, of course, be decided through empirical investigation, one or both parents may be plagued by a lack of confidence in the soundness of their own judgment, by a lack of experience in exercising independent judgment or in expressing personal taste or preference, by a fear of being socially conspicuous by virtue of being different, or by an inability to think with originality in some or in most matters. Some names that are currently modish and may, therefore, be chosen for the above reasons are Deborah, Susan, Lisa, Steven, and Jeffrey.

Desire to Display Uniqueness, Distinctiveness, or Novelty: Here the motivation is the obverse of the foregoing in that the primary consideration in the selection of a name is the uniqueness of the choice. This determinant reflects a need in one or both parents to assert their own individuality or originality by maintaining an attitude of non-conformity to the dictates of current fashion. Coupled with or substituting for this attitude may be a wish to confer an air of distinctiveness or individuality upon the offspring bearing the atypical

name. Examples of names chosen for this characteristic 1
Thane, Kyle, Candida, Richardette, and Gaia. An exception to this
principle, however, would be the case in which current fashion pre-
scribes the use of novel names for infants (e.g., Morley, Myron,
Vilma, Lilith). In this latter instance, then, the inference would be
that selection of an unusual infant name is simply an expression of
the parents' need to conform socially.

Aesthetic Considerations: The infant's name may be chosen because
it is euphonious in itself or when taken in combination with the surname, or because it evokes happy mental associations with a pleasant concept, event, or object. A choice of name made on this basis
suggests the possession, in some measure, of aesthetic sensitivity by
one or both parents and is indicative perhaps of the position occupied by the aesthetic experience in the hierarchy of the parental
value system. On the other hand, selection of a name mainly on
aesthetic grounds may simply reflect a strain of parental pretentiousness betraying itself in the desire to be regarded socially as
"aesthetes." (Names like Dew, Mist, Dawn, Campanella, Sonella,
Coral, Rhondine, Alouette, Cybelline might serve as illustrations of
this category.)

Psychological Connotations: Falling into this category are names
chosen because their sound connotes to the parent certain desirable
traits or characteristics, or because the parent believes that the
name will evoke in others an image or an impression of the desirable
characteristic. (E.g., certain names, such as Frank, Grace, Hope,
Charity, August, Prudence, and Victor, may be regarded as connoting virility, femininity, morality, strength, etc. Related to this
phenomenon is the general issue of the stereotypical associations
elicited in others by the sound or the visual configuration of names.)
Arriving at a name on this basis points to the presence of a degree of
psychological concern, awareness, sensitivity, or preoccupation in
one or in both parents. It may also reflect the latent presence within
the parent of a measure of "magical thinking" — i.e., the unverbal-
ized and irrational hope or belief that the infant will in some way
acquire the trait connoted by its name. Moreover, such a ground for
choice suggests the existence in the parent of an attitude which can
be best described as "child-oriented" rather than "parent-oriented."
It is perhaps not unreasonable to entertain the possibility that a
distinct neurotic component resides within the personality structures

of those parents whose choice is guided solely by psychological considerations.

Naming for Real or Fictitious Eminent Persons: The name chosen here is commonly associated with a real or fictitious person of some renown. Parents who make their choice on this basis may be somewhat naive, perhaps unimaginative, possibly prone to engage in magical thinking, and perhaps unduly given to hero-worship; or conceivably they may be the precise converse — sophisticated, well-educated, and possibly somewhat pretentious. In the latter instance where most likely the name selected is that of a fictitious person, probably esoteric in its reference, there may co-exist an unconscious desire to achieve an aura of uniqueness or novelty in the name by this tactic. Moreover, an impression of learning, of literary taste and astuteness, can be conveyed to others by this kind of practice. Lincoln (or Abraham Lincoln), Washington (or George Washington), and Jefferson (or Thomas Jefferson) would probably be chosen by the less imaginative, more naive parent, whereas Baudelaire, Rimbaud, Trilby, Medea, Zen, Zeno and Zarathustra might be preferred by the knowledgeable and pretentious one.

Idiosyncratic Names With Cognitive Connotations: The motive underlying the choice of this kind of name is usually highly personal and frequently readily apparent. Names such as "Last Chance," "No More," "Number One," etc., though certainly not common, do occur, displaying concrete and obvious meaning. Where such name choices are made, the parents may be found to be unimaginative, undereducated, perhaps unintelligent individuals; or, conversely, whimsical, highly individualistic, and clearly exhibitionistic people. In the latter instance, they are undoubtedly strongly driven to achieve uniqueness and social distinction, perhaps occasionally even at the price of appearing to be bizarre or ludicrous to others. Relatively little concern for or sensitivity to the future social and emotional needs of the infant so named is evinced by such parents.

Arbitrary, Expedient, and Concrete Names Without Personal or Psychological Connotation: Names in this category are chosen through indifference, lack of imagination, lack of intelligence, or purely in the interests of expedience. Occasionally, as in the preceding category, an element of whimsy may be contained in the choice. In any event, here, too, the future effect of the name upon the infant recipient is not taken into account, the fundamental attitude being "parent-oriented" rather than "child-oriented." Entries in this category are probably rare but would include names such as "Boy, Girl, Laddie, Sonny, Sister, Daughter," and to a lesser extent the names of months, i.e., "April, May, June, etc." Names falling under this rubric, with the possible exception of the month names, probably are found most commonly among educationally and culturally deprived groups such as the Southern white and negro share-croppers and the so-called "hill-billies" where the reproductive rate is high and the offspring lose their individual identity and high emotional significance to the parent through the stultifying weight of numbers. The parental attitude is one of indifference, if not outright hostility, because the child is regarded as an unwanted social burden and responsibility, the unfortunate and unwelcome by-product of a highly-valued biological act.

Multiple-Determined Choices: While perhaps not logically a distinct and separate category in the same sense as the foregoing ones, this category is identified and included here both in the interests of comprehensiveness and by way of explicit acknowledgement of the fact that — as is true in all other aspects of human behavior — name selection need not necessarily nor invariably reflect the influence of but a *single* underlying motive or attitude. Thus it is probably more often than not the case that the choice of a particular name is the result of a delicate compromise among conflicting or complementary psychological needs characteristic of both parents. Nevertheless, a reasonably discerning motivational and attitudinal analysis should provide insight into the nature, intensity, and hierarchical position of these needs within the family unit as they are reflected in the final name choice.

Summary

It is hypothesized that parents whose choice of an infant name is determined solely by considerations of family tradition, religious or ethnic custom, or current fad or fashion will, in general, by empirical test, show themselves to be essentially middle-class in their values, standards, and aspirations; socially conforming and accepting of the social status quo; and psychologically dependent upon others for emotional support, approval, and for guidance. Intellectually they will be found to range from below average to slightly above average in capacity, but it is unlikely that they will include among their numbers individuals of outstanding endowment. By and large, as a group, they will probably show themselves to be better adjusted personally and socially than the members of the other groups to be discussed below.

Those parents whose choice of an infant name is based on a desire for uniqueness or novelty, or on aesthetic considerations, or on the psychological connotations of the name, or on a regard for the real or fictitious eminent person with which the name originally was identified will generally reveal themselves to be highly individualistic, socially nonconforming, rebellious, or even defiant, and essentially self-involved, or self-conscious in their outlook. A measure of genuine or feigned idiosyncracy will characterize them; and a degree of intellectual, and, perhaps social and artistic pretentiousness will mark them. As a group they will be found to be more intelligent, better-educated, more sensitive and appreciative aesthetically, and more inclined to personal and social maladjustment than are other people considered in this discussion.

Parents who choose idiosyncratic names with cognitive connotations, or arbitrary, expedient, and concrete names without personal or psychological connotations — with the exceptions noted — will be found to be of low intelligence, of relatively poor educational attainment, unimaginative, and indifferent to the presence or the needs of the offspring. In many instances, psychological rejection and outright hostility are evident here; and the child may be viewed as a social and financial burden.

Multiple-determined name choices require and lend themselves readily to individual analysis.

In conclusion, it should be noted that this postulation leans heavily on the assumption that the same motives or attitudes, or configurations of motives and attitudes, will persist in time and will be found to underlie the choice of the names of all children in a given family unit. Where the motives or attitudes behind the selection of a name are found to vary from time to time and, hence, from child to child in a particular family, it is hypothesized that this will be a manifestation of the occurrence of some personality change in one or both parents, or an expression of a significant change in the relations between the parents. Intensive analysis of such instances might lead to the uncovering of additional psychological material of considerable interest.

New York, N. Y.

Beer Brand Names in the United States

JOHN R. KRUEGER

Recent popular works on the advertising industry (e.g., *Madison Avenue, U.S.A.*, or *The Hidden Persuaders*) have told how admen create an image for a product by selecting names that evoke customer feelings resulting in purchase, and by otherwise suggesting the desirability of the given product. In these brief lines, it is proposed to examine brand names of beer, a widely sold and widely advertised product, in an effort to discover the chief bases of appeal in marketing this beverage through name selection.

What does one think of when beer is mentioned ? Leaving aside that segment of the population for whom this refreshing drink still has overtones of alcoholism and all that Prohibition was meant to correct, one may sketch the popular image of beer as follows. Beer is a German drink, above all – it is associated with the Germans; Germans are good brewers; Germans drink lots of beer; therefore, a beer strongly suggestive of Germany must be a good beer. Beer is light, cool and refreshing on hot days – therefore, a beer name which evokes images of cold, lightness, flavor, etc., must also be a good beer, since these are qualities that beer has.

Any encyclopaedia will inform one that brewing is a very ancient art. Germans, nonetheless, are closely linked in the popular mind with beer, just as wine makes one think of France, and vodka of Russians.

In these notes the results of an investigation of beer brand names will be given. First and foremost, beer is intimately associated with Germans, things German and Germany. About half of all brand names are either unmistakably German (and are even so identified as such by a person knowing no German), or evoke in some way German regions or German brewing craftmanship. About one quarter of remaining brand names imply that beer is refreshing, mellow, tasty, cold or thirst-quenching. The remaining names are divided among such categories as local names from states or regions, numbers or letters, or descriptions of the label or an identifying feature of the container. It should, however, be mentioned that not all advertising centers on the brand name as such; some stresses other slogans or features which are made the basis for campaigns.

Data for this brief study have been drawn from my files of over 200 brand names collected since 1960 while resident and traveling on the West Coast and in the Mid-West. These names fairly represent, I believe, the naming practices of the brewing industry. From telephone books and industrial directories only a few names have been obtained, as it was often difficult to distinguish between the names of brands and those of companies, breweries or distributors. Furthermore, some large brewers bottle what appears to be the same product under an assortment of names. As some brands are marketed nationally, and others are unknown outside their home cities, no place of origin is indicated except where pertinent. The inclusion or exclusion of any particular commercial name does not constitute an endorsement or lack of one.

Names of German Families or German Words. Most numerous in the categories here are brand names of beer which are proper names clearly identifiable as German, or which are other German words. The element *-brau* (*-bräu*) "brew" occurs several times. These names include *Augustiner, Becker's Mellow, Blatz, Blitz-Weinhard, Braumeister, Budweiser, Bürgermeister* (always carefully spelled with the umlauted ü), *Coors, Durst* (means "thirst"!), *Edelweiss, Esslinger, Fehr's, Fisher* (perhaps from *Fischer*?), *Gluek* (note spelling), *Goebel, Goetz* (pronounced "gets"), *Gunther, Hals, Hamm's, Heileman's Lager, Hudepohl's, Karl's K, Köl* (spelled with ö), *Krueger* (no relation; means "publican, innkeeper"), *Knickerbocker* (has Dutch overtones, to be sure), *Leinenkugel's, Meister Bräu, Miller's High Life* (perhaps originally *Müller*?), *Pabst Blue Ribbon, Pfeiffer, Piels, Prager, Rheingold, Ruppert's, Schaefer, Schlitz, Schmidt, Schoenling, Steinbrau* (an invented word?), *Stroh's* and *Wiedemann's*. Others are *Berlin, Gettelman's, Hauenstein, Reisch, Rheinlander, Rhinelander, Schell, Storz, Waldeck* and *Walter's*.

German Locale. Among the names of American beers which are based on or refer to Germany or German-speaking regions are *Alps Brau, Bavarian's Select, Bohemian, Dutch Lunch, Dutch Treat,*

Hapsburg, Heidelberg, International Old Dutch, Old Dutch, Old German (twice), *National Bohemian, Old Heidelbrau* (note invented word), *Old Vienna* and *Weiss Bavarian*. It should be pointed out that the word "Dutch" is used in many areas of the Mid-West as a synonym for German (stemming from *deutsch*) and does not refer to a Hollander. This is the usage of my native region of eastern Nebraska, heavily populated by Germans from the migrations of 1848.

Quality or other Feature of the Product. Next most numerous after names having a connection with Germany is this classification, in which brand names seek to show that the product is superior, tasty, well-prepared, of good ingredients, fit for a king, well-aged or of ancient origin, and, if none of these, cold. These names include *Best, Brewer's Best, Champagne Velvet, Cold Brau* (note the blend of English *cold* and German *Brau* "brew"), *Excell, Glacier, Golden Grain, Happy Hops, L & M* (Light and Mellow), *Lucky Lager, M B* (Mellow Brew), *Maid-Rite, Old Export, Old English, Old Timer's, Old Tankard* (Pabst), *Regal, Regal Select, Rex* (whether the connection with Latin *rex* "king" is evident would be hard to say), *Royal 58, Sterling, Supreme Pilsner, Velvet Glow*, and *Western Gold*. Most of these names have some logical connection with beer or its qualities.

Features of the Container. Some brand names make use of the color of the can, or of some object on it, or of the label, in the case of bottles. Among these names are *Black Label, Black and White Label, Gold Label, Red Top, Silver Bar* and *Silver Top*. Closely allied with these names is another group of brands which denote tangible objects or use some identification which is usually on the container. Most of these do not have any logical connection with beer. One is reminded of the names of inns and coffee houses in times before reading was widespread among the people, e.g., "St. George and the Dragon," or "The Golden Arms," and so on. Among these names are the following: *Banker's, Brown Derby* (has a hat), *Crystal Rock, Country Club, Falcon, Fox Deluxe, Highlander* (has Scotch plaid), *Iroquois Ale, Keeley's* (uses a green color, implying Irish), *Old Abbey, Old Gibraltar, Red Cap Ale* (has a head wearing a red cap), *Tudor, Tech*, and *Twenty Grand*.

The American Scene. A number of brand names make use of what might be called local color, using names meaningful in specific localities. Here not as many have been included as might be, because the local significance of some names was not recognized by me. Among those in this category are *Buckeye* (Ohio), *Camden Beer* (New Jersey), *Canadian Ace, Cincinnati Cream, Dixie* (New Orleans), *Duquesne, Eastside Old Tap, Erin Brew, Falls City* (Louisville, Ky.), *Genesee* (upstate New York), *Great Falls Select* (Montana), *Grain Belt, Hollywood Ranch Markets* (Los Angeles), *Iron City* (Pittsburg, Pa.), *Olympia* (Washington State), *Padre* (California, implies the old Spanish missions), *Rainier* (Washington State), *Santa Fe Lager, Tivoli, Valley Forge* and *Wisconsin Premium*. Others are *Butte Lager* (Montana), *Cascade* (mountains in western Washington), *Dakota, Grain Belt* (Minnesota), *Old Milwaukee* and *Western*.

Miscellaneous Names. A few brand names are difficult to classify under any rubric, and to be sure, some of those given above might well be included under different headings. A few names do not suggest, at least to me, anything particularly German or "beery." Here I would place *Ballantine, Drewry's* (uses picture of Canadian mounted policeman), *Kingsbury*, or *Sheridan*. In this group fall a few names employing numbers, as *102*, or *Oertel's 92* (i.e., 1892), or *Brew '52* (presumably 1852, but possibly 1952), or the simple name *ABC*. Requiring some local knowledge are the names of *Simon Pure* beer (made by the Simon Brewery of Buffalo) or *Jax Beer* (brewed by Jackson Brewery of New Orleans). Finally, one should not neglect *Falstaff*, Shakespeare's jolly drinker and wencher. This category, too, could no doubt be expanded by additional research.

In this survey, drawn from several hundred brand names in my files (which I plan to continue), I think it has been demonstrated that beer is definitely associated with Germany, because German names and references to German regions are the most numerous among brand names. In second place come references to the refreshing qualities of beer, with names of local significance and some oddments bringing up the rear. It would, of course, be possible to undertake a very comprehensive study, with correspondence to these firms which might reveal additional information or corrections, that would no doubt form an interesting chapter in the history of the brewing industry in America, but this work must be left to a later date.

Indiana University

Place-Names on the Moon: A Report

HAMILL KENNY

I. Growing Public Attention

Ever since 1957, when the International Geophysical Year began, the moon's place-names have, to some degree, been in the news.[1] Perhaps the first example of such publicity occurred in November 1958,[2] when newspapers mentioned ALPHONSE, the moon crater where, so Soviet Dr. N. A. Kozyrev believed,[3] volcanic action had lately taken place. This news, when it was discussed in December, 1958, by the Italian magazine *Oggi*,[4] led to the mention not only of ALPHONSE ("Alfonso"), but of ARISTARCHUS ("Aristarco"), ARZACHEL, COPERNICUS ("Copernico"), KEPLER ("Keplero"), PLATO ("Platone"), POSIDONIUS ("Posidonio"), and "Coda del pavone" (Galileo's *Cauda Pavonis* or Peacock's Tail). Then in September, 1959,[5] came press notice of three of the moon's "seas": MARE SERENITATIS (Sea of Serenity), MARE TRANQUILLITATIS (Sea of Tranquillity), and the MARE VAPORUM

Symbols and abbreviations: * = Earlier name, now either changed or deleted; I. A. U. = International Astronomical Union; Kuiper = Photographic Lunar Atlas; LAC = U. S. Air Force Chart; *Memoir* = "Who's Who in the Moon"; Pamphlet = pamphlet accompanying *Photographic Lunar Atlas.*

[1] Public attention was attracted to the moon's place-names in the times of Jules Verne (c 1865), when Verne in chs. 12, 13, 17, and 18 of *Around the Moon* (English version by Mercier and King, 1947), using Beer and Mädler's *Mappa Selenographica,* has his moon voyagers mention and fictitiously describe thirty-one lunar features, including "Mount Helicon," "Gulf of Iris," "the Black Lake or Pluto," "the annular mountain of Short," and "the circle of Neander."

[2,3] Nov. 3, 1958 (see W. L. Lawrence, *N. Y. Times,* Jan. 25, 1959). Dr. Kozyrev's report: AP, Moscow, Nov. 13, 1958; *N. Y. T.,* Nov. 13, 1958.

[4] "Nella Coda del Pavone Un Nuova Enigma Lunare," *Oggi,* Dec. 4, 1958, pp. 43–44.

[5] Lunik II was launched Sept. 12, 1959 (*Compton's Encyc.*; *N. Y. T.,* April 3, 1963). It struck Sept. 13, 1959 (*World Bk. Encyc.,* Ann. Supplement, 1960; *N. Y. T.,* Oct. 1959). *World Bk. Encyc.,* 1961, and AP (Wash. *Star*), Moscow, April 2, 1963, both give the date of striking as Sept. 14, 1959.

(Sea of Vapors).[6] For it was near these "seas," on September 13, that Lunik II struck the moon.[7] Little more than two years later in 1962,[8] a flash of light activated by a ruby laser also struck the moon, an event that led to public mention of the crater ALBATEGNIUS. On January 13, 1962, in a discussion of ideal moon sites, the press[9] noticed the LEIBNITZ MTS. ("Leibnitz mountain range"). The same year, a second Italian magazine, *Incom*,[10] in a feature article on the moon, spoke of RHAETICUS ("Retico"), SCHICKARD, PHOCYCLIDES ("Focilide"), ERATOSTHENES ("Eratostene"), PLATO ("Platone"), and the APENNINES ("Appennini lunari," "Appennini seleniti"). Scanty as they are, such instances suggest on the part of the public an increasing acquaintance with the moon's place-names.

II. Need for Lunar Place-Names

Astronomers need these place-names to enable them to refer to and discuss the moon's visible features. Eppa Loretta[11] declares: "If the craters or the seas had no names, the study of them would be practically impossible..." New lunar features are, of course, continually being identified. Moreover, the possibility that the moon may be visited makes it likely that our satellite, from the standpoint of its place-names, will soon cease to be merely "le *cimetiere des astronomes* et la *Pantheon des savants*."[12]

---

[6] *N. Y. T.*, Sept. 14, 1959, and *Compton's Encyc.* (1962) have Seas of Tranquillity, Serenity and Vapors, and Maria Serenitatis, Tranquillitatis, and Vaporum, respectively. *The Washington Post* (Sept. 15, 1959), and lately the *N. Y. Times* (April 3, 1963) have, respectively, Seas of Tranquillity, Vapors and Clarity, and Seas of Clarity, Serenity, and Vapors. Thus, the *Post* translates MARE SERENITATIS as "Sea of Clarity"; and the *Times* translates MARE TRANQUILLITATIS as "Sea of Clarity." So far as I know, astronomers do not recognize "Sea of Clarity" for either.

[7] See 5 and 6.

[8] Stuart H. Loory, "The Incredible Laser...," *This Week Magazine*, Nov. 11, 1962, p. 8.

[9] *The Washington Star.*

[10] Anno XV, N. 47 (Nov. 25, 1962), pp. 40–43, p. 45.

[11] "Proposal for Naming the Rays of the Lunar Craters," *Popular Astronomy*, 43, No. 1 (January 1935).

[12] Abbé Moreux, *Etude de la Lune avec Dictionnaire Selenographique*, Nouvelle Ed. (Paris, 1950), p. 45.

III. History of Lunar Place-Names

"Who's Who in the Moon"[13] gives a history of lunar place-names, and contains explanatory and biographical notes on the names of all the formations adopted in 1935 by the I.A.U. For "I.A.U." and the like see *Symbols and abbreviations* preceding footnote 1 on p. 73. The *Memoir* points out that Langrenus of Brussels (*Map*, 1645) first gave names to the moon's features, and that the names on a Paris copy of his map come to more than 300. On the map (*Selenographia*, 1647) of Johann Hevelius of Danzig, whom Agnes Mary Clerke calls the founder of lunar topography,[14] the named features number 250. Departing from the method of Hevelius, Riccioli of Bologna (*Almagestum Novum*, 1651) named lunar features not only for contemporary astronomers, but also for astronomers of the Middle Ages and antiquity. He lists about 236 features named for persons (e.g., ARISTO-TELES), and about seventy-eight features, mainly geographical, which are named impersonally (e.g., *PALUS HYPERBOREA, *TERRA SAPIENTIAE). Riccioli kept Kepler's idea[15] of the moon's *maria* or "seas"; but he gave them names that describe the moon's supposed influences on the earth (e.g., MARE CRISIUM, MARE IMBRIUM, and MARE NUBIUM). Moreover, Riccioli had a system: he named the northern lunar features for the ancients (e.g., PLATO); the moderns he put below. Since – as a Jesuit – he disbelieved in the Copernican theory, he gave to an important southern feature the name TYCHO, and relegated the names of the Copernicans to features situated in the OCEANUS PROCEL-LARUM (Sea of Storms). As for later innovators, Johann Schröter (*Selenotopographische Fragmente...*, 2 v., 1791, 1802) first began the use of Greek and Roman letters to identify minor lunar formations.

IV. Present Status, Visible Side

Noting that today's lunar maps keep six of Hevelius' names (e.g., ALPS, APENNINES), and more than 200 of Riccioli's, "Who's

---

[13] "Who's Who in the Moon," *Memoirs of the British Astronomical Association* (Edinburgh, 1938), 34, Pt. I. The work is definitive and makes further biographical study largely superfluous.

[14] "Johann Hevelius," Eleventh *Britannica*, 13.416.

[15] See Clyde Fisher, *Story of the Moon* (N. Y., 1943), p. 104. He states (*loc. cit.*): "Possibly ... 'Maria' ... goes back to Kepler (1571–1630), who wrote ' Do *maculos* esse *maria*, do *lucidas* esse terras'."

Who in the Moon" (p. 5) states that "an authoritative list" of the
moon's named formations amounts to 672, of which 609 are personal
names. The *Memoir* bases its figures on what it calls "our latest
standard work," Mary A. Blagg and K. Müller's *Named Lunar Formations*,[16] which lists the lunar names drawn up for Commission 17
and approved at a meeting of the I. A. U. in 1932, at Cambridge,
Massachusetts. Gerard P. Kuiper[17] describes the 1935 I. A. U. system as having 680 named formations and some 8000 additional
features "with letters and symbols . . . regionally attached to named
features . . ." This is, of course, the nomenclature[18] of the two latest
definitive lunar guides, one of which (*Photographic Lunar Atlas*) has
been called "the first complete lunar atlas since 1910,"[19] and the
other of which (*U. S. Air Force Lunar Charts and Mosaics* [*Charts
of the Moon*]) began appearing in 1962 and, upon completion, will
consist of eighty-four detailed maps.

The *Photographic Lunar Atlas* omits the alphabetical symbols of
the 1935 I. A. U. system. Instead of printing lunar names on its
photographs, it divides the moon into forty-four sections and provides index maps (sheets 1–11) and a reference list ("Pamphlet,"
Table V, pp. 19–23) of the moon's numbered and named formations.
On the eighty-four Air Force Lunar Charts and Mosaics (Charts of
the Moon), being published, [20] both the major names and the names
of lettered formations are given. Here, as with Kuiper, the moon is

---

[16] (London, 1935). See also Mary A. Blagg, . . . *Collated List of Lunar Formations
Named or Lettered in the Maps of Neison, Schmidt, and Mädler* . . . (Edinburgh, 1913).

[17] . . . ed., *Photographic Lunar Atlas Based on Photographs Taken at the Mount
Wilson, Lick, Pic du Midi, McDonald, and Yerkes Observatories*. . . (Chicago [1960]).
23 p. tables (pamphlet 28 cm.) and atlas of 230 photographs . . . Pamphlet, p. 6.

Dr. Kuiper has since edited two supplements: (1) *OrthographicAtlas of the Moon.
Supplement No. 1 – to the Photographic Lunar Atlas*. Edition A, . . . Tucson, 1960 to
61 (. . . Chiefly photos); and (2) *Orthographic Atlas of the Moon, Supplement No. 1
to the Photographic Lunar Atlas*. Edition B, . . . Tucson, 1961. Chiefly photos.

[18] Complemented by resolutions and decisions published in the Transactions of
the I. A. U. (1950: 7, 63, 160, 166, 169; 1952: 8, 216; 1955: 9, 263), and revised by
Gerard Peter Kuiper (see Pamphlet).

[19] Folder describing *Photographic Lunar Atlas*, Univ. of Chicago Press.

[20] They are being published by the Aeronautical Chart and Information Center,
U. S. Air Force, St. Louis 18. In Jan. 1962, Charts LAC 58 and 76 were available.
LAC's 57, 59, 60, 61, 74, 75, 77, 78, 79, 93, 94 were planned for 1962. LAC 61 was completed on March 22, 1963. LAC's 78, 59, 79, 77, and 56 were to be printed by July 1,
1963.

divided into sections, and two "reference mosaics" and a lunar chart index are included. On the Air Force Charts not all of the I. A. U. 1935 standard lunar features are identified. "Eminences" are marked by Greek letters (see LAC 94, May, 1964); *Rima* is used for *Rille*. Following Blagg and Müller's system, the Charts utilize capital letters to designate the names of major craters (e.g., COPERNI-CUS). Smaller neighboring formations, when designated, have lettered names in lower-case letters, with the identifying letters usually single and capitalized (e.g., Copernicus A).[21] In some instances adjacent formations are given two alphabetical letters, with the second letter not always capitalized (e.g., Copernicus BA; *but* Grimaldi Ga).[22] In these lettered names each part has a meaning – Copernicus BA, for instance, denotes a crater (A) near another crater (B), the latter itself near the major crater COPERNICUS.

The *Photographic Lunar Atlas* (see Table III, "Pamphlet") makes the following seventy-one changes in the I. A. U. 1935 list: (1) there are forty-five changes in spelling and typography – ALTAI SCARP is changed from *ALTAI MTS., because it is a *scarp*, not a mountain; (2) *Cleft* is replaced by *Rille*, because *Cleft* implies cleavage – *HYGINUS CLEFT becomes HYGINUS RILLE; (3) thirteen names are deleted – ROOK MOUNTAINS, for instance, because they are on the moon's edge and are not "readily identifiable"; (4) DESLANDRES[23] has been added – the only name that has lately been recognized by the I. A. U. and added to the 1935 list; (5) *HENRY (FRERES) has, for clarity, been replaced by HENRY, PAUL and HENRY, PROSPER; (6) the boundaries of five named features have been changed – e.g., *WILKINS, a small 'bay,' is no longer included; and (7) five names are used that are not explicit on the I. A. U. map, but are identifiable from their respective original authorities – e.g., WOLFF (MT.), identifiable from Schröter. These changes have been adopted by the U. S. Air Force Charts, which were prepared with the advisory assistance of Dr. Kuiper and the staff of the *Photographic Lunar Atlas*. However, the Air

---

[21] This is not invariable. The lettered formations near the crater WICHMANN (LETRONNE LAC 75) have, for example, single letters, uncapitalized: Wichmann a, Wichmann b, Wichmann c, and Wichmann d.

[22] Air Force Charts COPERNICUS LAC 58, GRIMALDI LAC 74.

[23] Henri Alexandre Deslandres (1853–1948), French physicist and astrophysicist, noted for his contributions to spectroscopy and solar physics.

Force Charts (see LAC 58, COPERNICUS, July 1961) add to the
I. A. U. list thirty-two new lettered formations, ranging from Copernicus A, J, and R, to Tobias Mayer M, N, T. and S.

V. *Present Status, Hidden Side*

Probable the liveliest single event ever to attract public attention to the moon's place-names was the photographic achievement
of Russia's Lunik III in October 1959.[24] Decked out with brand new
place-names, Lunik's snapshots of the moon's hidden side soon appeared in American newspapers. The *Washington Star*[25] gave these
names as MOSCOW SEA, ASTRONAUTS BAY, TZIOLKOVSKY
HILL, LOMONSOV HILL, JOLIOT-CURIE CRATER, SOVIETS-
KY MOUNTAIN RANGE, and DREAM SEA. The *New York
Times*, three weeks after the feat,[26] told of a photograph with eight
spots named by the Soviet Sciences Academy, including a spot
called "Moscow Sea." And on March 19, 1960, the *New York Times*
described the new nomenclature as celebrating T. A. Edison and
eleven others, including four Russians. The map of the moon's
hidden side in *Compton's Encyclopedia*[27] seems, among those in reference books, to have the fullest number of the new Russian names:
EDISON CRATER, GIORDANO BRUNO CRATER, HERTZ
CRATER,[28] JOLIOT-CURIE CRATER,[29] KURCHATOV CRA-
TER,[30] LOMONSOV CRATER,[31] MENDELEEV CRATER,[32]

---

[24] Launched Oct. 4, 1959 (*World Bk. Encyclopedia, Ann. Suppl.*, 1960). Photograph released: *N. Y. Times*, Oct. 27, 1959; *Wash. Star*, Oct. 27, 1959. Russian
stamp with map of hidden face: *N. Y. Times*, May 3, 1960.

[25] "Moon Pictures Herald Planet Study . . .," Oct. 27, 1959.

[26] Oct. 27, 1959.

[27] 1962, vol. 9, p. 482.

[28] Richard B. Rodman, translator of *An Atlas of the Moon's Far Side*, informs me
that the man honored by this name is Heinrich Rudolph Hertz (1857–94), who
studied electromagnetic transmission and developed Faraday's electromagnetic
theory of light.

[29] French nuclear scientist. Frederic and Irene Joliot-Curie discovered artificial
radioactivity in 1934.

[30] Igor Vasilievich Kurchatov (1903–60), Russian physicist.

[31] Mikhail Lomonsov, believed in Russia to have developed the first working
model of a helicopter.

[32] Dmitri Ivanovich Mendeleeff (1834–1907), Russian chemist notable for his
researches on the Periodic Law.

PASTEUR CRATER, POPOV CRATER,[33] SKLODOWSKA-
CURIE CRATER,[34] TSU-CHUNG-CHI CRATER,[35] JULES
VERNE CRATER, SEA OF MOSCOW, BAY OF ASTRONAUTS[36]
SOVIET MTS., and SEA OF DREAMS.[37]

In November, 1960, the Associated Press told of the publication
of a Soviet Atlas of the far side of the moon, containing thirty pictures and identifying 500 objects.[38] This atlas, translated by Richard B. Rodman, and entitled *An Atlas of the Moon's Far Side;
the Lunik III Reconnaissance;*[39] appeared in the United States in
1961. The photographs in the atlas occasionally overlapped the
historic lunar features. Therefore there still is some use of the I. A. U.
nomenclature (with Kuiper's amendments). For names not yet
certified by the I. A. U., the terminology of H. P. Wilkins was
adopted. "Pending IAU decision," the names of the newly charted
maria, or "seas," have been kept in non-Latinized form (e.g., SEA
OF MOSCOW). One gathers from the Index of the Rodman atlas
(p. 143) that – in addition to the seventeen new names given in
Compton's Encyclopedia (see above) – the Russians named two more
new features: LOBACHEVSKY[40] and MAXWELL (Clerk Maxwell, Brit. physicist, 1831–79). The entire list of the formations
photographed by Lunik III is serially numbered on pp. 31–141 and
amounts to 498.

---

[33] R. Aleksandr Stepanovich Popov (1859–1906), Russian engineer and exper-
imentalist, credited in Russia with the invention of radio.

[34] Marja (Marie) Sklodowska Curie (1867–1934), Polish physical chemist and
physicist.

[35] Tsu Ch'ung – chih, Chinese mathematician and astronomer (430–500), a re-
viser of the calendar.

[36] Cf. the extinct *MARE ASTRONOMORUM, now MARE FRIGORIS, on the
visible side.

[37] Cf. LACUS SOMNIORUM (Lake of Dreams) and PALUS SOMNI (Marsh of
Sleep), both on the visible side. The *Wash. Star* (Oct. 27, 1959) describes the Russian
feature as "a so-called sea" on "the very edge of the moon's hidden side, called
'Mechta' (dream)."

[38] *Wash. Star,* Nov. 16, 1960.

[39] Akademiia Nauk SSSR ... Editorial board: N. P. Barabashov, A. A. Mik-
hailov and Yu. N. Lipsky ... New York, ... 1961 vii, 147 p., 30 photographs;
loose end map of the Far Side...

[40] Nikolai Ivanovich Lobachevski (1793–1856), Russian mathematician. He contributed to the theory of non-Euclidean geometry, and made geometric researches
on the theory of parallels.

VI. Conclusion

Upon studying the moon's place-names the layman is struck by the fact that many of them are misnomers (SINUS IRIDUM, PALUS SOMNI, LACUS MORTIS, MARE NUBIUM, OCEANUS PROCELLARUM). He notes that the crater names, most of them personal,[41] do not always do justice to their namesakes – NEWTON, on the moon's limb, is almost invisible, whereas ARISTARCHUS is the moon's brightest crater.[42] The layman notices, besides, that some of the crater names (ATLAS, HERCULES, HELICON, even PLATO) have little practical lunar connection. He may feel, indeed, that historical lunar nomenclature is neither very scientific nor very appropriate.[43]

Astronomers themselves have now and then shown dissatisfaction with the moon's place-names. *MARE ASTRONOMORUM (Langrenus) has become MARE FRIGORIS, both of them misnomers.[44] *PHILIP IV has become OCEANUS PROCELLARUM; and *PONTUS EUXINUS (Hevelius) has become the MARIA TRANQUILLITATIS and SERENITATIS. Dr. Kuiper's recent amendments to the I. A. U. nomenclature amount to about seventy-six. In 1955, Commission 16, of the I. A. U., decided to withhold official recognition of all new lunar place-names – until, at least, the completion of "the proposed photographic map of the Moon."

A fault of the present system, Dr. Kuiper suggests, is that there are continual proposals to add the names of contemporary scientists to the crater names. In May, 1955, for example, it was urged that a

---

[41] The moon's most misleading personal place-name is probably HELL, for Father Maximilian Hell (1720–92), Hungarian Jesuit and astronomer. Owen J. Gingerich (*Collier's Encyc.*, 1962, 16: "Moon") seems to refer to this crater when he remarks that the moon's craters "range in size from 150 miles for Bailly, Janssen, *Hellplain*, Grimaldi, and Clavius, to a few hundred feet."

[42] This memorial to Aristarchus is more suitable, however, than one at first realizes. For he appears to have been the first astronomer (Samos, 250 B. C.) to perceive that the earth moves around the sun.

[43] One of the more appropriate lunar place-names is HARBINGER MOUNTAINS. Citing Dr. Joseph Ashbrook, Cecilia Payne-Gaposchkin – Professor of Astronomy, Harvard University – informs me (letter, April 16, 1959) that W. Birt gave the name in England in about 1865. The sun's rays reach the Harbinger Mountains before they rise on Aristarchus. The Harbinger Mountains are therefore the *harbingers* of "the approaching visibility of Aristarchus."

[44] MARE is certainly a misnomer, since evidently the moon has no real seas.

crater near NEWTON be named for Albert Einstein.[45] However, says Dr. Kuiper: "The current 'historical' system ... has acquired some value because many careful observations have been described in its terms."

By commemorating scientists, and by conforming to the fiction of the moon's oceans by such names as SEA OF MOSCOW and BAY OF ASTRONAUTS, the Russians have followed the traditional pattern of the I. A. U. 1935 system. Dr. Kuiper ("Pamphlet," p. 7) states, however, that "in the face of modern requirements" the I. A. U. will soon probably wish to "re-examine the entire problem of lunar nomenclature..." It seems to the present writer that the real worth of the traditional system will get its fullest test when the moon is actually visited, a date that has been estimated to be perhaps 1980.[46]

Hamill Kenny

University of Maryland

---

[45] Meir H. Degani, *Astronomy Made Simple* (New York, 1955), p. 150.

[46] AP, *Wash. Star* (dateline Philadelphia), Dec. 26, 1959. A later item in this paper ("Moon Map-Guide for a Lunar Landing," Sun., April 21, 1963) states that the area to be visited will probably be OCEANUS PROCELLARUM (Ocean of Storms), where there are the three easily recognized craters, KEPLER, ENCKE, and KUNOWSKY.

The Names of U.S. Industrial Corporations:
A Study in Change

J. BODDEWYN

To MANY PEOPLE, corporations are "nothing but a name." All they know about these firms is inscribed within the few words which form the corporate name – a rather typical situation. As Boulding points out in *The Image*, it is not so much extensive factual knowledge that governs human behavior as the messages filtered through a value system from a reality often too complex to be readily grasped.[1] Corporate names impart this type of boiled-down, subjective information so much appreciated by modern business.

Unlike individuals who may be recognized by their physical peculiarities, a corporation – said to be intangible, invisible and existing only in contemplation of law – is identified solely by its name. Since, in general, things are felt to be what they are called, the corporate name is an important element in the image projected by the firm, and it helps sell its products as well as its stocks and bonds.[2] Symbols also make groups conscious of what they are, facilitating unity of purpose within the firm. Thus we witness today the spending of tens or hundreds of thousands of dollars to change letterheads and signs, to register a new name in dozens of states and on stock exchanges, and to pay lawyers and new name consultants.[3]

One may thus agree with the man who, in response to Shakespeare's much-used question "What's in a name?" replied, "Everything!"[4] Yet, we know relatively little about trends in corporate names and name changes, notwithstanding their abundant and

---

[1] K. Boulding, *The Image* (Ann Arbor: University of Michigan Press, 1956), 14.

[2] E. Sapir, *Culture, Language and Personality* (Berkeley: University of California Press, 1958), 9; D. Roma, "Experience of Two Name Changers," *American Business* (May, 1958), 26–27; "The Yankee Tinkerers," *Time* (July 25, 1960), 62–68.

[3] J. Maritain, "Language and the Theory of Signs," in R. N. Anshen (ed.), *Language* (New York: Harper & Brothers, 1957), 88; "The Name Game," *Time* (April 3, 1964), 90; J. F. Lawrence, "What's in a Name? 4-Year Study, $10,000 Fee, Poll of Clerks," *The Wall Street Journal* (March 21, 1960), 1, 15.

[4] G. M. Loeb, "What's in a Name?", *Dun's Review* (October, 1960), 90.

piecemeal reporting in business publications.[5] Hence, there is need for the following analysis of three groups of industrial corporations at various periods of American business history: (1) the first eight manufacturing corporations (1789–1800); (2) the 115 manufacturing and mining firms incorporated in New England until 1860; and (3) the 500 largest industrial corporations in 1960.[6]

The components of corporate names (first, middle and last as in "Ford Motor Company"), their word-length and their alterations are examined in this analysis. For the onomatologist, corporate names provide a special opportunity to study name *change* – and relatively rapid change at that. More than half of *Fortune*'s 500 Corporations have altered their names one or more times, and all have kept theirs for an average of only 27 years.

Early Corporations

Colonial corporations had long names such as "The Proprietors of the Boston Pier, or the Long Wharf in the Town of Boston in New England" (1772), often detailing the headship and membership of the corporate body, its purpose and location. Since colonial and even later charters were granted on a special basis, there were no statutory requirements regarding corporate names apart from

---

[5] While new names of large industrial corporations have regularly been reported and examined in magazines, financial pages and stockholders' reports, a comprehensive study covering a large number of names over an extended period of time has not been made.

P. H. Erbes, Jr. ["Modernizing the Company Name," *Printer's Ink* (June 11, 1943), 15–17, 68–69] has analyzed the names of 399 leading advertising firms in 1942. There are also several lists of "lead words" such as "American, United, National, New, General, Standard" [e.g., Daniel Roma, "Experiences of Two Name Changers," *American Business* (May 1958), 26–27]. These analyses, however, provide little or no historical perspective as they simply detail the components of corporate names at particular times. Fairly frequent references can also be found to the number of name-changing companies listed on the major stock exchanges. See, for example: A. Merjos, "Investors' Scoreboard," *Barron's* (April 2, 1962), 9, 22.

[6] J. S. Davis, *Essays in the Earlier History of American Corporations* (Cambridge: Harvard University Press, 1917, II), 269 ff.; E. M. Dodd, *American Business Corporations Until 1860; With Special References to Massachusetts* (Cambridge: Harvard University Press, 1954), 462–63; "The 500 Largest U.S. Industrial Corporations," *Fortune* (July, 1960), 131–50. This last list was extended to include names adopted up to December 31, 1960. The Appendix defines the key terms used in this study, and provides some additional information about methodology.

the general provisions of common law and equity protecting names against misrepresentation. Under these special charters, commonly allowed for narrowly defined purposes, it was difficult to change the corporate name. As a matter of fact, reincorporation was often simpler than obtaining an amendment.

The first eight manufacturing firms to be incorporated (1789 to 1800) had names almost twice as long (6.4 words) as those of corporations in 1960.[7] Their names clearly identified the economic activities in which they engaged. No persons were cited, except impersonal "Proprietors," "Directors", or "Inspectors." Geographical names provided the only common type of first name although corporateness or ownership was often the first thing mentioned – a practice still fairly common in other countries (e.g., "Société Générale de Belgique"). There was no "Corporation" but plenty of "Society"[8] besides the already mentioned "Proprietors," "Directors" and "Inspectors."

The term "Company" became the overwhelming favorite in the nineteenth century when titles began to be shorter. Personal and geographical names increased in popularity, following the incorporation of proprietorships and partnerships facilitated by the passage of general incorporation laws after 1795. These laws made it possible for a greater variety of firms to obtain corporate charters. They also provided more explicit rules regarding the choice of corporate names and simpler procedures for their change.

The following analysis of pre-Civil War names reveals (1) the predominance of personal and geographical names; (2) a preference for narrow descriptions of the firms' activities; and (3) the popularity of "Company."[9]

(Footnote 9, see next page)

[7] Davis (*op. cit.*) considers the following firms to be the first manufacturing corporations in the United States: "The Directors, Inspectors and Company of the Connecticut Silk Manufacturers" (Connecticut, 1789); "The Proprietors of the Beverly Cotton Manufactory" (Massachusetts, 1789); "The New York Manufacturing Society" (New York, 1790); "The Society for Establishing Useful Manufactures" (New Jersey, 1791); "The Proprietors of the Newbury-Port Woollen Manufactory" (Massachusetts, 1794); "The Proprietors of the Calico Printing Manufacture" (Massachusetts, 1796); "The Hamilton Manufacturing Society" (Massachusetts, 1797); and "The Salem Iron Factory Company" (Massachusetts, 1800).

[8] "Society" is still used in Romance language nations where "Corporation" is rendered by the initials "S.A.," the familiar "Société Anonyme" or "anonymous society" – a reference to the fact that the stock certificates are to the bearer and that, therefore, the owners are unknown.

Table 1. Name Components of the 115 Manufacturing and Mining Firms
Incorporated in New England Until 1860

Name Components	Proportion of 115 Firms
First Names	
Personal or Geographical names	93%
Other names or no first name	7%
References to Product, Operation or Function	
Specified	58%
Unspecified "Manufacturing"	37%
No mention	4%
References to Corporateness	
"Company"	80%
Other words* or no mention	20%

* Including at least two "Corporation."

Fortune's 500 Corporations

Most of *Fortune*'s firms were incorporated after the Civil War although they were often heirs to ante-bellum proprietorships and partnerships.

Name Components

In the nineteenth century, three-part names such as "Bridgeport Brass Company" were common. Typically, the first name indicated the owner, promoter or location; the middle name identified the firm's products or processes, while the last name was usually "Company" or some variation thereof. By 1960, quite a few names had departed from this original pattern, and only 58% of the names contained all three elements.

First Names

A hundred years ago, more than nine out of ten corporate first names referred to a person or locale. Today, less than 60% make such a reference, with the decline particularly pronounced in the

---

[9] The list of corporate names obtained from Dodd's study of pre-Civil War firms is not quite accurate as he occasionally recorded an abbreviated version of the complete name.

case of geographical names. Nevertheless, personal names remain the most common type of first name. Since they no longer serve the purpose of identifying the owners, surnames have acquired a highly abstract character which suits the need of diversified corporations that do not want to be identified with particular products or processes (e.g., The Bendix Corporation).

On the other hand, denotations of broad market coverage have remained fairly constant after reaching a peak around 1900. The frequent adoption before the turn of the century of names such as "National" and "International" reveals the expansion of markets served by industrial firms. Large-scale marketing made reference to particular locales inappropriate unless some advantage could be derived from such association (e.g., "Corning Glass Works"). The first merger movement created firms intent on serving all or most of the national market, and on indicating their control of entire industries – hence, the multiplication of ambitious first names such as "American," "National," and "United States" around the turn of the century.

Table 2. First Name Components

Types of References	Frequency of References[a]				
	1880 28 names	1900 158 names	1920 323 names	1940 475 names	1960 500 names
Geographical Identification[b]	29%	22%	19%	17%	14%
Market Coverage[c]	7%	14%	14%	13%	13%
Persons[d]	54%	43%	47%	43%	44%
Others[e]	21%	21%	21%	27%	32%

[a] As in other tables, totals may add up to more or less than 100% because some names include more than one type of reference, and because percentages were rounded to the nearest point.

[b] Mentions of particular places, rivers, towns, states or sections of the country are included here (e.g., "Chicago").

[c] Examples: "United States, National, Republic, American, Continental, International, Universal."

[d] Fictional names such as "Revlon" or historical names such as "Laclede" were classified under "Others."

[e] *Adjectives* indicating excellence (e.g., "Ideal"), combination (e.g., "United") or diversity (e.g., "General") were listed here together with *acronyms* (e.g., "ACF") and *composite* names (e.g., "Midland-Ross").

The use of first names classified in Table 2 under "Others" has definitely increased since the First World War. The terms "United," "Union", and "Allied" reflect external expansion through mergers and combinations. "General" was often chosen to indicate diversity of products and processes – particularly, after 1910. Brand names such as "Pet" or "Certainteed" were included in corporate names in the 1920's and 1940's in order to capitalize on already well-known names at a time when new and expanding communication media were diffusing brands everywhere.[10]

The recent interest in research and development, together with the necessity of finding names for very diversified firms, has led to the adoption of another type of abstract name, i.e., the acronym. This term applies to the telescoped names made of the first letters or syllables either of a previous name or of fields of endeavor. Thus, we have "FMC Corporation" instead of "Farm Machinery and Chemical Corporation"; "Genesco Inc." instead of "General Shoe Corporation"; and "Chemetron" for *ch*emicals-*me*tals-elec*tro*nics. While no acronyms were adopted by *Fortune*'s 500 before 1921, eighteen corporations used one in their 1960 names.[11] These appear quite appropriate for the Buck Rogers-type corporations whose purposes now encompass the future as well as the world.

Worth noting in the "Others" category is the steady increase in hyphenated names from none in 1880 to 11 % in 1960. The firms that merged after the First World War have been seemingly content to adopt less ambitious names than their turn-of-the-century predecessors who often chose monopolistic-sounding names. Composites such as "Owens-Illinois Glass Company" (1929) or "Sunray Mid-Continent Oil Company" (1955) certainly sound more prosaic than "United States Steel Corporation" (1901), yet all three firms resulted from mergers. It appears, however, that composite names are often temporary and represent an intermediate stage before the adoption of a new name – frequently an acronym.

Middle Names

The names of the eight industrial firms incorporated between 1789 and 1800 indicated their products, processes or broad functions such

---

[10] R. K. Otterbourg, "Who's Who in Industry," *Barron's* (December 22, 1958), 9–10.

[11] Cf. "The Acronymous Society," *Time* (July 28, 1958), 39.

as manufacturing. Of the 115 firms incorporated until 1860, only
4 % failed to mention product, process or function in their name.
In 1960, this proportion had decupled, with 43 % of the names of
Fortune's 500 Corporations making no reference to the nature of
their activities. The middle name is obviously on its way out.

Table 3. Proportion of Names Making no Reference to Product, Operation or
Function*

Year	Frequency
1880	14 %
1900	29 %
1920	32 %
1940	33 %
1960	43 %

* Corporate names including coined brand names such as "Coca-Cola" were not
considered here as referring to a product, operation or function.

This abandonment of the middle name illustrates the trend
towards diversification (i.e., *more* products, processes or functions)
and evolution (i.e., *new* products, processes and functions), which
has been documented in the literature of American business history.[12]
An analysis of 435 name changes reveals that 55 % could be associated with broader corporate purposes either because (1) the new
names make reference to *additional* activities as when the "Food
Machinery Corporation" became the "Food Machinery and Chemical Corporation," or (2) they *eliminate* reference to products,
operations or functions as when the "Anaconda Copper Mining
Company" became simply "Anaconda Company," or (3) they *combine* the names of several firms as when the "Zellerbach Corporation" became the "Crown-Zellerbach Corporation" after absorbing
the "Crown Willamette Paper Company." In the 1940's and 1950's
approximately two-thirds of corporate name changes featured such
alterations.

Also noticeable is the appearance of "Products" (e.g., "Evans
Products Company") and "Industries" (e.g., "Engelhard Industries,
Inc.") in names of the 1930's and 1950's, as a new way of expressing
broader purposes. Since 1945, no new name has been chosen that

[12] A. D. Chandler, Jr., *Strategy and Structure* (Cambridge: The M.I.T. Press,
1962).

includes the word "Manufacturing." This probably reflects the integration of large firms into distributing their own products and supplying their own raw materials requirements.

Last Names

In 1880, none of the firms studied by the writer included "Corporation" or "Incorporated" in their name. Eighty years later, close to half had one such term in their title. Such a major name change is readily explained by recent and increasingly common state requirements that corporations indicate their corporateness.[13] In the twentieth century, the terms "& Company" as well as "& Sons," usually associated with partnerships, became inappropriate unless followed by "Inc." or replaced by "Corporation." Names such as "Johnson & Johnson," having no reference to their corporateness, are rarities of before the turn of the century.

Table 4. Last Name Components

Year	Frequency			
	"Company"	"Corporation"	"Incorporated"	Others*
1880	79%	0%	0%	21%
1900	85%	1%	1%	13%
1920	68%	13%	2%	17%
1940	50%	29%	7%	14%
1960	42%	34%	13%	11%

* Under "Others" are included combinations such as "Co., Inc."; other appellations such as "Limited"; or the absence of a reference to the corporate form of enterprise, as in "Johnson & Johnson."

"Corporation" was adopted by many of the combinations that resulted from the various merger movements. The merged may have wanted to differentiate themselves from the smaller firms that made the new combines, or to indicate that the new firms were of the "holding" variety.[14] Erbes explains the swift rise of "In-

---

[13] For current requirements regarding the corporate name, see American Bar Foundation, *The Model Business Corporation Act Annotated* (St. Paul: West Publishing Company, 1960).

[14] The writer is indebted to Professor Alfred O. Chandler of M.I.T. for this tentative explanation of the shift to "Corporation."

corporated" after 1920 as a protective reaction against the un-
popularity of the "soulless corporations." [15] Altogether, last names
have come to separate the corporate men from the boys – proprietorships and partnerships.

Name Length

Changes in the first, middle, and last names of the 500 Corporations
were bound to affect their word-lengths. A comparison of the number of words in corporate names chosen in each decade after the
Civil War shows a continuous decrease from 4.7 words in the 1870's
to 3.2 words in the 1950's – a decline of about one-third. This
shrinking can be ascribed to a number of causes, the main one being
the elision of the middle name. The adoption of "Corporation" and
"Incorporated" in lieu of composite last names such as "Company,
Inc." also shortened the coporate name. In 1960, the 500 names contained an average of 3.5 words, larger firms having slightly longer
names than smaller firms. The shortest names, however, were those
of two very old firms: "Stanley Works" (1852) and "Crane Company" (1890). During the period 1871–1960, close to half of the
name changes resulted in fewer words.

Number of Names

Fortune's 500 corporations have shared 935 names, thus aver-
aging a little less than two names per firm. While the "Rexall Drug
and Chemical Company" has had seven names, most firms have
used only one or two.

Table 5. Number of Names per Firm

Number of Names	Percentage of Firms
1	43%
2	35%
3	16%
4	4%
5 or more	2%

[15] Erbes, *op. cit.*, 68.

The 500 firms averaged close to 50 years of age, in 1960.[16] Among them, 285 name changers have utilized 723 names, or 2.5 names per firm. The time interval between the 435 name changes has averaged 19 years although the most frequent occurrence of name change took place less than ten years after the adoption of the previous name.

Frequency of Name Changes

The frequency of name changes has increased over the years, only tapering off in the last two decades.

Table 6. Frequency of Name Changes

Period	Number of Name Changes (1)	Number of Firms at End of Period (2)	Average Number of Firms* (3)	Frequency of Name Changes (1)/(2) (4)	Frequency of Name Changes (1)/(3) (5)
1881–1900	22	158	93.0	14%	24%
1901–1920	71	323	240.5	22%	30%
1921–1940	160	475	399.0	34%	40%
1941–1960	180	500	487.5	36%	37%

* This is the average of the number of firms at the beginning and end of each period: [(2) + (3)]/(2). There were 28 firms in 1880.

As far as 1960 names are concerned, the firms, on the average, adopted them some 33 years ago. The 200 largest firms have had theirs for a somewhat longer period (36 years). The most tenacious name bearer is the Pepperell Manufacturing Company (1844). Close to two-thirds of the present names were adopted after 1920, and more than one-fifth are of post-1950 vintage. The 1920's and 1950's were obviously decades of active change.

Selecting and Changing Names

Symbols such as names are specific enough, but often it is difficult to analyze what lies behind them.[17] Names have different meanings

---

[16] Age refers to the time elapsed since the first name considered in this study was adopted, not necessarily to time since the inception of the firm or one of its predecessors.

[17] A. N. Whitehead, *Symbolism; Its Meaning and Effects* (New York: The Macmillan Co., 1927), 63.

for different people. The periodical literature, however, throws some
light on the process of name selection and change. Usually, the
names are suggested by insiders or consultants who may use com-
puters to fabricate acronyms. After preliminary screening, the
results are tested on a variety of people. A legal check to establish
that the preferred names do not trade on the good will and reputation of other corporations, precedes final selection.[18]

The requirements of a good name were adequately defined by
Paul K. M. Thomas[19] who in 1924 admonished against choosing too
general or too specific names which hamper correct identification of
a firm's activities. Further, in naming a corporation, one names
something that is expected to grow. Besides, names ought to be
memorable, readable, pronounceable, and free from confusion.
They should also correspond to the desired corporate image.[20]

Colloquial designations and the abbreviated forms used on stock
exchanges and financial pages (e.g., "Philco," "Socony") seem to be
driving out formal names, as if by some new application of Gres-
ham's Law.[21] Fads occasionally result in nothing changed but the
name,[22] and there are firms with a new name but no business to go
with it.[23] Such action adds up to what one observer has called "a
musical comedy librettist's notion of what a corporation name
should be."[24]

---

[18] J. F. Lawrence, *op. cit.*, 1, 15; "The Name Game," *op. cit.*, 90; Otterbourg, *op. cit.*, 9–10.

[19] Paul K. M. Thomas, "The Importance of Choosing the Right Name for Your Business," *Printer's Ink* (February 21, 1924), 117.

[20] Lawrence, *op. cit.*, 1, 15.

[21] J. M. Vicary, "What's in a Company Name," *Dun's Review* (June, 1957), 56; C. S. Scott, Jr., "Corporate Nicknames in the Stock Market," *American Speech* (October, 1960), 193–202.

[22] A. Abelson, "What's in a Name?," *Barron's* (May 21, 1956), 9–10; W. C. White, "New Words Come and Go," *Electronics* (March, 1948); "The New Horatio Algers," *Time* (November 16, 1962), 85; "The Yankee Tinkerers," *Time* (July 25, 1960), 65. Some enterprising onomatologist may want to study the names of business firms in novels and plays.

[23] "Corporate Cards of Identity," *Financial World* (December 28, 1960), 6–7. This article mentions that "National-U.S. Radiator" became the "Natus Corpora-tion" after selling its operating assets, at a time when it was still uncertain of the nature of its future activities.

[24] "What They See in a New Name," *Business Week* (March 28, 1959), 103.

Among the motives for changing a corporation name, mergers and diversification appear to lead the band.[25] Most name-changers feel that their firm has outgrown its name. Other wish to simplify a cumbersome name, or capitalize on a well-known brand name, or reflect a change in ownership, and – last but not least – do what other firms are doing if only because name change symbolizes growth, energy and aggressiveness.[26]

Conclusions

1. *Corporate names have become shorter* due to the waning of the middle name; also to the need for shorter names in advertising copy.

2. As such, *the first name has increasingly become the single distinctive part of the firm's title*. More and more, the first name is an abstraction, either because of the use of acronyms or because of its newly gained isolation (e.g., "Admiral Corporation").

3. Where the last name is concerned, *corporateness has progressively come to be expressed by "Corporation" or "Incorporated" rather than by "Company."*

4. *Corporate names generally evolve from purely descriptive tags into evocative ones*. Practically and legally, all corporations need a name for identification and differentiation. However, the corporate title transcends these requirements and becomes "a symptom of the state of the speaker, a signal for the listener, and a substitute symbol for the facts."[27] Much is expected nowadays of corporate names. The coporate "monicker" is sometimes required to convey at the same time diversity of products, aggressive management, financial stability and farsightedness – preferably in two words.

5. *These changes in corporate names reflect rather faithfully the transformations wrought in their bearers by a host of environmental factors* – namely, the constant diversification and evolution of industrial corporations oriented to changing technologies, broader markets and future transactions. The study of corporate symbols,

[25] Abelson, *op. cit.*, 9.

[26] "The Name Game," *op. cit.*, 90; "Why Firm Names Are Being Changed to Brand Names," *Printer's Ink* (November 10, 1927), 191–92. This last article also lists reasons for *not* changing a corporate name.

[27] E. Pulgram, *Theory of Names* (Berkeley: American Name Society, 1954) 7.

such as the name, the emblem, the trademark or the motto. provides a handy mirror to this changing reality which is often difficult to identify and measure.

6. *Diversification and evolution will in the future continue to require fewer narrowly descriptive and more "all purpose" names.*

7. *As more firms adopt shorter names without very specific denotations of purpose, a limit will be reached as far as length is concerned.* It seems unlikely that official corporate names will ever contain fewer than two words,[28] although one-word code names of the types used in cabling or on stock exchanges are a possibility (e.g., "Nabisco"; "Alcoa").

8. *The truly international corporation will require names pronounceable in any language. having no bad meaning or connotation in foreign languages, and with letters that fit most alphabets.*[29]

Naming is a continuous process that is never finished. Therefore, the demand will remain for "[corporate] names that will stir the pulse like a trumpet call, set the brain awhirl like a movie star, inspire reverence like a cathedral," as French playwright Giraudoux said of "the only social unit of which our age is capable – the corporation."[30]

APPENDIX

Scope

While the three groups of industrial corporations examined here do not in any way represent a statistical sample of U.S. industrial corporations, they constitute recognizable and eminent sets that warrant generalization about the naming of large industrial corporations. The names of antecedent firms merged into a surviving corporation or combined to form a new one were not considered as it would have entailed a complex and lengthy tracing back of corporate names, in view of the frequency of mergers and combinations.

---

[28] In 1960, some 12% of the firms already had a two-word name – the majority of them less than twenty years old.

[29] *Business Week* (June 4, 1960), 135.

[30] Jean Giraudoux, *The Madwoman of Chaillot,* translated and adapted by Maurice Valency (New York: Random House, 1947), 7–19.

Sources

Data about names and dates were obtained from the following sources: (1) corporation manuals such as *Moody's* and *Standard & Poor's* which usually include a historical section on each company listed; (2) reports to stockholders and company histories; (3) histories of American industry; and (4) letters to the companies involved. Lack of readily available information about the first two groups of industrial corporations has restricted the analysis of their names.

Definitions

Corporate name: the name recorded in the corporate charter.

Name change: the official recording of a different name either through charter amendment or through the procurement of a new charter, however small the difference in wording but not including the adoption or abandonment of abbreviated forms.

Name length: the number of words in the corporate name. Each separate part of the name was counted as one word, including initials. A few coined words such as "Coca-Cola" were treated as a single word.

Name components: the first, middle and last elements that traditionally compose corporate names (e.g., "Ford Motor Company").

As with persons, the *first name* constitutes the truly distinctive part of the corporate name that sets it apart from those of other firms engaged in similar activities. All firms have a first name in one of the following forms:

1. A *personal* name ("Ford")
2. A *geographical* name ("Pittsburgh")
3. An *adjective* denoting or connoting either *market coverage* ("National"); *excellence* ("Ideal"); *combination* ("United"), or *diversity of activities* ("General")
4. An *acronym* ("ACF"; "Chemetron")
5. A *composite* name ("Midland-Ross").

The *middle name* (when present) usually indicates the *products* ("Steel") or *processes* ("Brewing," "Optical") in which the firm engages. The *last name* (when present) commonly describes the legal form of the firm ("Company," "Incorporated," "Corporation").

New York University

Lucifer's Landholdings in America

L. B. SALOMON

IT WOULD TAKE THE DEVIL'S OWN TIME and tirelessness to track down all the United States terrain features (Rocks, Caves, Lakes, Dens, Punch Bowls, Tea Tables, Half Acres, etc.) listed either in his or in Hell's name. I myself, without going beyond standard road maps, guidebooks, and a random sample of toponymic treatises, have counted upwards of 350 such parcels of Satan's acknowledged property. In American onomastics the Devil not only *owns* a lot of the landscape; he even displays parts of his anatomy here and there for the tourist trade, e.g., humping up his Backbone in at least ten states, turning up his Nose in California and New York, poking out his Thumb from a mountain in Alaska and one of his Horns as a butte in Oregon, pricking up his Ears in North Dakota, bending his Elbow all over the continental United States.

Americans' eagerness to give the Devil his due has even engendered some interstate rivalry, of which a couple of examples may be cited. Missouri, for instance, has its champion in R. L. Ramsay, who writes,

> A large proportion of the territory of Missouri ... is still recognized as the property of the Devil, if place names are sufficient evidence of ownership. More than thirty localities attest the healthy respect we have for His Satanic Majesty. We have the *Devil's Elbow*, the name used for a sharp river bend; one of his *Boots*, in a boot-shaped cave in Warren County; three *Devil's Dens* and two *Devil's Tea Tables*, great smooth flat slabs of rock; a *Devil's Washpan, Washboard and Wash Basin*. Five pieces of his *Backbone* are found in as many different counties. The *Devil's Toll Gate* stands in a narrow opening at the foot of *Tom Sauk Mountain*; and the *Devil's Race Ground*... was mentioned ... in the journals of the Lewis and Clark Expedition.[1]

---

[1] *Our Storehouse of Missouri Place Names* (Columbia: University of Missouri, 1952), p. 112.

But California, next to Texas of course, always has the most of everything, Hell's holdings not excepted. "There are in California," says E. G. Gudde, "between 150 and 200 topographic features which are named for the Prince of Darkness. Probably no other state can equal this number."[2]

I am not so much concerned, however, with which state carries off the honors in Tophetic toponymy as with the contrast between this Devil's plenty and the very meager selection of landscape features attributed to God or any of his unfallen angels. Gently rolling farm-land and placid meadow brooks may be privately credited to divine provenience, but let the water foam white, let breathtaking rock formations thrust upward from the ground or multicolored strata paint the walls of a baroque chasm – in short, let the delighted eye be presented with *scenery* – and, if any supernatural agency gets credit for it, the chances are it will bear the hallmark of Hell. Even where, as in the North Dakota badlands, one tract of erosion forms may be called God's Gardens, Hell's Hole is not far away. Nobody seems to have taken up Thoreau's suggestion that Walden Pond be called God's Drop; yet the grateful citizens of South Dakota's Minnehaha County, who have an enchanted glen so lovely that the ordinarily matter-of-fact W. P. A. guidebook speaks of it as "a sanctuary of charm and inspiration," have named it Devil's Gulch, and the natural trail at the head of the ravine the Devil's Stairway. Gudde, to be sure, reports that California has about 50 features (including towns) named either just plain Paradise or Paradise this or that because of their supposed resemblance to the abode of the blest – but to some, he remarks dryly, "the name was no doubt applied in irony."[3]

George R. Stewart has a theory, which he applies mostly to the West, about this one-sided habit of naming:

---

[2] *California Place Names* (Berkeley: University of California Press, 1949), p. 93. Texas, by the way, is one of the seven states in the continental U.S.A. in which I have not yet found any features listed under *Devil* or *Hell*. The others are Alabama, Delaware, Kansas, Pennsylvania, South Carolina, and Tennessee.

[3] *Ibid.*, p. 253. The town of Paradise in Butte County, for example, was recorded on the Official Railway Map of 1900 as Paradice, and according to an old story was named for the Pair o' Dice Saloon. Helltown is not far away. Gudde reports, in-cidentally (p. 11), that Angel Island and Angels Camp were both named for settlers whose family name happened to be Angel.

The Devil's western holdings became varied and numerous. However profane he might be in speech, the American did not apply the name of God to places. When he wished to give any idea of the supernatural, he resorted to the Devil. If the Sioux *wacan* indicated that a body of water was spirit-haunted, the American usually translated it as Devil's Lake. When he saw a mass of columnar basalt so gigantic as to suggest more than human power, it became the Devil's Postpile. More often the idea of the torture of hell was involved, half-humorously. A dike of hard rock projecting from a mountainside often presented a regular curve suggesting a giant slide. But its jagged top also suggested an extremely painful process. So it became the Devil's Slide with the implication that his imps would put poor lost souls to sliding down it.[4]

Such names had been fairly common in the East, but the spectacular western scenery suggested them more frequently. Probably every mountain state has at least one Devil's Canyon. The usage survived into recent enough times to provide the Devil's Golf Course. Hell was often used with much the same ideas as Devil. With the aid of alliteration, any bad stretch of trail or river became Hell's Half-Mile, and any particularly desolate area was Hell's Half Acre.[5]

Now, there may well have been, in both East and West, a touch of bravado in the assigning of diabolic provenience to topographical features; a dash of conscious irreverence; even a bit of schoolboyish perversity, as in writing forbidden words on walls. But I should like to propose an alternative motivation: namely, an uneasy conviction that the Devil really does have much more than squatter's rights to the land lying between the Atlantic and Pacific Oceans. As a matter of historical record Satan's claim to all American real estate, both wild and improved, is attested by some very eminent authorities.

---

[4] In Montana, at least, Satan seems to have been more playful. The W.P.A. guide quotes the following poem about a Devil's Slide on Cinnabar Mountain:

> Ages ago, one can easily see,
> Old Yellowstone Valley went on a spree;
> The mountains had risen, the valleys had sunk,
> And old Mother Nature got roaringly drunk.
> The Devil, as drunk as the Devil would be,
> Slid to the bottom of Cinnabaree.

[5] *Names on the Land* (New York: Random House, 1945), p. 316.

Puritan theologians thaught that "the wicked one in whom the whole world lyeth" (Cotton Mather's phrase) had this continent all to himself from earliest times; that he managed to lure the Indians into his overseas territory so that for a good many centuries at least they could not possibly be exposed to the glorious news of the Evangel. "This American continent," wrote Jonathan Edwards, ". . . was wholly urïknown to all Christian nations till these latter times. It was not known that there was any such part of the world, though it was very full of people: and therefore the devil had this part of the world as it were secure to himself, out of the reach of the light of the gospel, and so out of the way of molestation in his dominion over them. . . . It is certain that the devil did here quietly enjoy his dominion over the poor Indians for many ages."[6]

Once the waves of Christian immigration began to erode his dominion he fought a relentless campaign of harassment and infiltration against the invaders. In 1632 John Winthrop reported a great combat at Watertown between a mouse and a snake, with the mouse emerging victorious. "The pastor of Boston, Mr. Wilson, a very sincere, holy man, hearing of it, gave this interpretation: that the snake was the devil; the mouse was a poor contemptible people, which God had brought hither, which should overcome Satan here, and dispossess him of his kingdom."[7] Two years later Winthrop noted in his journal that "Satan bestirred himself to hinder the progress of the gospel."[8] By the end of 1638 the cold war was coming to a furious boil, as "The Devil would never cease to disturb our peace, and to raise up instruments one after another" (a woman at Salem, for example, persistently refused to bow at the name of Jesus). "At Providence, also, the devil was not idle" (husbands there were finding difficulty in controlling their wives). "Another plot the old serpent had against us, by sowing jealousies and differences between us and our friends at Connecticut, and also Plymouth." And early the following year, during a violent hurricane, "The Indians near Aquiday being pawwawing in this tempest, the devil came and fetched away five of them."[9]

---

[6] *Works* (London: Ball, Arnold, and Co., 1840), I, 600.

[7] *Winthrop's Journal*, ed. J. K. Hosmer (New York: Charles Scribner's Sons, 1908), I, 83—84.

[8] *Ibid.*, I, 121.

[9] *Ibid.*, I, 285—297.

Cotton Mather marveled at the divine favor which permitted the Pilgrims and Puritans, despite such a redoubtable enemy, to build churches and settle towns "in a place where, time out of mind, had been nothing before but *Heathenism, Idolatry, and Devil-worship.*"[10] Yet neither he nor Jonathan Edwards had any fears as to the ultimate outcome of the struggle between newcomers and original owner, nor did Edwards even respect Satan as a really worthy adversary. "Although the devil be exceeding crafty and subtle," he said, "yet he is one of the greatest fools and blockheads in the world, as the subtlest of wicked men are."[11] And Mather, reflecting on the progress made by the Puritans once "the sound of the *silver trumpets* of the Gospel"[12] had been made audible in the land, exclaimed, "Surely of this *work*, and of this *time*, it shall be said, *what hath God wrought*? And, *this is the Lord's doings, it is marvellous in our eyes!* Even so (O Lord) *didst thou lead thy people, to make thyself a glorious name!*"[13]

But the glorious naming hasn't always worked out that way, not even in New England. *Towns* could be named for a benevolent creator, like Providence, or for sacred places, like Sharon, Canaan, or Salem; but, just as the Devil notoriously has all the good tunes, the great blockhead still maintains his title to what the road maps call points of interest.

Indeed, the eternal adversary seems more firmly entrenched in Massachusetts than in almost any other eastern state. South of Worcester, in an awesome fissure called Purgatory Chasm, the Devil has a Corn Crib, a Coffin, and one of several Pulpits from which be presumably hurled forth his own *firstly*'s, *secondly*'s, and *thirdly*'s in answer to sermons preached against him by black-clad clergymen in the towns. He has left his cloven Hoofprint in a rock beside the Congregational Building in Ipswich, and two huge Footprints pointing southward, two miles apart, near Upton. Near South Hadley is the Devil's Football, a 300-ton magnetic boulder which Satan is alleged to have kicked from the Devil's Garden at Amherst Notch several miles away.

---

[10] *Magnalia Christi Americana* (Hartford: Silas Andrus and Son, 1855), I, 13.

[11] *Works*, II, 612.

[12] *Magnalia*, I, 42.

[13] *Ibid.*, I, 13.

[14] He also has a Pulpit on Monument Mountain, and another on a ledge overlooking the Deerfield River.

Offshore, on No Man's Land, a small island eight miles from Martha's Vineyard, the Devil has a rocky Bed and Pillow. And at Gay Head, on the Vineyard itself, a bowl-shaped depression in the hillside facing the sea is the Devil's Den. Here, according to Indian legend, once lived a giant named Maushope, a benevolent tutelar deity who broiled whole whales over fires built with huge trees torn up by the roots. He kept the Gay Head Indians supplied with fish, and once even agreed, reluctantly, to build them a bridge across the sound to Cuttyhunk, five or six miles away – but only pledged one night's work, during the time between sundown and cockcrow. The Cuttyhunkers wanted no part of this, but only one old woman among them knew how to thwart the project. An hour or two after dark she held a lighted candle before the eyes of her rooster, which let out a lusty cockadoodledoo; whereupon Maushope, who had been tossing tremendous boulders outward from the shore to form a causeway, went home to bed. The line of rocks with which he fulfilled the letter of his contract is called the Devil's Bridge.[15]

Besides the Den at Gay Head, the Devil has two Dens on the Massachusetts mainland: one, a cave near Wilmington; the other, a rocky gorge with beatiful mossy walls and deep pools, right in the Northampton-Amherst area where Edwards fought him to a forensic standstill and Emily Dickinson reported,

> The Only One I meet
> Is God.

No, the old Devil who snatched away those five "pawwawing" Indians near Aquiday is not about to give up his possessions even though he may have to manage them only as an absentee landlord. Furthermore, the Americans who preserved so many hundreds of Indian names for the places from which they so ruthlessly expelled their Iroquois or Cherokee or Sioux or Apache inhabitants seem more than willing to let the Devil's name stand as long as they enjoy an easement to visit the property, including the right to scrawl their initials and chip off pieces as souvenirs.

It may be the merest token compensation, but perhaps it's the American way.

Brooklyn College

---

[15] B. A. Botkin, *Treasury of New England Folklore* (New York: Crown Publishers, 1947), p. 450.

Obscene Names and Naming

in Folk Tradition

ROBERT M. RENNICK

I<small>N</small> <small>HIS</small> <small>BRIEF</small> <small>INTRODUCTION</small> to that pioneering venture into serious consideration of traditional erotica which appeared in a recent issue of the *Journal of American Folklore*,[1] Frank Hoffman pointed out that this field of study had received virtually no recognition by folklorists until the symposium of which he was chairman met to consider this matter in the winter of 1960. Hoffman and his colleagues made us clearly aware of the problems inherent in the systematic study and analysis of this area of folklore. They also reminded us of our obligation as scholars to consider all facets of folk experience and expression as objectively as possible and that, if mass acceptance of scholarly findings is not yet upon us, they should at least be made available to serious students of the discipline by way of articles in professional journals.

This paper will, therefore, be a consideration of erotica, or preferably *obscenity*, in the area of *nomenclature*. To my knowledge this has not yet been seriously attempted. Although much is known on this subject, and even more is assumed, very little if anything has been brought together in any systematic fashion for careful and considerate analysis. I hope, in this paper to present a brief, objective, and necessarily cautious introduction to obscene nomenclature by first presenting some kind of theoretical framework for its examination, followed by a tentative typology of such names, and a representative sampling of the relevant folklore.

I

At the outset, it is necessary to define and delimit our subject and to place it in the proper perspective. As implied above, I

---

[1] "Symposium on Obscenity in Folklore," *Journal of American Folklore*, LXXV (1962), 189–265.

prefer the term *obscene* to *erotic* to avoid the more obvious limitations of the latter word. *Erotic* tends to be confined to the sexual realm, referring to the amatory desires and practices of human beings. It usually excludes those other acts or objects of a "private nature," those having to do with the bodily functions of elimination. Both sets of behavior, however, have come to be defined as obscene or offensive in our culture and to be regarded as inimical to the standards of common decency and morality, if not good taste or refinement. *Obscenity* is thus a more inclusive term.

What makes something obscene ? I accept the proposition that there is nothing inherent in any act or symbol which suggests obscenity but that it is arbitrarily regarded as such by a particular group of persons in a particular cultural context. As the anthropologist Leslie White has pointed out, the meaning of any symbol is never "derived from or determined by properties intrinsic in its physical form."[2] There is nothing about the word *shit* (or the name *Schitt*), for instance, that would in any way denote the excretory function. There is nothing about the excretory act which would account for the meaning of the symbol attached to it. Neither is there any reason why the excretory function in itself should be regarded as obscene. Indeed, in many societies and among medical persons in our own, it is considered a perfectly natural topic for ordinary conversation. But the *average* person in our society is inclined to assume a negative attitude toward the excretory symbol and its referent, as toward the sex act and its relevant symbolism, defining them as stimuli likely to arouse feelings of lust. This seems to be even more true of excretory behavior, for the increased lessening of restraints which tend to characterize the new sexual morality in this country has not yet extended to the bodily functions. Most Americans are still self-conscious about elimination and feel uncomfortable when they must communicate this type of experience to others; as when one may have to mention, say, to a physician that he's "been having difficulty moving (his) bowels," or that he "has an unbearable itch just above the testicles." It is all apparently a reflection of our attitude that sex and bodily functions are "private affairs," not to be shared among persons, even close friends. So married couples often prefer to eliminate in private;

---

[2] "The Symbol: The Origin and Basis of Human Behavior," *Etc: A Review of General Semantics*, I (1944), 229–237.

children are not encouraged to dress or undress in the presence of their brothers or sisters of the opposite sex; bathroom doors are often closed, even for washing or shaving.[3]

A symbol's meaning, according to White, has been arbitrarily determined by the persons who have created the symbol and make use of it. Certain types of behavior have been popularly defined or evaluated in our culture as "obscene" because they are feared to arouse sex feelings which are viewed as unhealthy to the society. But such arousal need not occur and would not if such definitions were not given. (*Whence* this definition is an historical problem which does not concern us here.) Bodily elimination and the sex act are vital processes, and thus universal and necessary. An obscenity definition of them, however, is not. "Obscenity" comes with the suppression of a behavior – its characterization as "forbidden" or "taboo" (as with belching in our society) or with its restriction to certain sectors of human experience – in the privacy of the bedroom or the bathroom and with a minimum of vocalization about it. Violations of the obscenity taboos are generally responded to negatively. When we hear certain words, defined as "obscene," uttered in ordinary conversation or when we are confronted with its referent behavior, we are likely to feel shocked or embarrassed, or we may pretend that we really didn't hear it or that it means something else.

On the other hand, under certain conditions, these same behaviors and/or their symbolic representations may be treated humorously. Instead of avoiding the taboo symbols they may be joked about, perhaps reflecting either the popular tendency to make light of a serious matter or (as Allen Walker Read suggests) the desire to seek a thrill by "doing the forbidden."[4] But the very

---

[3] Moreover, euphemisms are freely employed for such "private affairs"(itself the classic euphemism). See H. L. Mencken's discussion of "Forbidden Words" in his *American Language*, Supplement I, (New York, 1945), pp. 639 ff.

[4] Allen Walker Read, *Lexical Evidence from Folk Epigraphy in Western North America: A Glossarial Study of the Low Element in the English Vocabulary* (Paris, 1935), p. 9.

The use of offensive nomenclature may also serve as a political weapon. In the early nineteen twenties, at the peak of the Socialist fervor in Italy, some parents are known to have vented their hostility toward the existing political, religious, and moral systems of the country by giving their children ridiculous or offensive (and even obscene) names. Though, somehow, it was felt that this would be suf-

fact that we find humor in *these* behaviors and symbols connotes obscenity. When we ridicule persons bearing certain kinds of names, saying how we'd die if we had to go through life with a name like "Mary Schitts," for instance, so that Mary is made to feel that she should change it as soon as she can, we are demonstrating our sensitivity to this sort of thing. Telling stories such as those related in this paper for their titillating effect when their humor is no more intrinsic than an account of a man shaving or brushing his teeth, or laughing at names like "Mary Schitts," whereas surnames like Toothaker or Shaver, not uncommon in this country, are met with matter-of-factly, is no different from leering at pictures of nude women instead of accepting them as being as natural as a still life or a pastoral scene.

Thus it is the context in which any symbol is used rather than the symbol itself which makes it obscene; how, for instance, a transmitter of an item of folklore may regard that item or how his audience may receive or define it should determine its obscene significance. By implication, then, what is defined as obscene or offensive will necessarily vary from group to group or even from individual to individual within a group as well as from one time to another. For instance, certain names which Americans today tend to define as obscene had no such connotation in Medieval England when they were more common. Charnock, in his classic and reasonably reliable *Ludus Patronymicus* (London, 1868), an etymology of curious

---

ficiently insulting to the despised regime, apparently no thought was given to the effect such names as Massacre, Anarchy, Lucifer, Freethought, and Lustful would have on the children. Finally, when the practice seemed to be getting out-of-hand, a law was passed prohibiting the indiscriminate selection of children's names and providing for the substitution of "acceptable" names for those already given. (*The New York Times* [July 18, 1927], p. 6: 7.)

Paul Tabori, in *The Art of Folly*, notes a similar practice during the French Revolution when the disavowal of the traditional Saint's Calendar and anything else smacking of clericism led to a new patriotic fervor encouraging the adoption and assumption of names reflecting a new free spirit of creativeness and imagination. Some of the "oddities" to come out of this movement are given on pages 152–153 of his book.

Another example of the insult function of offensive naming was sent to me by Louis Feipel of Brooklyn, New York who pointed out that "Mrs. Barbauld, the sister of Dr. Aiken, was facetiously called 'that pleonasm of nakedness' by Coleridge, the idea of nakedness being reduplicated and reverberated in the two syllables of her name — 'bare' and 'bald.'"

English surnames, points out that the origin of such names as *Goose* (and *Goosey*), *Cock*, *Bottom*, *Puss(e)y*, *Rape*, *Sex*, *Suckbitch*, *Urine*, *Pisse*, and *Vulgar* were not at all what they now suggest to us.

Bottom, for instance, referred to a bottom or valley and appears also as part of such not uncommon names as Bottomley, Higginbottom, and Winterbottom.[5] *Cock*, alone or as the stem of many other names, may be derived from the rooster (the French *coq*) or is, more likely, an appendant term of endearment as in *Hitchcock* (little Richard) or *Allcock* (little Hal, for Henry).[6] *Puss(e)y* comes from *Pewsey* or *Pusey* which are parishes in Wiltshire and Berkshire.[7] Similarly, *Goosey*, is a tithing in the parish of Stanford-in-the-Vale, Berkshire, while *Goose* comes from the Cornish *gûs* (a wood), or else is a corruption of *gasse* (Danish for gander) or even a translation of the German *gans*.[8] *Rape*, Charnock suggests, is a corruption of *Rolfe*.[9] *Sex* (like *Six* or *Sax*) might stem from the Anglo-Saxon *Seaxa*, meaning a Saxon, which, itself, might derive from *seax* (a dagger or short sword) suggesting that the Saxons were persons who used such implements.[10] *Urine*, which has a Cornish counterpart in *Euren*, derives from the Cornish *voren* (strange); or it could be a corruption of *Uren* (not uncommon as a surname in many parts of the United States) from the old personal name *Urwyn* (Irvine); or it could have come from *Irvine*, a parish in Ayrshire (also spelled *Irwyn* and *Irwine*).[11] *Pisse*, according to Charnock, is a variant of the name *Piesse*, and he quotes Lower to the effect that the *Piesse* family came to England from Bretagne following the revocation of the Edict of Nantes and that their "name was derived from the order of knighthood created in 1560 by Pope

---

[5] Charnock, p. 10.

[6] *Ibid*, p. 17. (Charnock claims, erroneously, that Hitchcock derives from *Isaac*. Actually, *Hitch* is a pet form of Richard.)

[7] *Ibid*., p. 79. (*Pussy* once referred to a girl, much as "broad" does today; in this country it signifies the female copulative organ.)

[8] *Ibid*., p. 41.

[9] *Ibid*., p. 82.

[10] *Ibid*., p. 91. (Cf. Robert Ferguson, *English Surnames and Their Place in the Teutonic Family* (London, 1858), p. 218.)

[11] Charnock, p. 125. (Henry Barber, in *British Family Names, Their Origin and Meaning* (1903), p. 267, suggested that the name might have had a Welsh antecedent in *Urien* [heavenly]. *St. Urien*, a locality name, was of probable Norman origin.)

Pius IV" and corrupted into *Pies* or *Piesse*.[12] Even the name *Vulgar* may be traced to the Saxon *ulf-ger* (very helping.)[13]

Sometimes, obscene-sounding names occur as variations in spelling or distortions of other names due to a misunderstanding in oral transmission. Lillian Lowry tells of a white female from western Kentucky whose name *Feelyer* might have been a corruption of *Ophelia*.[14] *Crap* and such related forms as *Crapp, Crappe, Krapp,* and *Krappe* were probably orthographic variants of the name *Crabbe* (or *Krabbe*, the German or East Frisian spelling) which suggests one who dealt in crustaceans; or else it refers to persons who walked like crabs or who were ill-tempered, irksome, or unpleasant (alleged crab-like qualities; hence persons who "crab a lot.")[15]

It may not be too unlikely that some of our "obscene" names in English have followed what Robert Ferguson once suggested is "the tendency to corrupt toward a meaning."[16] A name which has no apparent meaning in the language of a particular generation is likely to be forgotten or as little ready to be brought to mind as one whose meaning is clear to those who must deal with it. A name which refers to a familiar item or action is often the better remembered. This might explain the presumed derivation of such names as (1) *Death* from *D'Aeth*, denoting one who came from the city of Ath in Belgium's Hainault Province;[17] (2) *Body* from the Anglo-Saxon *Boda* (a messenger) or the Old Norse *Boddi*, a diminutive of *Bödvarr* (wary in battle);[18] (3) *Smellie* from *Smeley*, an Essex place name, or possibly from *Semilly*, a Norman name, or from the Anglo-Saxon *smala, smael,* or *smel* meaning small;[19] (4) *Ass* which Ferguson suggests may derive from the Old Norse *assa* (eagle), if not from the animal of that name, better known to us as the

---

[12] Charnock, p. 75.

[13] *Ibid.*, p. 127.

[14] "Christian Names in Western Kentucky," *Midwest Folklore*, III (1953) 131–136.

[15] P. H. Reaney, *A. Dictionary of British Surnames* (London, 1958), p. 81. (Cf. Ferguson, *op. cit.*, p. 183.)

[16] Charnock, *op. cit.*, p. xiv.

[17] Reaney, *op. cit.*, pp. 91–92.

[18] Barber, *op. cit.*, p. 98; and George F. Black, *The Surnames of Scotland: Their Origin, Meaning, and History* (New York, 1946), p. 85.

[19] Barber, p. 243; and Ferguson, *op. cit.*, p. 303.

donkey (Old Norse *ess* or *esse*);[20]   (5) *Belch* or *Belcher* from the
French *belchere*;[21]   (6) *Bare* from the Old English *baer* meaning un-
armed, defenseless, deserted, or indigent;[22]   (7) *Gotobed* which, according to Lower, might have been derived from the example of a
lazy person who slept too much,[23] but which might also have come
from the Old Germanic *gott-bet*, meaning "pray to God," or from
Guth-beade (Anglo-Saxon "war counselor"), or from *Boda* (see
above);[24] and (8) *Suckbitch*, a family name in the west of England
which has been traced back to the fourteenth century and may have
been derived from *sokespic* which may be nothing more than chaw-
bacon.[25] [Charnock, however, believes it came from *soc* (liberty)
and *spic* (bacon) or possibly the Old French *spec* (an inspector)].[26]
In any case, it has nothing whatever to do with bitches sucking.

Still other names found in Medieval English sources and current
in our day have derivations that lack any significance of the obscene. Those milder forms of obscenity encountered as American
surnames – *Hell* and *Damm* – were not unknown in the 13th century. *Hell* and *Helle* were surnames denoting residence at the side
of a hill, or were possibly variants of *Ellis*.[27] Most of the *Hell*(s) in
America, however, are of German descent; *Hell* denotes an ancestor's origin in *Halle* or near *Halle*, a city on Saxony-Anhalt.
Similarly, *Damm*, of Old English as well as modern German or

---

[20] Ferguson, pp. 94, 164.

[21] M. A. Lower, *Patronymica Britannica: A Dictionary of the Family Names of
the United Kingdom* (London, 1860), p. 30.

[22] *Ibid.*, p. 18.

[23] *Ibid.*, p. 135.

[24] Charnock, *op. cit.*, p. 41.

[25] E. S. in *Notes & Queries*, 1st Series, V (May 1, 1852), 425.

[26] Charnock, *op. cit.*, p. 108. (A similar sounding name was *Sucksmith*, borne by at
least one family in the West Riding, Yorkshire. A correspondent to *Notes & Queries*
(4th series, III, [June 19, 1869], 579) believed that this name was a corruption of
Soke Smith (i.e. parish smith, from the Danish "*sogn smed*").) Just as in feudal times
lords often gave a local miller a monopoly over the milling of flour and meal for the
parish (the mills were called "soke mills") similar exclusive franchises may have been
given to smiths, and this could have accounted for the name. Thus, *Sucksmith* may
simply have been "blacksmith." Another correspondent (*Ibid.*, V [June 18, 1870],
590) suggested that the Sucksmith progenitor was a country blacksmith who
specialized in making coulters, called "sucks" in local dialect; this word coming
from the Norman-French "soc" meaning a ploughshare or coulter.

[27] Reaney, *op. cit.*, p. 160.

Dutch derivation, was a name given to dwellers at the site of a dam or dike.[28]

Other offensive-sounding names not infrequently found today but which had more innocent origins are *Bowel(ls)*, *S(c)hit(t)* and its many other variants, *Outhouse*, *Backhouse*, *Leak(e)*, *Fock* (*Foch*, *Focke*, *Fook*, *Fooke(s)*, *Fowke*, *Fewkes*, *Fuke*, *Fuchs*, etc.), *Rape*, *Hug*, *Kiss*, *Hoar*, *Loose*, *Pickup*, *Virgin*, etc.[29]

Bowel(ls) might be derived from *Bouelles*, the name of a town in the Seine-Inférieure which was brought to England by the Norman invaders and preserved as *Bowells* in Essex. It is also the Welsh patronymic form of *Howel(ls)* as *ap Howel(ls)* (much as *Pew* or *Pugh* formed from *ap Hugh*.)

Schitt, the English transliterative form of the German *Schütt*, refers to a heap or pile of anything (e.g. straw). Reaney suggests, as well, a derivation in Old English *scytta* (shooter or archer).

Outhouse is relatively modern as a name and derives from the German *althaus* (old house), but *Backhouse* was the 14th century English *bakehouse* and was given as a name to a person who worked in or for a bakery. *Leak(e)* may be the Old English *lēac*, referring to a plant similar to the onion; and a person with this name would have been a dealer in leeks.

Fock and its many variants, as names, may go back to the 12th and 13th centuries and were English derivatives of the Old German *Fulco* meaning people. More recent sources are the Germanic *Fuchs* (fox) and the Dutch *Fokker* (cattle or stock breeder). *Rape*, from *Raper*, is the north England form of *Roper* and is derived from *rāp* (Old English, meaning rope or rope maker).

Hug stems from the Old English *ugga*, a diminutive of *ūhtrǣd*, while *Kiss*, comparatively recent as surnames go, is from the Hungarian *kis* (or *kicsi*) meaning little. It is often found as a surname in Hungary.

Hoar(e) and *Hore* (though not *Whore*) can be traced to the Old English *hār* meaning grey-haired or to *ore*, a Sussex place name referring to a dweller by the bank. *Loose* is a Kentish place name.

---

[28] *Ibid.*, p. 88. Cf. Cecil L'Estrange Ewen, *A History of Surnames of the British Isles* (London, 1931), p. 323.

[29] The following paragraphs are derived from Reaney, *op. cit.*, pp. 41–2, 295, 18, 197, 123, 276, 171–172, 166, 204, 251, and 336, respectively.

Pickup was a Lancashire place name. *Virgin*, as a not infrequent surname in England, even to the present time, probably has nothing whatever to do with the sexual purity of its original bearers. Bardsley suggested that the name nay have been bestowed on the man who played the Holy Mother in a Medieval miracle play. Ferguson, however, claimed a Scandinavian origin with a different meaning which was also manifested in the names *Virgo* and *Virgine*.

Although, as we have seen, most obscene-sounding names were not intended to signify what they seem to today, there were a few isolated examples in the Middle Ages of the witting bestowal of obscene names for the purpose of ridicule. These were given originally as nicknames with a few being passed on as surnames to succeeding generations. One such sobrename which probably did not become hereditary was *Bastard*, having the same meaning it does today. However, in the eleventh and twelfth centuries it did not have the stigma it later came to have and was even proudly borne by some of the more influential Englishmen of the time, including William the Conqueror.

Some names of this variety were simply caricatures of their bearers; e.g. *Smallbyhynd*, which might have been a fitting indication of the size of the so-named's buttocks. Similarly, Alan *Swete-in-bedde* and John de *Halfnaked* may suggest some discernible characteristics of these persons.[30] *Rump(e)* was not uncommon as early as the eleventh century and derives from the Middle English, in which it denotes the hindquarters or buttocks of any animal. According to Reaney, it was used as a mark of contempt for the person so named.[31] *Butt*, a Middle English personal name as early as the twelfth century, was probably derived from a nickname referring to a heavyset individual; the word denoted the "thicker end" or stump of something.[32] *Belch(er)*, at least in some cases, may have testified to the bearer's habit of eructating after a heavy meal (from the Old English *baelc* or *baelce*, meaning a belch).[33]

---

[30] Both of these names were listed in old Oxford registrars.

[31] Reaney, *op. cit.*, p. 278.

[32] *Ibid.*, p. 29. It may also have come from the French *but* denoting a target for shooting, the name referring to a person who resided "near the archery butts," or even signifying the archer himself. (Reaney, p. 29.)

[33] *Ibid.*, p. 28.

II

A *working typology* of what today might be considered "obscene"-sounding names in England and America would consist of four categories[34]:

(1) a type of *general obscenita* which would include such names as *Vulgar, Queer,* and *Sewer,* as well as *Hell* and *Damm;*

(2) names alluding to the more *intimate parts of the human body,* which may be subdivided into

(a) *general body names* like *Body* itself and *Bodily,* as well as *Bare* and *Wetebody;*

(b) names denoting or suggesting the *male sex organs* like *Prick(e)* and *Pricksmall, Balls, Dick, Badcock* and *Highcock* (or any other cock), and *Crotch;*

(c) names deriving from the *female sex organs* like *Teat(es), Teet(es), Ti(ts),* and *Titter, Nipple, Bust, Papps, Utter, Bosom, Breast, Puss(e)y,* and *Maidenhead;* and

(d) names referring to the *rear end* such as *Ass, Rump(e), Butt, Rear, Smallbyhynd, Sourbut(ts), Sowerbutts,* and *Bottom;*

(3) names suggesting the *intimate bodily functions* like

(a) those of *urination* such as *urine* and its variants (including *Uren, Uran,* etc.), *Leak(e)* and *Leakey, Holdwater, Outwater,* and *Passwater, Peed, Pisse, Pistor,Piddle, Pesewips,* and *Pissant, Wiwi, Bladder,* and *Wetmore.*

(b) those of *defecation* such as *Bowel(ls), Schitt* and its variants, *Krapp(e),* as well as *Laxative* and *Constipation;*

(c) those having to do with the *outcome of bodily functions* such as *Decay* and *Dekay, Odor* and its variants, *Smelly* and *Smellie, Stink(er)* and *Stank(er, y,* and *o), Reaks,* and *Filth(y);*

(d) those relating to the *place* where such functions occur such as *Outhouse, Backhouse, Latrina, Commode;* and

(e) those having to do with *eructation* like *Belch(er),* and *Spitfathom;*

(4) names suggesting *erotic activities and their personnel* such as *Sex, Intercourse, Gotobed, Vice, Fock* and variants, *Rape* and *Wrape, Laid, Screw, Quicklove, Hug, Kis(s), Kisswetter, Buss, Popkiss, Goose(y), Suck* (and *Sucklick* and *Sucksmith), Virgin, Pickup, Bitch, Hoar(e)* and *Hore,* and *Loose(ly),* and, finally, *Bastard.*

---

[34] These are actual names. Each has been authenticated by the writer who has, in his possession, particulars on their bearers.

III

What follows is a sampling of obscene name lore in the English language, drawn from the unsolicited contributions of correspondents as well as gleanings from casual conversations and systematic ventures into the field. Informants, though for the most part matter-of-fact about their contributions, offering few apologies and manifesting little embarrassment over them, generally preferred to remain anonymous when asked if their names could be mentioned as sources of data. In identifying their own sources, they would limit their remarks to "a friend told me this" or "it's common knowledge hereabouts." Thus, few sources will be given for the items in this accumulation. In a few cases, however, variants in published literature will be referred to, and related items and issues will be presented as asides. No attempt will be made to deliberately structure the items in the sample around the conventional folklore genres, for most of them are simply anecdotal in form.

In view of the "indelicate nature" of the material in his collection, the writer feels that it might be discrete to begin with the less offensive references to *Hell* and *Damm*. Here punlore, in particular, is nonpareil as it recounts the name-changing predilections and efforts of those burdened with such names; like a Mr. *Damm* of Tennessee who was permitted to change his name after he'd complained to a local court that a publisher of souvenir postcards was selling his family's portrait under the title "the whole *Damm* family."

Several classic cases of changes in the name *Hell*, which seems to be more likely than *Damm* to inspire such acts, are often recounted in lawyer circles. A German-born resident of Portland, Oregon named *Otto Hell* was permitted by a local judge to take the name Hall when he pointed out how his neighbors and associates took pleasure in calling him by his surname and the initial of his given name. Another *Otto Hell* was an optometrist who complained that persons in need of glasses were always being told to "go to Hell and see." This is analogous to the numerous punning references to *Helen Hunt*. As a folk type she seems to have had more than her share of allusions. She is, for example, nearly always in charge of lost-and-found departments, especially in department stores, and of pharmacies in hospitals, and supply closets in public schools; and new personnel, as part of their institutional "initiation," are always being sent to her. Similarly, it seems that nearly every hospital has (or used to have) its *Helen Highwater*, head nurse, and interns beginning their service are always advised to consult with her in learning their way around the wards. One also can't help mentioning in this context the nineteenth century American novelist who inspired irreverent punsters to announce that they were going to *Helen Hunt Jackson's grave*. Typical of the *Helen Hunt* anecdotes in oral circulation is the one about Mrs. Jackson who, while still Hunt, is said to have once found a money purse in a church pew after the morning's service. The preacher, when she informed him of it, advised her to hold on to it and that he'd announce it at the evening's service. That night, he addressed the congregation to the effect that a money purse had been found in the church and that the owner can go to *Helen Hunt* for it. The preacher, we are told, was met with a tittering response from his congregation.

Sometimes the humor in a name like *Hell* comes from an error in spelling. One of the several possible ways of responding to a person whose name one happens not to have caught on the first introduction is to ask if it's spelled with an "e" or an "i." Though this is often effective, there was at least one time when it didn't work. The narrator relates that "at a recent party I was introduced to a young woman whose name was rather hastily given. When asked whether she spelled it with an 'e' or an 'i' she got very angry and refused to speak to me for the rest of the evening. I later found out that her name was *Hill*."

A story once popular in Nashville, Tennessee is of the grammar school principal who was escorting the members of the local school board around to his various classrooms. In an effort to show his guests how effective the instruction had been under his administration, he asked the teacher in one classroom if she would question her pupils on what they had been learning. She started off with some fairly simple questions, and working up to the progressively harder ones, she began to focus her attention on the brighter pupils of her class. But one especially difficult question had even her best pupils stumped. Immediately, however, a hand shot up from the back of the room. It belonged to the class dunce whose name was *Dammit* Jones. "Why, *Dammit*," the teacher said, "you know you can't answer this question." "Oh, hell," said the principal, not knowing the boy's name, "he can try."

The use of initials may have humorous effects, especially with names like *Damm*. A popular nineteenth century anecdote, on both sides of the Atlantic, recounts the trials of a young lawyer (or doctor or tradesman) who is setting up his practice by performing the most obvious initial act of hanging a sign outside his office door with his name, "*A. Swindler*" (or any other derogatory name). His first client can't help remarking that his sign is bound to deter potential clients, and advises him to write out his first name in full. "Oh I couldn't do that," the lawyer answers; "as bad as this must seem to be, it would be infinitely worse if I added my full given name – Adam."

Still on initials, Elsdon Smith tells of an attorney named Daniel Ashton Martin whose secretary, Irene Thompson, in characteristic fashion, would type in the lower left hand corner of his dictated letters: "Dict. DAM/it." [35]

Hell is even the name of several places in the United States, and at least one is known to have successfully capitalized on it. A village in southeastern Michigan (population 45) has, for years, been enjoying a tourist boom. People would come from all over just to be able to mail a card postmarked *Hell* or to purchase bumper stickers for their cars stating "WE'VE BEEN THROUGH HELL!" In addition to this attraction, the village has lately acquired a reputation as a marriage mill. Seventy two couples were wed there in 1965 and 61 the following year, a large percentage of them having been divorced at least once. One couple is alleged to have told the local justice of the peace that since they'd already been through Hell twice, they might just as well *start* there. In October of 1967, the Michigan Seventh-Day Adventists conducted a Bible camp there for youngsters, calling it "Bible Study in Hell." Their theme was, of course, "How to Go to Heaven."

It would not do to leave this discussion without that classic of punlore alluding to "his Satanic Majesty." Popular in nineteenth century England was the story of the mother who lisped so badly in pronouncing the name of her baby at its baptism that instead of coming out "Lucy, Sir," as she intended, it sounded like "Lucifer." The clergyman, of course, would have none of this and christened the child "John."

---

[35] *The Story of Our Names* (New York, 1950), p. 241.

Let us proceed now to a consideration of the "more flagrant violations of onomastic propriety" (as one of my informants recently put it) – the name-lore relative to and suggested by the bodily functions and erotic behavior of human beings. A good starting point for such consideration could be an examination of the reactions of persons to the embarrassment and discomfort felt by bearing some of the names we listed before, whatever their origins and inherent meanings may have been. We may begin with some of the anecdotes associated with efforts at name-changing.

A story once current arount Monroe, Louisiana, was of an immigrant named *Schitt* who settled in that town, prospered, and finally had a bill enacted in the state legislature to change his name to *Sugar*. Whereupon some local wit was inspired to compose the following couplet, which tormented the changer's children throughout their school days:

> "Shit by name, shit by nature
> Changed to Sugar by the Legislature."[36]

In June of 1964, the Roger Gordon *Smellie* family of London, England went to court and secured a change-of-name to the less odious one of *Hurst* because, as they put it, "we got tired of hearing our children referred to as 'little stinkers.'"

Sobratsky, a Russian, came to America and settled in Michigan. Soon he shortened his name to *Subar* and apparently got along quite well with it. In the meantime, a kinsman had gone to Israel; but instead of taking the name *Subar*, he chose a similar sounding but more impressive name, *Sover* (meaning "thinker"). Besides, it is said, *Subar* in Arabic refers to the "male organ."

The *Elisheivitz* family of a certain Midwestern city became *Ellis* so that their son would no longer have to suffer being called "*ishytits*" (or "*itchytits*") by his schoolmates.[37] Similarly, in nineteenth century England, we know that a Josiah *Badcock* took the name *Elliot* and Samuel *Highcock* assumed the name *Condon* to avoid the playful references to copulation which their names inspired. So did James *Balls*, who preferred to be known as *Woolsey*. Edward

---

[36] The same thing is said to have happened in North Carolina to a Mr. *Hogg* who had also petitioned that state's legislature to allow him to bear the name *Hoge*.

[37] H. Allen Smith tells of the school girl who had to suffer *her* classmates' snickers whenever the teacher called her name in class – *Helen Zahss*. See *People Named Smith* (Garden City, New York, 1950), p. 48.

Sagarin tells us of a Mr. *Balze* who effected an accent on the "e" to insure that both syllables would always be pronounced.[38]

On occasion, an extremely hypersensitive person will react to the suggestiveness of his name by performing some rash and uncalled for act. Some years ago in a small Wisconsin village there lived a family of six boys named *Luberschitz*. The kids in town called them "Shits" and were always making fun of them. The older boys finally prevailed upon their parents to change their name, and the new family name, *Mueller*, was proudly borne to the local school, particularly to the seventh grade classroom where young Fritz informed his teacher of the official change. "I am now Fritz Mueller," he said, and he spelled it out for her very carefully, "M-U-E-L-L-E-R." Then he sat down, feeling very proud of himself. But the teacher could not contain her anger and blurted out "You can't just change your name whenever you wish..." Fritz jumped up from his seat — "I can too," he said. "My father had to pay a judge, and the court said that now our last name is M-U-E..." "Sit down!" the teacher snapped. "I don't care what the court said. Your school records are in the name of Fritz *Luberschitz* and *Luberschitz* they will stay until you pass from my class. Sit down, I said!" Fritz glared at her. Then, grabbing his books out of his desk, he shouted, "Then you don't have even a Fritz *Luberschitz* in your class, *no more!*" He marched to the door of the classroom; then, turning to his teacher, he hissed, "You old bag!", and out he went. He never returned to the school, my informant tells me, and years later his classmates discovered that this dropout had made a very successful career for himself as a high rank officer in the United States Army.[39]

The sensitivity of persons to uncomplimentary names often extends to other persons who bear them. Jewish trial lawyers in New York City have a favorite story about a once noted jurist named Peter *Schmuck* who possessed, to Yiddish-speaking persons, a name roughly referable in that language to the copulative organ.[40] Jewish attorneys were rather hesitant about appearing before the Dutch-American (though Gentile) magistrate, or else they sought

---

[38] *The Anatomy of Dirty Words* (New York, 1962), p. 87.

[39] Letter from Miss Ellen M. Woicek of Manteno, Illinois.

[40] *Smuk*, in Dutch, refers to finery. In German, *Schmuck* denotes an ornament or decoration, or jewelry, adornment or embellishment.

to avoid direct reference to his name by subjecting it to mis-
pronunciations of various kinds – *Schmook, Schmack, Schmaak,* etc.
but never pronouncing it the correct way, simply *Schmuck*; for
Schmuck, to a Jew, is an epithet directed at a damn fool or a sex
pervert. The use of the word, even as a name, was just too painful
to the Jewish lawyer's ears. The judge, apparently in complete
ignorance of this significance of his name, was, however, quite
proud of it and at the end of at least one particularly trying day is
known to have indignantly slammed his fist on the bench and
shouted: "My name is Schmuck! I am a Schmuck! And I want to
be referred to as a Schmuck!"

The above accounts are all alleged to be true. Some are more
than alleged, as I can vouch for their genuineness; however, a
number of stories frequently told of persons who seek to minimize
or avoid the effects of an uncomplimentary name are told with no
attempt to justify their authenticity. Jewish joke tellers, for
instance, are fond of recalling the businessman who progressively
alters his name as he travels from country to country. For humorous effect, however, the chronological order of the story is usually
reversed: "As a successful textile merchant in New York, he went
by the name *Mortimer Brooks*; in London, he had been *Morris
Fountain*; in Paris he was *Maurice La Fountain*; in the Rhineland,
Moritz Wasserspritzer; but back in Warsaw he was just good old
Moisher Pisher."[41]

---

[41] Variants of this tale with different settings come to my attention every so
often. I recently received this account of the Jewish family named *Pischer* who, as
they became more affluent, changed their name to *Fountain*. When they got really
affluent, they moved to Chicago's North Shore but only after they had changed
their name again – to *De la Fontaine*. Mrs. Harry Golter of Chicago tells me that
this same story circulated among the refugees from the Nazi tyranny and was
descriptive of the hopes which accompanied their change of environment and of
their upward mobility: "*Moshe Pish*," the peddler, left Warsaw after the First
World War and settled in Britain where he became a salesman and called himself
Moritz Wasserstrahl. During the thirties, he made his way to France, got a job in
Paris as a hotel manager and called himself "*Maurice de la Fountain*." Jews, Mrs.
Golter informs me, have the habit of laughing at their own misery. Many jokes circulated among the refugee community. They often arose out of the need to express
frustration, the way many folk-songs are born. Many of these jokes have been col-
lected and published, but Mrs. Golter could not tell me by whom.

At least once to my knowledge has the *Pisher* joke been in print. A variant of it
appears in Richard Dorson's "Jewish-American Dialect Stories on Tape" in *Studies*

By far the most frequently told of all onomastic jokes and the one with the greatest number of variations is that involving a person named *Stink* who goes to court to change his name. The judge, of course, being quite sympathetic, asks what name he would like instead, and invariably the request is for a change in his given name. All county clerks who read change-of-name petitions can swear that they've at least once come across a version of this, "*in fact*." If not *Stink*, perhaps the name is *Stank*, or *Stanko*, or *Stinkewich* ... And even *Schmuck* (Joe *Schmuck*, in at least one version known to the writer, prefers the name *Cecil*). *Herbert Hoover Stinks* seeks a change to *Joe Stinks*. *Franklin Stinks* wants to become simply *Frank*, while *Frank Stinko* has always wanted to be known as *George*. A Mr. *Stanko* changes his Italian name to the more euphonious one of *Stanks*. A popular variant of this is the account of a Joe *Stinks* (or any other uncomplimentary name) who seeks some other given name because he's tired of people saying, "Hello, Joe, what do you know?"

The *Stink* joke is one of a class of onomastic anecdotes involving the surprise ending effect, where the punch line is not what the listener expects. Another example of this was told some years ago in Virginia: A preacher asked the parents by what name they wished their son baptized. They said, "Odious D." When asked why, they replied that the "D" really didn't stand for anything. They merely "thought it would be distinguished to give him a letter in the middle of his name."

"Obscene" name-giving to children has certainly produced its share of folk anecdotes. Representative of these is the story of the colored lady with lots of babies who is given a book on birth control by the local public health nurse. A year later, the nurse returns to see if the book has been of any help to her. "It sure has," says the lady. "I had twins since I read your book, and it gave me such nice names for them – *Phyllis* and *Gonorrhea*." There are variants of this tale in nearly every collection of southern Negro name lore. A. P. Hudson, for instance, mentions the twins *Si* and *Phyllis*.[42]

in Biblical and Jewish Folklore, edited by Raphael Patai, Francis Lee Utley, and Dov Noy, Indiana University Folklore Series 13 (Bloomington, Indiana, 1960), p. 139.

[42] A. P. Hudson, "Some Curious Negro Names" *Southern Folklore Quarterly*, II (1938), 179–193.

Many of the names allegedly given to Negro babies are of "obscene" significance. Hudson's collection includes a *Commodius* (who was a premature baby named for the receptacle in which he was placed at birth); as well as *Stink* and *Stunk*, the twins sons of a Rocky Mount, North Carolina, shovel man on the local sanitary wagon which, in "pre-sewer" times, would drive through the streets of the town.[43] *Laxative* Jones and *Strawberry Commode* have been reported from the records of the Alabama Board of Health. Alleged, but probably fictitious, is little *Fertilizer* who was named for her parents – Ferdinand and Eliza. Then there are the inevitable *Lotta Crappe*, *Tiny* and *Rosie Bottom*, *Tiny* and *Rosy* Butt, and *Ophelia Dick* that many communities in this country claim to have among their citizenry. And some of them actually do. *Tiny* and *Rosy* are the daughters of a Mr. and Mrs. *Butt* of Rochdale, Indiana. Robert St. John, in *This Was My World* (Garden City, New York, 1953, pp. 235–36) tells of the *Bottom* family of Rutland, Vermont whose oldest daughter was named *Rosie*; not *Rose* but *Rosie*, and woe to any who thought otherwise. An active socialite, "Rosie Bottom [often] flitted through the pages of the *Rutland Herald*" on which paper St. John was for a time employed. *Ophelia Dick* is a middle-aged woman living on Main Street in Richwood, West Virginia.

It is often said that the situation in which parents find themselves at the time of the pregnancy or events leading up to the birth of the child often suggests a name for it. A Marietta, Ohio mother is said to have named her child *Morphie* which is short for Morphine. As everyone knows, morphine is a product of a wild poppy; and, according to her mother, if ever a child had a wild poppy, this one had.

A popular theme in naming-tales reflects the fear of a new father that his child will be given an obscene name by a thoughtless or even intolerant clergyman. Told especially of new arrivals to this country to illustrate this fear and their distrust of American functionaries, or possibly their lack of facility with the English language, is the story of the father who brings his new baby to the local priest to be baptized. "Now, see that you baptize heem right," he cautions. "Last time I here I tell you call my boy Tom, but you name heem Thomas. Thees time I want heem be call Jack. So you better no call heem *Jackass*!"

---

[43] *Ibid.*

As implied above, school teachers have often had their share of difficulties with "obscene-sounding" names. A fictional case in point involves a teacher's disbelief in such a name as borne by one of her pupils. Asked his first name by a new teacher at the beginning of the school year, the little boy answered, "*Snotnose McGee*." "Oh come now," said the teacher. "That's not your real name. What are you really called?" "*Snotnose McGee*," the child repeated. "Now look here," said the teacher angrily, "I'm in no mood for games. I want you to tell me your real name; and if you don't, I'll send you right down to the principal's office. Now, what is your name?" "*Snotnose McGee*." "Okay, I've had it with you," said the teacher, and she sent the child downstairs to have it out with the principal. On his way to the office, he passed his brother, saying, "You'd better come along, too, *Shithead*; they won't believe you either." [44]

The schoolroom, as we have seen, is a popular setting for "obscene" namelore. In one story, a teacher is taking attendance at the beginning of the semester – *Teacher:* Brown. *Brown:* Here. *Teacher:* Johnson. *Johnson:* Here. *Teacher:* McDonald. *McDonald:* Here. *Teacher:* Rosenberg. *Rosenberg:* Here. *Teacher:* Sally Jones. *Sally Jones:* Here. *Teacher:* Wannamaker. *Everybody:* Yes.

A former Yale University student (circa the turn of the century) recently recalled a professor by the name of *Glasscock*. "A very likeable chap was he and quite undeserving of the alias which we twenty-year-olds bestowed upon his dignified being. I am almost ashamed to tell it, but it seemed real funny then... we called him 'Professor Crystal Pecker.'"

Similarly reflecting on his own college days the writer recalls that the students would attempt to enroll fictitious persons in their classes and other activities under "phony" names, the most popular of which was *Lena Genster* who was pledged by at least half a dozen sororities before someone got wise. [The editor of this issue recently informed me that "dirty names" (not this one but ones like it) would be given as library pranks at Michigan State and Indiana universities. "You turn in a call-card with a fictitious name on it, and the circulation desk people will yell it out loud and clear."]

---

[44] H. Allen Smith gives a version of this in *People Named Smith* (Garden City, New York, 1950), p. 52, in which the child's last name is, of course, *Smith*, and her brother is *Fartface*.

In spite of the popularity of this anecdote, another colleague swears that this actually occurred at his institution. A girl named *Linda Sexauer* was being sought by one of the administrative offices. A call was made to the Music Department in which she was thought to be enrolled to see if they had a *Sexauer* there. "Why no," answered the secretary, "we don't even have a coffee break."[45]

Folk humor relating to obscene names often appears in the form of the pun. In addition to the several examples already given we can cite these, from oral tradition.

A variation of the popular traveling salesman and farmer's daughter joke is the one about the drummer who is told by the innkeeper, affectionately known as "Father Inn" by his employees, that he will have to sleep with one of the kitchen help as all the guest rooms in the place are occupied. The usual love-making preliminaries are carried out, but when the matter begins to get serious, the girl loses her aplomb and calls out, "Father Inn." Misinterpreting her outcry, the drummer replies, "Damn it, it's going in as far as it can!"

This is kin to the joke about the hired hand named Fuckerfaster who, instead of performing his required chores around the farm, is seen taking his employer's daughter behind the barn. The farmer, missing him, calls to him by name, only to be acknowledged with, "Keep your shirt on, I'm fucking her as fast as I can!"

Another farmer sends his daughter off to college, and on her first visit home during the semester break he notices that she has been putting on a little weight. "Ain't you gotten a lot fatter than you was when you went away?" he asks. "Yes, Papa," she answers. "I guess I have. I now weigh a hundred and thirty pounds stripped for gym." After studying on this for a minute, her father angrily shouts, "And who the hell is Jim!"

---

[45] The writer is unable to resist, at least in the form of a footnote, this classic, though published, piece of onomastic punlore: "Peters was the college's star fullback. But a few days before the big game he injured his leg in scrimmage, and he was told he wouldn't play in *the* game of the year. The college paper announced the sad news with this headline — 'Team Will Play Without Peters.' The dean, however, spotted this bit of college headline writing before it went to press and gave orders to change it or get kicked off the paper. The editor changed it, and Saturday morning the paper hit the campus with this headline — 'Team Will Play With Peters Out.'" (J. M. Elgart, editor, *Over Sexteen* (New York, 1951), p. 25.)

Mr. *Brown* and Mr. *Huggs* were partners in the operation of a
school many years ago, and in their promotional literature they
would inform the parents of prospective pupils how they divided
their teaching responsibilities – "*Brown* trains the boys and *Huggs*
the girls!"

Sportscasters in the early nineteen fifties are said to have had a
field day with North Carolina State basketball player Bernie *Yurin*,
finding it the height of wit to announce, "And there goes *Yurin*
dribbling down the court."

Cincinnati University medical students are proud to have on
their faculty a Professor Robert S. *Leake* in no other capacity than
as a urologist. He's for real. Questionable, however, is the Wyoming
physician named *Dekay* who, according to local accounts, named his
daughter *Diane*.

In the eighteenth century a Russian admiral named *Puke* is
said to have asserted when resigning his commission in the Russian
Navy:

> "I'm sick of the service – so tell the Grand Duke.
> I've thrown up my commission – your servant, John Puke."[46]

A motel owner in Comfort, Texas, which is located somewhere
between the towns of Alice and Louise is said to have advertised
his place of business by erecting a large sign reading "Sleep in Comfort between Alice and Louise."

The matter of *euphemism* should not be ignored in any consideration of obscenity in namelore. There are known to the writer a
number of examples of place names which have been changed or at
least modified in sound ostensibly to "protect the sensibilities of
the innocent." Here are some of these examples from the folklore
of Nevada and California:

> On a secondary road leading from Beatty, Nevada down
> into Death Valley, there is a very narrow passage through
> rock formations which appears on some maps now as *Titus
> Canyon*. However, the early prospectors in the area had
> named it *Tight Ass Canyon* and some still call it that and are

---

[46] The rhyme has been traced to Edward Nares' *Heraldic Anomalies* (London,
1823), Vol. I, p. 186. According to Nares, though apparently to nobody else, the
Grand Duke was Constantine who presided over the Admiralty.

indignant that civilization has chosen to modify it. In the Goshute Mountains of Eastern Nevada there are some natural mineral springs discovered and named by the Indians of the area many years ago. Whatever their Indian names may have been, they translated out as *Hard Cock*, due to the extremely aphrodisiac nature of the water. While the springs were so designated on early maps of the area, the modern maps merely show *H-C Springs*. In Yolo County there is a stream named in pioneer days *Puta Creek*. It is said to have been so-named because a group of Mexican prostitutes had their place of business located on its banks. Later residents apparently were offended at the name and compromised by calling it *Putah Creek*, thus making it appear to be an Indian name, which it is not.[47]

Neither should a consideration of obscene namelore omit the so-called "bawdy book titles" which grace the repertories of college students and summer campers. Representative of these are such gems as "The Man Who Put Salt in the Ocean" by I. P. Freely (and its more popular variant, "The Yellow Stream" by I. P. Daily); "The Spots on the Wall" by Who Flung Shit (or Hu Flung Dung); "The Fatal Accident, or the Tiger's Revenge" by Claude Balls; "The Anxious Lady" by Mister Period; "The Glorious Sight" by Eileen Dover (or "The Easiest Way" by Eileen Back); "The Open Kimono" by Seymore Hare; and "The Chinese Pervert" by Peiping Tom.[48]

Any conclusion to a discussion and presentation of obscene namelore in folk tradition should reflect if not reiterate the closing remarks of the participants of the Obscenity Symposium whose enterprise was mentioned at the outset. That is, that the anecdotes just given are but a sample of the relevant folklore of obscenity in names; that they await further collecting efforts; and that such lore should be considerably easier to come by in the present genera-

---

[47] F. W. Nance of Elk Grove, California in a letter to the writer, November 8, 1967.

[48] According to Louis Feipel, former staff member of the Brooklyn Public Library, this type of name combination that tells a story is often borne by real persons; for example, the American bankers *Russell P. Knightly* and *I. P. Moore*, as well as *Joe P. Little, Isora P. Moore, Mary Peed*, etc. of New York City.

tion than the more conventional types of lore (i.e. ballads and tales) *if only* people would no longer feel shocked or embarrassed by them to the point of withholding them from collectors or showing their aversion by restricting their availability in printed form to the public. Of course, as we have implied, if this occurred, they would no longer be "obscene."

DePauw University

The Names of the Canterbury Pilgrims

P. BURWELL ROGERS

In the General Prologue to the *Canterbury Tales,* Chaucer gives names to only two of the pilgrims; and elsewhere he names only six others. Even when we add the Host and Chaucer to the eight named, the number is not very impressive, whether we take Chaucer's "nyne and twenty" or a larger number as comprising the company.

However, in examining the names of these few we may come to a partial explanation of why Chaucer did not name all the pilgrims; and at the same time, we may see something of Chaucer's intentions and accomplishments in writing the *Canterbury Tales.*

The Prioress, Madame Eglantine, and the Friar, Hubert, are the two pilgrims named in the Prologue. At the beginning of his description of the Prioress, Chaucer says, "And she was cleped madame Eglentyne" (I, 121), thereby giving us her name.[1] Chaucerians have speculated much about her name, which is ultimately derived from Latin *aculenta,* "prickly." *Eylantine* is also a name for the sweetbriar, or the wildrose. It is much more suitable for a heroine of a romance than for a prioress, but in the light of the lady's character and temperament the very incongruity of the name to its bearer is one of the delights of the Prologue. As a personal name, Eglantine appears in England as early as 1213; but it does not appear as the name of the sweetbriar until about 1400. Regardless of whether Chaucer was inspired by the name of the wild flower or by the name of a heroine of a romance, the fanciful name fits the Prioress perfectly.

Presumably the Nun's Priest, who tells the tale of Chauntecleer and Pertelot, is included in Chaucer's enigmatic "and preestes thre" (I, 164), who accompany the Prioress. After the Knight has interrupted the Monk's dreary accounts of the fall of great men, the

---

[1] All quotations are from F. N. Robinson, ed., *The Works of Geoffrey Chaucer,* 2nd ed. (Boston, 1957).

Host calls to the Nun's Priest, "Com neer, thou preest, com hyder, thou sir John!" (VII, 2810). While in the Middle Ages Sir John was a common name for any priest, that this priest is really named John is made clear in the narrator's remark introducing the tale:

> And thus he seyde unto us everichon,
> This sweete preest, this goodly man sir John.   (VII, 2819—2820)

Since John is the name of both the Baptist and the Evangelist, it has double reason for being the most popular masculine name in Christendom. Here the coincidence of its being the Nun's Priest's name, even though Harry Bailey seems not to have known it, is in keeping with Chaucer's dealing with the priest as a type who is not described or individualized at all.

As far as his name is concerned, the Monk is treated very much as the Nun's Priest is, for the Host fumbles for his name too. When Harry Bailey calls upon him for a tale, he addresses him as "My lord, the Monk" (VII, 1924); and he goes on to say,

> But, by my trouthe, I knowe nat youre name.
> Wher shal I calle yow my lord daun John,
> Or daun Thomas, or elles daun Albon ?   (VII, 1928—1930)

Here we see the Host beginning with John, the commonest of names, and moving on to two less common ones as he apparently tries to guess at the Monk's real one. It is noteworthy that here he employs the names of three saints, two being apostles and the third being St. Alban, the first martyr of Britain. However, after the Knight's interruption, with careful courtesy the Host addresses the Monk as "sire Monk, or daun Piers by youre name" (VII, 2792), thus making it clear that Piers is the Monk's name – although we do not know how the Host learned it. In Piers, Chaucer chooses the name of one of the most popular of the apostles, and he uses the French form common in England after the Norman Conquest. The names of two favorite apostles are appropriate to the two religious men, the Nun's Priest and the Monk. That they also are common masculine names is in keeping with Chaucer's general practice of characterizing the pilgrims as representatives of types before making them individuals.

A third religious, the Friar, though, is given a name much more indicative of an individual than of a type, for at no time has Hubert been very common in England. Professor Charles Muscatine has argued that Hubert is fitting for the Friar because it is the name of rascally clerics in the Old French *Roman de Renart* and other poems in the Renart tradition.[2] Perhaps the rise of something like a cult of St. Hubert (c. 656–728), Bishop of Liège and patron of huntsmen, contributed to bringing the name into a certain prominence in Chaucer's time. Altogether, though, we feel that whether Chaucer was influenced by the Renart tradition or by the popularity of the saint, Hubert is not an unsuitable name for the Friar.

Chaucer himself leaves us wondering about the Friar's name, because after finishing the characterization of the man he informs us, almost as if it were an afterthought, "This worthy lymytour was cleped Huberd" (I, 269). This bare statement stands disconnected from what precedes and what follows; but it is evident that Chaucer deliberately placed the description of the Merchant after that of the Friar, for he concludes his remarks about the Merchant with a final line that reminds us of his last statement about the Friar: "But, sooth to seyn, I noot how men hym calle" (I, 284). It is a distinction of the Merchant that he is the only pilgrim about whom this kind of statement is made.

While Chaucer the narrator tells us the Friar's name, the Cook reveals his own when he exclaims at the conclusion of the Reeve's Tale,

> I pray to God, so yeve me sorwe and care
> If evere, sitthe I highte Hogge of Ware,
> Herde I a millere bettre yset a-werk. (I, 4335–4337)

Hodge was a popular nickname for Roger; and the Host calls the Cook Roger when he speaks to him, and the narrator likewise calls him Roger (I, 4345, 4353, and 4356). But later in the lively episode in which the drunken Cook falls off his horse and cannot tell a tale, he is called only "thou Cook," "This Cook," "sire Cook," and "the Cook" (IX, 15, 20, 26, 46, 85, 88, 92).

It is also the Cook who gives us Harry Bailey's name (I, 4358). While the Host's is perhaps the most familiar name in the *Canterbury Tales*, it appears only this one time. Everywhere else Harry Bailey is addressed and referred to as the Host. Since Harry is a nickname for Henry, the Host has been associated with Henri Bai-

---

[2] "The Name of Chaucer's Friar," *MLN*, LXX (Mar. 1955), 169–172.

liff, an innkeeper in Southwark, 1380–1381;[3] but such an association is no value to us here, and the name seems suitably plain for
the plain man who carries it.

While not a pilgrim on the way to Canterbury, the Host's wife,
even though a type, for a moment becomes a real woman for the
readers of the *Canterbury Tales*. After Chaucer's tedious moral tale
of Melibee, the Host cries,

> I hadde levere than a barel ale
> That Goodelief, my wyf hadde herd this tale!   (VII, 1893–1894)

Today's editors and scholars accept Goodelief as the name of Harry
Bailey's wife, but at an earlier time Professor Skeat did not. He interpreted the words "goode lief my wife" as a phrase of four separate
words meaning "my dear good wife."[4] Professor Kittredge related
the name Goodelief with that of Godelieva, a virgin martyr of
French Flanders noted for her wifely patience, whose day is April
eighteenth.[5] Since in the Introduction to the Man of Law's Tale the
narrator says that it is April eighteenth (II, 5–6), the connections
are interesting; and scholars today generally take note of them. In
the end, though, the irony in the name Goodelief, whether it means
"dear to God" or refers to the patient saint – or both, is appropriately comical when we think of the Host's characterization of
his wife.

When the Miller insists upon telling his tale immediately after
the Knight's, the Host tactfully tries to quiet him and calls him by
his name, "Robyn, my leeve brother" (I, 3129). Robin was a nickname, originally a diminutive, for Robert; and it was a favorite in
England for nearly a thousand years. In the later Middle Ages,
Robin was even more popular than Robert; so Chaucer's choice
here is that of a common name to fit a common man.

It is the Miller who first calls the Reeve by his name: "Leve
brother Osewold" (I, 3151). The narrator repeats the name twice,
once immediately following the Miller's Tale (I, 3860) and again
in relating the Reeve's words, "'Now sires,' quod this Osewold the

[3] Robinson, pp. 668 and 689.

[4] Walter W. Skeat, ed., *The Complete Works of Geoffrey Chaucer* (Oxford, 1894–1897), V, 244.

[5] John Matthew Manly, ed., *Canterbury Tales by Geoffrey Chaucer* (New York, 1928), p. 635.

Reve" (I, 3909). Oswald probably never has been a very popular name, and it seems to have had but little currency around London during Chaucer's lifetime. Moreover, it is not found in the Norfolk records of the fourteenth century; but it was more common farther north, where undoubtedly St. Oswald (c. 605–642), King of Northumbria, and St. Oswald (d. 992), Archbishop of York, helped to popularize it. The Reeve Oswald has traces of northern dialect in his speech not inappropriate to his place of origin in Norfolk, and it can be added that his northern name goes fittingly with his northern speech.

The wife of Bath is well known by her name Alice, which she reveals in her Prologue, when she quotes what she would have one of her husbands say to her, "I knowe yow for a trewe wyf, dame Alys" (III, 320). However, after Jankin has floored her, he calls her "Deere suster Alisoun," a nickname of endearment (III, 804). Alice was very popular in the later Middle Ages in England; and because of its numerous appearances in the fourteenth-century records of Bath, Manly saw Chaucer's giving it to the Wife of Bath as perhaps of no particular significance.[6] Once again we see Chaucer's using a common but popular name for a plain person.

Most of us tend to think of Chaucer himself as going on the pilgrimage and relating all that he saw and heard, and it is perhaps with conscious effort that we remind ourselves that the first-person narrator is the narrator, the *persona*, and not necessarily Chaucer the man and the poet. The humor in the *Canterbury Tales* rises to one of its highest points when the Host calls upon Chaucer for a tale, for we think of Chaucer himself then as well as the pilgrim and the *persona*. However, Chaucer does not name himself anywhere in the work. Harry Bailey speaks to him bluntly, as if he did not know him and had scarcely been aware of his presence before: "What man artow?" (VII, 695). After addressing him with a contraction of *thou*, the pronoun used with inferiors and sometimes with equals, the Host does not again extend his courtesy in using either *thou* or *ye* in speaking to him. But when he can no longer stand the tale of Sir Thopas, he softens his interruption with thou: "Namoore of this, ... for thou makest me So wery ..." (VII, 909–911). He apparently does not know Chaucer's name even though the poet had come to the Tabard Inn alone before the crowd of pilgrims ar-

---

[6] Manly, p. 527

rived. Nor are the pilgrims aware of his identity, in spite of his
having spoken to every one of them at the inn. The Man of Law
makes it evident that he does not know that Chaucer is present when
he refers to Chaucer and his poetry in the introduction to his tale.
The very ambiguity with which Chaucer presents himself and relates his part in the pilgrimage only tends to increase the humor
and irony of the narrative. But the scribes were meticulous to inform us of Chaucer's presence when they wrote such headings as
"Bihoold the murye wordes of the Hoost to Chaucer" and "Heere
bigynneth Chaucers Tale of Thopas" (p. 164). On the other hand,
the "Retractions" are headed with a reference to "the makere of
this book," while Chaucer's name appears below in the colophon:
"Heere is ended the book of the tales of Caunterbury, compiled by
Geffrey Chaucer" (p. 265).

Most of us today think and speak of the various pilgrims not by
their names but by their generic titles: the Knight, the Squire, the
Yeoman, and so on. And Chaucer the narrator also generally uses
the generic designations: "the Knyght" (I, 845), "The Cook of
Londoun" (I, 4325), "This dronke Millere" (I, 3150), "This worthy
clerk" (IV, 21). The Host almost always addresses the pilgrims by
their generic titles; but he often shows courtesy in such forms as
"Sire Knyght" (I, 837) and "my lady Prioresse" (I, 839). On all
occasions the Wife of Bath is addressed as "dame" (III, 164, 184,
830, 853, and 1270). But with no intention of discourtesy the Host
refers to her as "the woman" (III 851); and the narrator speaks
of her as "the wyf" (III 1269). In speaking to pilgrims he considers
not his superiors Harry Bailey can be blunt and direct in addressing
them: "Marchaunt" (IV, 1240), "Squier" (V, 1), and "Frankeleyn"
(V, 696). In inviting the Monk to tell a tale, he courteously addresses him as "My lord, the Monk" (VII, 1924); but after the
Knight's interruption, he rudely refers to "this Monk" (VII,2781).
However, this is immediately softened by addressing him as "Sire
Monk" (VII, 2788). The Knight sooths the tempers of the Pardoner
and the Host by addressing them by the overly polite terms "Sire
Pardoner" and "sire Hoost" (VI, 963 and 964). So we see the way
in which the generic titles lend themselves to a great variety of
distinctions.

While we are impressed by the names that Chaucer gave to
selected pilgrims, we are even more greatly impressed by his lack

of concern for taking advantage of numerous opportunities in which the use of names would be natural and realistic. For example, in the quarrels that spring up between the Miller and the Reeve, the Friar and the Summoner, and the Pardoner and the Host, the use of names would seem to be very natural; but names play a very minor part in the quarrels, if they appear at all. The Cook's name is given in the prologue to his fragmentary tale, but it is not used later where it would naturally be expected when the Cook is too drunk to keep his seat on his horse. Since Chaucer usually did not use the pilgrim's names and since he used most of the names given only once, it is clear that he considered naming the pilgrims of but little importance in his overall plan.

Thus, we see that his naming the Host and eight of the Canterbury pilgrims follows no pattern and has but little intrinsic significance. Names appear only infrequently and often only incidentally, while generic titles prevail and are used generally by both the narrator and the pilgrims themselves. Without depending upon names, the pilgrims make perfectly clear their relations with each other through their use of generic terms with appropriate modifiers.

The derivations of the pilgrims' names appear to have no particular significance, and they have not been considered here. However in the names of characters in some of the tales there are interesting echoes of names of a few of the pilgrims. The Host addresses the Monk as "Daun John" and the Nun's Priest as "Sir John" after the Shipman has told his tale about the monk Daun John, but the Monk's and Nun's Priest's prologues are so widely separated from the Shipman's Tale that any carry-over in the names must be remote. The boy who is the servant of the carpenter in the Miller's Tale is named Robin (I, 3466, 3555), which is the Miller's name. Alison in the Miller's Tale may be very much what the Wife of Bath was in her youth, but Chaucer makes nothing of using the same name for the two women. In addition, it is curious, as Professor Manly noted many years ago, that the "gossip" of the Wife of Bath is also called Alice and Alison (III, 530, 548).[7] Since there seems to be no immediate accounting for the repetition of these names, we may presume that most likely they only represent the frequent use of popular names.

---

[7] Manly, p. 579.

In the end we may say that Chaucer was not particularly concerned about giving names to the pilgrims. They were ordinary people representing a cross-section of society, and most of the few that are named are given plain names well suited to the plain people who are primarily representatives of their class and who are individuals only secondarily.

Bucknell University

Coca-Cola: The Most-Lawed Name

PETER TAMONY

A S HE STANDS IN THE STREETS of Atlanta, Georgia, U.S.A., the chief executive of the Coca-Cola Company may say with Alexander, the Romans, and rulers of Spain, Holland, and Britain that the sun never sets on his empire – modern, twentieth century style. For the 1967 Report of his organization shows its drink downed 95 million times a day in 138 countries, and that for the first times sales exceeded one billion dollars.

The basis of this productive structure was formulated in 1886 when John S. Pemberton, a Confederate veteran who had struggled through Reconstruction as a retail druggist, patent-medicine wholesaler, and vendor of a non-alcoholic drink, worked on yet another potable. During testing, after infusion of soda, at Willis Venable's fountain in Jacob's drug store at Five Points, comments and suggestions of patrons were considered, the consensus result being scripted Coca-Cola by F. M. Robinson, a penman-bookkeeper, who had been told the drink's taste was based in coca leaves and the kola nut.

Coca-Cola was first bottled by Joseph A. Biedenharn at Vicksburg in 1894. In 1899 Asa Chandler, who had bought the formula and business from Pemberton in 1888, gave two Chattanoogans, Ben Thomas and Joe Whitehead, a franchise in perpetuity for bottling the drink in most of the United States outside New England. Able merchandising and advertising, just after the turn of the century, stimulated national consumption of the beverage. Such fanfare and commercial success added myth and fantasy to the actual ingredients of the drink to the extent it early became a focus of controversy and remains so to food faddists and agitators to this day.

The alkaloid *cocaine* was first separated from the leaves of the shrub *Erythroxylon coca* by Wohler in 1860. For a decade or so it was considered a wonder stimulant and anesthetic, especially in England, where Arthur Conan Doyle, before he got wise, allowed

Sherlock Holmes cocaine as a pick-me-up after a hard day's sleuthing. In the U.S. the use of cocaine appears to have been widespread in the South. By 1886, however, the drug was proclaimed "the worst slavery known," and advertisements of safe cures appeared in the press. Traditionally, an important article of commerce throughout Central Africa was the cola, kola or goora nut (*Cola acuminata* [Sterculiaceae]). From trees native to tropical Africa, numerous varieties of these nuts were used as stimulant condiments, all containing varying percentages of caffeine.

Such are the names in which the alliterative Coca-Cola is based. Whatever may have been the original formula of the drink, i.e., utilization of the decocainized leaf – the refuse product discarded in the manufacture of cocaine – and the cola nut for flavoring and stimulation, these seem to have been eliminated in the first decade of this century. Harvey W. Wiley, who was honored in 1956 by a U.S. postage stamp, in *Beverages and Their Adulteration* (1909), writes that the government, after seizing 40 barrels and 20 kegs of Coca-Cola, alleged that the merchandise as advertised by the company was misbranded in that it did not contain any coca or cola, and further that it was adulterated in that it did contain an added ingredient, caffeine, which was deleterious to health. After the usual legal hassel to the U.S. Supreme Court, the case was dismissed without prejudice, the company agreeing that its product would not be sold contrary to the provisions of the Federal Food and Drug Act, et cetera.

This was the decade during which the Pure Food and Drug Laws were being crusaded, Upton Sinclair's *The Jungle* (1906) and the writings of the muckrakers then characterizing American print. Wiley notes that the Report of the President's Homes Commission, appointed by Theodore Roosevelt, issued in 1908, listed about 50 beverages labeled with the words, *coca cola, cola, coke, koke,* and *ola,* in combinations, including *Loco Kola.*

It was to stem the flood of such imitations of its name, label and product, and to preserve its lucrative business, that the Coca-Cola Company went to law. The first of a 55 year series of suits, according to John J. Riley, appears to have been filed in 1912. This was against the Gay-Ola Co. of Memphis, Tennessee (200 Fed. 720; 119, C.C.A. 164). Gay-Ola was not among the brand names listed in the 1908 Report. Nor does this suit appear to have stemmed a rising tide of imitations. In January of 1916 five new cola drinks were named, the *National Bottlers' Gazette* appearing to endorse the concept that infusion of "and" between the words coca and cola could describe another's beverage without infringing the nationally known trademark.

Prior to passage of the Harrison Narcotics Law of 1914 many standard home remedies were liberally dashed with derivatives of opium, cocaine, et cetera, *hop joint* being a Southern allusion to a drug store. Among nineteenth-century assertions, Coca-Cola's first label claimed it "a valuable brain tonic and a cure for nervous afflictions – sick headache, neuralgia, hysteria, melancholy. . . ." Service at soda fountains, a usual appendage of drug stores around the turn of the century, and word association with *cocaine*, engendered *dope* as a nickname of Coca-Cola. A variant was *cold dope*, while *shot*, or *shot of dope*, was employed, *tonic* being colloquial in New England. *Coke* is recorded in *A Dictionary of Americanisms* (1951), the first example of usage cited being from the *Coca-Cola Bottler* (Phila.), November 17, 1909. Priorly, the brand names *Cola Coke* and *Koke Ola* were listed in the 1908 Report of President Roosevelt's Commission. An impressive decision won by Coca-Cola was that against the Koke Company, terminated in 1920. In the finale, Justice Oliver Wendell Holmes held that *Koke* was an infringement on Coca-Cola's nickname, and described the plaintiff's beverage as "a single thing coming from a single source and well known in the community." J. H. Spingarn, writing in *The Nation* (June 7, 1941), notes that 143 beverages registered with the U.S. Patent Office used *cola* as an identity-form, and that the Coca-Cola Company had been filing a lawsuit a week for over 30 years to protect its trademark, nickname, et cetera. On the whole, such suits seem to have been calendared to sustain the image of Coca-Cola power, and to discourage small, granite-utensil mixologists. Such woodshed and basement entrepreneurs dotted towns and cities, supplying local saloons with sarsaparillas and carbonated mixtures for boozes prior to Prohibition, being wiped out in the 15-year eclipse of the poor man's club, by local sanitary and building codes, and costs of distribution. Further to terrorize competitors and their counsel, Coca-Cola's long-tentacled legal forces had Justice Holmes' pronunciamento buckrammed along with 700 pages of comparable decisions and injunctions for distribution to law libraries and attorneys.

Such formidable authority, however, did not deter Charles G. Guth of New York, who was what Wall Street today would term a wheeler-dealer. As president of Loft, Inc., a chain of soda fountains and confectionaries, Guth thought he was entitled to a jobber's discount from Coca-Cola. In the tangle over refusal of this concession, Guth bought in bankruptcy proceedings, common during the Depression, the brand name and formula of Pepsi-Cola, an 1890's label listed in the 1908 Report of President Roosevelt's Commission. On losing a proxy battle in 1935, Guth pulled out of Loft, taking the Pepsi-Cola "property." In the court battle that ensued, a Chancery decree in Delaware awarded Guth most of the stock of the Pepsi-Cola Corporation.

Pepsi-Cola became involved in the plethora of lawsuits generated by Coca-Cola to protect its business – charges of imitation of color, labeling a product *cola*, scripting the name of a competitive drink, service of other than Coca-Cola when a patron asked for a Coke, et cetera, such matters constituting deliberate and fraudulent attempts to appropriate its good-will, custom, and what-not. Pepsi-Cola filed countersuits to restrain Coca-Cola from instituting harassing litigation, charging Coca-Cola had over the years attempted to exhaust the resources of competitors by nuisance lawing, and had thus bulldogged a monopoly by rushing to law. An example: to prosecute a suit in the Federal courts against a careless soda-jerk who had served another brand when asked for a Coke, Coca-Cola flew to San Francisco 18 executives and attorneys, including two representatives of Steve Hannigan's flash-fire public relations brigade. This had to be the world's-record-champion higher-ups air-hegira to December, 1940.

Finally, Pepsi-Cola, well heeled, took the offensive in the battle of the colas, filing registration of its trademark in Canada. In the legalese common to special pleaders, Coca-Cola had claimed the word *cola* was descriptive only of a nut which was unknown to the general public at the time its trademark was adopted, that it denominated a minor, unimportant constituent of the drink, and thus had no meaning in the beverage field except as part of its registered trademark. And that if cola did have another meaning it was because of the efforts of Coca-Cola, and the widespread advertisement of its trademark. Pepsi-Cola countered that no one could preempt usage of an English word, even if it had become common and current to describe a whole class of drinks. Considering, no doubt, the authority of a pillar of empire, *Oxford English Dictionary*, which records a 1795 example of usage in an *Account of Sierra Leone*, "Cola is a famous fruit, highly esteemed by the natives, to which they attribute the same virtues as to Peruvian bark," the Supreme Court of Canada declared the word *cola* a generic and descriptive term, which, as part of the common tongue, was open to anyone who wished to employ it as part of a trademark to indicate a type of beverage. On March 19, 1942 the Judicial Committee of the Privy Council, highest tribunal of the Empire, upheld the Canadian decision. Coincidentally, the very next day the Chancery Court of Delaware recorded a comparable decision in a suit involving the Nehi Corporation.

In April of 1942 Nehi took full-page magazine and newspaper space to tell the world "Court Decides in Favor of Royal Crown Cola." On June 8, 1942, *Newsweek* newsed a "Cola Armistice," recording that Coca-Cola and Pepsi-Cola, as a result of the London decision, had agreed to drop two suits in the U.S., and one or more in each of nearly 40 other countries.

Coca-Cola, however, retained its adjudicated right to the verbalism *Coke*. Perhaps forseeing the handwriting of the Canadian justices, it appears to have decided in 1941 to use the colloquial form of its name in its advertising. On the back cover of the *Saturday Evening Post* for January 10, 1942 an apple-cheeked pageboy with a bottle-top cap, wide-eyed, blazons, "Hello ... I'm 'Coca-Cola' known, too, as 'Coke'." A paragraph, headed "P.S.," succinctly outlines the word-clipping function of the American mind in its production of the caressive Coke, "the friendly abbreviation for the trade-mark 'Coca-Cola'." As our Armed Forces spread over the whole of the landed world during World War II, other peoples okayed the drink and the word as they became familiar with a second American universal, *okay*.

Since 1942 the principal activity of the legal arm seems to be protection of the vocalism, "Coke." If the word is enunciated in an order, only Coca-Cola must be served. Apparently, a vendor, if he is one of the many old timers who will not sell Coca-Cola because of alleged aid to the Prohibitionists, must tell a customer he does not purvey Coke, and must get consent to a substitution. In an action entered in the U.S. District Court at San Francisco on October 16,

1967, the defendant was "perpetually enjoined and restrained" in a consent decree in less than a month "from selling and supplying on calls for 'Coca-Cola' or 'Coke' any product other than the plaintiffs. . . ."

As he touches his lips to the patented bottle (1915) for the "pause that refreshes" (1929) the Americano amazes the world. His mouth must ever be in action, smoking and chewing making a trilogy as the pause that refreshes becomes the pause that enriches Coca-Cola and all its competitors, plus the American Tobacco Company and Wrigley.

SOURCES

Federal Digest, Vol. 61A, *Trade Marks and Trade Names and Unfair Competition.*
    Coca-Cola; page of actions, 484 (St. Paul, Minn.: West Publishing Co., 1953).
Fortune, December, 1938, pp. 64—67.
Life, June 23, 1952, p. 79.
Riley, John J. *History of the American Soft Drink Industry, 1807—1957* (Washington, D.C.: American Bottlers of Carbonated Beverages, 1958), p. 234.
San Francisco Examiner, December 22, 1940, p. 4/2.
Scarborough, Dorothy. *On the Trail of Negro Folk Songs* (Cambridge: Harvard University Press, 1925), pp. 89—90: "The Hop Joint."
Shepard's Federal Reporter Citations. Fifth Edition, Supplement 1953—1965. Coca-Cola: one hundred forty actions (Colorado Springs, Colo., 1965).
Spingarn, J. H. "Of Coca, Cola, and the Courts." *Nation*, Vol. 152 (June 7, 1941), pp. 666—668.
Time, April 27, 1942, p. 41 (adv't, Nehi-Royal Crown Cola).
— — May 15, 1950, pp. 28—32 (cover article).
Wharton, Don. "Coca-Cola: Its Fame and Fortune." *Reader's Digest*, June, 1947, pp. 33—37.
Wiley, H. W. *Beverages and Their Adulteration* (Philadelphia: Blakiston, 1919), pp. 109—114; 405—408.
Also:
    U.S. District Court for the Northern District of California, San Francisco: The Coca-Cola Company vs. Red Chimney, Inc., etc., Civil Action No. 48041, filed October 16, 1967. Plaintiff relies on trade-mark registrations: 22,046 issued January 31, 1893; 47,189, October 31, 1905; 238, 145 and 238,146, January 31, 1928, "Coca-Cola"; and 415,755, August 14, 1945, covering the trade-mark "Coke": all incontestible pursuant to the Lanham Trade-Mark Act.

    General information: Coca-Cola is indexed in *Reader's Guide to Periodical Literature* (New York: Wilson), and *New York Times Index*. E. J. Kahn's *The Big Drink, An Unofficial History of Coca-Cola* (1960: New York, Random House), lacks an Index. Nor have I referred to *Big Beverage*, W. I. Campbell (1952: Atlanta, Tupper and Love), a novel, reviewed in *New York Herald Tribune Book Review*, November 9, 1952, 14.

Shakespeare's "Nell"

LARRY S. CHAMPION

IN THE THREE PLAYS depicting the reigns of Henry IV and Henry V, Shakespeare sets before his audience "the hostess of the tavern at Eastcheape," a character whose growth in name – from simply "the hostess" to "Mistress Quickly" and finally to "Mistress Nell Quickly" – parallels a significant development in her delineation as a comic character.[1] The most striking feature of this development is the consistent pattern of events through which she is degraded and through which she is left little more than a common prostitute who dies of the "malady of France." As Shakespeare in *Henry V* sketched her character with more vivid comic pejoration, he evidently chose to dub her Nell because the name connoted to his audience a loose woman, a wench, or a strumpet.

Evidence concerning *Nell* and the other variants of *Helen*, though scant, is significant. While there is no entry under *Nell* in Edward Lyford's *The True Interpretation of Christian Names*, published in London in 1655, *Eleanor* is defined as "pitifull from the Greek." As for the reputation of Helen in popular usage, Charlotte M. Yonge, in *The History of Christian Names* (London, 1884), states that, although the name remained popular as a result of the proverbial beauty of Helen of Troy, the name also connoted "any amount of evil or misfortune."[2] More recently, E. G. Withycombe in *The Oxford English Dictionary of English Christian Names* (Oxford, 1947), after explaining *Nell* as "a pet form of *Ellen, Eleanor, and Helen,*" asserts without explanation or description that the name "gradually fell out of upper-class use" (p. 105). Significant also is the connotation of the name so consistently suggested in the literature of the period. John Skelton's "bowsy-faced" brewer and

---

[1] See my article "The Evolution of Mistress Quickly," *Papers on English Language and Literature,* I (Spring, 1965), 99–108.

[2] p. 68. Miss Yonge further suggests that the reputation of Queen Eleanor of Acquitaine and also the legend of Elaine and her illicit pleasures with Launcelot contributed to the pejoration of the name.

barkeeper in "The Tunning of Elinour Rumming"; John Rastell's "Little Nell, a proper wench who danceth well," and with whom Humanity is told by Sensuality to eat, drink, and be merry in *The Nature of the Four Elements*; Francis Beaumont's naive and bumbling Nell, the Grocer's wife, in *The Knight of the Burning Pestle*; the almost random examples in Renaissance literature which reflect the tradition of Helen as "the supreme pagan incarnation of lust" [3] – such instances point to a similar character type and suggest more than one is able to explain as mere coincidence.

Certainly the most convincing evidence comes from Shakespeare, who – in the six dramas in which the name occurs – uses *Nell* consistently to describe a woman of questionable reputation, frequently of the lower class. In *The Comedy of Errors* (III, ii) Nell is "a kitchen wench and all grease" who mistakenly lays claim to Dromio of Syracuse. In *2 Henry IV* the name on three occasions connotes a woman of low social status and of less than desirable reputation. In a letter read comically in Poins' presence (II, iii), Falstaff – obviously envious of Ned's close friendship with his own "Sweet Hal" – warns the Prince to "be not too familiar with Poins; for he misuses thy favours so much that he swears thou art to marry his sister Nell." In a later use of the name (III, ii), Cousin Silence tells Justice Shallow that his daughter Ellen is "a black ousel." In the final act, Pistol, in reporting to Falstaff that Doll Tearsheet and Mistress Quickly have been imprisoned, uses Helen as a synonym for mistress or prostitute: "Thy Doll, and Helen of thy noble thoughts, is in base durance and contagious prison" (11. 35–36). In *Romeo and Juliet* (I, v) Nell is the name of a serving-woman hotly called for to help prepare the Capulets' house for the fateful ball. In *2 Henry VI* Eleanor, the Duchess of Gloucester, "second woman in the realm," is a vicious social climber whose aspirations for her husband involve the throne of Henry VI. Gloucester, forced later to expose her machinations, speaks of "Sweet Nell's" "hammering treachery" which casts her "from top of honour to disgrace's feet" (I, iii). On two occasions in *Troilus*

---

[3] A glance through either Douglas Bush, *Mythology and the Renaissance Tradition in English Poetry* (Minneapolis, 1932), or Dewitt Starnes and E. W. Talbert, *Classical Myth and Legend in Renaissance Dictionaries* (Chapel Hill, 1955), will reveal the remarkable frequency of the allusion to Helen as the epitome of the disreputable woman.

and Cressida Paris dubs his famous paramour "my Nell"; he "would fain have arm'd today, but my Nell would not have it so" (III, i, 150; see also 1. 50). Diomed later brands her "bawdy veins" and "contaminated carrion" (IV, i, 69, 71); Ulysses scornfully remarks that Helen can never "be a maid again" (IV, v,50); and Thersites taunts Ajax with the remark that he has not enough brains "as will stop the eye of Helen's needle" (II, i, 87).

It is the evolving character of the hostess, however, which most clearly suggests Shakespeare's connotational intentions for the name *Nell*. Arthur Acheson states flatly that two characters are involved: "In *Henry IV Part I*, the hostess of the tavern is referred to as a young and beautiful person . . . In *Part II*, she is represented as Mistress Quickly, an old, unattractive, and garrulous widow."[4] While such an assertion is an exaggeration, it does bespeak the qualitative difference between the amorphously sketched hostess of *Part I*, married and reasonably respectable, and Mistress Quickly of *Part II* and *Henry V*, a widow with aspirations for Falstaff but who is willing to settle for Pistol, who vaunts the respectability of her tavern while playing the common procuress for Falstaff and Doll Tearsheet, and who – made the comic butt of various slurs upon her sexual activities – becomes extremely defensive about the purity of her own character, though she subsequently dies "i' the spital of malady of France." In *1 Henry IV* (III, iii) there are numerous references to her honest husband and to the respectability of their inn. In *2 Henry IV*, Falstaff's branding her a "quean" (II, i, 51) and the pun on quick-lie boisterously signal the pejoration in her character as Mistress Quickly.[5] She now claims to be a "poor widow of Eastcheape" and asserts that Falstaff, whom she has known for twenty-nine years and "who has practised upon the easy-yielding spirit of this woman," has promised to marry her. The circle of acquaintances has widened to include the prostitute Doll Tearsheet, and together they entertain Falstaff before he sets

---

[4] *Shakespeare's Lost Years in London, 1586–1592* (New York, 1920), p. 203. He explains the single mention of the name *Quickly* in Part I (III, iii, 88) as a later interpolation during revision.

[5] There are no spelling variants of "Quickly" in the quarto and folio texts to clarify such a pun in *2 Henry IV* and *Henry V*. Helge Kökeritz points out, however, that the "y" ending in Shakespeare frequently is rhymed with "eye" and that such practices "would make a pun like *Quickly — lie* almost unavoidable" (*Shakespeare's Pronunciation* [New Haven, 1953], p. 220).

out for Gloucestershire In V, v, she is carried off to prison with
Doll, vaguely on the charge that the brothels are being torn down
with the advent of the new king, specifically on the charge that
"the man is dead that you and Pistol beat amongst you." In
Henry V "Nell" Quickly has married Pistol, although in doing so
she has been false to Nym, who was trothplight to her – a marriage
in itself curious since Dame Quickly in *2 Henry IV* could not abide
the sight of Pistol and implored Falstaff to drive him from her inn.
While the social gain to have been realized as the wife of Sir John
Falstaff is humorously suspect, there can be no question that Pistol
is indeed a comedown for this woman. And, of course, Nell reaches
the nadir of her social fortunes in the report of her death – in the
hospital of venereal disease. The Mistress Quickly of *The Merry
Wives of Windsor*, who by intrigue manipulates affairs to her own
profit, is of no central concern to us here because Shakespeare never
uses the name *Nell* in the comedy. This evidence does suggest,
however, either that Shakespeare wrote *The Merry Wives* between
2 Henry IV and *Henry V*, that is, before Mistress Quickly became
known as Nell Quickly, or that he specifically avoided the name
Nell in *The Merry Wives* because of the intended difference in
characterization in the comedy.

The question, then, is obvious: did Shakespeare, as he determined the development of the character of the hostess throughout
these plays, choose the name *Nell* by sheer coincidence or by conscious design? The evidence appears to lead in a single direction.
The classical traditions reflected in the literature of the period, the
numerous instances from Shakespeare's contemporaries, and above
all the remarkable consistency of character delineation by Shakespeare for which he used the names *Nell*, *Ellen*, and, to some degree,
Helen suggest that the dramatist was quite cognizant of the psychology of the name and its associated meanings.

And, if one may assume that the name *Nell* implied a woman of
easy virtue, as Doll demonstrably did in Shakespeare's day, it is
unlikely that either Shakespeare or the printer has erred in having
Pistol report in *Henry V* (V, i, 86–87): "News have I my Doll is
dead i' the spital of malady of France." Likewise unnecessary is the
silent editorial emendation to Nell which has been practiced since
Johnson's edition in 1765. The probability is that the dramatist
used *Doll* (italicized in the folio text) metaphorically for *Nell* in

clear reference to the similar associated meaning and that he punned on the ladies' names even as he reported Nell's death from the disease which all too clearly signaled the extent of her social and moral decline. Such an assumption has the virtue of being at least equally as plausible as J. Dover Wilson's assertion that Falstaff was in *Henry V* as it was originally written, that he had to be written out of the work when Kemp departed from the Lord Chamberlain's Company, and that Pistol's remark (originally to have been Falstaff's allusion to his wench Doll Tearsheet) is a vestigial remnant of the older play which Shakespeare failed to alter.[6]

North Carolina State University

---

[6] See the New Cambridge edition of *Henry V* (1947), pp. 113–116.

Humours Characters and Attributive Names in Shakespeare's Plays

WILLIAM GREEN

SHAKESPEARE'S INTEREST IN NAMES as more than tags for distinguishing one character from another manifested itself early in his career. In general, he carried over names from his source works, or when altering such names or adding characters with new ones, chose his invented names on grounds of propriety for poetic utterance, or of mood, or of national origin. There are, however, a number of names throughout the canon which have figurative overtones. One such group clusters around personality traits or around the character's occupation. English has no one technical term for describing this type of nomenclature. Label names, charactonyms, or attributive names are some that have been used.[1] The device, of course, belongs to a very old literary tradition.

Early English drama abounds in examples. The morality plays or works such as Bale's *King John* and Udall's *Ralph Roister Doister* well illustrate the technique. Yet Shakespeare's immediate predecessors – Lyly, Greene, Peele, Marlowe, and Kyd – showed little interest in such nomenclature. Shakespeare's fascination with the possibilities of attributive names, therefore, was partially a return to an older tradition. As he played the name game, Shakespeare did not limit himself to any one genre. The comedies, tragedies, and histories all contain characters whose appellations have been determined by their traits or occupations.

Two examples from early works will show how deliberate the technique is. In *2 Henry VI* there is a scene (II.iii) in which Peter, an armorer's apprentice, is to fight his master. It is a serious scene because Peter has accused the armorer of treason. In calling for the bout to begin, the Earl of Salisbury asks the apprentice, "Sirrah,/what's thy name?"

> *Peter* Peter, forsooth.
> *Sal.*   Peter! what more?
> *Peter* Thump.
> *Sal.*   Thump! Then see thou thump thy master well.

---

[1] G. Wilson Knight prefers *label names*. See his "What's in a Name?" *The Sovereign Flower* (New York: Macmillan, 1958), pp. 170–172. Harry Levin employs the term *charactonyms*. See his "Shakespeare's Nomenclature," *Essays on Shakespeare*, ed. Gerald W. Chapman (Princeton: Princeton University Press, 1965), p. 64.

It is not the play on words alone which is significant here, but the origin of Peter's last name, taken from a necessary activity in making armor. Shakespeare underscores this by having Peter refer to his hammer in the speech preceding the above-quoted question of Salisbury.

In *Love's Labour's Lost*, a comedy of approximately the same period, the comic characters have a scene (V.i) in which they plan their presentation of the Nine Worthies. At the conclusion of their pseudo-learned discussion of who will play whom, Holofernes, the schoolmaster, addresses the constable whose name is Dull: "*Via*, goodman Dull! thou hast spoken no word all this while." Dull replies, "Nor understand none neither, sir." They interchange additional remarks in this vein. Then Holofernes tops off the conversation with the comment, "Most dull, honest Dull." There is nothing particularly brilliant in these two examples; Shakespeare is playing with words and does so using minor characters in minor episodes. Yet the trend to the employment of charactonyms is established.

Shakespeare usually reserved the device for characters of his own creation rather than for those retained from his source works. With brand new characters not only did he know precisely why he was adding them to his story line, but also how the name designation could aid in achieving the effect he was after. With few exceptions, he restricted attributive names to the lower class characters. This applies both to those who have speaking roles and those who are only alluded to such as Master Smooth, the silkman, and Jane Nightwork (whose calling is obvious) in *2 Henry IV* or to Jane Smile in *As You Like It*. Such appellations, moreover, appear almost exclusively in the comedies and in the comic scenes of two history plays – *2 Henry IV* and *Henry V*.

Within drama, comedy offers the most potential and freedom for working with attributive names. History is bound by its very subject matter. Tragedy does not offer much scope because the characters, particularly the leading characters, have to be treated as complex individuals. A charactonym tends to reduce the many facets of a character's personality which the playwright wishes to explore. It may also destroy individuality. The same holds true in general for the upper class characters of Shakespeare's comedies. For brushstroke techniques, however, and for quickly limning a character whose function in the script is limited, the charactonym has great flexibility. And there is one form of comedy that it becomes particularly suited to: humours comedy.

Humours comedy has its origin in medieval medical theory in which the body was thought to contain four fluids which controlled man's behaviour: blood, phlegm, yellow bile, and black bile. In proper proportion these fluids produced a well-balanced individual; an excess of one could cause a distortion of personality.

By the 1560's the strictly medical conception had begun to break down, with a broader psychological definition replacing it. The term *humour* was extended to eccentricities of character, even to a whim or a caprice. It was taken into literature in this sense, and by 1592 writers were placing the actual word in their works to express any number of aberrations in personality.[2] Just about this time the word begins to appear with some frequency in the dialogue in Shakespeare's plays. These early plays, the first of two groups in which frequency count reveals a sensitivity to this new "in" word,[3] do not show a corresponding use of attributive character names or of humours-style characterizations. In other words, so far as our subject is concerned, in the period 1590–1594 Shakespeare was working on two different tracks. The link up between attributive nomenclature and humours terminology or characterization remained to be made.

[2] For an account of the humours movement in English literature, see Charles Read Baskervill, "English Elements in Jonson's Early Comedy," *Bulletin of the University of Texas* (1911), pp. 34–75; Benjamin Boyce, *The Theophrastan Character in England to 1642* (Cambridge, Mass.: Harvard University Press, 1947); Percy Simpson, ed., *Ben Jonson's Every Man in his Humour* (Oxford: Oxford University Press, 1919), pp. xxxvi–lxiv.

[3] The count for the following chart has been taken from Marvin Spevack, *A Complete and Systematic Concordance to the Works of Shakespeare* (Hildesheim: Georg Olms Verlagsbuchhandlung, 1968–1970), 6 vols. The variant forms of *humour* — *humoured, humorous, humors,* and *humour letter* — have been included in the total figures.

Periods	Plays	Frequency
I	*The Comedy of Errors*	6
(1590—1594)	*Love's Labour's Lost*	9
	The Taming of the Shrew	7
	The Two Gentlemen of Verona	0
	1 Henry VI	0
	2 Henry VI	3
	3 Henry VI	0
	Richard III	5
	Titus Andronicus	4
II	*A Midsummer Night's Dream*	1
(1594—1600)	*The Merchant of Venice*	2
	The Merry Wives of Windsor	25
	Much Ado About Nothing	7
	As You Like It	8
	Twelfth Night	3
	Richard II	2
	King John	5
	1 Henry IV	8
	2 Henry IV	7
	Henry V	13
	Romeo and Juliet	5
	Julius Caesar	9

In 1596, the new fashion for humours-type characterizations – in which interest had further been fanned through Casaubon's translations of some of Theophrastus' character sketches back in 1592 – spread to the drama through the work of George Chapman. His *The Blind Beggar of Alexandria* appeared in February, 1596, followed a year later by *An Humorous Day's Mirth*.[4] The success of *The Blind Beggar of Alexandria* – it established a performance record for the Lord Admiral's Men in the period 1594–1597 – probably prompted Shakespeare to try his hand at incorporating the new humours techniques into his plays. He first attempts humours portrayals in *2 Henry IV*. I believe he was working on this play in early 1597 and put it aside to turn out *The Merry Wives of Windsor* that same spring in answer to a special command of Queen Elizabeth.[5] His work, *2 Henry IV*, is a history play. Yet on its fringes appear characters possessing traits commonly assigned to humours types. The very label applied to Falstaff and his cronies in the *dramatis personae* of the Folio text shows the playwright's interest in the new fad. Here Falstaff and company are called "Irregular Humorists." Actually, there is only one real humours character among them – Pistol, the braggart. And his name pinpoints his eccentricity of character. In the words of Oscar J. Campbell, Pistol "shoots

Periods	Plays	Frequency
III	*Troilus and Cressida*	3
(1600—1608)	*All's Well That Ends Well*	0
	Measure for Measure	0
	Pericles	0
	Hamlet	1
	Othello	3
	King Lear	0
	Macbeth	0
	Timon of Athens	3
	Antony and Cleopatra	0
	Coriolanus	1
IV	*Cymbeline*	1
(1609—1613)	*The Winter's Tale*	1
	The Tempest	0
	Henry VIII	0

[4] In both these plays not only is there deliberate use of humours psychology in character delineation, but the word *humour* is freely bandied about in the dialogue. Yet in neither work does Chapman employ attributive names, with the possible exception of Lemot in *An Humorous Day's Mirth*. From his function in the play as a practical joker and manipulator of a series of love intrigues, Lemot must rely on words. Hence his name represents a combining of the French *le* and *mot*.

[5] See my *Shakespeare's Merry Wives of Windsor* (Princeton: Princeton University Press, 1962), Chap. IX.

off his store of verbal ammunition at the slightest provocation."[6] This
high-flown rant in "Cambyses vein" he preserves in both *The Merry
Wives of Windsor* and in *Henry V*.

Though not listed among the "irregular humorists," other humours
characters – regular humorists – appear in the play, and, significantly,
each bears an attributive name. We meet the empty-headed, old country
justice, Master Shallow and his taciturn compatriot, Justice Silence. And
what could be a better appellation for that piece of mutton who says of
herself that she is meat for Falstaff (II.iv.135) than Doll Tearsheet? Even
the minor characters of the comic scenes, although not completely developed as humours characters, bear attributive names. The recruits whom
Shallow has gathered for Falstaff are called Mouldy, Shadow, Wart,
Feeble, and Bullcalf. As Falstaff addresses each of them (III.ii), he man-
ages to make some remarks reflecting on their names. Earlier in the play
(II.i), the constables selected to arrest Falstaff are called, appropriately
enough, Master Fang and Master Snare. And then there are those characters who are merely alluded to, Master Smooth, the silkman and Jane
Nightwork.

In Shakespeare's use of attributive names, *2 Henry IV* stands as pivotal.
On the one hand it reflects his earlier interest in charactonyms in their
simplest form – mirroring a specific personality or occupation trait of a
character who has no significant role in the play. On the other, it shows
him combining the possibilities of humours characterization and character
appellation. *The Merry Wives of Windsor* shows greater sophistication in
these respects than does *2 Henry IV*. Several humours characters appear
in *The Merry Wives*. Three hold important roles in the plot: Master Ford,
Dr. Caius, and Master Slender. Ford's humour is jealousy. All Windsor
knows, as Mistress Quickly relates, that "he's a very jealousy man." Ford
even talks of it openly with others, and in private says of himself, "God
be praised for my jealousy" (II.ii.308). So intense is this emotion that
Ford becomes despicable enough to hire another man, Falstaff, to seduce
his wife. In this action Shakespeare exploits Ford's humour to increase
the complications of the main plot.

Dr. Caius and Slender appear in the subplot where they serve as the
second and third wooers, respectively, to Anne Page. They are basically
the two grotesques frequently found as suitors to the *amorosa* in Italian
comedy.[7] By casting them as humours figures, Shakespeare has skillfully
retained their grotesque function. Dr. Caius is portrayed as a choleric

---

[6] *Shakespeare's Satire* (London and New York: Oxford University Press, 1943), p. 74.
[7] Oscar James Campbell, "The Italianate Background of *The Merry Wives of Windsor*,"
Essays and Studies in English and Comparative Literature, University of Michigan Publications in Language and Literature, VIII (Ann Arbor: University of Michigan, 1932),
pp. 99–112, *passim*.

Frenchman.[8] It is his choleric nature that causes him to send the challenge to Parson Evans, thereby setting that subplot in motion. Slender is the country gull: no sooner does he arrive in town than he is robbed. He is completely passive in the suit to Anne Page, and cannot even woo her without his Book of Songs and Sonnets. As his name implies, he is slender, and "he hath but a little wee-face; with a little yellow beard." Slender of body and slender of mind is this country gull. From a psycho-medical point of view, just as Caius is constructed along the lines of a choleric individual, Slender follows the pattern of the phlegmatic. His stupidity, complexion, and yellow hair would instantly identify him to an Elizabethan audience as one with an excess of the phlegmatic humour.[9]

Slender is the only one of these three characters with an attributive name. One cannot second-guess Shakespeare here as to why he did not use the device with Ford and Caius. All the other humours characters in the play bear attributive names. They do, however, have decidedly minor roles. Two we have met before, Shallow and Pistol. Shallow is still the talkative, empty-headed country justice of *2 Henry IV*, and Pistol is the blusterer full of sound and fury. Simple, Slender's servant, though scarcely delineated, lives up to his name. While not a true humours character, Mistress Quickly cannot be overlooked as in line with her name she rapidly flits around town in her capacity as go-between.[10] The last to consider is Nym, who, as his name proclaims (it is from Middle English *nimen* "to take") is a rogue and filcher. And his overworked phrase "That's my humour" serves to clinch his generic origin.

The Merry Wives of Windsor becomes Shakespeare's first major contribution to the comedy of humours genre. And it clearly shows that in 1597 Shakespeare was experimenting with the permutations and combinations of charactonyms and humours delineation. In this, he was following in the footsteps of George Chapman, with Ben Jonson hard on his heels. Though Shakespeare was writing humours comedy before Jonson, it was Jonson who developed a scheme for this type of drama and built out of the genre a carefully constructed theory of characterization. His work could not have escaped Shakespeare's attention, for the Lord Chamberlain's Men (Shakespeare's company) produced Jonson's first humours comedy, *Every Man in His Humour*, in 1598. The following year they did *Every Man out of His Humour*.

---

[8] John L. Stender, "Master Doctor Caius," *Bulletin of the History of Medicine*, 8 (January 1940), 133–138.

[9] J. B. Bamborough, *The Little World of Man* (London and New York: Longmans, Green, 1952), p. 95.

[10] She bears the same name in the three *Henry* plays, but the connotative attribute of her name is most forcefully demonstrated in *The Merry Wives of Windsor*.

Shakespeare's interest in humours comedy in the years 1596–1601 is further demonstrated by the frequency with which he uses the word *humour* in his plays at this time. A count reveals that this is the second and last period of his career in which it appears significantly, especially in *The Merry Wives of Windsor* and *Henry V*.[11]

I suggest this close exposure to Jonson's work is responsible for the masterful linking of humours characterization and attributive names manifest in Shakespeare's last romantic comedies, *As You Like It*, dated around 1599–1600, and *Twelfth Night*, about 1600–1601. *As You Like It* has three characters with attributive names: Jaques, Touchstone, and Oliver Martext, the latter two not being humours figures. Martext is a slight character whose name reflects on him as a bumbling country priest. Touchstone, as a witty jester, occupies himself with a great deal of discourse on court and country life. In this sense he is little more than a commentator whose function is revealed in his name, for a touchstone is "that which serves to test or try the genuineness or value of anything" (*NED*).

But Jaques has a new dimension to him. He is a full-fledged humours character with an apt charactonym. Jaques is the malcontented traveler who can "suck melancholy out of a song, as a weasel sucks eggs." He exhibits all the symptoms described by Jonson in the prologue of *Every Man out of His Humour* of both the individual suffering from melancholia in the psycho-medical sense and the individual affecting a pose. In this blend he is the most complex humours character yet created by Shakespeare.[12] And with his constant railing and his disposition to shun company, he functions as the anti-love figure of the play. At the end he is the only one who will not be present at the weddings. In satirizing this satirist, Shakespeare has given him a most appropriate name. Unfortunately the passage of time has caused its meaning to be lost and its pronunciation changed. Jaques, as it was pronounced in Elizabethan English, puns on *jakes* "a privy." Students and many actors give it the French pronunciation [ʒɑːk] or make it disyllabic, which on occasion it is.

The punning is involved. It reflects on the character of this melancholy traveler through an allusion to Sir John Harington's pamphlet of 1596, *The Metamorphosis of Ajax*, which is about the introduction of the toilet. Harington himself is punning on the ancient warrior's name (a jakes) with ill-smelling intent. The name also links Jaques' melancholy humour with the privy in more scientific fashion. "Melancholy," notes J. B. Bam-

---

11 See chart, note 3.

12 See Oscar James Campbell, "Jaques," *Huntington Library Bulletin*, No. 8 (October, 1935), pp. 71–102; Z. S. Fink, "Jaques and the Malcontent Traveler," *Philological Quarterly*, 14 (1935), 237–252; E. E. Stoll, "Shakspere [*sic*], Marston and the Malcontent Type," *Modern Philology*, 3 (1905–1906), 281–303.

borough, "both caused dyspepsia and was caused by it. Ill-digested food bred corrupt humours, which by definition were kinds of melancholy; on the other hand the natural function of the melancholic humour in digestion, which was to assist the retention of the food, led in excess to constipation."[13] These connotations would have been instantaneously apparent to an Elizabethan audience.

What Shakespeare accomplished with one character in *As You Like It*, he extends to three in *Twelfth Night* – and in more artistic fashion. For not only are Sir Toby Belch, Sir Andrew Aguecheek, and Malvolio humours characters with perfectly matched attributive names, but unlike Jaques, they are also very much a part of the action line of the play. As humours characters, each has been constructed around a different psycho-medical humours trait while at the same time reflecting social affectation or eccentricity. And two of them are of the nobility.

Sir Toby Belch has the least subtle name of the three. In characterization, his affinity for wine – obviously reflected in his name – is not solely an eccentricity. He is in personality and physical makeup the sanguine individual.[14] His build, complexion, movements, even his voice match the stereotype of the sanguine man. Predominating in his personality are such traits as merriment, quickwittedness, and a fondness for eating and drinking.

Sir Andrew Aguecheek is the country gull, affecting the manners of a sophisticated courtier. In appearance and manner, he is the phlegmatic individual. Maria's description of him before he enters (I.iii) as a fool, a quarreller, and a coward sets the keynote instantly. Upon Andrew's entry, Toby calls attention to his long, blondish hair – a physical attribute of the phlegmatic. Phlegmatics were thought to have white, unhealthy skins; they also were supposedly susceptible to respiratory ailments.[15] While Andrew's health is not commented on in the play, Shakespeare, I believe, was drawing upon a stock portrait which an Elizabethan audience would have conjured up from his name, Aguecheek. Add his gullibility and cowardice and we get the typical phlegmatic of the day, a character well worth lampooning.

Malvolio too is a gull, but a more complex one. Maria aptly describes him as "an affectioned ass, that cons state without book and utters it by great swarths; the best persuaded of himself, so crammed, as he thinks with excellencies, that it is his grounds of faith that all that look on him love him" (II.iv.161–164). To his social affectation must be added his self-love. From a psycho-medical point of view, Malvolio is almost a text-book

---

13 Bamborough, *op. cit.*, p. 70.

14 *Ibid.*, p. 92.

15 *Ibid.*, pp. 94–95.

portrait of the choleric man. He has the physical as well as the mental characteristics associated with this humour. The traits can be summed up thus: "[I]n moderation choler made men bold, valiant, warlike, rash, ambitious and quarrelsome; in gross excess it produced violent, causeless rages, arrogance, envy, jealousy, suspiciousness, discontent, malice and revengefulness." [16] Indeed, these are the very traits we see Malvolio display before our eyes. What more appropriate appellation for this character, then, than Malvolio, ill-willed ? [17]

As noted, each of these characters is constructed around a different humour and labeled with a name that reflects it. To complete the quartet of humours, Shakespeare portrays Orsino as a melancholic duke. However, as was his custom, Shakespeare did not endow his upper class major character with a charactonym, [18] even though Orsino is ridiculed for his attitude as a melancholy lover.

In *Twelfth Night* Shakespeare successfully superimposed a humours comedy on a romantic comedy. After this play he abandons humours characterization. At the same time, his interest in attributive names falls off, although it never disappears completely. Of the works of the period 1601 to the end of his career, only *Measure for Measure* (1604) has a noticeable number of characters with attributive names.

Shakespeare's handling of attributive names and humours characterization follows a cycle that runs throughout his career. He perceives a new dramatic trend, form, or character type on the Elizabethan stage; he experiments with it, perfects it, and then goes off in a new direction. So having given his audiences what they willed with such consummate skill in *Twelfth Night*, it was time for our Will to embark on a new way.

Queens College, the City University of New York

---

[16] *Ibid.*, p. 93.

[17] Leslie Hotson believes Shakespeare was satirizing Sir William Knollys, Comptroller of the Queen's household, in Malvolio. Hotson thus sees the name as a commentary on Knollys' character, i.e., *Mala-voglia* — "Ill Will *or* Evil Concupiscence"; he also sees it as an allusion to Knollys' pursuit of Mall Fitton, i.e., *Mal-voglio* — "I want Mall." Aguecheek, Hotson proposes, comes from *Agu-chica*, i.e., "Little-wit," a shortened form of *agucia chica* or *agudeza chica*. This is a reflection on what Hotson theorizes is Aguecheek's Spanish origin. See *The First Night of Twelfth Night* (New York: Macmillan, 1954), pp. 108, 115.

[18] Compare Don John in *Much Ado About Nothing*, another melancholic without a charactonym.

Afro-American, Spanglish, and Something Else: St. Cruzan Naming Patterns

J. L. DILLARD

THE TENDENCY OF ONOMASTIC RESEARCH, especially in the United States, to concentrate on place-names has caused over-emphasis upon the influence of the official or majority culture and under-emphasis of the contributions of the minority, disadvantaged, and "power-"less groups. Such a bias causes the by-passing of acculturation processes in naming. American Indian place-names, for example, are often dealt with; but these are either aboriginal or, in many cases, the result of self-conscious restoration. Important intermediate stages, lacking in exoticism, may be overlooked. Other minority groups, like American blacks for instance, do have clear onomastic patterns – in personal names,[1] in vehicle names,[2] and in church names,[3] if not in place-names. Research outside the United States, especially in the West Indies, has shown that the Afro-American populations which speak varieties of English (particularly Creole and Creole-related varieties) have striking patterns of their own.[4] Further, some perspective from these patterns may prove useful in understanding patterns in the United States.[5] Even the Nova Scotian black population

---

[1] For the Afro-American population, the clearest case is that of the day-names. See David DeCamp, "African Day Names in Jamaica," *Language* 43 (1967), 139–147; Frederic G. Cassidy, *Jamaica Talk* (1961), 157–8; J. L. Dillard, "The West African Day-Names in Nova-Scotia," *Names* 19:4 (December, 1971), 257–261.

[2] See J. L. Dillard, *Afro-American and Other Vehicle Naming Practices*, Institute of Caribbean Studies Special Study No. 1, 1965; "Names of Slogans? Some Problems from the Caribbean, Burundi, and the United States," *Caribbean Studies* 9, No. 4 (1968), 104 to 110.

[3] James B. Stronks, "Chicago Store-Front Churches: 1964," *Names* 12:2 (June, 1964), 127–128; R. S. Noreen, "Ghetto Worship: A Study of the Names of Chicago Storefront Churches," *Names* 13:1 (March, 1965), 19–38; J. L. Dillard, "On the Grammar of Afro-American Naming Practices," *Names* 16:3 (September, 1968), 230–237.

[4] See David DeCamp, "Cart Names in Jamaica," *Names* 8:1 (March, 1960), 15–23; Dillard, "Names or Slogans?" *Caribbean Studies*, 1968.

[5] See Dillard, *Caribbean Studies*, 1968. In a novel like William Melvin Kelley's Black-Joycean *Dunfords Travels Everywheres* (Random House, 1968), we find ghetto bar names like

B. Q.'s
HARE'S LAIR
The BROWN TURTLE
THE OASIS PALM
JESSE B'S JOYCE CLUB
BROWN'S

has participated in naming patterns which are usually associated with the West Indies and West Africa.[6]

With recent interest developing in St. Croix,[7] it may be of some interest to look at the naming patterns of that island in the U.S. Virgin Islands. Populated by black descendants of slaves – complicated by a supercargo population from various European nations and from the

> MR. MITEY'S BLESSED DINER
> MELVIN'S JAZZMATAZZ GALLERY
> SMOKEY'S SMOTHER ROOM
> RINEHART'S RESTAURANT
> TM'S DREAM ROOM
> SONNY R'S BOOM BAR
> THE JOHNSON JONES JAIL HOUSE

Although fictional, these names occur in the context of quite self-conscious concern about black culture and identity.

[6] Dillard, "The West African Day-Names in Nova Scotia," *Names* 19:4 (December, 1971), 257–261.

[7] Robert J. DiPietro, "Multilingualism in St. Croix," *American Speech* 43, No. 2 (May, 1968). In spite of the fact that DiPietro's article deals only with "bilingual" and "diglossic" aspects of the co-existence of Cruzan English, (American) Standard English, and Puerto Rican Spanish on the island, there is observable a wide range of St. Cruzan English dialects. The relatively few remaining Danes tend to speak English with a slight but easily perceptible accent; even a French accent or two may be heard on a short stay. U.S. retirees and resort workers, etc., come mainly from the middle class professionals of the East Coast and typically speak something rather close to consensus (Network) Standard. (A surprising number of the room clerks and other such workers are former professionals with college degrees, working at such jobs to supplement retirement income.) So do a great number of the tourists — in fact, an impressionistic survey would place most of them in Westchester County. Puerto Ricans usually speak the hybrid sometimes called "Spanglish"; but some of them, who grew up in St. Croix, speak "Cruzan talk" like the natives, in addition to Spanish.

The Black Cruzans themselves manifest a wide range varying from "Cruzan talk" to Standard English, with varying amounts of interference from the former on the latter. Radio announcers, for example, may be identified as Cruzans by stress patterns (*something*, *airpórt*) and by over-careful pronunciation [kángrɪsmæ̀n]. Children reading in a service in the Lutheran church retained [dæt] and [tɪŋ] in their formal reading styles, although because of the Biblical text being read no grammatical or lexical effects of Cruzan were observable.

Probably the most extreme "deviations" from Standard English (and from any of the well-known non-standard dialects of the United States and England) can be found in the speech of children. Aida Rouss, "Don't Yank, Taak Yoh Cruzan Taak" (unpublished) hypothesizes that the *do*-support rule does not apply to Cruzan, and cites sentences like

> You know rubber tree?
> You see dat stretch de?
> You hear me fuss wid anybody?
> He wid he madda?   (Is he with his mother?)
> De nenyam ready?   (Is the food ready?)

In my own talk with children in Christiansted, I was asked "You does got to walk?" and, when I pretended not to understand after several repetitions, the exasperated "If you

United States – the island has seen a recent influx of Puerto Ricans, many of them dark-skinned.[8] As in the other islands, especially those with a heavy tourist trade, the Afro-American naming patterns must co-exist with many other patterns; and they tend to occupy the "private" end of a kind of diglossic naming-practice scale, showing up in the names of small, unimpressive business establishments, in vehicle names, and in the place-names of rural areas.

This is not to say that the Afro-American patterns go underground; they are enough in evidence to be noticed by visitors interested in chronicling the (basically white) social whirl. Horace Sutton, for example, in his Chicago *Tribune* article "St. Croix: A Danish Delight" (April 18, 1971) reported

> Places are called Upper Love ... Lower Love ...
> Jealousy ... Dots Folly ... Hannah Rest ...
> Judith's Fancy ... Bethlehem ... Slob.

He could have added *All For The Better* and *Profit*, among others. Sutton, who called these "balmy" place-names and who also wrote of their "Oz-like" air, hesitantly attributed them to Danish influence. But, since similar names are to be found in West Indian islands with no conceivably great Danish influence,[9] it is reasonable to conclude that the islander black population deserves the credit for these naming patterns. Sutton, like many another visitor, probably over-generalized from the Danish names of the major towns – Christiansted and Fredericksted – and from the Holger Danske Hotel.

---

does got to walk?" which contains a quasi-auxiliary *do*-form, but hardly in the syntactic function of Standard English. Cruzan children also say things like

"That's your bike. That's what bike you ridín'." Informants have uniformly maintained that the "deep" Creole feature

NP de Verb (You de ride)

does not occur in Cruzan, and have readily volunteered the information that

NP Verb-ín' (You ridín')

substitutes — thus perhaps indirectly indicating that they are aware of the *de* forms. Rouss cites "You de de" ["You are there"] which would be an at least marginal use of auxiliary *de*. This is, of course, a well-known shibboleth; and informant reports may not be trustworthy.

Rouss reports that Cruzan talk is regarded as "bad" (i.e., probably "deeper" Creole) by other islanders. The tendency to stigmatize the speech of other islanders, and to report one's own island as having the "best" (i.e., most nearly Standard, or least Creole) English is, however, a stereotypical West Indian pattern.

[8] A few undoubted Africanisms, like nenyam "food," are in Cruzan talk; and Creole structures like the post-posed third person plural marker are also found: Me know me people-dem. Gloria E. Encarnacion's "Cruzan Calypso," a more or less comical use of Cruzan for the tourist trade, features expressions like *knackin' daag* "in crowds, in great abundance" which remain unexplained and may well be Africanisms.

[9] See, for example, Richard and Sally Price, "A Note on Canoe Names in Martinique," *Names* 14:3 (September, 1966), 160.

There is, however, another element which is clearly identifiable and easily attributable to the Puerto Ricans who are increasingly migrating to St. Croix. The Puerto Rican naming pattern has been reported,[10] and some account has been taken of its probable cause: the special confrontation, often a kind of tug of war, between English and Spanish on the island. Although the Puerto Rican language contact situation is actually a rather simple one compared with those of other West Indian islands – and would séem even more absurdly simple to West Africans or to some Asians – Puerto Ricans constantly marvel at their own virtuosity, commemorating it in names of mixed English and Spanish content ("Spanglish"). In many cases, there is reason to doubt that intelligibility for monolingual English speakers and readers is the motivating force for "Spanglish" names; in cases like *Yunk, Bird Land's Tabern, Charlie's Melodie's Bar*, etc., such devices as the exaggerated use of apostrophes are hyper-Anglicisms which can hardly aid the understanding of outsiders. How many *gringos* are really enlightened because *Cuchilandia*, probably on the analogy of *Yanquilandia*,[11] contains an English etymon in its third syllable ? But *Chuchilandia Bar and Restaurant* has been transferred to Christiansted. We also find

EL COMETA GROCERY	JORGE'S PLACE
JOSE'S GARDEN	GARCIA'S MARKET
EL RUBI BAR	BORINQUEN BAR
PLAZA LECHONERA	MORALES' GROCERY
BAR 2 LUCES	MIGUEL'S PHOTO STUDIO

along with the vehicle name *Bad Jose* and the *Santa Cruz Pharmacy*. The term *Bar* is,. of course, the usual one in Puerto Rico; I have never seen *Cantina* in a name on that island.

Despite the efforts of *Independentistas* and crusading Hispanists, the home-island Puerto Rican pattern remains one of aggressive acculturation toward the United States, with concomitant insistence upon the Puerto Ricans' use of English to "Americans" (who may include for-

---

[10] J. L. Dillard, "Spanglish Store Names in San Juan, Puerto Rico," *Names* 12:2 (June, 1964), 98—102, and "Spanglish Store Names Again," *Names* 14:3 (September, 1966), 178—180. The cliché "The more it changes, the more it's the same thing" is borne out by Puerto Rican "English" names. The *Rainbow Grill* gets a few more neon lights and becomes *New Bronx Casino Club* (the clientele of which is entirely Spanish-speaking); *Bird Land's Tabern* becomes *Chick.N.Bar.B.Q.* and then just *Pizza*, but

House
BIRD LAND'S
Restaurant

has reappeared over a door. The *Time Square Quick Lunch* (Río Piedras) has one new sign which reads *Times Square*, but the old *Time Square* still appears elsewhere.

[11] The suffix *-landia* is at least mildly productive. There is, for example, the *Gomilandia* (from *gomas* "tires") *Refreshment Center*, located in the same small sub-building as the stock of tires, in a Texaco station in Santurce.

eigners from as far away as India, and even an occasional Argentinian) rather than the latter's use of Spanish to Puerto Ricans.[12] The same feeling of language appropriateness has extended itself to St. Croix, and some younger Cruzans of Puerto Rican ancestry (especially the blacks) are bilingual in St. Cruzan English[13] and Puerto Rican Spanish.[14] Despite the general discouragement of Cruzan use of Spanish, there is an occasional attempt (not too well realized) on the part of the English-speaking Cruzans to use Spanish for Puerto Ricans:

        NILA'S SHOP
DRESSMAKER   CUSTURERA [sic]

The Cruzan tradition itself, besides being apparently manifest in the place-names already referred to, is strikingly evident in vehicle names

BABY SHAF   MR. LIGHTNING
SAD MOVER   THE DIFFERENT
APOLLO II   BUCCANEER
CONSIDER ME
LOVE BUG [a Volkswagen, of course]
   Come and See Me

Puerto Ricans in the San Juan area often paint names like *Demon El Coqui*, and *Cobra* (with a picture of the snake) on their automobiles, with pictures and in bright letters but smaller and less prominently displayed than the typical names of the English-speaking islands. There is at present no clear evidence linking the Puerto Rican to the Afro-American tradition of naming automobiles. Especially in the case of *Demon* (a brand name), the Puerto Rican names probably refer to the cars. The Cruzan names, on the other hand, refer primarily to the drivers – like *Baby Shaf* which is probably best explained as a boast of virility ("the maker of babies"). As DeCamp[15] has pointed out, the most notable characteristic of this naming tradition is its reflection of the inner states of the owner or driver (*Consider Me, Sad Mover, The Different*), although current events (*Apollo II*) also get some attention, in Jamaica as in St. Croix. (But the driver in this case is probably claiming reflected glory from the astronauts – or offering to reflect some of his own glory on them! – rather than merely seeking to commemorate an historical event.)

---

[12] J. L. Dillard, "Standard Average Foreign in Puerto Rican Spanish," in E. B. Atwood and A. A. Hill (eds.), *Studies in Language, Literature, and Culture of the Middle Ages and Later*, Austin, Texas, 1969, pp. 97–108.

[13] For these purposes, it is not necessary to resolve the issue of whether this is "perfect" bilingualism – or whether that is possible. These young people are, at the least, capable of fooling all but the most perceptive listener.

[14] For some observations on the variable nature of Puerto Rican "folk" Spanish, see J. L. Dillard, "Sobre Algunos Fonemas Puertorriquenas," *Nueva Revista de la Filologia Española*, XVI (1962), 422–424.

[15] "Cart Names in Jamaica," *Names* 8:1 (March, 1960).

Cruzan business names are characterized primarily by a certain floridity :[16]

DE [sic] HIVE RESTAURANT AND BAR
WEEKE'S TEN GRAND BAR AND RESTAURANT
DODIE'S SUN AND MOON FASHIONS
HUMMING BIRD LAUNDROMAT
WRINGER ROOM BAR
BARON SPOT CHRISTIANSTED
FALLEN STAR BAR AND RESTAURANT

It seems obvious that the kinds of names noted constitute a separate naming tradition from mainstream American business names (although, obviously, some resemblances can be found). It may be only *a posteriori* reasoning which separates out a name like *The Stone Balloon* (a very white, very touristy bar and restaurant). But, in comparison to a mass of other data from West Africa and the West Indies,[17] West African survival for, especially, the vehicle names[18] does not seem like an at all extreme hypothesis. The three traditions (West Indian, "Spanglish," and tourist) are basically distinct and each has its own functional domain. Crossing, as in the case of the vehicle name *Bad Jose*, is more frequent between Cruzan and Spanglish than between either of those two and tourist. (This should be no more surprising than that intermarriage follows the same pattern.) Danish hardly exists at all, except for the older, very official place and street names (and the latter are quite regularly translated into English). The islanders themselves (like the St. Thomas taxi driver who once explained to me that [sent krɔɪ] was the French pronunciation of the name of the other island, the Danish pronunciation having been [sent krwa]) are hardly aware that Danish was ever there.

Like that of the continental United States, the Afro-American population of the West Indies has received little attention – onomastic or otherwise – from researchers. What research has been done has been subject to preconceptions which were in fashion at the moment, and to a great degree it has been limited to Jamaica. The promise of comparative studies in the area is, however, bright; and the field is wide. Important contributions to the understanding of black language, cultural, and onomastic patterns in the United States can also result.

University of Puerto Rico

---

[16] Florid names are especially characteristic of storefront churches like *Sacred Heart Spiritual Church of Jesus Christ, Inc.*, in Washington, D.C.

[17] See the discussion in Dillard, "Names or Slogans ?" 1968.

[18] Although there are no general studies, enough information is available to show that the same practices are to be found in West Africa. John Diggers, *Anansi, The Web of Life in Africa*, 1962, p. 36, shows Fanti fishing boats with "proverbs and symbols expressing the philosophy of each boat crew" carved on the sides. On the relationship of boat names to other vehicle names, and on the relationship between names, slogans, and "proverbs," see Dillard, "Names or Slogans ?" 1968.

Anent J. Alfred Prufrock

ROBERT F. FLEISSNER

T HE NAME OF ELIOT'S ANTI-HERO J. ALFRED PRUFROCK is indeed an imposing one, thus ironically befitting the self-important figure for whom it is a label. Yet no attention to speak of has been paid to the aesthetic implications in the name of this "aestheticist" person, let alone to the historical sources. It has been tacitly accepted that "the name Prufrock. . . was borrowed for him by Eliot from a St. Louis family,"[1] specifically from the Prufrock-Littau Company, furniture dealers, and that that is all there is to it. Yet Eliot is on record for having said that he was not aware of any single, basic origin of the name: "I did not have, at the time of writing the poem, and have not yet recovered, any recollection of having acquired the name in this way. . . ."[2] Since it is perfectly clear that other names of Eliot's have symbolic meanings,[3] let us look more deeply into the connotations of Prufrock's full name and see what emerges. An extraordinary richness reveals itself, one that hitherto has been ignored. It is convenient to take the name in sequence, starting with the initial, then the middle name, and finally the surname.

I: The Beginning Initial

What is Prufrock's Christian name? We do not know, only have a "secretive J." confronting us. In terms of Prufrock's problems in accepting Christianity—difficulties that Eliot himself then later resolved—the hint in the initial already points at either latent Christianity or, what is more likely, a resistance to accepting a "Christian" first name. Since Prufrock asks himself the Christ-like question of whether or not he should accept life after death (with specific reference to the miracle of Lazarus), it is possible that the "J" stands for a potential similitude with Christ, thus "J". for Jesus. Since Eliot grew up in St. Louis, he could well have been aware of the implications of the initials S. J. (Society of Jesus) following the names of Jesuits teaching at St. Louis University. Still, in terms of Prufrock's own wavering attitude toward formal religion,

---

[1]Grover Smith, Jr., *T. S. Eliot's Poetry and Plays: A Study in Sources and Meaning* (Chicago: University of Chicago Press, 1956), p. 17. The standard article on the matter is Stephen Stepanchev, "The Origin of J. Alfred Prufrock," *Modern Language Notes*, 66 (June, 1951), 400-401.

[2]Stepanchev, *loc. cit.*

[3]For example, Gerontion, names in *Old Possum's Book of Practical Cats*, the Rock (comparable with *Prufrock*), Marina, and The Hollow Men. It is hardly necessary to review their import here.

the initial might be taken as standing potentially for Judas as well as Jesus. There must be more, therefore, behind the initial than a hidden allusion to religion.

Grover Smith, Jr., tells of "the somewhat precious and for America, at least, esoteric quality of his name, with its obtrusive initial *J*" and makes the point that it recalls "the signature T. Stearns-Eliot which Eliot used."[4] Since some readers, notably Pound, felt that there was much of Eliot in Prufrock, this connection cannot be ignored. But it still does not account for the particular letter used in the initial. Why should it be so secretive or "obtrusive"? One evident reason, suggested by one of my students, is that Prufrock is the type of reticent individual who would cover up his first name simply because he did not like it, in much the same way as many persons hide their middle names with initials (including the writer of this paper.) On the other hand, if Prufrock just wanted to be different or snobbish, he could have used an initial initial for no other reason than to distinguish himself from the run-of-the-mill type that uses an initial only for the middle name. I suspect that this latter reason is the one that would come to most readers' minds.

Nonetheless, there is a better reason yet, one that provides deeper insight into Prufrock's character. If he wanted to hide his first name, he may have had a very understandable reason: he may not have liked it because it had feminine or girlish connotations. Although admittedly this is a conjecture, there is some good evidence behind it.

For the conjecture to have any validity, certain questions must be raised and answered. Firstly, what basis might there have been for Eliot's having imputed girlish tendencies to Prufrock? Secondly, what kind of a girlish name might then reside behind the initial? Thirdly, how might this name have been picked up by Eliot? I believe that all these questions can be tentatively answered.

To begin with, as I mentioned earlier, it has often been accepted that there are some resonances of Eliot himself in the character of Prufrock as well as in the name. Now, a leading question regarding Eliot's personal life is whether he was bisexual. T. S. Matthews has dismissed the problem out of hand, calling the rumor of Eliot's homosexuality "easy to refute,"[5] yet he has to admit that "to the anonymous, rather nasty mind of the reviewer of the *Times Lit Suppl*, some of the suppressed lines [of *The Waste Land*, recently brought to light in The New York Public Library] blow the gaff on Eliot's guilty secret: that he hated and feared women—in short, that he was a homosexual."[6] Matthews' biography, however, is generally regarded as special pleading and certainly not definitive. The question of Eliot's sexual or emotional life cannot be properly answered unless John Peter's argument is reintroduced.

The case put by John Peter[7] is rather curious. Dealing with Eliot's most controversial poem, *The Waste Land*, Peter tells us that the object of the speaker's love is a young man who soon afterwards met his death, it would seem by drowning. The

---

[4]Smith, p. 17.

[5]*Great Tom: Notes Towards the Definition of T. S. Eliot* (New York: Harper and Row, 1974), pp. 75-76. Matthews also notes (p. 36) that the title of *The Love Song of J. Alfred Prufrock* derives from Kipling (but not the name in the title).

[6]Matthews, *loc. cit.*

[7]"A New Interpretation of *The Waste Land* (1952)," *Essays in Criticism*, 19 (1969), 140-175.

speaker himself, Tiresias (at least in most cases),[8] is described in hermaphroditic terms. When Peter first suggested this interpretation in print, Eliot had it suppressed, and it was not republished until after Eliot's death, when it appeared with an introductory paper[9] and alongside another discussing Mr. Eugenides, a character in the poem often considered a decadent homosexual, and citing Peter's article in the process.[10] Allusions in *The Waste Land*, particularly that to the "hyacinth girl" (described as having wet hair as if related to the drowned male object of the speaker's love), have been made much of, particularly now by G. Wilson Knight, who accepts Peter's interpretation. With regard to *Prufrock*, however, only a few of these points are relevant. Of particular interest are Peter's assertions that "we should note, I think, that Marie mentioned early in *The Waste Land* is on the Continent a name given to both sexes"[11] and that "as with Hallam and Tennyson, so with Jean Verdenal and Eliot. . . ."[12]

For the initial "J." in Prufrock's name "stands for" *Jean*, plausibly if he was named after Jean Verdenal, who may have been Eliot's lover in Paris. The first name is covered up not only to hide the identity, but because *Jean* is a name with feminine connotations (that is, it is male in French but female in English, an association also frequently encountered with the English names *Jean* and *Gene*, insofar as the latter may embarrass some men because it sounds the same as its feminine counterpart). Eliot dedicated both *The Waste Land*, unofficially and *Prufrock* to Jean Verdenal, and he did not complete *Prufrock* until after his relationship with the Parisian youth who was subsequently drowned. Compare then the allusion to drowning at the end of *Prufrock*. Although it is impossible to know for certain whether or not Eliot invented the first initial of Prufrock's name before he met Jean Verdenal, the "J." surely assumes some of the resonance of Jean's name if for no other reason than that the intent behind a work of literature cannot be ultimately determined until it has been completed. *Prufrock* clearly contains other French echoes, notably from the writings of Laforgue. And Peter points out that Eliot's dedication of the monopog to Jean is uncommonly fervent: "the measure of the love which warms me towards you' (in translation).[13] Grover Smith indicates that though *Prufrock* was begun at Harvard, it was not finished till Eliot's Paris year, and that he showed his manuscript poems most probably to his new male friend he encountered at Paris, memorializing him in his dedication to *Prufrock and Other Observations* some four years later. Still, I would agree with Elizabeth Schneider, in her recent monograph on Eliot, that there is not enough evidence to know if the poet was homosexual or went through such a phase. Yet Prufrock and Eliot are not entirely the same, and whereas I would reject the view that Prufrock is bisexual *per se*, he appears latently that way. In sum, then, since it is common knowledge that Prufrock's love is either ironic and/or related more to the speaker's self than to any of the women mentioned, why should we not see it as also

---

[8]Stephen Spender, in *T. S. Eliot* (New York: The Viking Press, 1976), questions Grover Smith's view that the "I" of the poem is the Fisher King (p. 113).

[9]An editorial comment by F. W. Bateson, the editor, and a Postscript by Peter. The article first appeared in 1952 (see n. 7).

[10]William H. Pritchard, "Reading *The Waste Land* Today," *Essays in Criticism*, 19 (1969), 176-192.

[11]Peter, p. 145. The obvious analogy that comes to mind is the poet Rainer-Maria Rilke.

[12]Peter, p. 168.

[13]*Ibid.*, p. 169.

directed toward Jean Verdenal (spiritually at least, if not physically), whose first name subtly completes the hidden first name of J. Alfred Prufrock?

II: The Middle Name

Peter's reference to Hallam and Tennyson leads directly to a consideration of Prufrock's middle name. For does not *Alfred* echo Tennyson's first name? We may be tempted to consider other possibilities, like that of King Alfred perhaps, but since Prufrock disclaims being a prince, it would be presumptuous to give him a royal role, even nominally. There are actually a number of good reasons for contending that Eliot had Tennyson in mind in writing the poem and devising the name of the protagonist apart from the Eliot-Verdenal/Tennyson-Hallam connection. Let us consider these in turn.

(1) Tennyson's own poetry, notably his *Idylls of the King*, has been charged with having the same kind of precious effect that Prufrock's own character evokes, indeed to the extent that Eliot's American contemporary, Edwin Arlington Robinson, decided to write his own Arthurian idylls, following Tennyson's lead but attempting to overcome the prissiness.

(2) Eliot's pronounced debt to Tennyson throughout his work cannot be ignored. He made use of Tennysonian subject matter not only in the Arthurian grail myth of *The Waste Land*, but in the hints that he borrowed from *Maud*, "The Lady of Shalott," and other lyrics, especially those dealing with the dichotomy of Art and Life, including *Prufrock*.[14]

(3) Tennyson's own difficulty in reconciling faith and doubt, in *In Memoriam*—a consideration that is now best recalled through Eliot's familiar critique of that elegy as more memorable for the quality of its doubt than that of its faith—is intimated also in *Prufrock*.

(4) Most obviously, Eliot wanted to follow in the Victorian Poet Laureate's footsteps and thus, in Alfred Prufrock, appropriated Tennyson's first name. The infernal setting of the poem in a macabre but delightful way recalls the story about Tennyson's Calvinist aunt who informed her Alfred that looking at him reminded her of the biblical text about sinners damned to everlasting fire.

(5) Finally, and most importantly, if Prufrock appropriated Tennyson's first name as his middle name via Eliot, what happened to Tennyson's own "middle" name? *It too was appropriated.* It must be recalled that Prufrock goes out of his way to stipulate that he is not "Prince Hamlet, nor was meant to be"; instead Alfred was meant to be "an attendant *lord.*" Alfred *Lord* Tennyson. The resonance is clear.

III: The Surname

Prufrock's last name is more complicated. Stephen Stepanchev tells us that "the name Prufrock is so rare that a thorough search of the telephone directories of fifteen

---

[14]See W. K. Wimsatt, Jr., "*Prufrock* and *Maud:* From Plot to Symbol," reprinted in *Hateful Contraries: Studies in Literature and Criticism* (Lexington: University of Kentucky Press, 1965). pp. 201-212; also Donald J. Weinstock, "Tennysonian Echoes in 'The Love Song of J. Alfred Prufrock,'" *English Language Notes*, 7 (March, 1970), 213-214. Neither article deals with any influence of nomenclature.

other large American cities [other than St. Louis] failed to discover a single representative of the family."[15] And Eliot's refusal to admit that he borrowed the name from real life suggests that it is more than a "representative name." There are undoubtedly psychological overtones. As George Williamson writes, "in this poem. . . we have the love song of a certain character, whose very name is suggestive of qualities he subsequently manifests."[16] He goes on to note, rather too cavalierly, that "if Eliot's proper names do not acquire meaning from history or literature or etymology, they are used for their generic or social suggestion."[17] As has been pointed out, Eliot's names, for example in *Gerontion*, do have etymological suggestiveness: "But can it be fortuitous that these names, enumerated in connection with the Eucharist, nearly all of them carry a religious suggestion (de Silvero: thirty pieces of silver. De Tornquist: the Crown of Thorns and the Thorn in the Flesh. Von Kulp: culpa)?"[18]

Elsewhere I have suggested that the surname is portmanteau, in Lewis Carroll's use of the term, but that rather than considering the combination effect as pointing to a "*prude* in a *frock*," with the womanly and even clerical[19] connotations implied by such a conflation, the more serious reader would think of the speaker's quest for "proof of rock," for a firm foundation for his wavering beliefs.[20] This distinction is, I believe, a good one still to maintain critically, particularly because it elicits positive rather than merely negative facets of the protagonist's personality. But there is more involved in the surname than such name-play. Thus, I have also considered, in a different article, the affinity of the name Prufrock with that of Touchstone;[21] that is, to touch a stone for proof of rock makes some sense too. When we take into account that both Prufrock and Touchstone were described in anti-romantic ways (at least insofar as Prufrock's hesitancy to accept women is concerned) and that Touchstone, as a court clown, may represent the "Fool" that Prufrock admits to being sometimes, the parallel does not seem overly far-fetched. It has recently been suggested to me[22] that the name Prufrock could just as well, or better, derive from that of Montefeltro, however, in that this reference in the poem's epigraph suggests a combination of the Italian *monte* (mountain) with English *felt*[23]—thus "proof of rock" in the sense of a mountain that is felt! But that association, aside from the humor it evokes, has not much to do with the poem except insofar as both Prufrock and Montefeltro inhabit their own infernos. An even more amusing suggestion, I submit, is that the portmanteau effect of Prufrock's name recalls that of some of Dickens's characters, notably David Copperfield. For we all know (or should, I suppose) that Eliot found *Copperfield* second only to *War and*

---

[15]Stepanchev, *loc. cit.*

[16]*A Reader's Guide to T. S. Eliot: A Poem-by-Poem Analysis*, 2nd ed. (New York: Farrar, Straus and Giroux, 1969), p. 58.

[17]*Ibid.*

[18]See the review of Williamson by C. A. Bodelsen in *English Studies*, 35 (1954), 90.

[19]Cf. "de-frocked."

[20]See my review-article of John Harrison's *The Reactionaries: A Study of the Anti-Democratic Intelligentsia* entitled "Reacting to *The Reactionaries:* Libertarian Views," in *Journal of Human Relations*, 17 (First Quarter, 1969), 138-145.

[21]"Prufrock as Touchstone" (reply to query-note), *American Notes and Queries*, 11 (December, 1972), 56-57.

[22]By Prof. Richard Knowles of the University of Wisconsin (Madison).

[23]The Italian word *feltro*, which refers to felt in the sense of a felt hat, would have no symbolic value here.

Peace, and is not a "field of copper" "proof of rock" too? Obviously this suggestion cannot be taken seriously, but I reject the association with Dickens's own leading autobiographical work only with regret because there seem to be other Copperfieldean elements in *Prufrock.*[24] Moreover, there is much that is Dickensian about Eliot's poem,[25] like the animism in the yellow fog that acts in a manner recalling not only Carl Sandburg's fog but various scenes in Dickens, for instance the wind at the outset of *Martin Chuzzlewit.* The name Prufrock seems to reflect other Dickensian names somewhat, such as Pecksniff (also in *Chuzzlewit*) and Chadband. There is a decidedly Victorian quality about both Dickens's and Eliot's names; the hypocritical quality is evident in their very pretentious sonorousness.

From a formalist point of view, Prufrock's last name is certainly more important than his first two. If there is, as I have indicated, an indication of hushed-up girlishness in the initial, of further preciousness in the hint of Tennyson in the middle name, there is at least a comic[26] conclusion in the Dickensian effect of the last name. For Prufrock is indeed after "proof of rock" in a Touchstone-like way, but he never makes it, ending up ironically as a kind of "prude in a frock" in spite of himself. Behind the pretentiousness and effeminacy, however, a man is trying to assert himself, and that man is T. S. Eliot. It is not until he finds himself in his later work that his quest approaches completion, but a modest start was made shortly after *Prufrock* was finally completed. For at that time Eliot entered into his first marriage. Whatever his earlier dissipations,[27] he tried to mend his ways, for the weakness of Prufrock is

----

[24]There are allusions to Lazarus and Hamlet in the opening two chapters of this novel, ones which curiously parallel the same association in *Prufrock.* Moreover, the character of Littimer in Chapter XXI, described as "deferential, observant, always at hand when wanted," looks ahead to Prufrock "Deferential, glad to be of use." Littimer places great importance on his watch, suggesting Prufrock's concern about time; his "pattern of respectability" suggests Prufrock's, and that "no one knew his Christian name" invites comparison with Prufrock's first initial. Littimer is also a kind of "attendant lord," waiting on Steerforth. (Was Old Possum full of . . . Dickens?)

[25]It is now well known that Eliot's original title for *The Waste Land* was "He Do the Police in Different Voices," taken from Dickens. For more on *Prufrock* and Dickens, see Barbara Everett, "In Search of Prufrock," *Critical Quarterly,* 16 (Sumer 1974), 101-121.

[26]In *The Overwhelming Question: A Study of the Poetry of T. S. Eliot* (Toronto: University of Toronto Press, 1976), which is one of the most interesting studies of his work to appear in some time. Balachandra Rajan argues that *Prufrock* must be considered as largely in the comic mode.

[27]After this paper was accepted, George Watson's interesting article on Jean Verdenal, "Quest for a Frenchman," appeared in "The State of Letters" section of *The Sewanee Review,* 84 (Summer 1976), 465-475. Watson objects to hints of Eliot's friend in *The Waste Land* (a view which has now also been accepted by Robert Sencourt, Eliot's Catholic friend and biographer, in his *T. S. Eliot: A Memoir*) on the grounds that Verdenal did not drown and that: "there is no reason to suppose that Eliot ever thought he was drowned" (p. 473). I question that last statement. True, Eliot's dedication to *Prufrock and Other Observations,* "For Jean Verdenal, 1889-1915/mort aux Dardanelles," could mean *at* the Dardanelles and not *in* the Dardanelles, but the poet's later reference to the friend in the *Criterion* of April 1934 suggests that at the time Eliot wrote the dedication, at least, he thought the Frenchman had drowned: "a friend who was later (so far as I *could* find out) to be mixed with the mud of Gallipoli" (cited by Watson, p. 466, with my italics). The phrase "mud of Gallipoli" (a seaport) suggests, to me at least, water; otherwise, if Eliot had known his friend was presumably

shunted aside in favor of a stronger sense of individuality and a deliberate acceptance of political, religious, and poetical values.

Central State University (Ohio)

---

shot while ashore, he would have said "dirt," for it is unlikely that there were battlefields of mud at a seaport. Moreover, the kinship between his description of the friend ("waving a branch of lilac") and the crux in *The Waste Land* "they called me the hyacinth girl" is certainly curious, if not absolutely factual. Further, would not Eliot, in his far-ranging poetic mind (and having composed *Prufrock* when William James's theories of mental associations were dominant at Harvard), have linked death and the Dardanelles with death and the Hellespont, hence with the drowning of the lover Leander in the same straits? That the most famous lyric about this mythic love affair was written by a reputed homosexual, Christopher Marlowe, from whose *The Jew of Malta* Eliot quoted elsewhere in a headnote, would not have escaped his attention. Watson also contends that "Eliot's sympathy for the emotional difficulties of a homosexual friend, for which an anecdote at second hand is quoted by Mr. Peter in the postscript of 1969, is hardly evidence for anything more than Eliot's kindliness of heart" (p. 473); however, aside from the matter of authenticity, the anecdote pointedly provides some evidence for Eliot's having had "a homosexual friend." Although I tend to agree that the washing of dirty linen in public is not always commendable (though its fascination with regard to famous men of letters cannot be denied either), I see nothing wrong in separating the person from the *persona* to the extent of noticing hints of male friendship in what Eliot wrote. Naturally I cannot profess to pass judgment on his personal life, except to suggest that some of it was sensibly sublimated in his art. In the same manner, Elisabeth Schneider has questioned whether Eliot's early poem *The Death of Saint Narcissus* had any such hidden meanings; however, the Narcissus symbol is used with such meanings in *Death in Venice*. Eliot's likewise sequestered lyric *King Bolo and His Big Black Queen* (which, like Peter's article in *Essays in Criticism*, Eliot did not want to have published) has unmistakable reference to bisexual bawdiness (e.g. "airy fairy hairy' un "/"Cardinal Bessarion"). At the time of writing, I had not yet seen James E. Miller's new study, *T. S. Eliot's Personal Waste Land: Exorcism of the Demons* (University Park: Pennsylvania State University Press, 1977).

From Classic to Classy:
Changing Fashions in Street Names

JOHN ALGEO

FROM THE NAMES PEOPLE give to the places they live, we can tell something about the people themselves. Changes in those names, in turn, reveal changes in the lives of the people. Normally, place-names are relatively long-lasting, and thus changes have to be observed retrospectively at a great distance. However, in a time of expanding population, new areas of settlement are opened, new towns founded, and new streets laid out, all of which are given new names. Street names are doubtless the most abundant kind of place-name and consequently they are the most convenient sort in which to observe changing fashions. They are not merely convenient, but also revealing. The population of our nation is increasingly an urban one, and the street is the place most characteristic of the city-dweller and most influential in his life. If clothes make the man, streets make the urbanite. The names he chooses for his streets reveal his relationship to his most immediate environment.

The sample community investigated here is Athens, Georgia, a small city in the northeast section of the state and the site of the University of Georgia. Now slightly more than 175 years old, Athens is in many respects a typical American town. The kinds of names its streets are given have changed sharply in recent years. During the 1960s, the town and the university both had a period of very rapid growth. New residential subdivisions were started and new streets created in large numbers during a relatively short time. Most of the new residential areas are subdivisions, more or less planned by their developers. A contrast of old Athens street names with new ones points up some significant differences and some notable changes in naming patterns.

HISTORICAL BACKGROUND

In 1801 a committee consisting of Abraham Baldwin, John Milledge, and three others selected a site in northern Georgia, on the Oconee

River at a spot known as the Cedar Shoals, to be the location of the University of Georgia.[1] Milledge bought 633 acres from the owner, Daniel Easley, and presented the land to the trustees of the university, which had been chartered by the state legislature in 1785. In the 16 years between its chartering and the actual beginning of its operation, Abraham Baldwin was nominal president of the institution, which had no students, no other faculty, and no buildings—but did have 40,000 acres of land, with which it had been endowed by the state even before it was chartered. The fact that the site committee agreed unanimously upon the Cedar Shoals location, despite the fact that it had to be bought while the embryonic university was already land-poor, suggests that either the area was extraordinarily attractive or Easley was an extraordinarily gifted real-estate dealer. However that may be, the site was called Athens, and a town began to grow up immediately to the north of the new college yard.

The history of the town is reflected by a number of maps showing the increase of platted lots and streets in Athens. The first of these is a town plan drawn by Josiah Meigs, the president of the college, and the Reverend Hope Hull, a member of the board of trustees; it appears in the minutes of the trustees for 1805 and shows two east-west and four north-south streets, all unnamed. There is a seventh street leading out of town and labeled "Road to the Bridge."[2] The second map shows the old town as of 1826 but not the new part that had begun as early as 1813 (Minutes, November 9, 1813, p. 213); in the part shown the east-west and the north-south streets have increased to six each. There is still a road to the bridge, although it has shifted slightly in location from the 1805 map. Front Street, which divides the college yard from town, is the only street that is named. The third map, from 1854, shows both the old and new parts of town. It includes 41 named streets and several unnamed ones.[3] The fourth map, showing the town

---

[1]   Unless specifically noted otherwise, the historical information that follows is based on the following accounts: Kenneth Coleman, *Confederate Athens* (Athens: University of Georgia Press, 1967); E. Merton Coulter, *College Life in the Old South*, 2d ed. (Athens: University of Georgia Press, 1951); Augustus Longstreet Hull, *Annals of Athens, 1801-1901* (Athens: Banner Job Office, 1906); Ernest C. Hynds, *Antebellum Athens and Clarke County, Georgia* (Athens: University of Georgia Press, 1974); Sylvanus Morris, *Strolls about Athens during the Early Seventies* (n.p.: n.p., n.d.); H. J. Rowe, ed., *History of Athens and Clarke County* (Athens: McGregor, 1923); Mary Bondurant Warren, "Athens: Its Earliest History," *Papers of the Athens Historical Society*, ed. by Marion West Marshall and Mary Bondurant Warren, 1 (1964), 6-10.

[2]   Minutes of the Trustees of the University of Georgia, vol. 1, May 31, 1805, p. 107 (University of Georgia Library).

[3]   I am indebted to Charlotte Marshall for copies of the 1826 and 1854 maps, as well as many leads about early Athens street names.

in 1874, names some 60 streets.

On February 5, 1859, a motion was passed in the town council to create a committee of three members "to name the different streets of Athens." On March 5, the committee requested additional time to carry out their task, and finally reported their action to the council on April 2, 1859, with the following preface:

> To the Intendant and Wardens of Athens
>
> Gentlemen—The Committee to whom was referred the naming of the streets of Athens, have discharged that duty, and have the honor to submit for your approval, the subjoined report. It will be seen that streets with well-known [names] have had them retained. The design in the others, has been to perpetuate the names of some of the early citizens of our town—particularly of those now dead—and also of some who have done service to the University of Georgia and the State.
>
> > A. A. Franklin Hill,
> > A. H. Childs,
> > W. G. Delony.

The following report named 46 streets and identified them, chiefly by the houses or other structures built on them. "The whole report was received and unanimously adopted. The Chairman of the Committee was authorized to write the names on the map of the town."[4] This was the first official naming of Athens streets.

After the 1859 naming of streets and the 1874 map, the town continued to grow. Today there are over 850 named streets in the city and its surrounding suburban areas. For a comparison of changing fashions in street onomastics, the 46 names adopted in 1859 are matched with 46 street names in one of the newer residential parts of town, an area to the southeast of the city limits, but well within greater Athens, from three to six miles from the center of town. First the old street names are analyzed for their types, then the new street names, and finally a comparison of the two is drawn.

THE OLD STREET NAMES

Over three-quarters of the old street names (35) commemorate persons associated with the early history of the town or the university.

---

4 Minutes of Intendant and Wardens of the Town of Athens, Georgia, Book 1, 1847-1860.

They include the first five presidents of the university, the man who bought and donated the land on which town and university came to stand, and a large assortment of business men and politicians of the early nineteenth century:

Baldwin Street: Abraham Baldwin, first president of the University of Georgia, 1785-1801, was one of the principal authors of the university's charter and proposed the bill in the state legislature authorizing its foundation.

Barber Street: Wethersby Barber was a town character. His given name is variously spelled *Wethersby* (Morris, p. 49) and *Weathersby* (Rowe, p. 32) and is given as *Wetherford* in Hull's *Annals* (p. 480). The confusion is appropriate. According to a story attributed to Barber himself, "his father lived in the Cherokee Nation, and Chief Wethersby was his friend, and he named his son Wethersby after the Indian" (Morris, p. 49). The story is perhaps to be taken with a grain of salt, Barber being notorious as a jokester. He is supposed to have gotten five dollars from the journalist Henry Grady for a cock that could stand flat-footed and eat corn off a table four feet high (provided the corn and the cock were both on the table top). He also offered to sell bottom land for two dollars an acre and, when challenged with the fact that the land was a rocky hill, explained that it was indeed bottom land since rain had washed off all the top soil (Coulter, p. 226).

Baxter Street: Thomas W. Baxter settled in Athens in 1831.

Billups Street: The site-selection committee for the university began their work by meeting at Billups' tavern on June 29, 1801, probably somewhere south of modern Athens.[5]

Brown Street: Bedford Brown was an early merchant in the town and was captain of a home guard company during the war of 1812. John and Samuel Brown were town commissioners in 1815. The Rev. John Brown was the third president of the university, from 1811 to 1816. It is not clear which of these gentlemen the street was named for. In any event, the name did not last. By 1874 the one-block stretch, which was near a small cemetery, was called Graveyard Street; on recent maps it appears as Magazine Street, but the road no longer exists, having given way to university construction. All that remains is a staked off entry way to a parking lot.

Chase Street: Albon Chase was a business man in insurance and paper manufacture, a warden (or city councilman), and publisher and editor

---

[5] *The Augusta Chronicle and Gazette of the State*, June 20, 1801, p. 3/2.

of newspapers in antebellum Athens.

Clayton Street: Augustin S. Clayton was in the first graduating class of the university in 1804. He was prominent in local business and politics.

Cobb Street: A Cobb family was in the area from early times, a John Cobb having sold the land on which the original county seat, Watkinsville, was located. In 1834 John Addison Cobb developed Cobbham, a residential area immediately to the west of the original plat of Athens. One of his sons, Howell Cobb, became governor of Georgia, speaker of the U.S. House of Representatives, Secretary of the Treasury, and finally a general in the Confederate Army; another, T. R. R. Cobb, was a lawyer who codified the state laws, a delegate to the Confederate Constitutional Convention (the original draft of the constitution being in his handwriting), and finally also a Confederate general (Rowe, p. 32).

Dearing Street: William Dearing was an officer of the Georgia Rail Road and one of the founders of the Athens Factory (see Factory Street below).

Dougherty Street: Major Charles Dougherty settled in Athens in the 1820s. In 1811 the street was called Walton Street (Hull, p. 6).

Espy Street: James and John Espy were Revolutionary soldiers who were founding members of the first Presbyterian Church in Athens. The street, which was on the outskirts of town, had disappeared by 1874, and the name along with it.

Finley Street: The Rev. Robert Finley was the fourth president of the university, though he did not live long enough to exercise his office. He was hired for the position from Princeton and was apparently given a sales pitch that the reality failed to live up to. He was told the climate was so wholesome that, although the college was 16 years old, "the grave of a student is not to be seen" (Coulter, p. 23), hardly surprising in view of the fact, of which he was not informed, that the student body had shrunk to 28 by that time. Disillusionment set in when he discovered that it took 15 days to travel from Savannah to Athens, about as long as the trip from Princeton to Savannah. He contracted typhus and died the year of his arrival (1817). The trustees of the university gave his widow two town lots in Athens and his children free tuition, the family remained in town.

Franklin Street: Leonidas Franklin was a town warden in 1848.

Fulton Street: The Fultons were not as prominent in the early records as some of the other street-namesake families; however, Fulton is only a modest one-block lane. M. C. Fulton married Virginia F.

Hamilton in 1851 (Hull's *Annals*, p. 484).

Gilmer Street: Governor George R. Gilmer was a friend of the university in its early, difficult days. By the early 1970s, the original Gilmer Street had been renamed White Street (doubtlessly commemorating the family of John White, a businessman who settled in Athens in 1833); since then, the street has been closed to allow the expansion of a Holiday Inn. Present-day Gilmer Street, in a different part of town, is considerably more recent than the original one.

Hancock Avenue: Thomas Hancock came to Athens in 1819; he was an innkeeper who helped to organize the first Methodist Church. In 1811 the street was called Green Street (Hull, p. 6).

Hill Street: A Hill family was long prominent in the area. Blanton Hill was a merchant in the 1840s; A. A. Franklin Hill served on the street-naming committee.

Hoyt Street: James Hoyt bought one of the first town lots in 1804, and the Rev. Dr. Nathan Hoyt was minister of the Presbyterian Church for over 30 years in the early and mid nineteenth century.

Hull Street: Hope Hull was a Methodist preacher and a trustee of the university who built the first college chapel in 1807-08; he was also one of the first town commissioners, designated in the act of incorporation.[6]

Jackson Street: Dr. Henry Jackson was a professor of mathematics at the university.[7]

Lumpkin Street: Wilson Lumpkin was a member of Congress, governor of the state, and a trustee of the university. Atlanta, earlier called Marthasville, was twice named for his daughter, Martha Atalanta Lumpkin. His house, built of granite blocks, an unusual form of construction for the area, is now a part of the campus.

Meigs Street: Josiah Meigs, second president of the university, served from 1801 to 1811.

Milledge Avenue: Governor John Milledge was one of the committee that selected the site of Athens for the university. It was he who bought the land on which the university and the town now stand and gave it to the trustees. Buildings are also named after him in all the older units of the state university system, including the University of Georgia.

---

6 *Compilation of the Constitutional Provisions and Acts of the Legislature Incorporating and Relating to the City of Athens, and Codification of the Ordinances of Said City*, ed. H. H. Carlton (Athens: Southern Watchman, 1881), p. 67.

7 By the latter half of the nineteenth century, the area east of Jackson Street to the river and between Hoyt Street on the north and Clayton on the south was known as *Lickskillet* (Morris, p. 45), a nickname that is still used elsewhere for a poor section of town (Frederic G. Cassidy, "Notes on Nicknames for Places in the United States," *American Speech*, in press).

Mitchell Street: William Mitchell came to Athens in 1803, and the family was prominent throughout the antebellum years. The original Mitchell Street was in the northwestern part of town; its exact location is uncertain and it was not recorded on the 1854 or 1874 maps. The present-day Mitchell Street is a different one, in the southeastern sector of the old town.

Nesbit Street: The family name was variously spelled *Nesbit, Nesbet, Nesbitt, Nisbet.* John Nisbet was a founder of the Athens Factory, a director of the Georgia Rail Road, and a bank director. In 1874 the street was called Cemetery Street, because it was the access way to the Oconee Cemetery. Today it no longer exists, modern Cemetery Street being in a different location, albeit with the same function. The original name has also disappeared.

Newton Street: Elizur L. Newton and John Newton came to Athens about 1810. They were prominent as merchants, churchmen, innkeepers, and bankers.

Phinizy Street: Major Ferdinand Phinizy bought four town lots in 1805. Jacob Phinizy was a banker and a warden of the town in 1848. What was called Phinizy Street in 1859 was apparently known simply as the Elberton Road (the road to a nearby town) on the 1874 map; today sections of it are variously called the Athens (or Winterville) Road, Spring Valley Road, and the old Elberton Road. In 1874 a different road, one bordering the property of Ferdinand Phinizy, Jacob's son, was known as Phinizy Street; today it is an extension of Hancock Avenue.

Pope Street: Nicholas Pope bought one of the first town lots in 1804, and Burwell Pope was a well-to-do resident of Athens in the 1830s.

Prince Avenue: Oliver Prince had a farm in the northwest of the town; Prince Avenue was the road to it. He was connected, by a chain of literary borrowing, to Thomas Hardy, the novelist. Prince wrote a satirical sketch describing the drilling of the Georgia militia and published it in 1807 in his uncle's newspaper, *The Washington* (Ga.) *Monitor.* It was quickly reprinted in Massachusetts as a pamphlet entitled *The Ghost of Baron Steuben.* An Englishman, John Lambert, came across the satire and in 1810 reprinted it in his *Travels through . . . the United States*, from which it was borrowed by C. H. Gifford for his *History of the Wars Occasioned by the French Revolution* (1817). In 1835, Augustus Longstreet printed it as a chapter entitled "The Militia Company Drill" in his *Georgia Scenes*, crediting it to his friend, Oliver Prince. In 1879, when writing *The Trumpet-Major*, Hardy incorporated the account into his novel by taking it word for word from Gifford's *History*, under the mistaken impression that the English yeomanry was being described. The plagiarism, which says more for Hardy's sense of literary merit than for his conscience about literary property, was discovered in the United States by readers who were familiar with the Longstreet book. It haunted Hardy for the rest of his life, and afterward.[8] The residents on modern Prince Avenue, however, are unconcerned with the literary misadventures of their street's namesake.

Pulaski Street: Casimir Pulaski, the Polish patriot and hero of the American Revolution, came to this country through the mediation of Benjamin Franklin, who was on a diplomatic mission in France. In 1779 he defended Charleston and was mortally wounded in an attack on Savannah. The motive for the naming of the Athens street has sometimes been questioned: "Why Count Pulaski should have been honored by having an Athens street named for him is one of the 'amiable and admirable secrets' of history" (Rowe, p. 32). The naming need, however, not be regarded as a mystery. The association of Pulaski with Benjamin Franklin, for whom the first permanent building on the university campus was named, from which the institution itself came to be called the Franklin College, and Pulaski's heroic death in the Revolutionary cause in Georgia are reasons enough to count him among those "who have done service to . . . the State" (as the naming committee characterized some of their honorees).

Strong Street: Elisha Strong was an early Athens merchant.

Thomas Street: Stevens Thomas, who was one of the first town commissioners (Carlton, p. 67) and the most prominent merchant of early Athens, had his house and store on this street, which was called Alley No. 2 in 1811 (Hull, p. 6).

Waddell Street: Moses Waddel (or Waddell) was the fifth president of the University of Georgia (1819-29); his son, William Henry Waddel, was a professor of ancient languages.

Williams Street: William Williams was a business man in antebellum Athens. The street originally called Williams Street is present, though unnamed on the 1874 map; today it is called Madison Avenue. The present-day Williams Street is in a different part of town.

Wray Street: Thomas Wray was an early citizen of Athens; the street is a one-block road that led to his house.

---

8 This tangled web is laid out by Carl J. Weber in *Hardy of Wessex* (New York: Columbia University Press, 1940), pp. 115-22. I am indebted to George O. Marshall, Jr., for this information and for many other suggestions embodied throughout this paper.

Fewer than a quarter of the original 1859 street names (11) have other than family names for their specifics. Most of them are named for some feature, man-made or natural, to which they lead. They were consequently strictly functional in origin. Some of the streets bearing family names were doubtless likewise originally functional, denoting the road one takes to get to, for example, the Prince farm, or Mr. Wray's house. Only the first of the remaining streets is clearly descriptive in origin:

Broad Street was presumably named for its width, although in fact it is not conspicuously wider than some of the other streets of the central town. The name must have been adopted not long before the 1859 action that officially designated the streets of Athens. Earlier it was generally known as Front Street because it was the boundary that divided the original college yard from the town lots and was thus the front of both. At one time it was also called Public Street (Hull, p. 148).

College Avenue is the street that leads through town to the college entrance.

Factory Street was the road that ran eastward of the college yard from the central town to the Athens Factory, which was proudly acknowledged locally as the first mill for the manufacture of cotton cloth south of the Potomac (Morris, p. 11). The name was still on the 1874 map; but, with the disappearance of the Factory, the street was renamed. Today the upper portion of it is known as Spring Street (this portion running by what once was the town spring, no longer to be seen), and the lower portion has been renamed Mitchell Street, originally the name for a different street apparently no longer in existence.

Foundry Street ran from Broad Street to the Foundry, an important manufactory of early Athens. The most famous product of the Athens Foundry was the Confederate double-barreled cannon. Produced in 1862 at a cost of $350, it consisted of two barrels cast together and diverging by approximately three degrees. The cannon was simultaneously to fire two balls connected by a chain; the divergent angle of the barrels was to send the balls in slightly different directions, stretching the chain between them, and mowing down a whole line of Yankee troopers with one shot. "When the cannon was test fired on the Newton Bridge Road near Athens, one ball left the muzzle before the other, and the two balls pursued an erratic course. According to a contemporary report, 'It had a kind of circular motion, plowed up an acre of ground, tore up a cornfield, mowed down saplings, and the chain broke, the two balls going in opposite directions. One of the balls killed a cow in a distant field, while the other knocked down a chimney from a log cabin.' The observers 'scattered as though the entire Yankee army had been turned loose in that vicinity' " (Coleman, p. 96). The cannon was declared a success locally and sent off to the Confederate Arsenal at Augusta, where, however, it was declared unsatisfactory because of the difficulty in getting the two barrels to fire simultaneously. The cannon was returned to Athens, where its saga continued to unfold. "During the unpleasantness between the North and South there was a fear that the enemy were coming to Athens. A meeting was held and resolutions adopted, that on the approach of danger, Dr. Moore should fire the double-barrel cannon, then in front of the Town Hall. All the women were to get inside and the men were to form a circle and fight the foul invader to the death. One calm Sunday when the women were at church, and the men lying around home with little clothes on, some devilish boys fired that gun. The ensuing scene baffles description. The women ran screaming, the churches broke up, and the men appeared as they were. After the excitement subsided the hall was found packed with men, not a woman could get inside. The number wounded in the scuffle to get inside has never been reported" (Morris, p. 15).

Market Street was the site of the false alarm just recounted. A combination town hall and public market had been built in the middle of Market Street, hence the name, which remained on the 1874 map, but later was changed, probably when the market was closed. The street was then renamed *Washington*, in honor of the first president of the nation. The new designation, suggested by Eustace W. Speer, Professor of Belles Lettres at the university, makes it one of the few streets named for persons who did not reside in Athens.

Oconee Street runs from the old town to the lower bridge over the Oconee River.

River Street ran from the northeastern corner of the old town to the upper bridge over the Oconee River and thence on toward the neighboring town of Danielsville. Today the street is called North Avenue. The present day River Road is a completely different street, paralleling the Oconee River in the south part of town.

Rock Spring Street is on the west side of town. It ran southward to and crossed a small branch and may, therefore, have been named after the branch's wellspring. On the other hand, the 1805 map identified the town spring, which was near the center of town, as Rock Spring; either there was more than one spring of that name or the street's name is purely commemorative.

School Street ran from the western edge of the old town to the Lucy

Cobb Institute, named in memory of the eldest daughter of T. R. R. Cobb. The school was opened in January 1859, the same year that the streets were officially named, and eventually became one of the most distinguished women's finishing schools in the South. The coincidence of the opening of the school with the adoption of street names doubtless accounts for the name of this street; it did not, however, endure. On the 1854 map the street had been called *Taylor*; on the 1874 map, the western portion of the street was called *Taylor* and the eastern portion *Reese*. Today the entire stretch is known as *Reese Street*. The name *School Street* seems to have been a topical enthusiasm that failed to take hold.

Wall Street is perhaps the smallest street in Athens, being one short block in length and relatively narrow. It is located in the oldest part of town in the middle of one of the original blocks; it does not, however, appear on any of the early maps, even that of 1854. After having been named in 1859, it does appear on the 1874 and later maps. Possibly it began as an alley and only came to be regarded and used as a regular street after its naming. The name itself is a mystery. There is no clear motive for it, unless perhaps it refers to the wall of a building by which the alley ran.

Water Street, on the south side of town, ran from Baldwin Street to the lower bridge over the Oconee River. A street in the same area today is known as *Williams Street*. The present-day Water Street parallels the east bank of the Oconee from Broad Street to the upper bridge in the northeast. Hynds (p. 143, n. 20) records the name of the 1859 street as *Waler* or *Wales*, perhaps as a result of difficulty in reading the handwriting in which the Council Minutes were kept.

It is possible that the committee naming Athens streets in 1859 overlooked some—either as too insignificant or simply through oversight. Although not mentioned by the committee, a short street running east-west near the town spring was called Spring Street on the 1854 map. Today the same street is called South Street (going on the south side of Broad Street), whereas what is called Spring Street today runs north-south by the old spring site. It is likely that the streets around the spring in the early and mid nineteenth century were ill-defined.

Two other streets not mentioned in the 1859 naming are present and named on the 1854 map and still exist: Church Street and Harris Street. Church Street was certainly named for Alonzo Church, the sixth president of the university (1829-59). Church's 30 years in office make him the longest tenured of all the presidents of the university and would certainly have qualified him as the namesake for an Athens Street during his lifetime, but perhaps the city fathers shared Thomas Jefferson's prejudice against naming places or institutions after living persons—it being more decorous and safer to await their demise, after which honorees can do nothing to change one's good opinion of them. As much is implied by the preface to the committee's report, quoted above. Church lived until 1862; it is possible that the street was popularly called by his name during the later years of his life, but was deliberately passed over by the committee of 1859, who left its naming for a more decorous time. The namesake of Harris Street is uncertain. Rowe (p. 31) thinks it was either Col. Jeptha V. Harris or the Hon. Stephen W. Harris: "For which of these two the street was named is not recorded." Harris was a common name in early Athens history, so there are still other potential candidates for the honor.

By 1874, most of the 1859 streets still existed and maintained their names, as they do even today. Fifteen new streets had appeared, most of them on the outskirts of town. The name categories are approximately the same as those of the earlier streets. Many commemorate persons: *Adams, Carr, Erwin, Habersham, Miller, Phinizy*, and *Reese* streets. Others were directional: *Armory, Bobbin Mill, Buena Vista* (leading to the Buena Vista farm, there being also a Buena Vista Baptist Church), *Georgia Factory, Monroe* (town), and *Plantation* roads, and the *Road to Harmony Grove and Clarksville. Nowhere Road* should probably be regarded as a directional name too. A new category, the propaganda name, appeared with *States Rights Street*, although 1874 was rather late for the message to have much effect; the street is called *Henderson Avenue* today.

THE NEW STREET NAMES

The 46 new street names are all apparently post-1960. They thus are at least a hundred years later than the old names discussed in the preceding section. These names were chosen for study not quite, but almost, at random. They are all of the streets known to exist or mapped in four contiguous subdivisions and an apartment complex in one of the largest new residential areas. The area is typically suburban.

The most recently named street in the area is *Cedar Shoals Road*. The name *Cedar Shoals* itself has strong historical associations with Athens. The first settlement in the county was on the banks of the Oconee River at the spot called Cedar Shoals (not for decorative purposes, but because the river ran shallow and there was a grove of cedar trees). It was there that Daniel Easley had constructed a mill on part of his 1000 acres, of which he was to sell 633 as the site of the University of Georgia and the town of Athens. The name for this street is therefore commemorative or perhaps directional since it leads to the Cedar Shoals High School, a new institution built about the same time as the street. Two small streets branching off Cedar Shoals Road serve the Tivoli Apartments, the only structure, other than the school, located on the road. The apartment complex is named apparently not for the Italian community, but for the Danish park, for the streets have a Scandinavian theme: *Viking Court* and *Skandia Circle*.

Immediately to the north of *Cedar Shoals Road* is the Cedar Creek subdivision, which is named after a small branch that flows through it. One of the two main entry streets to the subdivision is named *Cedar Creek Drive*; it leads to and crosses the creek, but is less a directional name than a decorative one. "Cedar Creek" was adopted by the developers of the area as a term for the subdivision and one of its streets not to direct persons to the creek, but because of the picturesque value of the name. Spin-off names are *Cedar Creek Court*, *Cedar Springs Drive* (there is no spring in the area), and *Cedar Circle*. There is a dominant arboreal theme for street names in the subdivision. Others derived from trees are *Chinquapin Place* and *Way* (the specific term being of Algonquian origin and not especially characteristic of north Georgia), *Ponderosa Drive* (the second main entry street to the subdivision, named after a Western tree), *Spruce Valley Road* (there is no valley in the area), *Sweet Gum Drive*, and *Torrey Pine Place* (a California tree). Generalized tree names are *Arbor View Drive* and *Orchard Knob Lane* (there are no arbors to be viewed in the area and no knobs on which orchards might be planted). Hardly named for a tree, although at least for vegetation, are *Broomsedge Court* and *Trail*. Suggestive of trees because of the morpheme *wood* in their names are *Dunwoody Drive*; *Ravenwood Court*, *Place*, and *Run*; and *Rollingwood Drive* (which curves, if it does not quite roll). Trees suggest birds (and the name *Ravenwood* is at least semi-avian), thus: *Mockingbird Circle* and *Whippoorwill Circle*. *Sunnybrook Drive*, although in no sense a tree name, is aquatically linked to the second part of the subdivision name, *Cedar Creek*. A few names seem to have no connection with the dominant theme: *Sandstone Circle*, *Court*, and *Drive*; and *Horseshoe Circle* (which is shaped like neither a horseshoe nor a circle, being only slightly curved).

Jockey Club Estates is a small four-street development to the east of Cedar Creek. The main entry, *Jockey Club Drive*, sets the theme, which is followed by *Churchill Circle* (suggesting Churchill Downs, site of the

Kentucky Derby), *Shoemaker Court* (Willie Shoemaker, the jockey who holds the record for winning races), and *Citation Court* (the winner of the triple crown in 1948).

To the south of Jockey Club Estates is Plantation Estates, with a pioneer theme. The main street is *Plantation Drive*; smaller streets are *Homestead Drive, Frontier Court,* and *Doe Run.*[9] Adjacent to these streets are *Orchard Circle* and *Indian Lake Court* (needless to say, there is no lake in the area).

Still further to the south is the subdivision Waverly Woods, from which one might have expected a literary theme. In fact, the theme is again arboreal. Some streets in the area have specific tree names: *Tamarack Drive* and *Great Oak Drive* and *Court*; others have generalized or suggestive names: *Shady Grove Drive, Woodstock Drive,* and *Deertree Drive.* One sport is *Longview Drive,* although a long view of anything hardly seems possible amid so much vegetation.

COMPARISON OF THE OLD AND THE NEW

What is most characteristic of all the early names, whether they commemorate prominent citizens (like *Lumpkin Street*), identify places to which they lead (like *Foundry Street*), or otherwise reflect the local scene (as *Broad Street* describes itself), is that they speak an attachment to the area, its history, geography, and culture. Nineteenth-century street names "belong" to the locality; they are appropriate names, being commemorative, functional, or descriptive. A striking change has come over the names given to streets in recent years. With the exception of *Cedar Shoals Road*, which commemorates the original settlement in the Athens area, and possibly *Cedar Creek Drive*, which at least leads to Cedar Creek, all of the new names lack the kind of appropriateness the old names have. Instead, the new names are decorative. They are chosen for their pleasant associations and hence for their commercial value. They do not relate to the land or the community, but are synthetic concoctions that might as well be used to name streets in Arizona, Wisconsin, or Maine. They seem, indeed, to be deliberately unlocal.

On the other hand, the new names have a kind of internal patterning that the old ones lack. Although most of the old names commemorate persons, they are not grouped so that, for example, all the streets

---

9 Although deer are occasionally still seen in the area, this name is probably decorative; it is unlikely that the street was the site of a deer path. On the other hand, the town of Doerun (pronounced to rhyme with *florin*), Georgia, surely preserves a bit of natural history.

named for university presidents are in one place, all those named for bankers in another, and so on. The old names are distributed without pattern, relative to one another. Not so the new names. Each subdivision has a dominant theme to which its street names relate: trees, horse racing, pioneering, Scandinavia. In effect, then, the use of a theme has replaced the older custom of naming streets appropriately (whether commemoratively, functionally, or descriptively). One of the new names is "appropriate" if it relates to the dominant theme of its subdivision. The "appropriateness" of the new names is linguistic, relating a name to other names around it; the appropriateness of the old names is referential, relating a name to the thing it designates or to the history of the community.

A third striking difference between the old street names and the new ones is the choice of generics. Among the old names, *street* is the overwhelming favorite (42 of 46), with *avenue* a very distant second (4). Neither of those generics is used in the new street names, which have far greater variety: *drive* (18), *court* (10), *circle* (8), *place* (3), *road* (2), *run* (2), *way* (1), *lane* (1), and *trail* (1). The new generics are clearly chosen for variety and for their associations of rusticity or exclusiveness and opulence. The generic *street* in the old names is purely functional, being the most usual common noun for the referent. On the other hand, the several generics in the new names aim to be like the specifics, decorative. They are chosen for effect, not for usefulness.

These three differences between old and new names all result from a single cause. In the early nineteenth century, it was usual for settlement to precede naming. First came the people, building houses, setting up businesses, organizing a community; then, after a street was already in use, someone would decide it was high time for an official name. A long while might lapse between those two events; the first streets in Athens were laid out in the early 1800s, but it was not until 1859, three generations later, that names were officially chosen. When the time came for official action, perhaps a name had already become attached to the street by popular consensus; if so, only official adoption of that name was needed. On the other hand, no name might have developed spontaneously, or a scattering of different names; in that case, to settle the matter, the official namers could look to the history of the street and the larger community or to the uses and characteristics of the street. Thus developed the commemorative, functional, and descriptive names—the classic sort of name in earlier Athens, as in earlier America generally.

Today the order of events has been reversed. Now naming precedes settlement. Typically, a developer subdivides a large plot of land into residential lots, lays out the streets and paves some of them, and gives names to his creations, which become the official designations of those streets before there are any people living on them. When the first suburbanites settle in the new area, it has no history or existing institutions, and the streets are likely to be indistinguishable from one another in appearance; but the streets have names. The developer has had a *tabula rasa* to write upon, limited only by his sense of style and of what will help to sell the lots. The result is the new naming pattern for streets.

Whereas once a street name was an integral part of the history and life of the community, today it is often an artificial appliqué, a mere decoration of doubtful taste. Popular culture in the second half of the twentieth century can be characterized, in part, as one of prepackaged, plastic ostentation. The new street names are part of that new culture. They have few or no local associations. Like clothing from the mail-order house, packaged food from the chain store, and news over the national networks, there is a uniformity of street names everywhere. Local distinctiveness in them is going the way of local distinctiveness in dress, cookery, and opinion—a victim of democratic homogeneity. Classic names have given way to classy ones.

How will the future regard these names we are giving our streets today? Time smooths over many a rough edge and mellows a gaudy hue with its patina. Will the passing years lend dignity to *Doe Run?* Will they build up historical associations for *Broomsedge Trail?* Will they improve the esthetics of *Jockey Club Drive?* Or are such names destined to remain artificial and slick—classy names, not classic ones? Some onomatologist of the year 2100, some student of place-names with the dedication and skill of Claude Henry Neuffer, will have to answer those questions.

University of Georgia

Names as Verbal Icons[1]

W. F. H. NICOLAISEN

> "And in the end, their names were only names and
> names — and nothing more.
>
> Or, if their names were something more than names ..."
> Thomas Wolfe, *Of Time and the River*.

In a detailed discussion of the process of semantic change involved when words become names, I have suggested elsewhere[2] that names reflect at least three levels of meaning:

(a) the *lexical* level, i.e. the dictionary meaning of the word or words comprising the name;

(b) the *associative* level, i.e. the reason or reasons why the particular lexical (or onomastic) items were used in the naming process – this, incidentally, is also the level on which connotative names operate;

(c) the *onomastic* level, i.e. the meaning of a denotative name as a name, or its application based on lexical and associative semantic elements, but usually no longer dependent on them.

If this assumption of a threefold semantic tier is correct, *naming* might be paraphrased as "the process by which words become names by association." It is also worth reiterating that as part of the final stages of this process the end-product, the name,[3] frequently loses its lexical meaning and, divested of the associations which initially caused the transition from word to name, more often than not operates, from a semantic point of view, on the onomastic level alone. Consequently, while for the correct usage of a name it is necessary, indeed essential, that the user know it, it is not expected of him that he also understand it, since that would demand a survival or at least a recovery of the lexical meaning. Such a reduction to the lexical level is, however, normally uncalled for, in view of the fact that even when the word meaning of a name is accessible

---

[1] This is a considerably revised version of a paper read at the Annual Meeting of the American Name Society in Chicago on December 30, 1973. It is affectionately dedicated to Margaret Bryant, not only because she did not hear the first version.

[2] "Linguistics in Place-Name Studies," in *Current Trends in Onomastics in the United States* (in preparation).

[3] Or, in Algeo's terms, "a word people use to call someone or something by." See John Algeo, *On Defining the Proper Name*, University of Florida Humanities Monographs, no. 1 (Gainesville, Florida), p. 87.

without any special effort or knowledge, it is ordinarily ignored by the name user, to the point of total unawareness; therefore the fact that Mr. Baker is a butcher does not bother anyone.

While the linguistically oriented onomastician – and practically all name scholars have so far almost by definition, but certainly by training, been linguists, and especially linguistic historians – shows a primary concern in the task of making a name lexically meaningful again, the creative writer, and particularly the poet, has gladly accepted the lexically meaningless name as a literary device of no mean possibilities. This is not to say that all writers and poets have in fact seen the creative possibilities of names in this way; indeed, many have approached and employed them rather like the linguistic historian – it did matter to them what the real or perceived lexical meanings of the names of their characters or localities were, and it is therefore quite a legitimate pursuit on the part of literary onomastics to ferret out the author's etymological intentions, as an important aspect of the literary function of names.

However, what this paper is attempting to do goes beyond such direct relationship between name etymology and quality of character or place; its concern is to be rather the deliberate poetic usage of the lexically meaningless name as a foregrounding device by the creative artist who seizes upon the onomastic item as a welcome means of enriching and condensing the texture of his work. This is true of both oral tradition and written composition, and it is therefore just as helpful to illustrate our line of argument by examples from, let us say, popular balladry[4] as from conscious art poetry, whether imitative of the ballad or not.

At its simplest, in such usage, the name – and I am obviously thinking particularly of place-names in this context – becomes a convenient localizing device, pinpointing the external or internal event of the poem:

> "The king sits in Dunfermling town / Drinking the blude-reid wine"
> (Sir Patrick Spens)
> "There lived a wife at Usher's Well, / and a wealthy wife was she"
> (The Wife of Usher's Well)
> "I have a bower at Bucklesfordberry, / full daintily it is dight"
> (Little Musgrave)
> "There dwelt a man in fair Westmoreland, / Johnie Armstrong men did him call"
> (Johnie Armstrong)
> "There lives a lad in Rhynie's lands, an' anither in Auchindore"
> (Lang Johnny More)

These randomly chosen lines from Sir Francis James Child's canon of traditional ballads,[5] can easily be matched by instances from art poetry:

---

[4] "Place-Names in Traditional Ballads," *Folklore* 84 (1973), pp. 299–312.

[5] Francis James Child, *The English and Scottish Popular Ballads* (New York: Houghton, Mifflin and Company, 1882–1898).

"In Xanadu did Kubla Khan a pleasure dome decree"
      (Samuel Taylor Coleridge, *Kubla Khan*)
"All in the Downs the fleet was moored, / The streamers waving in the wind"
      (John Gay, *Sweet William's Farewell to Black-eyed Susan*)
"Let Observation, with extensive view, / Survey mankind, from China to Peru"
      (Samuel Johnson, *The Vanity of Human Wishes*)
"Sweet Auburn! loveliest village of the plain"
      (Oliver Goldsmith, The Deserted Village)
"Ye flowery banks of bonie Doon, / How can ye blume sae fair"
      (Robert Burns, *Bonie Doon*).

In calling such usage "simple," one may with justification be accused of trivialising the poet's or singer's intent and of neglecting important facets of poetic strategy. In order to answer such criticism, the quotations just listed were therefore chosen deliberately to represent various degrees of simplicity or complexity. Dunfermline, Westmoreland, Rhynie, Auchindore, and the Downs are very real and identifiable geographical locations, some of them more widely known than others, which serve the purpose of localisation and that alone. China and Peru are just as real and identifiable, but in the context of the Johnson poem are clearly not meant as actual locations but rather as limiting geographical references. Usher's Well and Bucklesfordberry sound real, and certainly are real as locations anchoring the respective ballad narratives "to the ground," so to speak, within the ballad "world," but to the best of this writer's knowledge have never been identified and might consequently just as well be termed imaginary in the same sense in which, in spite of its basis in historical reality, Xanadu might be called imaginary. Sweet Auburn and Bonnie Doon are by no means localities invented by Oliver Goldsmith and Robert Burns but the epithets added, as well as the evocative address, intimate that our two poets had obviously more in mind than a toponymic shorthand for a geographical setting, a more limited kind of poetic technique which is akin to the place-name rhyme of oral tradition.[6]

As regards lexical meaning, English-speaking readers – and these ballads and poems are, after all, in English – may recognise certain elements in such names as Usher's Well, Bucklesfordberry, Westmoreland, Auburn, and the Downs, and are likely to be aware of at least partial meanings. There is, however, no poetic significance in such partial transparence, and these names might on the whole be as semantically opaque as the others – Dunfermline, Rhynie, Auchindore, Doon, and Xanadu, China and Peru, although the opacity of the first four of these is, of course, less formidable to speakers of Celtic languages. The main point to remember is that etymologies, or attempts at etymologisation, simply do not enter into the picture.

---

[6] See, for example, W. F. H. Nicolaisen, "Some Gaelic Place-Rhymes," *Scottish Studies* 7 (1963), pp. 100–102.

The hints contained in Goldsmith's "Sweet Auburn" and Burns' "Bonnie Doon" are sufficient to make us realise that a name may function in a poem in more than one way, quite regardless of its etymology, real or perceived. In addition to is localising effect, it may have other qualities, notions, feelings, impressions to convey which may or may not have a direct connection with its location. Instances in the first category, i. e. in the group for which it does matter where the names are located, would be, it seems, Westmoreland, the Downs, Dunfermline, Rhynie, Auchindore, Xanadu, China and Peru which, in their own different fashions, provide the reader or listener with some of the flavor of the places so named, whether it be the peculiar scenic beauty of the English Lake District, the historical associations of the royal residence on the River Forth, the cultural landscape of the farming communities of the Scottish northeast, or the exotic appeal and otherness of places and countries far from home. Much will depend in each case on the knowledge which the reader or listener has of the places concerned. It is more than likely, for instance, that names like Dunfermline, Rhynie, and Auchindore convey very little topographic or cultural detail to most people outside Scotland or Britain, whereas their isolating onomastic burden is far greater for a Scot, especially for Dunfermline, less so for Rhynie, and least for Auchindore, although the general picture of the landscape of the north-east of Scotland still remains.

To the second category, i. e. to those names which have a secondary function not directly related to their location, would belong such names as Usher's Well, Bucklesfordberry, Auburn and Doon. For the first two examples, no location is known anyhow, and any secondary role, apart from the apparent authenticity conferred on a ballad narrative by the mention of a place-name, however unidentifiable or fictitious, will for that reason have to be deduced from internal evidence. For the name Usher's Well there is next to no information of this kind, and we must come to the conclusion that it only has a localising function, albeit a fictitious one, in the ballad.[7] For Bucklesfordberry, on the other hand, the night of love and morning of disaster for Little Musgrave and Lady Barnard (they spend the night together at Bucklesfordberry and are both killed by the irate and jealous Lord Barnard on his unexpected return in the early morning) creates a new literary meaning which one can no longer ignore or dismiss from one's mind whenever the name is mentioned. Auburn and Doon, too, although primarily this English village in Yorkshire and that Scottish river in Ayrshire, take on a new literary role as a result of the poems in which they occur so that Auburn, as "Sweet Au-

---

[7] In his adaptation of this traditional ballad under the title of "The Sea-Wife," Rudyard Kipling, for instance, substitutes the equally unidentifiable *Northern Gate* for *Usher's Well*.

burn, loveliest village of the plain," becomes the poetic prototype of a Deserted Village, and Doon, as "Bonnie Doon," can no longer be disassociated from false love and deceit which makes mockery ·of appearances. Bucklesfordberry, Auburn, and Doon carry out this their secondary function successfully, whether their location is known and appreciated or not. For those who do know the Yorkshire Auburn and/or the Ayrshire Doon, their empirical personal knowledge will allow them to appreciate the poetic works in question on an additional level which generates visual association with topographic detail. The point at issue, however, is that such knowledge is not essential for a full understanding of these poems.

There would undoubtedly be considerable justification in detecting in this latter group traces of metonymic transference of meaning, although the contrast literal versus figurative is so much more easily handled with regard to non-onomastic lexical items. When somebody says "The whole village rejoiced,"[8] it does not need much experience in the language of literature to understand the noun phrase "the whole village" as standing for "all the people in the village." When a newscaster tells us that "Washington has reacted cautiously to the latest peace proposals," most of us also realise that the place-name Washington here represents "the people in Washington who run the American government," but since Washington has no, or at best partial, lexical meaning, the literal use to which the figurative one is here contrasted must of necessity be a purely onomastic one, i.e. Washington, capital of the United States, situated at such and such a latitude and longitude, of the following size and extent, administrative status, etc., whereas the derivation of the name from that of the first President of the United States, the conversion of a personal name into a place-name, does not come into play at all. For most names there is no "literal" usage-cum-meaning in the ordinary sense. Because of the shift in the level of meaning outlined at the beginning, most names, even when accessible on the lexical level, are basically figurative in so far as their application tends to vary from orthodox language usage and introduces a measure of noticeable linguistic abnormality or even downright audacity, as when a place is given the name of "Wounded Knee."

It is against this background of onomastic "figurativeness" that we have to contrast the figurative usage of names in a literary sense, a poetic deployment which permits the writer to build a name into his general metonymic and symbolic strategies, even to the extent of metaphorical application, stimulating and encouraging the thinking in names, in onomastic images, rather than in words. The onomastic metaphor "Wounded

---

[8] This example and the next are used by Geoffrey N. Leech, *A Linguistic Guide to English Poetry* (London: Longmans, 1969), 148–149.

Knee," for example, turns into a literary metaphor in the last line of Stephen Vincent Benét's toponymically oriented poem "American Names," in the injunction "Bury my heart at Wounded Knee" (which, recently, moved further along the figurative route as the title of a book). In the context of Benét's poem, "Wounded Knee" becomes the culminating, ultimate, non-reducible distillation of a cultural essence. Together with "the plumed war-bonnet of Medicine Hat, Tucson and Deadwood and Lost Mule Flat" and such others as Harrisburg, Spartanburg and Painted Post, it is molded by the poet into a set of verbal icons, of pseudo-sacred images, in both sound and sense, not only foregrounding his self-confessed love for American names but also removing them irrevocably from the realm of lexicographical definition and from the normal linguistic processes of encoding and decoding.

Similarly, the opening two lines of Carl Sandburg's poem *Localities* – "Wagon Wheel Gap is a place I never saw / And Red Horse Gulch and the chutes of Cripple Creek" – in their insistence on the enumeration of quaint onomastic reminders of the romanticised life of the American frontiersman and the great move west, are an attempt at creating a particular atmosphere through metaphors that turn what are to all intents and purposes recognisable, meaningful lexical compounds into semantically denuded poetic sound symbols of American geography and popular culture.

Perhaps the strongest and most densely textured examples of what might be called the poetic prose of name worship, i.e. an iconically perceived accumulation of figurative geographical names turned metaphors, occur in Thomas Wolfe's epic *Of Time and the River*. Having in an earlier passage put into words his conviction as to the identity of name and place, at least in a French setting ("... what name could more perfectly express Arles than the name it has – it gives you the whole place, its life, its people, its peculiar fragrance ...")[9], the author extols in several ecstatic paragraphs "the thunder of imperial names, the names of men and battles, the names of places and great rivers, the mighty names of the States."[10] Battles, states, Indian nations, railroads, engineers, engines, sleeping-cars, tramps are pressed into service, savored, proudly offered to tongue and ear and mind as thundering hymns of worship and intoxicating songs of patriotism in onomastic garb; and all are just a preparation, a prologue for the concluding hydronymic extravaganza, echoing the main theme of the book[11]:

---

[9] Thomas Wolfe, *Of Time and the River* (New York: Charles Scribner's Sons, 1935), p. 698.

[10] *Ibid.*, p. 866.

[11] *Ibid.*, p. 867.

Finally, the names of the great rivers that are flowing in the darkness (Sweet Thames, flow gently till I end my song). By the waters of life, by time, by time: the names of the great mouths, the mighty maws, the vast, wet, coiling, never-glutted and unending snakes that drink the continent. Where, sons of men, and in what other land will you find others like them, and where can you match the mighty music of their names. – The Monongahela, the Colorado, the Rio Grande, the Columbia, the Tennessee, the Hudson (Sweet Thames!); the Kennebec, the Rappahannock, the Delaware, the Penobscot, the Wabash, the Chesapeake, the Swannanoa, the Indian River, the Niagara (Sweet Afton!); the Saint Lawrence, the Susquehanna, the Tombigbee, the Nantahala, the French Broad, the Chattahoochee, the Arizona, and the Potomac (Father Tiber!) – these are a few of their princely names, these are a few of their great, proud, glittering names, fit for the immense and lonely land that they inhabit.

No historical dilutions or delusions here, no search for origins, just locations and sounds, sounds, sounds – to use the author's epithets "princely, great, proud, glittering" sounds, a "mighty music ... fit for the immense and lonely land." A poetic illusion, perhaps; a linguistic distortion, possibly; a perpetuation of a myth, probably; an aesthetic pleasure, certainly – but also a feast (or is it a surfeit?) of names as metaphors, and a delight for the onomastic iconographers – us.

The State University of New York at Binghamton

Soviet Russian Given Names

PATRICIA ANNE DAVIS

Russian onomastics is a field in which there is much opportunity for scholarly research. Given names, in particular, still need much investigation. Only about a dozen scholars in Russia and the Soviet Union have concerned themselves with the problem of personal names, and even less research has been done abroad. In recent years, some research has been done in the Soviet Union mainly on what the Soviet researchers call "new names." This term is generally meant to include those names which became popular in Russia only after the Revolution of 1917 and which are not found in the Russian Orthodox Church Calendar of Saints.

Only one book has been written entirely on the subject of Soviet names. This one, *Novye imena*[1] ("New Names"), by D. Delert, published in Rostov in 1924, is out of print today and not available even in Moscow's Lenin Library. Among the other Soviet scholars who have dealt with the problem of names, A. V. Superanskaja and L. V. Uspenskij are the best known. Both have written articles and books on various aspects of Russian onomastics, and each has at least one chapter concerned with Soviet names.

One other Soviet work contains a chapter on the "new names." This is *Russkie imena* ("Russian Names") by A. A. Ugrjumov, published in Vologda in 1962. This book, however, was written on a popular rather than a scholarly level, and it contains errors resulting from the strong influence of Soviet attitudes upon the author. In addition, some Soviet names appear in various dictionaries, including the Russian-Ukrainian dictionary of names published by S. F. Levčenko in 1961, and the Russian-White Russian dictionary of names published by M. R. Sudnik in 1965.

---

[1] Transliteration of Russian words and names will conform to the system used in the *Slavic and East European Journal*.

In 1964, the University of Pennsylvania Press published a *Dictionary of Russian Personal Names* which, although concerned mainly with surnames, contains a list of given names, including some "new names." This work, compiled by Morton Benson, is the only American dictionary of Russian names.

The only one of these works that included statistics was the book by Delert. His statistics were designed to prove that workers and peasants were progressively rejecting calendar names in favor of the new Soviet names. He claimed that in 1920, 25.5 per cent of the children born in the Don region received non-calendar names, and in 1923, 49.8 per cent received non-calendar names.[2] His figures seem extremely high and are, in all likelihood, not correct.

The statistics in this paper are based on a study of the names of about 11,000 Russians living in the Soviet Union. These names were found in the divorce notices listed in *Večernjaja Moskva*. This is a Moscow evening newspaper, published every day but Sunday. At present, divorce notices are not listed. Previously they appeared five times a week with approximately 25 notices each time. For the present study, the year 1964 was used. About 11,000 of the persons listed bore Russian (not foreign) patronymics and surnames; these were included in this study. The source itself, however, contains a basic weakness in that the ages of those seeking divorces are not given. It was assumed that an overwhelming majority of persons seeking divorces in Moscow in 1964 were born between 1918 and 1940.

The statistics obtained in this study show a far smaller use of "new names" than those of Delert. Briefly, the numbers are as follows: Of the 5,500 men listed in the divorce notices, 5,356 or 97.4 per cent had traditional Russian Church names. Of the 5,500 women, 5,200 or 94.6 per cent had calendar names. This shows little change from pre-revolutionary practice. Statistics obtained in the same study indicate that 99.3 per cent of men and 97.7 per cent of women born in Russia between 1700 and 1917 bore calendar names. Pre-revolutionary statistics were based mainly on the names of persons found in encyclopedias and biographical dictionaries.

Thus, of the 11,000 Soviet Russian citizens listed in the divorce notices, only 4 per cent had non-calendar names. These names may be discussed under two headings – borrowed names and invented names.

---

[2] *Pravda*, review of *Novye imena* by D. Delert, June 12, 1924.

Three fourths of the non-calendar names are borrowed names. These are mainly Russian adaptations of names used in western countries. Some of these became relatively popular in Russia, particularly those that had some political significance. The given names of widely known revolutionary figures, such as Inessa Armand, Clara Zetkin, Rosa Luxemburg, Robert Eiche, and Felix Dzerzhinsky, appeared several times. A number of other non-calendar names of western origin also appeared more than once. These were *Al'bert, Alina, Alisa, Dina, Èduard, Èrnest, Èmma, Genrix, Nelli*, and *Žanna*.

Besides these fairly popular western borrowings, another 34 western names – some of them Russianized – occurred once each in the 11,000 names considered. They originated in various languages. Sometimes the direct source-language cannot be definitely ascertained, because the name has been Russianized or because it exists in the same form in several western languages. Following are the western names which were recorded and the languages from which they probably came into use in Russia.

1) From French: *Al'bertina, Amelija, Artur, Diana, Èmil, Èmilija, Izabella, Lilija, Luiza, Violetta, Žannetta, Žozefina*.

2) From English: *Džoja, Èdgar, Èlla, Èrik, Frank, Garri, Meri, Tomas, Vil'jam*.

3) From German: *Dora, Èl'za, Gertruda, Irma, Iza, Izol'da, Lora*.

4) From Italian: *Džemma, Floria, Paola, Stella*.

5) From Spanish: *Èl'mira, Konsuèla*.

It can easily be seen that some of these names could have come into Russian from a language other than the one with which they are identified here. For example, *Tomas* might have come from French, German, or even Spanish, rather than from English. Some of these names were known in Russia long before the Revolution of 1917. Foreign names had always been fashionable among the Russian nobility. In the early nineteenth century, names such as *Al'bert, Leonard, Robert, Èduard, Adolf, Karl*, and *Ludwig* were relatively popular. With the Revolution, however, came one very noticeable change. German names, such as those mentioned above, disappeared almost entirely, and names of English origin, previously extremely rare, began to be recorded more frequently.

The increase in foreign names following the Revolution may be attributed in part to the enforced separation of church and state, and in part to increased literacy. A number of the borrowed names recorded only after the Revolution were introduced into Russia through literature. The Italian name, *Gemma*, appeared in Russian as *Džemma* following the translation of Estelle Voynich's novel, *The Gadfly*.[3] *Èdgar* may have been introduced through a translation of *King Lear*. *Èl'za* and *Isol'da* were heroines of Wagnerian operas. *Meri* was used by the Russian author Mixail Lermontov in his novel, *A Hero of Our Time* (1839).

The increase of literacy among Russians is reflected also by the fact that some children received names used only in literature. Oscar Wilde's *The Picture of Dorian Gray* produced the forms *Dorian*, *Dor*, and *Graj*, all found in the 1964 divorce notices. Some Russian children were named for Shakespearian heroines. The name *Ofilija* was found in this research, and Superanskaja noted also *Dezdemona* and *Džul'etta*.[4]

Russian children were named for some of Puškin's heroes. The story has been told that the father of Russian cosmonaut German Titov (born 1935) was a great admirer of Puškin, and, therefore, named his son *German* for the hero of *The Queen of Spades* and his daughter *Zemfira* for the heroine of *The Gypsies*.[5] This story may or may not be true. The hero of *The Queen of Spades* is named *Germann* and not *German* – etymologically a different name. Puškin chose the name carefully to indicate that his hero was of German background. But *Zemfira* is undoubtedly taken from Puškin.

The most popular non-calendar name found in this research is *Svetlana*. This is also a literary name. Its origin is obscure. Soviet scholars consider it a pre-Christian Slavic name, but it is not found in Old Church Slavic or Old Russian sources. It was used by the Russian poet Žukovskij and may have been his creation. It was not recorded before the Revolution, but appeared in twenty-fourth place among names found in the divorce notices. Its popularity continued to increase, and, since the Second World War, it has been one of the most popular names in the Soviet Union. The fact that

---

[3] A. V. Superanskaja, *Kak vas zovut? Gde vy živete?* (Moscow, 1964), p. 25.

[4] *Ibid.*

[5] This story is told by Superanskaja (p. 24) and others. It came originally from *Pravda* (August 7, 1961).

Stalin's daughter was named *Svetlana* undoubtedly helped to increase the popularity of this name.

The other type of "new name" is the invented name. This is the more interesting type and also the rarer. Only one per cent of the 11,000 Soviet Russians considered here bore invented names. These names were created to honor the Revolution or some revolutionary figure. They were most common in the early days of Soviet power when enthusiasm for the cause was at its height. In general, these Soviet neologisms are of several types. Here, they will be considered in the following groups: 1) Names taken from the name of Lenin; 2) Names taken from the names of other well-known revolutionary figures; 3) Scientific terms used as names; 4) Revolutionary terms used as names; 5) Acronyms; 6) Names of unknown origin.

The most common type of Soviet neologism is that formed from some part of Lenin's name. Many persons in the Soviet Union wanted to name a child for Lenin. The majority of them simply used his given name, *Vladimir*, which, consequently, became the most popular name in the country. Almost ten per cent of the men listed in the 1964 divorce notices were named *Vladimir*. Other parents made up their own forms as tributes. Among persons considered here, the following were recorded: *Lenian, Leniana, Vilen, Vladilen, Vladilena, Vladlen,* and *Ninel'*. The last is *Lenin* spelled backwards. It is a feminine name and the most popular of Soviet neologisms. Soviet citizens are generally familiar with it. It seems to have reached its peak of popularity in the thirties, and to be declining at present. Superanskaja recorded the following additional forms, composed from parts of Lenin's name: *Vilena, Vilenina, Vilora* (from *V. I. Lenin, organizator revoljucii* "organizer of the Revolution"), and *Lenina*.[6]

Other revolutionaries were also honored with namesakes. It has already been shown that the given names of various revolutionary figures became popular in Russia. In addition, various forms of surnames were used as given names. Those recorded here were *Èngel'sina, Èngelina, Marks,* and *Marat*. The last was previously one of the most popular Soviet names. Other interesting names of this type were noted by Delert. Some of these are *Dzerž* (from Dzerzhinsky), *Ledav* (from *Lev Davydovič Trotskij*), *Lunačara*

---

[6] Superanskaja, p. 85.

(from Lunačarskij), *Marksina,* and *Èngfrid* (a reverse acronym from *Fried*rich *Eng*els).[7]

At this time, many common nouns were given to children as names. Most of these nouns were either scientific terms or words expressing something important to the Revolution. The following scientific terms were recorded here: *Gelij* "helium," *Granit* "granite," *Stal'* "steel" (Also recorded was *Stalij* with the suffix used in the names of chemical elements. It is possible that this name was given in honor of Stalin.) Superanskaja mentioned a few similar ones, such as *Radij* "radium," *Torij* "thorium" (an element used in making atomic weapons), and *Nikel'* "nickel" (probably a feminine name). She also noted other scientific terms which were apparently used as names. Some of these are *Traktor* "tractor," *Èlektrostancija* "electric power station," and *Èlektrofikacija* "electrification."[8] Ugrjumov supplied *Èlektron* "electron," *Raketa* "rocket," and *Differencial* "differential."[9]

In addition to those who used scientific terms as names, there were also parents who used words intended to glorify the Revolution or some aspect of it. Some examples of this type of name found in the divorce notices are *Èra* "era," *Genij* "genius," *Ideja* "idea," *Iskra* "spark" (from the name of a revolutionary newspaper of which Lenin was an editor), *Oktjabr'* "October" (the month of the Revolution), *Oktjabrina* (feminine name from *Oktjabr'*), *Pioner* "pioneer" (also the name of a Soviet youth organization), and *Simvolika* "symbolics." Other names of this type (not recorded in the divorce notices) include *Fevralina* (given in honor of the February Revolution), *Maj* "May" (a masculine name given in honor of the First of May), *Nojabrina* (from *nojabr'* "November," the actual month of the October Revolution), *Volja* "will," *Svoboda* "freedom," *Smena* (a word whose primary meaning is a change of workers in a factory and then, by analogy, the younger generation as replacement for the old), *Dekreta* "decree," *Barrikada* "barricade," and finally *Revoljucija* "Revolution."[10]

It has already been shown that many of the Soviet neologisms were acronyms formed from parts of the names of revolutionary

---

[7] *Pravda,* June 12, 1924.

[8] Superanskaja, pp. 22–23.

[9] A. A. Ugrjumov, *Russkie imena* (Vologda, 1962), p. 36.

[10] Superanskaja, pp. 21–22.

leaders. Word-acronyms were also formed. The following were found in this study: *Kim* (a masculine name known to most Soviets and considered to be formed from the initial letters of *Kommunisti-českij Internacional Molodeži* "Communist Youth International," 1919–1943), *Novomir* (probably from *novyj mir* "new world," constructed to appear as a pre-Christian Slavic name), and *Rèm* (from the initial letters of the Russian words for revolution, electrification, and mechanization). Other acronyms noted by Superanskaja include *Revmira* (*revoljucija mira* "world revolution"), *Junarma* (*junaja armija* "army of youth"), *Revdit* (*revoljucionnoe ditja* "child of the Revolution"), *Mjuda* (*Meždunarodnyj junošeskij den'* "International Youth Day" 1915–1945), *Nèra* (*novaja èra* "new era"), *Lenèra* (*Leninskaja èra* "era of Lenin").[11]

There have been other similar acronyms composed by parents for their children. One of the strangest and possibly the most complicated ever recorded was *Lorikèrik* composed of the initial letters of the Russian words for the following: Lenin, October Revolution, industrialization, collectivation, electrification, radio installation, and Communism.[12]

Several of the non-calendar names which appeared in the divorce notices may be considered either western borrowings or invented names. They are basically Western European names which could be given a Soviet political reinterpretation. Among these is the very popular name *Majja*, a pre-Christian name appearing as *Maia* or *Maja* in various European languages. In the Soviet Union it is probably given in honor of the First of May.[13]

Two other names, listed here as western borrowings, have possible political connotations. They are *Gertruda* (reinterpreted by some as an acronym from *geroinja truda* "heroine of labor"), and *Izol'da* (sometimes given in the arctic parts of Russia by parents who mistakenly interpreted it as *izo l'da* "out of ice").[14] There is also one name which is sometimes reinterpreted in the opposite direction. It has been suggested that the popular Soviet neologism *Rèm* is not a Soviet acronym but a Russianized form of the Latin name *Remus*.

---

[11] *Ibid.*, pp. 21, 23.

[12] L. V. Uspenskij, "Zovut zovutkoj," *Literaturnaja Gazeta*, November 14, 1959.

[13] Superanskaja, p. 88. See also: Vera Inber, "Maja," *Short Stories by Soviet Writers*, p. 21.

[14] Superanskaja, p. 23.

This is unlikely because the vowel used in constructing *Rèm* is almost always the same vowel as the initial letter of the Russian word for electrification rather than that of the first syllable of *Remus*. However, the form *Rem* has also been recorded.[15]

It must also be noted that there appeared among the names listed in the divorce notices a significant number of names of unknown origin. They may possibly have been created by an imaginative parent. Those found here are listed below, usually with some suggestion as to their origin.

Alij: possibly a Russian transliteration of the Arabian name *Ali*, the son-in-law of Mohammed.

Damir: possibly an acronym composed of *mir* "world" or "peace" and some other element – perhaps *daj* "Give!"

Èverest: probably from Mt. Everest.

Galija: an alternation of *Galja,* hypocoristic form of *Galina*, or possibly a feminine name derived from gallium, the name of a metallic element.

Geliona: possibly a misspelling of the calendar name *Geliana* or a form derived from *gelij* "helium."

Gèma: probably an alternation of the Italian *Gemma*.

Genofefa: phonetic alternation of German *Genoveva* or a misspelling of the calendar name *Genovefa.*

Junna: possibly an alternation of English *June*.

Lenarij: possibly formed from Lenin. It contains a common suffix for masculine names, seen in *Valerij, Jurij*, and others.

Ljusja: hypocoristic form from *Ljubov', Ljudmila*, or *Ol'ga*, used as a given name.

Min'ko: possibly a Ukrainian surname used by a parent as a given name.

Neriga: possibly a phonetic alternation of the modern Lithuanian feminine name *Neringa* from *neringa* "isthmus."

Reva: possibly from *revoljucija* "revolution."

Rida: This form is known to Superanskaja, who feels that it was used by someone accidently because it sounded like a foreign name. It may be a mispelling of *Rita*, diminutive of *Margarita*.[16]

Romèna: probably a feminine name formed from the given name of French author Romain Rolland.

---

[15] Inber, *Short Stories by Soviet Writers*, pp. 20–22.
[16] Superanskaja, p. 26.

Rudi: a feminine name, possibly a Russian transliteration of English *Rudy* – mistakenly thought to be feminine because of the ending.

Sim: possibly a Russian transliteration of English *Sim,* hypocoristic form of *Simon,* or an acronym formed from the initial letters of *Socialističeskij internacional molodeži* "Socialist Youth International" 1907–1914.

Stènmar: unknown – possibly an acronym.

Suslanna: possibly a misspelling of *Susanna,* perhaps from association with *Svetlana.*

Taja: possibly a hypocoristic form from *Tat'jana* or *Taisija.*

Tanina: possibly derived from *Tanja,* hypocoristic form from *Tat'jana.*

Zira: unknown.

Granik: possibly an alternation of *Granit* "granite," a known Soviet neologism.

Ilijana: possibly a misspelling of the calendar name *Julijana* or a feminine name formed from *Il'ič,* Lenin's patronymic, with the suffix *-jana,* which is found in many feminine names.

One cannot conclude a paper on Soviet names without mentioning some of the most unusual ones. Uspenskij, writing in *Literaturnaja Gazeta* (November 14, 1959), gives three such examples. He tells of a boy incongruously named *Milèdi* (milady), and of a person whose passport bore, as a given name, the words *Cvet višnevogo dereva v mae* "The color of the cherry tree in May." He writes of an incident in which a girl asked the principal of her school if he intended to read the full names of students at the graduation exercises. When he answered affirmatively, the girl burst into tears and ran from the room. Puzzled, the principal checked the file of this student whom he knew as Velira, and found that her official given name was *Velikij Rabočij* "Great Workman."

Use of such Soviet neologisms was at a peak in the twenties and thirties when the Soviet Union was new and many of its young people were filled with over-zealous patriotism. Twenty years later, the children who had been the innocent victims of this zeal had grown up and become parents themselves. Apparently remembering the difficulties they or their friends had encountered in childhood because of their unusual names, they did not wish to subject their own children to similar embarrassment. Many masculine bearers of

Soviet invented names, when they reached adulthood, changed their names so that their children would have proper patronymics.

This study included, as a supplement. lists of 400 boys and 350 girls born in the Soviet Union between 1947 and 1956 and presently living either in Moscow or in Kislovodsk. a town in the Caucasus. It also included a list of 19 boys and 22 girls born in Kislovodsk in 1964. The only Soviet invented name to appear among these children was *Oktjabrina* which occurred once on the list of school children in Kislovodsk. The only borrowed names to appear among the names of school children were *Artur, Èduard, Èleonora, Èmma, Nelli,* and *Žanna,* which occurred once each. In addition, the names *Majja* and *Žanna* each appeared once in the list of infant girls.

Although these samples are too small to indicate any definite conclusions about the fate of Soviet neologisms after 1940, it is probably accurate to assume that, while they have not yet completely disappeared, they are definitely disappearing. Probably before many more years have passed, they will have disappeared from use completely and be remembered only as a feature of Russian history.

University of Pennsylvania

BIBLIOGRAPHY

Below is a list of available books and articles which contain information on Soviet names.

Benson, Morton. *Dictionary of Russian Personal Names.* Philadelphia: University of Pennsylvania Press, 1964.

Fesenko, Tatiana. "Messaliny i Barrikady." *Novoe Russkoe Slovo* (New York), June 16, 1963.

Inber, Vera. "Maja," in *Short Stories by Soviet Writers.* Moscow: Progress Publishers (no date given).

Levčenko, S. F. *Slovar' sobstvennyx imen ljudej* ("Dictionary of Personal Names"). Akademija nauk Ukrainskoj SSR, 1961.

Pravda. Review of *Novye imena* by D. Delert. June 12, 1924.

Sudnik, M. R. *Slownik asabovyx ulasnyx imen* ("Dictionary of Personal Names"). Minsk: Akademija nauk BSSR, 1965.

Superanskaja, A. V. *Kak vas zovut? Gde vy živete?* ("What Is Your Name? Where Do You Live?"). Moscow: Izdatel'stvo nauka, 1964.

Ugrjumov, A. A. *Russkie imena* ("Russian Names"). Vologda: Vologodskoe knižnoe izdatel'stvo, 1962.

Uspenskij, L. V. *Ty i tvoe imja* ("You and Your Name"). Leningrad: Detgiz, 1960.

— — "Zovut zovutkoj." *Literaturnaja Gazeta.* November 14, 1959.

Is the Name *United States* Singular or Plural?*

ALLEN WALKER READ

IT IS REMARKABLE that the name *United States*, with such a high frequency of usage, should still be unsettled in its grammatical relations. The language has many simple cases of divided usage; but this problem has multifold ramifications in American history. At the Lincoln celebration in 1958 in Galesburg, Illinois, Carl Sandburg declared, "The United States *is*, not *are*. The Civil War was fought over a verb."[1] Let us examine the background of this statement.

There can be no doubt about the usage of the Founding Fathers. John Adams was typical when he wrote in a letter of November 13, 1783, from London: "The United States are another object of debate."[2] In 1833 Richard Rush, who had been American minister in London, asked the rhetorical question: "When were the United States subdued by England?"[3] An American lawyer noted in 1848 that "The United States stretch over thousands of miles of territory."[4]

The early British usage followed the same pattern. The English attaché in Washington, D. C., in 1805 declared that the British ambassador and his wife were "bored to death with these United States."[5] In 1833 the Englishman Edward Gibbon Wakefield wrote, "The United States are still colonies, according to the sense in which the word is used here."[6] Charles Dickens, on his visit to this country in 1842, reported in a letter after leaving Pittsburgh, "And I am quite serious when I say that I do not believe there are, on the whole earth besides, so many

---

* Paper read at the Fourth Annual Names Institute, sponsored by the American Name Society, Fairleigh Dickinson University, Madison, New Jersey, May 1, 1965.

[1] Reported by Herbert Mitgang in the New York *Times Magazine*, October 19, 1958, p. 27. Cf. also the New York *Post*, July 25, 1960, p. 23/3: "Carl Sandburg said last week that the Civil War was started over one word in the political platforms — whether it should be 'the United States is' or 'the United States *are*.'"

[2] *The Works of John Adams*, ed. Charles Francis Adams (Boston, 1853), VIII, 160.

[3] Richard Rush, *Memoranda of a Residence at the Court of London* (2nd ed.; Philadelphia, 1833), p. 220.

[4] Robert W. Russell, *America Compared with England* (London, 1848), p. xvii.

[5] Augustus John Foster, letter of September 2, 1805, in *Two Duchesses*, ed. Vere Foster (London, 1898), p. 238.

[6] Edward Gibbon Wakefield, *England and America* (London, 1833), II, 109.

intensified bores as in these United States."[7] In *Fraser's Magazine* in
1845 an Englishman wrote, "The United States of America are the greatest edifice ever achieved by the Anglo-Saxon race."[8]

Let us turn now to the statements of the commentators. The usage of
the early period was classically established in the famous "Index Expur-
gatorius" of William Cullen Bryant, by which he sought to purify the
journalistic writing in the New York *Post*. This list of forbidden terms
had the entry, *"The United States*, as a singular noun."[9] Before the end
of the century, however, a noted encyclopedist and professor of classics
at Columbia University, Harry Thurston Peck, remarked on the radical
change that had taken place. He wrote in 1899:

> Of late years "United States" has come to be employed in this country as a noun in
> the singular number, and this usage is entirely proper; for the term to most minds has
> ceased to have any suggestion of plurality about it, but is an expression for the nation
> as a whole, the unity of the thought blotting out the plurality of the form, and giving us,
> therefore, in two words a whole chapter of constitutional history; since fifty years ago,
> when particularism was in the ascendant, the plural verb was universally employed.[10]

He attributed this development, you will note, to the preceding 50 years.

When George Philip Krapp compiled his *Comprehensive Guide to Good
English* in 1927, he included the succinct observation, "United States,
n[oun], singular as the name of a country."[11] But four years later a
doctrinaire writer recommended the exact opposite. In *Scribner's Magazine* for August, 1931, Struthers Burt made an impassioned plea for
recognizing the diversity and variety of American regions. He backed
this by the following linguistic suggestion:

> Perhaps the next thing we must learn to do, or rather, relearn, is to regard the United
> States, and speak of them, as they once regarded and spoke of themselves. . . . One should
> never speak of the United States as it, she or her. That is a bad habit and a psychological,
> historical and geographical mistake. If you have to use a pronoun, you should use these,
> or they.[12]

A sample of his own usage is this: "The United States are facts; you
just can't argue them away or dismiss them."[13]

In 1949 a controversy on this subject broke out in the house organ of
the Columbia University Press, and the editors of the *Columbia Encyclopedia* were appealed to. One of them took a straddling attitude, writing,

[7] Letter of April 3, 1842, in *The Letters of Charles Dickens*, ed. Walter Dexter (London,
1938), I, 426.

[8] "England and Yankee-Land," in *Fraser's Magazine*, XXXII (October, 1845), 485.

[9] Printed by William Fraser Rae, *Columbia and Canada* (London, 1877), p. 58.

[10] Harry Thurston Peck, *What Is Good English?* (New York, 1899), p. 16.

[11] George Philip Krapp, *A Comprehensive Guide to Good English* (Chicago, 1927), p. 603.

[12] Struthers Burt, "This Subtle Land," in *Scribner's Magazine*, XC (August, 1931), 121.

[13] *Ibid.*, p. 121.

Both are right. When we are thinking of the separate states and their varied character-istics, "these" is OK (but seems a little tritish). When we are thinking of the nation, singular. The English language is pretty flexible, e.g., "none is" or "none are."[14]

A second editor, however, offered a different solution:

I think you should point out that in spite of your phraseology you are not an unrecon-structed rebel. Now, of course, my grandpappy fought in grey — that is, he was a colonel but didn't really fight much — and naturally I approve the usage, these United States. I feel I'm offering an olive branch when I say "the United States has" instead of "the United States have." Seriously, though, the question is one of rhetoric, not one of patriot-ism. The proper usage is the one that would seem most normal to most Americans who speak the accepted form of the language. In this case, in which the object is to stress diversity not unity, I should think most educated Americans would expect "these." But who can say ? Not the Gallup poll, certainly.[15]

It is curious how observers differ. It is especially revealing that he could say, "I should think most educated Americans would expect 'these.'"

H. W. Fowler in 1926 did not see fit to treat this problem, for no doubt it was not a problem to him. But when Margaret Nicholson revised his work in 1957 for an American audience, she included the following statement:

In usual contexts *these United States* is not only archaic (or pompous) but also apt to lead to a wrong verb or pronoun. *These United States* must be plural; *the United States* is usually singular.[16]

In the same year her competitors Bergen Evans and his sister declared,

But the *United States* is usually treated as a singular in English. We say *the United States is in North America*. The plural construction *these United States* is used, but it is felt to be poetic and it is avoided before a verb.[17]

A newspaper arbiter in 1959 was faced with the question: "Which is correct: the United States IS or ARE ?" His answer attempted to dis-criminate between two meanings:

There are a number of words that may be construed as either singular or plural; e.g., "series, species, alms, United States." In the case of U.S.A., use a singular verb when you are thinking of our combined states as a country: The United States has a population of . . . ; use a plural verb if you are thinking of our country in terms of individual states it is composed of: These United States are . . . . Ordinarily a singular verb is called for.[18]

The style manual of the United States Government Printing Office, in its latest revised edition (1959), included a model sentence with the

---

[14] *The Pleasures of Publishing*, XVI, no. 1 (January 10, 1949), 1–2.

[15] *Ibid.*, p. 2.

[16] Margaret Nicholson, *A Dictionary of American-English Usage* (New York, 1957), pp. 617–18.

[17] Bergen Evans and Cornelia Evans, *A Dictionary of Contemporary American Usage* (New York, 1957), p. 529.

[18] Carroll H. Jones, New York *Post*, November 12, 1959, p. 70, cols. 1–3.

clause, "if the United States is to have a stable economy."[19] The Merriam-Webster Third edition of 1961 in its entry *united states* notes, "pl[ural] but usu[ally] sing[ular] in constr[uction]."

Let us turn next to an examination of recent American usage. The usual form, "the United States is," is so well known to you that I need not cite examples of it. But the plural concord has a surprising amount of usage and deserves our consideration. It is my own feeling that most of the examples have a certain pretentiousness about them. The spirit of "now-I-take-my-pen-in-hand" leads to it, in the desire for a fine literary effect. In my less charitable moments, I regard it as arrant pedantry, on a par with *anybody's else* or *teeth-brush*. Clarence Stratton in his *Handbook of English* of 1940 expressed the situation well, saying, "Because of its archaic sound, speakers often use the phrase [in the plural] to add impressiveness to speeches."[20]

Let us now consider some sample quotations. Henry Van Dyke, in a conference of American and British professors of English at Columbia University in 1923, declared, "The native language of these United States is English."[21] Frank Lloyd Wright in his *Autobiography* of 1932 said that the Arizona desert will be "the playground for these United States some day."[22] Frank D. Graham, then president of the University of North Carolina, wrote in 1940, as war approached, "Without a British victory the world, these United States, can be, at best, but a workhouse or a prison."[23] Clyde Kluckhohn wrote in 1942, "The United States are unusual in their juxtaposition of the extreme of technological culture with groups which are still primitive."[24] A Roman Catholic prelate declared in 1943, "These men did not reflect that the Catholic Church has never been as free to prosecute her Divine Mission as in these United States."[25] A literary critic wrote in 1944, "I was given incontrovertible evidence that Seattle is really the literary center of these United States."[26] In the next year Elsa Maxwell said of President Roosevelt, "I believe him to be one of the greatest Presidents of these United States."[27] In 1947 Marya Mannes wrote, "Fifty to 70 million people in these United States read comic books regularly."[28] Max Lerner in a column in the

[19] *United States Government Printing Office Style Manual* (Revised ed.; Washington, D.C., 1959), p. 150.

[20] *Handbook of English* (New York, 1940), p. 325.

[21] Quoted in the New York *Times*, June 14, 1923, p. 7/2.

[22] Frank Lloyd Wright, *An Autobiography* (New York, 1932), p. 303.

[23] *The Nation*, October 5, 1940, p. 311/2.

[24] *Technology Review* (Mass. Inst. Technology), XLIV (February, 1942), 178.

[25] Francis E. McMahon, in *PM*, November 22, 1943, p. 4/2.

[26] L. E. Nelson, in Chicago *Sun Book Week*, December 3, 1944, p. 48/3.

[27] New York *Post*, March 7, 1945, p. 12/1.

[28] *New Republic*, February 17, 1947, p. 20/2.

New York *Post* has asked, "How did it happen that in so many years of wanderings among these United States, I have only now discovered New Orleans?"[29] Philip Wylie wrote in 1953, "These United States, conceived in liberty and dedicated to truth, are being assailed by the idea of communism."[30] Murray Kempton has said that the seniority system of the Senate has elected a senator *"de facto* president of these United States."[31] A supporter of Mayor Wagner declared in 1957, "These United States need more men like 'our mayor' in public office throughout our country!"[32] In a majority opinion of the Eighth Federal Circuit Court of Appeals, St. Louis, Judge Marion Matthes declared, "The time has not yet come in these United States when an order of a federal court must be whittled away, watered down, or shamefully withdrawn."[33]

I could continue with examples, but I trust that these are sufficient to demonstrate their nature. Most of them have a strongly oracular, orotund, magniloquent tone. These writers chose an archaic, abnormal pattern for rhetorical effect.

We may look next at some recent British quotations. In these there is no straining for effect, but the writers are simply carrying on an older tradition. Vera Brittain wrote, "The United States, at any rate, refused to resign themselves to adverse physical conditions."[34] On the floor of the House of Commons Hore-Belisha stated, "The United States are not a mercantile shipbuilding nation."[35] A. P. Herbert wrote, "We must say no more, in view of what the United States are doing just now."[36] Commander Stephen King-Hall has asked, "Why were the United States invented?"[37] An English Commonwealth fellow has recently stated, "The European lack of understanding of the U.S.A. is due largely to the United States themselves."[38] A professor at Oxford, A. J. P. Taylor, wrote in 1959, "The United States manage virtually without a closed period for public records."[39] This form of agreement is easy for the English partly because they are accustomed to say "The government are –," "The Corporation are –," etc. But Lawrence of Arabia expressed uncertainty in a letter to an American, by asking, "How is the States: or are the States?"[40]

---

[29] New York *Post*, April 28, 1952, p. 24/1.
[30] *Saturday Review*, August 29, 1953, p. 25/1.
[31] New York *Post*, February 21, 1956, p. 50/2.
[32] Leah Steinfeld, *ibid.*, February 1, 1957, p. 37/4.
[33] Quoted *ibid.*, August 20, 1958, Mag. section, p. 4/1.
[34] Vera Brittain, *Honourable Estate* (New York, 1936), p. 564.
[35] *Parliamentary Debates* (Commons), November 27, 1940, in *Penguin Hansard*, IV, 87.
[36] On April 1, 1941, *ibid.*, IV, 54.   [37] *North American Diary* (London, 1949), p. 10.
[38] A. Geoffrey Woodhead, in *Cousins and Strangers*, ed. S. G. Putt (Cambridge, Mass., 1956), p. 5.   [39] *Encounter*, December, 1959, p. 87.
[40] Thomas Edward Lawrence, letter of December 2, 1932, to F. N. Doubleday, in *The Letters of T. E. Lawrence*, ed. David Garnett (London, 1938), p. 754.

A secondary problem arises when the states are referred to separately. A well-spoken American feels that he has to say, "one of the states of the United States," while an Englishman tends to say, "one of the United States." This is an old dilemma. Even in 1838 a British traveler, David Stevenson, wrote, "These fertile valleys include nine of the United States of America."[41] Two years later James Mather, in a lecture given at Newcastle-upon-Tyne, said, "It may not appear improper to remind you, that each of the United States of America established a government for itself."[42] Even the editors of the *OED* fell into this pattern. Under *assembly*, the definition is "the name given to the legislature in some of the United States of America." And under *hamlet*, "In some of the United States, the official designation of an incorporated place smaller than a village."

Americans seldom fall into this pattern, although I did discover the following in the program at a Broadway theatre a few weeks ago, in the biography of a certain actor: "He has ... played in thirty-six of the fifty United States."[43]

A somewhat similar problem involves the term *Church of England*: an individual church must be referred to as "a church of the Church of England." The following colloquy, recorded by an Englishman, illustrates this: "'What is that church?' I asked a lady. Her reply was so unfathomably silly that I have never forgotten it. 'It is a church,' she said, 'of England.'"[44]

A rather rare eccentricity is found in the phrase *United State*. Thus, in Rome, an English correspondent of a London weekly in 1889 wrote concerning the American pilgrims there: "There were some from New York and some from Ohio, and some from Colorado, and some from Baltimore, and some from Illinois, and others from every existing United State."[45] In 1952 an Italian boy actor was quoted as saying the same sort of thing: "'The son of the Comtessa,' Vittorio reported, 'is 48 – one year for each United State.'"[46]

More surprising still is the suggestion that the country should change its name to *United State*. This indeed would solve the grammatical problem. The first glimmering of this that I have found is in an essay written in 1874 by a Scot, a cousin of the Duke of Argyle, J. F. Campbell. De-

---

[41] *Sketch of the Civil Engineering of North America* (London, 1838), p. 98.

[42] *Two Lectures, Delivered at Newcastle-upon-Tyne, on the Constitutions and Republican Institutions of the United States* (Newcastle-upon-Tyne, 1840), p. 28.

[43] *Playbill*, II, No. 2 (February, 1965), p. 34, at the Billy Rose Theatre.

[44] *Times Literary Supplement* (London), July 19, 1957, p. 436/2.

[45] The Rome correspondent of the London *Tablet*, quoted in *American Notes and Queries*, III (May 4, 1889), 12.

[46] New York *Post*, April 28, 1952, p. 33/1.

scribing American energy, especially as manifested in Oregon, he wrote, "The attractions and repulsions which drag and drive humanity ... tend to combine all men in one great future coming United State according to some philosophers here. Theirs is the 'Go-a-head' philosophy"[47]

But in 1881 a New Englander, C. H. J. Douglass, attempted to consolidate the results of the Civil War by suggesting the name *United State of America*. He wished that the founders of the country had adopted this form. As he wrote:

> It would have been more in accord with the principles of modern political science, perhaps, if the framers of the Declaration had seen fit to use the singular, *state*, instead of the plural, *states*; but they followed strictly the analogy of the "United Provinces of the Netherlands," and the "United Colonies of New England."[48]

He wished to squeeze out any hint of nullification or secession lurking in the plural *States*. He concluded his essay:

> Had the fathers of the republic chosen a specific instead of a generic name, they would have called the country the United Republic of America; but they chose instead the more comprehensive term ... ; and if, as is sometimes whispered, the Republican party in the United States should at some future time ... transform the republic into an empire, their Democratic friends may derive some consolation from the assurance that our future emperor will be under no necessity of changing the national name — a name dear to every American — for it would still be the

> UNITED STATE OF AMERICA.[49]

In 1942 an editor of *Time*, in searching for a heading to a discussion of national unity, hit upon the title, "United State."[50] In 1957 Randolph Churchill issued a *jeu d'esprit* that purported to tell of conditions in America in the year 2000. He began, "It is with pleasure that I accede to the request of *Encounter* to describe my recent visit to the United State."[51] He explained this development:

> It was as recently as 1975 that the Re-Founding Fathers, meeting in Philadelphia under the chairmanship of Mr. Adlai Stevenson, logically decided that ... the United States should cease to be plural. They were singularised by the 25th Amendment to the Constitution. In consequence, this amendment changed the name of the Flag to "Star and Stripe."[25]

Now a concluding word on form: the name *United States* developed from a description, and at first had the grammatical characteristics of a descriptive label. As it came to be accepted as a proper name, however, it developed the concord of a proper name. Probably it was vulgar at

[47] J. F. Campbell, *My Circular Notes* (London, 1876), I, 162.

[48] C. H. J. Douglass, "Our National Name — What Does It Mean?" in the *New Englander*, XL (September, 1881), 631.

[49] *Ibid.*, p. 634.

[50] *Time*, April 20, 1942, p. 8/3.

[51] "The Queendom of the United State," in *Encounter*, IX, No. 6 (December, 1957), 19/1.

[52] *Ibid.*, p. 20/2.

first to say "the United States is," but my material is not close-meshed enough to have caught this stage. In the latter decades of the last century, the strengthening of the federal ties caused the singular to become accepted in ordinary use. The English have held out against it, together with some Americans who prided themselves on their literary flourish.

The final stage of becoming a proper name would occur when *United States* drops the article. On rare occasions I have heard the colloquial form, "He lives in United States" or "He came to United States many years ago"; but I have not encountered this usage in print. (An exception is the application to language, the jocular "He talks United States.")

Students of usage will want to watch the name *United States* carefully. Its grammar has been in a fluid condition for a long time, and trends are deserving of close study. We must keep tab on them.

Columbia University

Onomastic Variety in the High Sierra*

FRANCIS LEE UTLEY

IN A SEARCH for a more extensive series of mountain names for a paper entitled "Mountain Nomenclature in the United States" (read at the Ninth International Onomastic Congress in September 1969, but still unpublished), I came across a fascinating and model study by Francis P. Farquhar: "Place Names of the High Sierra," published in three parts in the *Sierra Club Bulletin*, volumes XI and XII for the years 1920 to 1927.[1] Supplementing it with various collections of tales about the Yosemite and the Sierra Nevada, and with Erwin Gudde's more up-to-date *California Place Names*,[2] one comes up with a variety of accounts of aboriginal names, of systematic modern naming, and of place-name legends both authentic and romantically reworked.

Farquhar's study measures up to the four tests of a good place-name dictionary: geographical accuracy, historical knowledge and its cautious application,[3] linguistic concern,[4] and sympathy to the folktale where it exists. It is the ideal essay because it forms the basis for new work. There should, indeed, be a full-scale comparison of the place-names with the many collections of Miwok and Yurok texts which have been made since that time,[5] and with the popular legends which have been prettified by the white man, to show the process by which legends are converted from

---

* This article is a special tribute to a great linguist and onomastician, Elliott Dobbie. Though one associates him more with Morningside Heights than with the High Sierra, those who knew him know that there was no place or language by which he was not fascinated.

[1] XI (1920—23), 380—407; XII (1924-27), 47—64, 126—147. They were collected with additions in a book (San Francisco: The Sierra Club, 1926) which I have been unable to see. References to Farquhar and Gudde are given only in special cases, since the names appear in both in alphabetical order.

[2] University of California Press, 1962.

[3] The best evidence of this caution is the list of 60 place-names which are a puzzle, listed in XII, 48 — a treasure hoard for the speculative and the searching mind. Many of these were explained later by Farquhar and by Gudde.

[4] Not, of course, with the care shown by the model Indian studies of Franz Boas, *Geographical Names of the Kwakiutl Indians* (New York, 1934) and John P. Harrington, *The Ethnography of the Tewa Indians*, 29th Annual Report of the Bureau of American Ethnology (Washington, 1916), pp. 29—636. But the etymologies are sober and critically handled.

[5] For bibliography see Raffaele Pettazzoni, *Miti e leggende*, III (Torino, 1953), pp. 186—187; and Charles Haywood, *A Bibliography of North American Folklore and Folksong* (New York, 1951), pp. 1033—34, 1042—43.

their original tone and meaning. This brief paper can only scratch the surface of the ore to be found in Yosemite and the Sierra; perhaps this prospector will encourage a further rush for the gold that is there.

On the whole the naming in this mountainous country is recent; it owes much to systematic exploration by Joseph Le Conte of Berkeley and to John Muir of Wisconsin. Reversing the usual proportions, the names now resting there are predominantly personal; about 320 come from persons and about 120 from descriptive features. (In South Dakota I found on a recent search that elevation names run in the opposite ratio: about 430 descriptive against 120 personal names.) Only 31 on my count are Indian, and some of these are translations from the Indian rather than the original name.

Among these names there is much fancy and humor, much romance and legend. One spectacular group is a tribute to nineteenth-century scientific advance in biology and geology: the Evolution Peaks, named by Theodore Solomons in 1895, and comprising Darwin, Wallace, Huxley, Haeckel, Spencer, and Fiske. Solomons was probably following the lead of Clarence King in 1864 when, referring to his treasured copy of John Tyndall's *Glaciers of the Alps* (1860), he named the 14,536 ft. peak which he and others had ascended Mount Tyndall.[6] Since the time of Solomons, Lamarck and Mendel have been added to the range; and Dana and Lyell to peaks outside it. This, like the Presidential Range of New England, is an unusually systematic naming pattern; it reminds us of the praiseworthy naming of the streets of Stockholm by categories, so that one can easily locate a district by the street-name. The late Gösta Langenfelt, a fellow onomastician, made a life-work of such applied toponymy.

Many of the Sierra names have stories which, like that of the Evolution Peaks, are not fabulous. Our interest in folk etymologies and eponymous legends should not let us forget that von Sydow's "memorats" were eyewitness accounts in origin, with a large element of truth. Folklore is not necessarily false lore. The linguist or historian or geographer should, like the folklorist, attend to these stories whether they are true or false, though of course he should not himself falsify them, any more than he should reject them because of his special interest. Americans, somewhat deprived of the "chimerat" or *Märchen*, should not neglect the lowly *sage* or *memorat*. Truth is often quite as interesting as fiction. An excellent example is Sardine Lake. According to Chase, "It bears the inscrutable designation of Sardine Lake. I hailed Bodie with an inquiry as to the reason for the name, and received his illuminating reply in one word, 'Canned.' I learned later that years ago an ill-fated mule bearing a cargo of the delicacy con-

---

[6] William H. Brewer, "The Naming of Mount Tyndall," *Sierra Club Bulletin*, XII (1924–27), 443–444.

signed to a merchant in some mining camp of the Walker River region had fallen off the trail, and after a series of spectacular revolutions had vanished in the icy waters."[7]

Battle Creek in the Sierra records "a famous battle between a burro and a mountain lion," in which the burro was badly clawed but victorious, and the lion was drowned in the creek. The story was well-attested, yet one wonders whether the existence of a Battle Creek in Michigan, named after an obscure Indian battle of 1824, had anything to do with reinforcing the name or making it seem appropriate. According to James Clay (as cited by Farquhar, XI, 387), Cartridge Creek is a jesting commemoration of a man who had a good shot at a deer, but succumbed to buck fever and pumped out all his cartridges. Farquhar's Clouds Rest was named from a vista of clouds before a snowstorm, but his Cloudy Canyon is an error for Cloud Canyon or Cloud Creek, as he was informed later by Judge Wallace, the namer (XII, 47). The creek is "crystal clear" and the -*y* suffix is wholly misleading. The place was named after the Cloud Mine, which Wallace discovered and claimed, a mine in the clouds which proved too high to be workable.

So far we have had essentially true stories. But if we turn to the region of Half Dome we find a proliferation of fancy and legend. In 1911 Bunnell, reporting on earlier explorations, said, "The names 'North Dome,' 'South Dome,' and 'Half Dome' were given by us during our long stay in the [Yosemite] valley from their localities and peculiar configuration." There has been some shifting of names, and Half Dome or Cleft Rock, is now often "South Dome," while Bunnell's South Dome is now often Sentinel Dome (XI, 401). Two legends about Half Dome are widely different in episode and tone, though they seem to have a structural kernel in common – the eternal pursuit of female by male.

One, recounted by Bertha Smith in 1904, is in popular form, without indication of informant or time of collection. (Here – and elsewhere – I summarize, now and again interspersing quotations.) Tu-tock-ah-nu-lah, the Rock Chief, had his watch-tower on the Northern Wall of the Ah-wah-nee-valley. "In the spring he besought the Great Spirit to send rain that the wild corn might hang heavy with tasseling grain, the berries cluster thick on the branches of the manzanite, and the fish abound in the waters of the river. In the summer he fattened the bear and deer, and in the autumn he wandered through the mountains driving them from their haunts that the hunter might not return empty-handed from the chase. The smoke of his pipe spread like a soft haze through the air, sheltering the women from the sun when they went forth to gather acorns and wood for winter." One day at dawn our hero Tu heard a dovelike voice calling

---

[7] Farquhar, *op. cit.*, XII, 131.

his name, but the nymph of the voice fled when she was approached. In the evening he saw her on her throne and "knew that she was Tis-sa-ack, the Goddess of the Valley, who shared with him the loving care of the Ah-wah-nee-chees." (One wonders why two fertility figures had not got together by this time.) From that time his passion grew, and made him forget his people. Tis-sa-ack, sad at his neglect of the aborigines, prayed to the Great Spirit, who sent a storm and lightning which cleft the rock where she sat; the rain rushed to form Wai-ack or Mirror Lake. Now the valley bloomed once more, and the chief of the tribe ordered a feast for her. "But Tis-sa-ack was gone. She had sacrificed her love, her life, for the children of Ah-wah-nee," and "she left them the lake, the river and a fragment of her throne." Now still her spirit hovers at dusk "where at the Half Dome the sun slips over the western wall of the valley." Down from her wings floated the feathers which became white violets. Tu despaired, and "carved with his hunting-knife the outlines of his face upon the wall of his fortress, which the white man has named El Capitan." One passion led to another. This time he was drawn by a subtle fragrance sent by E-ee-he-no, who lived among the water-lilies "in the lake which the Three Brothers hold in the hollow of their hands," and he was drowned there.[8]

How much of this is a local Indian legend and how much romantic maidenly fiction we do not know. The Miwok of the region tell a quite different story, according to E. W. Gifford, a serious authority on Miwok anthropology and folk narrative,[9] even though his account appears in a semi-popular book.[10] "Half Dome lived with her husband, Washington Tower, on the bank of the Merced river. One day she quarreled with her husband, and taking with her a basket of seeds and her baby in its cradle, she ran away to the east. As she fled up through the mountains she formed the upper part of the Merced river and Yosemite valley." From the seeds in the basket came the flora of the valley. Washington Tower ran after her and beat her with a white oak club. In tears, Half Dome threw the basket to become North Dome, and the arched cradle, abandoned, became the Royal Arches. She was transformed into the peak which bears her name and which is marked by dark streaks – her tear-stains. Washington

---

[8] Bertha H. Smith, *Yosemite Legends* (San Francisco, 1904), pp. 47–54. Her other legends are about Yosemite "Large Grizzly Bear," Pohono "Spirit of the Evil Wind," Hum-moo "The Lost Arrow," Py-we-ack "The White Water," and Kom-po pai-ses "Leaping Frog Rocks." A slightly less rhapsodical version of the legend, going back to an Indian informant "Iota," is found in J. M. Hutchings, *In the Heart of The Sierras* (Oakland, California, 1886), pp. 387–390.

[9] *Cf.* note 5.

[10] Edward W. Gifford and Gwendoline H. Block, *California Indian Nights Entertainments* (Glendale, California, 1930), pp. 263–264. Gifford's Miwok stories are about Half Dome, El Capitan, and Yosemite Falls.

Tower turned into a great shaft of granite. Apparently the satirically treated Washington Tower is identical with To-to-kon-oo-lah (a name derived from To-to-kon, the sandhill crane), and hence with the hero of Bertha Smith's story, though I might be surer of all this if I were to visit the Yosemite valley and could identify the spots personally, and had time for some further burrowing in the recorded legends and the linguistic milieu. Farquhar does not list the name Washington Tower. If it is, as it would seem, the same as El Capitan, the Miwok have a different story for that feature. Once it was a small rock, and Bear and her cubs lay down on it and went to sleep. When they awoke they found it had grown so tall overnight that they could not descend. "In fact, it had scraped past Moon." The animals on earth, Mouse, Rat, Raccoon, Grizzly Bear, and Mountain Lion all tried to leap or climb to the summit for the rescue, and finally Measuring Worm, step by step, made it. But it took him a whole winter, and when he got there he found that Bear and the children had starved to death. He brought their bones back to earth for cremation. A fine story of the conquering of the mighty by the minute, like Aesop's Mouse and Lion or the Jewish legend of the gnat who slew Titus or Nimrod, by creeping up and destroying the tyrants' noses. It is not the Smith story, however.

The Mirror Lake of the Smith story is a prosaic displacement of Wai-ack or "Water Rock," just as Half Dome is a replacement for Ti-sa-ack. Bunnell presumably named the Lake which, though it is not particularly like Lake Tahoe or the thousand other sylvan mirrors, did have fine early morning reflections. Another name, Lost Arrow, is not a displacement, but a proper translation of the Pohonochee scout's name Hummo, which also involved the romantic legend of a misunderstood message (the arrow), and the death of lovers, reminiscent of the stories of Theseus and Tristan, with their black and white sails.[11]

Moro Rock in Sequoia National Park tempted men at the end of the last century to recall the Moros of the Philippines or the Morro Castle of Cuba, but the name in California was bestowed some time in the sixties because of a famous blue roan mustang, the *moro*, owned by a Mr. Swanson of Three Rivers. Sure evidence of the value, among other efforts, of checking the date of naming a natural feature.

The Three Brothers, said Hutchings,[12] is a commonplace name bestowed by "some lackadaisical person" on the feature with the Indian name of Eleacha, after a local food plant. Why the brothers are more commonplace than a food plant is not certain. We have encountered the

---

[11] Smith, *op. cit.*, pp. 19–30. See Thompson Motif Z 140.1 Color of flag (sails) on ship as message of good or bad news; Helaine Newstead in *Arthurian Literature in the Middle Ages*, ed. Roger S. Loomis (Oxford, 1959), p. 129.

[12] Farquhar, *op. cit.*, XII, 138.

three peaks in the Smith story of Half Dome, where they surround the lake where Tu-tock-ah-nu-lah was drowned, victim of the vampire E-ee-he-no. The Brothers were originally Kom-po-pai-ses, the Leaping Frog Rocks, according to many authorities. But Bertha Smith has her tale, a vanishing American tale directed against the white conquerors, who killed the noble chief Ten-ie-ya's three sons, which the mountains commemorate.[13] One wonders how the name could be a prosaic invention of the white man and also the center of a tale directed against his ruthless progress into the Indian's territory. Pompososus is apparently a folk-etymological rendering for Kom-po-pai-ses, the Leaping Frog Rock. The Whitney Survey of 1868 observes dryly that it has never caught the Indians at the familiar game of Leap Frog. Bunnell says the term means "mountains playing leap-frog," but adds, somewhat mysteriously, "a literal translation is not desirable."[14] Perhaps this is innocent confusion, but it seems dangerous silence to a generation brought up on Havelock Ellis and his prolific modern imitators.

Our next story similarly illustrates the white man's squeamishness in the presence of culture shock. It is attested by Gremke, Farquhar, and Gudde. According to Gremke (as quoted by Gudde and Farquhar), Tunemah Trail acquired its name in a peculiar manner. "The sheepherders frequenting that part of the country employed Chinese cooks. Owing to the roughness of the path they gave vent to their disgust by numerous Chinese imprecations. Gradually the most prominent settled itself onto the trail and it became known as 'Tunemah'." For this name, which has been extended to a lake, a pass, and a peak, Farquhar gives no clear translation. Suspecting the Gremke story to be folklore only, I called a friend, a Chinese expert. His own dialect, Mandarin, has an equivalent form. But the laborers were Cantonese, and so is the expression, /'tIUne"ma:/, "to have intercourse with mother."[15]

Farquhar's list of 60 puzzling names on which he seeks help look enticing to the folklorist: Inconsolable Range, Music Peak, Poopenaut Valley, Scaffold Meadow, Shuteye Peak, and Farewell Gap, to name but a few. Some find later explanations by Gudde and by Farquhar himself. Scaffold Meadow does not refer to a gallows, as it might be expected to do in the state which has produced a Hangtown Creek and Hangtown oysters (sheep's testicles), the latter served in the best hotels of San Francisco

---

[13] Smith, *op. cit.*, pp. 57–64.

[14] Farquhar, *op. cit.*, XII, 138.

[15] Gudde, *California Place Names*, p. 330; Farquhar in *Sierra Club Bulletin*, XII, 139. In one of his more recent works, *History of the Sierra Nevada* (University of California Press and Sierra Club, 1965), p. 236, Farquhar has the following note (18): " 'Tunemah' is a Chinese word of the vilest significance, given because of the expletive of a Chinese cook as he rode along it [the trail]." This does not bring us much closer to specifics.

today. The meadow contained a scaffold built by sheepmen to protect their supplies from bears and other predators. Nor are Shuteye Peak and Pass places where explorers took a nap, but rather memorials to Old Shuteye, a halfblind Indian through whose rancheria the trail passed. Farewell Gap and Inconsolable Range have no entry in Gudde; they would seem to mirror, like Desolation Lake, the nostalgias, frustrations, and despairs of early explorers. One hesitates to deal with Poopenaut Valley, which for a moment looks as Indian as it can be, but which might well reflect the broad humor of men tough enough to plow through these mountains for the first time. Strong as they were, one expects they were often "pooped out" at the end of a day. Or the valley, which we have not seen, might deserve the verb if it dwindled at one end, as with Lake Peter, the facetious coinage of Judge Wallace and Joe Palmer in 1877. "On one occasion when following a dim trail up the canyon above Wet Meadow it gave out, and Palmer named a little body of water they discovered, Lake Peter, because the trail petered out at that point." [16] Perhaps my guess about Poopenaut should not be taken too seriously; the Indian etymon may lie open to someone who knows the language of the district better than Farquhar or I.

Also among Farquhar's puzzles is Music Peak, which conjures up visions of natural Aeolian harps or a singing river on its sides or at its base. It turns out to be simply a misspelling, really named after Charles or Henry Musick, who were associated with a milling company at nearby Shaver. Similarly, Breeze Lake is not so called from its winds but from one William Breeze; Sing Peak not from another Aeolian harp but from a Chinese cook who worked for the namer; and Pleasant Valley is not charmingly descriptive but from a dairyman, James Cage Pleasant, killed on the spot by the Indians. June Lake remains a puzzle: does it refer to the time of the year or to its namer's daughter or wife, the sources of innumerable American place-names? Rush Creek likewise, which might owe its name to the famous Revolutionary War physician or to some of his many sons, namesakes, or relatives – or it might be merely a rapid stream. One cannot solve the problem in one's study.

Homers Nose has nothing to do with the primal poet. In Gudde, E. B. Homer tells the story: "As my father and the two government surveyors were looking at the mountain Mr. Powell laughingly remarked, 'Homer, that south projection looks like your nose.' 'All right,' said Mr. Orth, 'I am marking it on my map as Homers Nose' and so it was named." A final ambiguity is Mount Gabb, and its story justifies my belief that place-naming often involves more than one consideration. A name in short may be reinforced, a blend of *etyma*, or more properly "a compound

---

[16] Farquhar, *op. cit.*, XII, 63.

etymology," like *business* from Old English *besignis* and Old French *besognes*, "occupations,"; or *defy* from Latin *dis* + *fidāre* and *dēfæcāre*; or *hired man* from Old English *hyrian* "to hire" and *hired* "member of a household"; or *straight* from Latin *strictum* and Old English *streht*.[17] Mount Gabb was named after William More Gabb of Philadelphia, who joined the Whitney Survey in 1861 and died in 1878. He lived up to his name. On one occasion the serious Dr. Cooper "announced that he had discovered a new species of the old brachiopod genus, *Lingula*; and that in honor of his friend William More Gabb he had bestowed upon it the name of *Lingula gabii*." Clearly the name may have a double purpose, a simultaneous dual etymology – in short, and not to be loquacious, it may be a pun.

California, it will be remembered, is the heaven of the realtor, and the realtors have modelled their fancies on the poets who beautify the natural features. Upgrading or "swank naming," is a well-known process. We all remember how Minnesota progressed from "muddy water" to "cloudy water" to "the land of the sky-blue water," or Mississippi from "big river" to "the Father of Waters."[18] Less well-known is the transformation of the Pawnee Ki raru river in Nebraska, which meant "turbid river" or "manure river," from the buffalo dung it contained. This is now Republican River.[19] It is not our task here to say what justice there is in the transformation, or whether beauty is the result. But there is nevertheless beautification in California. The lovely Bridalveil Falls, a descriptive name which fits the object, was in Indian a prosaic tribal name Pohono, meaning a "puffing wind" or, in one discredited etymology, an "evil wind."[20] Cathedral Peak led John Muir to this fine prose: "No wonder the hills and groves were God's first temples, and the more they are cut down and hewn into cathedrals and churches, the farther and dimmer seems the Lord himself. The same may be said of stone temples. Yonder, to the eastward of our camp grove, stands one of Nature's cathedrals, hewn from the living rock, almost conventional in form, about two thousand feet high, nobly adorned with spires and pinnacles, thrilling under floods of sunshine as if alive like a grovetemple, and well-named 'Cathedral'."[21] As we have seen, El Capitan is a noble renaming of a word for the sandhill crane.

---

[17] George H. McKnight, "Some Compound Etymologies," *Journal of English and Germanic Philology*, XII (1913), 110—117. The editor suggests to me that *dēficere*, "to break loose, to become faithless, to rebel, to defect," is a better companion etymon than *dēfæcāre*, suggested by McKnight. And so it is, though the *NED* supports McKnight's view under *defy v²* "digest, dissolve."

[18] George R. Stewart, *Names on the Land* (New York, 1945), pp. 278—279.

[19] John Thomas Link, *The Toponymy of Nebraska* (Lincoln, Nebraska, 1932), pp. 80—81.

[20] See the story in Smith, *op. cit.*, pp. 11—18.

[21] Farquhar, *op. cit.*, XI, 386.

Another cheerful name is the Happy Isles, so named by W. E. Dennison because "no one can visit them without for the while forgetting the grinding strife of *his* world and being happy." [22] Happy Gap is more prosaic; it is on the "Jackass Route" and "those who succeed in getting a pack-train to this point at once perceive the appropriateness of the name." The Happy Isles have a ring as of the Greek Elysium, and they recall the few literary allusions of the kind in the Sierras. The geologist apparently once in a while read *belles-lettres*. On Disappearing Creek (recall Lake Peter and Poopenaut?) lies a water channel called The Enchanted Gorge, and our evolutionist Theodore Solomons named the peaks on either side Scylla and Charybdis. Homers Nose, we have seen, has nothing to do with Homer. But there are a Doré Pass and a Doré Creek at the bottom of Lundy Canyon, a scarp or wall a thousand feet high with cliffs which reflect Gustave Doré's famous pictures of Dante's Hell. This is an exaltation of the common pioneer awareness of the infernal, which here is manifest in Hell-for-Sure Pass, Desolation Lake, the Devils Bathtub, the Devils Crags and the Devils Postpile or Woodpile, the last "a splendid specimen of columnar basalt" in which "the sheepherder recognizes the handiwork of his Satanic majesty." A subtler reference to the demonic (and the daemonic) is a peak called Seven Gables near Mount Goddard. With this Puritan name we may balance such names as Kings River, originally Rio de los Santos Reyes, named perhaps because discovered on Epiphany by good Catholic Spaniards honoring the Magi, or the Merced River, Grove, Lake, Peak, and Pass, deriving from El Rio de Nuestra Señora de la Merced (1806), from the Blessed Virgin as in the full names of Guadalupe (a Mexican shrine) or Los Angeles, which has like Merced lost the element which described her. Moses Mountain is one more of Farquhar's puzzles; we presume it alludes in some fashion to Mount Sinai or Mount Horeb or Mount Nebo, for Moses was, as the prophet of Jahweh the thundering skygod, in every way a mountain man. The Royal Arches, which turned up in Bertha Smith's Half Dome story, were rocks once called Scho-ko-ni after the arched shade of an Indian cradle. Their present name is from a degree in Freemasonry, conferred under the eye of God which always is looking down from the rafters of the lodge.

There are many other charming names in Farquhar, a Dinkey Creek named after a dog, a J-O Pass from the initials of its Portuguese namer's long sought brother, [23] spectacularly descriptive names like the Hermit, the Minarets, Fin Dome, Sharktooth Peak, Sentinel Dome, the profiled crag which gave the name to the Lake of the Lone Indian, Picket Guard Peak, Scepter Pass, and the Videttes, East and West. Vividly descriptive

---

[22] *Ibid.*, XI, 402.

[23] For another explanation see Gudde, *op. cit.*, p. 168.

too is the name of the range, the Sierra Nevada, the snowy sawtooth range. One of the great parks of the region, Sequoia, owes its immediate reference to a descriptive association, the giant redwoods of'the California coast. But the tree itself was probably named after that famous Indian hero who assumed the massive task of inventing an alphabet and contributing to the education of his people.[24] Less sublime but quite as beautiful are Mariposa Peak, Grove, and County, named by the Spaniard Moraga in 1806 from the mass of butterflies found in the region. To give this paper a touch of the "relevant," we should note that the naming of counties has not been neglected by the free souls of Telegraph street in Berkeley. There one may buy a poster which, in obvious emulation of Mariposa, shows a blissful scene and a caption, "You are now entering Marijuana County." It brings butterflies to my stomach.

The Ohio State University

---

[24] The equation is not certain, and there has been much controversy about the naming of the tree. See Farquhar, *Yosemite, the Big Trees and the High Sierra* (University of California Press, 1948), pp. 8—9.

Names on the Ocean Bottom, or Some Observations on the Invisible Landscape

EUGENE B. VEST

Among the nearly wide-open spaces where the place-namer has been able to exercise his art increasingly in recent decades are, first, the universe, which, having bowed to Miss Fuller (in spite of Carlyle) and the march of science, the place-namer has accepted as his oyster; second, more specifically, the moon, both fore and aft, now the subject of frequent maps in the daily newspapers; third, the subcontinent of Antarctica, upon whose white surface, figuratively, hundreds of new names have appeared as a result of the extensive explorations following World War II; and fourth, the ocean bottom, where scientists are daily adding new names.

Although the oceans cover 71 per cent of the surface of the earth (about 140,000,000 square miles), the number of names labeling features of the land forming their bottom is extremely small. Accurate maps exist for only about one per cent of this area. Indeed, place names in the abyssal deeps, which occupy, at a guess, 90 per cent of the ocean area, were, until very recently, almost non-existent.

It is ironic to note, says one authority, that names for the constellations and signs of the zodiac, stretching through the depths of space, date from perhaps 3,000 B.C., while names still do not exist for countless sub-oceanic features comparatively so near us on our own planet. Moreover, much more is known about the surface of the moon, many of whose features have long been named, than is known about many parts of the nearby ocean depths.

Submarine place names on general and popular maps, depicting oceans and continents as apart from navigational charts, were almost unheard of a decade or so ago, and are not common now. Among map publications in the English language, the only area looked into in this investigation, most of the well-known world atlases still ignore the labeling of underwater features. The great *London Times Atlas of the World,* in five elephant folios, includes no such names. The *Encyclopaedia Britannica* atlas volume, in the edition of 1961, at least, shows no underwater place names. Strangely, in elaborate charts and tables accompanying the plates, the *Britannica* lists the oceans and seas of the world, the principal islands, the largest lakes, the longest rivers, and the highest mountains, but it says nothing at all about the greatest depths of the oceans, nothing about what they are called or where they are located, information certainly as interesting to the general reader as the names, locations, and heights of the highest land peaks (whose greatest heights the greatest ocean depths far exceed). A table naming the greatest depths can, however, be found accompanying the article "Ocean and Oceanography." In the recently published new edition of the separate *Britannica World Atlas* (1966) the two-page map of the world does, to be sure, grudgingly label a dozen large underwater features.

Rand McNally's *International World Atlas* (1961), with full-page maps of the Atlantic and Pacific, labels only some island dots, mentioning not a single underwater feature, not one of the great depths, not one of the great underwater mountain chains or peaks. (I might add that the two polar maps in this atlas are also nearly destitute of names, although hundreds are available to the mapmaker from scientific sources.)

The *Life Pictorial Atlas of the World* (1961), however, does indicate a few of the greatest land features of the ocean depths, especially in the Atlantic.

One well-known popular atlas, by contrast to these commercial ventures, one which is constantly re-edited and updated by the incorporation of the latest scientific data, has shown a steady rise in the number of underwater labels on its plates during the last decade or so. It is the *National Geographic Atlas of the World*, which has appeared as a long series of single plates and as complete editions dated 1963 and 1966. It is the only atlas which also includes explanatory notes right on its plates, as, for example, on the map of the Atlantic:

> *Mid-Atlantic Cordillera.* This submarine ridge is the world's longest mountain range, stretching 10,000 miles. Covered by water averaging a mile in

depth, it separates the Atlantic Ocean into eastern and western basins roughly three miles deep. Only a few of its highest peaks emerge to form islands, largest of which are the Azores.

This ridge was mentioned by the *New York Times* on Dec. 10, 1966, in connection with the discovery of a magnetic pattern frozen in the ocean floor. Again, on the *Geographic's* map of the Pacific Ocean, beside a marked spot just east of the southern tip of Mindanao, are the words: "World's deepest, Cook Depth, 6297 fathoms (37,782 feet)." This is the way intelligent mapmaking should be conducted. This depth, by the way, is named after *H. M. S. Cook*, a survey ship, which may itself possibly be named after the great explorer. (The Oxford Press's *Atlas of Britain and Northern Ireland* (London, 1963), also labels numerous features of shallow offshore Britain, but none of the abyssal deeps.)

In the field of gazetteers, the *Columbia Lippincott Gazetteer of the World* (1962 edition) includes names for only a handful of the greatest trenches, the Puerto Rico (with its Brownson Deep and Milwaukee Depth), the Marianas (with its Nero Deep), the Japanese (with its Tuscarora and Ramapo Deeps), and possibly a few more. Apparently no seamounts or guyots are listed. *Webster's Geographical Dictionary* (1965) lists the chief banks, deeps and trenches, though it is mistaken about the Mindanao Deep (35,400 feet) being the deepest yet found at the time of its publication (see the statement on Cook Depth above). Again I find no seamounts or guyots listed, but they may have been omitted because they were too low in the scheme of importance of items to be included in the volume.

To choose at random among popular books on the sea, G. E. R. Deacon's showy *Seas, Maps, and Men: An Atlas-History of Man's Exploration of the Oceans* (Garden City, 1962) contains several very poor relief maps of the ocean bottom which bear a few almost unreadable labels on large features.

Now a word on the history of underwater exploration, for the history throws light on the naming process. Measuring the depths of the sea apparently dates from remote antiquity, as Deacon says,[1] for plumb lines are shown in Egyptian wall paintings. This was a necessity from earliest times if sailors were to protect life, goods, and trade from shipwreck on rocks and sands. These measurements

---

[1] p. 190.

and accompanying place-naming occurred in shallow regions because here were the greatest dangers and because only here would
plumb lines reach. For the depths such sounding lines would not
suffice. Because the sea bottom in shallow areas was first plumbed,
therefore, and because these shallow areas were along the shores of
the Mediterranean and the Atlantic coasts of Europe, names are
thickest and oldest here.

I think of Antonio's bad luck on the Goodwin Sands, in the English Channel just south of the mouth of the Thames, as reported by
Salarino in *The Merchant of Venice*, 3.1.1–5:

> *Salanio:* Now, what news on the Rialto?
>
> *Salarino:* Why, yet it lives there uncheck'd that Antonio hath a ship of rich
> lading wrack'd on the narrow seas; the Goodwins, I think they
> call the place; a very dangerous flat, and fatal, where the carcases
> of many a tall ship lie buried, as they say.

(The Goodwins are still sometimes in the news, and probably always
will be. A story and a photograph in *Time* several years ago told of
a ship foundering on the Goodwins.)

The first study of the Mediterranean, the birthplace of Western
civilization and of the earth sciences, a sea to which Herodotus
referred in the fifth century B.C. and which Ptolemy mapped in-
accurately (employing latitude and longitude, however), was made
by Bartholomew Crescentius in his *Della Nautica Mediterranea*
(Rome, 1602).[2] It is a curious and paradoxical fact that in the next
century terrestrial mapmakers picked up the idea of contour lines
from a map drawn and published in 1725 by Luigi Marsigli in his
Histoire Physique de la Mer. Here he drew numerous lines from the
coasts of Provence and Languedoc into the deep Mediterranean,
joining points of equal depth, and so establishing the relief of the
sea bed in 'profile. He clearly showed the shallow shelf, already
named *La Plaine* by fishermen, and also a second one, sounding up
to 250 meters before the drop into the abyss. Others used and refined
the idea in mapping the coasts of Holland and the English Channel.
The science of measuring depths thus developed ahead of that of
measuring altitudes. Measuring altitudes had to await the development of the barometer, especially as improved by Laplace.[3] Many

---

[2] J. M. Houston, *The Western Mediterranean World: An Introduction to its Regional Landscapes* (London, 1964), p. 38.

[3] *International Yearbook of Cartography* (1962), pp. 152–53.

French and Italian studies followed, especially in the nineteenth century. Since 1910 an international commission, operating from the Oceanographic Institute at Monaco, has concentrated on the Mediterranean, yet the sea remains still largely unknown.[4]

Elsewhere, the first sounding beyond the Continental Shelf was made by Captain Constantine John Phipps (Lord Mulgrave) in the basin between Iceland and Norway as he voyaged toward the North Pole in 1773 in *H. M. S. Racehorse*. His sounding, 683 fathoms, is still on Admiralty charts. A half century went by before much further progress into the deeps was made.[5]

Matthew F. Maury, the American naval officer (1806–1873), was the first person to examine ships' logs and to organize their data systematically. One of the earliest and greatest expeditions was that of *H. M. S. Challenger*, directed by Sir Wyville Thompson, in 1872–76.[6]

It was only in 1920, with the development of echo sounding, that the configuration of the ocean bottom, long thought to be a flat, monotonous floor, became known, and the details of ocean bottom topography began to accumulate only during and after World War II with the use of positioning methods determined by electronics. Then came the revelation of great mountain chains, wide plains, large areas of rolling hills, deep rift valleys, and isolated mountains, many of them with flat tops, all features which called for names.[7]

In this connection Harris B. Stewart Jr. says that present deep-sea maps are at about the stage of maps of North America at the time of Lewis and Clark. He adds that when underwater features become fully charted (as they are not at present, even in major shipping lanes), ships will navigate by them with confidence. He gives a persuasive example of the importance of underwater charting. The *Explorer*, a ship of the U.S. Coast and Geodetic Survey, while on the major sea lane between Panama and Key West, passed directly over an uncharted mountain less than ninety feet under the surface. It turned back to chart and sample this great feature, which was then named *Explorer Bank*. The author speculates on what might have happened in the future if a large cargo-carrying submarine had run into it.[8]

---

[4] Houston, *op. cit.*, p. 37.　　[5] Deacon, *op. cit.*, pp. 190—91.

[6] *Collier's Encyclopaedia*, s.v. "Oceanography".

[7] *World Book. Encyclopaedia*, s.v. "Oceanography".

[8] *The Global Sea* (New York, 1963), pp. 14—15.

Increasingly, photographs from airplanes have proved useful. I myself, as an avid tourist, have flown over every ocean and many seas, and have constantly marveled at differing colors of water, indicating depths along continental coasts, at the mouths of great rivers (like that of the Nile recently, for example) and in the vicinity of the myriad islands of the sea (Tahiti, the Fiji group, and the small islands near Timor and Borneo not long ago, for another example). Now pictures from satellites in space are revealing many new facts about the sea floor, giving ideas of depth according to the depth of the color, locating unmapped shoals, and recording sudden changes of underwater topography such as channels created by hurricanes.[9]

Meanwhile the demand for undersea topographical information has expanded rapidly since World War II, and enormous data collecting and processing are going on. Oil and gas exploration forms one of the greatest demands. Said a *New York Times* headline on November 16, 1966, p. 65: "Use of Space Skill in Undersea Hunt for Oil Suggested." From the article itself we read:

> The aerospace and petroleum industries should combine their technological strengths for the joint exploration of offshore continental shelves... Within 35 years the world's population will have doubled... The oceans represent the last great resource for feeding it and providing the chemicals and minerals and water to meet all the future needs of man....

There will be bases 1000 feet deep "where 30 and 40 workers will live for extended periods." Indeed, shallow undersea areas have already become recreation spots, and John Pennecamp Coral Reef State Park, off the Florida Keys, which may be visited only by skin divers, has become America's first undersea park.

The terminology of strictly undersea topography includes at least the following 24 terms (some of them have their equivalents on dry land; some do not):

bank	guyot	rise
basin	hill	sands
canal	plain	seamount
channel	plateau	shoal
deep	province	sill
depth	reef	tablemount
escarpment	ridge	trench
fracture zone	rift	trough

---

[9] Paul B. Lowman, Jr. "The Earth from Orbit," *National Geographic* 130 (Nov., 1966), p. 656.

A word on two of these terms is called for.

> *guyot (Webster's Third New International):* Named after Arnold H. Guyot, died 1884, American geographer and geologist, born in Switzerland. Definition: A flat-topped submarine mountain or seamount, commonly found in the Pacific Ocean where the flat summits are at depths below the surface of the water as great as 5000 feet.

> *seamount (Webster's Third New International):* A submarine mountain rising above the deep sea floor commonly for 3000 to 10,000 feet and having the summit 1000 to 6000 feet below sea level.

Both of these terms sprang into prominence following World War II. Professor Harry Hammond Hess, of Princeton, in 1946, "showed that hundreds of flat-topped sea mounts are scattered over the Pacific," and gave them the name *guyot. Hess Guyot,* in the mid-Pacific, is named after Professor Hess who discovered it while commanding the *U.S.S. Cape Johnson,* "in honor of his maintenance of scientific interest under difficult wartime conditions and of his paper (Hess, 1946) which first called attention to guyots." *Cape Johnson Guyot,* near by, was named after the *U.S.S. Cape Johnson,* the ship on which Dr. Hess was navigator and commanding officer. This ship took the original line of soundings resulting in the discovery of Hess and Cape Johnson guyots.[10]

Here are samples of some of the older underwater names around Britain which I picked up from a British government hydrographic chart posted on the seafront at Margate, Kent, in the summer of 1966. The seafront, looking northward, faces the estuary of the Thames where it joins the Channel. Place names in these waters are scattered thickly, perhaps every quarter of a mile on an average.

> *Sands* named Gunfleet, Bachelor's Spit, Foulness, Maplin.
> *Shallows* named The Cant, Shingles Patch, Pudding Pan, Kentish Flats.
> *Channels* named Shipway, Sledway, Goldmer Gat, Wallet, East Swin.
> *Deeps* named Black, Knock, Ooze, Middle.

In spite of their name, these deeps were very shallow, under about 75 fathoms, compared to abyssal deeps. Elsewhere around Britain, on other maps, are *banks* named Buttock, Bligh, Bill Bailey's, Lemon, Broken, Indefatigable, Rosemary, Swarte (Dutch spelling), North West Ling, Little Halibut, Great and Little Fisher, Buchan,

---

[10] Edwin L. Hamilton, *Sunken Islands of the Mid-Pacific Mountains* (New York, 1956), pp. 14, 18.

Dogger, and Wee Bankie (east of the Firth of Forth). Still others
are The Warp, Le Colbart, Sandettie, North Hinder (Scottish for
hindrance?), Galloper, Gabbard, The Would, the Long Forties, and
The Smalls.[11]

When we turn to modern labels and the great features of the
abyssal deeps, we find that they are usually named after nearby
land features. *Examples in the North Atlantic* are, the Greenland-
Iceland Rise, the Labrador Basin, the Great Bahama Bank, and, in
the Caribbean arm of the Atlantic, the Cayman Trench, the Yucatan
Basin, the Colombian Basin, the Venezuelan Basin, the Tobago
Trough, the Barbados Trough, and the Puerto Rican Trench.

In the South Atlantic one finds the Pernambuco Abyssal Plain,
the Argentine Basin, the Angola Abyssal Plain, the Falkland Trough,
the South Sandwich Trench, and the Atlantic-Indian Rise. Seamounts and other isolated features, however, appear usually to be
named after persons or ships. Among the Altantic seamounts are
Faraday, Anton Dohrn, American Scout, Plato, Cruiser (called a
tablemount, actually; south of the Azores). A group of seamounts
roughly west of the Straits of Gibraltar are named Gettysburg,
Josephine, Ampere, Seine, and Dacia.

In the Pacific is the Gulf of Alaska Seamount Province. The Gulf
of Alaska, by the way, is one of the few areas of the globe where
systematic soundings are carried on: it is being explored under an
annual program of the U.S. Coast and Geodetic Survey. On December 27, 1966, for example, the *New York Times* headlined a news
item, "Mountains on Ocean Floor Around Aleutians Revealed,"
and opened its story, dated from Washington, by saying

> The existence of dozens of previously uncharted undersea mountains,
> ridges and basins was disclosed today with the publication of six new maps
> of the ocean floor surrounding the Aleutian Islands. The maps cover 400,000
> square miles of sea bed.... The newly discovered mountains rise as high as
> 6,510 feet from the ocean floor.

Published by the Environmental Science Services Administration
in the Department of Commerce, the maps "should prove valuable
in the study of earthquakes and of great aid to oceanographers and
commercial fisheries," the dispatch concluded.

---

[11] Oxford Press, *The Atlas of Britain and Northern Ireland* (London, 1963),
passim.

By contrast, the least known of the global seas is the far South Pacific, south of about 30 degrees south latitude, between New Zealand and South America.[12] This writer has been down there, east and south of New Zealand, and also south of Australia, in both the southern Tasman Sea and in the Great Australian Bight.

Sample names of large features in the Pacific include the Aleutian Basin, the Mendocino Escarpment (off Cape Mendocino, California), the Murray Fracture Zone (off southern California), the Tehuantepec Ridge (off southern Mexico), and the Guatemala Basin. Seamount groups in the North Pacific include Giacomini, Palton, Parker, Gilbert, Surveyor, Miller, Pathfinder, and Bear. In the South China Sea, an arm of the Pacific, west of North Borneo, occur banks named Prince of Wales, Prince Consort, Vanguard, Rifleman, Grainger, and Alexandra. Just off Saigon Pearl Bishop Bank must be well known today to American skippers.

In the Arctic Ocean are found the Eurasian Basin (at the Pole), the Canadian Ridge, the Chukchi Rise (north of Alaska), the Greenland Basin, the Lomonosov Ridge (very long and lying right across the Pole, with the Eurasian Basin, above, alongside), and the Murmansk Rise, among many others.

In the Indian Ocean it will suffice to name the Reunion-Seychelles Ridge (southeast of the Seychelles), the Somali Basin (east of the Somali Republic), the Mauritius Ridge (north of Mauritius), and the Crozet Basin (near the Crozet Islands, far to the south).

An Ocean Survey Program was begun by the ship *Pioneer* in February, 1961. It produced some accurate maps of undersea topography, but this was a mere start on a gigantic job. In the same year Unesco's Inter-governmental Oceanographic Commission was formed, with 44 countries sending representatives to its first meeting in Paris. It led to a good co-operative program among seven countries which explored the floor of the tropical Atlantic in 1963. A similar program was undertaken in the Indian Ocean.[13]

Once the world's continental shelves are conquered, predicts Stewart (p. 10), some ten million square miles, roughly equal to the area of Asia (p. 17), will be open for exploitation of its enormously rich animal, vegetable, and mineral wealth. It is the richest of all frontiers by far. The money now being spent on its investigation is

---

[12] Stewart, *op. cit.*, p. 21.　　[13] *Ibid.*, pp. 91–93, 122.

large, yet only a pinpoint compared with that being put into the space program. But progress continues as men not only multiply soundings but learn to live and explore underwater for longer and longer periods. In this area the Frenchman Jacques-Ives Costeau is the leader. Indicative of the growing interest in the watery underworld is the fact that the U.S. government is now choosing a site and building a new Federal institute of oceanography. All of this activity means that new names are sure to be set down in quantity on the invisible landscape in coming years.

Perhaps, moreover, the time is ripe for some organization to initiate the publication of a popular, exclusively underwater atlas and gazetteer of the world, one which would be periodically updated. Thus, the public would be kept aware of our growing knowledge of the invisible landscape.

University of Illinois
Chicago Circle

Biblical Place-Names
in the United States

JOHN LEIGHLY

REVIEWING KELSIE B. HARDER'S *Illustrated Dictionary of Place Names in the United States and Canada,* Eugene B. Vest commented that "[t]he comparatively few biblical names is surprising."[1] Harder's book contains a rather small sample from which to judge the frequency of biblical names, though the impression it gives of their low frequency in relation to the whole number of names in the United States is undoubtedly correct. There is no *a priori* basis, however, for judging the appropriate frequency of such names, or of any other class of names that might be defined. Vest's comment prompted me to investigate the relative frequency and distribution of biblical place-names in the United States.

I have worked from a sample of names in use in the middle of the twentieth century that is conveniently accessible and approximately uniform across the country. It consists of the names of civil divisions in the contiguous states used by the Bureau of the Census, supplemented by a list of post offices; the latter list adds names of unincorporated places to those of the Census Bureau's list of counties, incorporated places, and small civil divisions: townships, electoral districts, precincts, etc.[2] The total number of names—or, rather, of "namings," since many names are replicated—in my sample is 61,742, the number in individual states ranging from 51 in Delaware to 3,361 in Pennsylvania. The number of place-names in official use in a state varies not only with its area and the density of its rural and small-town population, but also with local customs of designating the smallest official districts or precincts. In Texas the administrative divisions of counties are numbered rather than named; as a consequence, my sample includes slightly fewer names from that state than from Kansas or New York. Names of post offices in Texas outnumber names of civil divisions. The same practice obtains in

---

[1] *Names,* 24:4 (December, 1976), 316.

[2] I used U.S. Bureau of the Census, *Sixteenth Census of the United States, 1940, Areas of the United States* (Washington: Government Printing Office, 1942), which contains detailed maps showing all names listed; and U.S. Post Office Department, *Directory of Post Offices* (Washington, Government Printing Office, 1958). The date of the census list is of little importance, since civil divisions have changed but little in the present century; post offices have declined in number from a maximum attained about 1910.

Mississippi and Tennessee, which in my sample have approximately the same number of namings as Maryland. Pennsylvania owes its large number of namings, far larger than that in Illinois and Ohio, which are closest to it in my sample, to its small townships and numerous chartered boroughs. In my total of nearly 62,000 namings I found only 803 from biblical place-names, 1.3 percent of the total.[3] The number of namings in my sample from some states is small, in view of the rare occurrence of biblical namings. Ten states have fewer than 500: the New England states other than Maine, Delaware, Utah, Wyoming, Arizona, and Nevada. Even among these, however, some differences are significant: that between 4.3 percent in Connecticut and 1.7 in Massachusetts certainly is; Utah, with 2.0 percent, ranks between Tennessee and North Carolina, whereas its neighbors (Idaho with 1.0 percent is nearest) have one percent or less. Its strongly religious original population, which spread into Idaho, is an adequate explanation of its relatively high rank among the western states. I shall proceed as if a sample of 250 namings suffices for my purposes. This limit excludes only Delaware, Nevada, and Rhode Island; my sample from Rhode Island contains no biblical names.

I consider only names used as place-names in the Bible, with the single exception of Paradise, which is not capitalized in the Authorized Version, but which has evidently been perceived as a place-name. Even among these, some should probably be excluded. Names found within the scene of the history of the ancient Hebrews, from Egypt (five occurrences) to Mesopotamia (one occurrence), larger than the proverbial range from Dan (one occurrence) to Beersheba (two occurrences), may be assumed to have become known to name-givers primarily from the Bible.[4] The New Testament extends this range to the north and west by its record of Paul's missionary travels and his eventual journey to Rome. A number of names from that record, as given in the book of Acts, appear as place-names in the United States, but some of them

---

3   Wilbur Zelinsky, "Classical Town Names in the United States," *Geographical Review*, 57 (1967), 463–495, permits a comparison of this percentage with that of a different class of names of infrequent occurrence. Using all namings he could find, disused as well as current, in official use since 1790, Zelinsky found 2.1 percent of them "classical." He counted, however, not only place-names from classical antiquity, but also personal names, modern coinages in classical form (*e.g.*, coined names ending in *-polis*), and names of letters of the Greek alphabet. His list of names contains only 44 place-names proper, 12 of which I have included here as biblical names. Namings from biblical place-names in current use certainly outnumber namings from classical place-names.

4   One name from this region, Palmyra, which I find 25 times in my list, does not occur in the Bible, and so was evidently known from other literary sources. Its Hebrew name, Tadmor, mentioned once in the Bible (I Kings 9:18), occurs once in my list, as Tadmore, Hill Co., Georgia.

might have been known from other sources. Athens and Rome were certainly widely known, and I have accordingly excluded them from my count. I have also excluded Syracuse, one of the stops made by the ship on which Paul traveled to Rome, and Alexandria, mentioned casually in Acts 18:24. But I have retained names from Greece other than Athens, and all from Anatolia, the "Asia" of the New Testament. The line I have drawn is arbitrary—I have counted Memphis and Smyrna, for example—but I have proceeded from the belief that the ordinary colonist or pioneer was more likely to know of a place in the ancient eastern Mediterranean region from the Bible than from secular literature.

REGIONAL DISTRIBUTION OF THE NAMES

The number of biblical namings in the individual states having 250 or more namings in my sample ranges from 69 in Ohio to none in Arizona. The first ten states in descending order of number of biblical namings are Ohio (69), Pennsylvania (51), Georgia (45), Illinois (44), North Carolina (37), Kentucky (32), Iowa (29), South Carolina (28), Indiana (27), and Missouri (26). These absolute numbers vary not only with the degree of acceptance of biblical place-names as appropriate for use in North America but also, very strongly, with the number of namings from the individual states in my sample. Five of the states just mentioned, Ohio, Pennsylvania, Illinois, Iowa, and Missouri, are among the first ten in total number of namings; Georgia and Kentucky are eleventh and twelfth, Indiana is fifteenth, but North Carolina twenty-first, and South Carolina, with only 894 namings, well below the median number of namings in the several states, twenty-ninth. At least formally, the influence of total number of namings in a state may be eliminated by expressing the number of biblical namings as a percentage of the total number of namings. Nine of the 45 states have percentages of 2.0 or more: Connecticut 4.3, South Carolina 3.1, Ohio 2.8, Vermont 2.7, Mississippi 2.5, Georgia and North Carolina 2.4, New Hampshire 2.1, and Utah 2.0. Some regularity appears: this list includes, first, three New England states, in two of which, Connecticut and Vermont, settlement was closely related, Vermont having drawn most of its pioneer population from Connecticut; New Hampshire, too, received settlers from Connecticut as well as from Massachusetts and directly from overseas. Next, four southern states; they do not quite form a continuous block, but Mississippi has only 609 namings in my sample, 37 percent of Alabama's 1,655, in which only 1.5 percent are biblical.

Besides these larger percentages in the East and Southeast, Ohio, with 2.8 percent, and Utah, with 2.0 percent, stand out above their

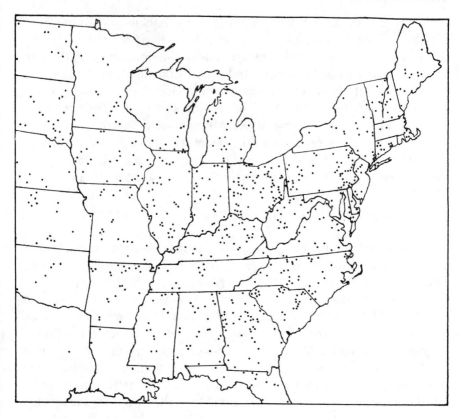

Fig. 1. Biblical place-names in the eastern half of the contiguous United States.

neighbors. Samples from the states bordering Ohio are good; they have the following percentages of biblical namings: Pennsylvania 1.5, West Virginia 1.3, Kentucky 1.7, Indiana 1.5, and Michigan 1.3. I have already discussed Utah; excluding Mississippi, it is the only state west of Ohio and Georgia in which biblical namings account for as many as two percent of the total number; the western state nearest to it is Oregon, with 1.4 percent.

Their great differences in area and internal homogeneity make the states unsatisfactory units for a numerical comparison of density of names. I have devised a better unit by plotting the names as dots on a working map of the United States in which areas are in their true proportions, a map about 70 cm. (28 in.) in its longer dimension. Figure 1, drawn on a greatly reduced scale, shows the distribution of the dots in the eastern half of the country. I then divided the map into arbitrary squares, each of which represents an area of 20,000 square kilometers

(7,722 sq. mi.), about halfway between the areas of New Jersey and Massachusetts, and counted the dots in each square. I drew the lines dividing the squares from an origin near the center of the map; they are thus wholly independent of state boundaries and of the clustering of dots. The number of dots in a square is a measure, uniform across the whole country, of the density of biblical namings, subject to the statistical uncertainty that afflicts the localization of events having a small probability of occurrence.[5] The entire area of the contiguous United States contains approximately 380 of the squares, of which about one-half, in my sample, are devoid of biblical names. Most of the empty squares are in the Great Plains and the mountainous and dry states of the West and Southwest, but there are also some in the thinly-settled country about Lake Superior and in northern Maine, as well as along the Gulf and south Atlantic coasts and in peninsular Florida. Most of the names are east of the Mississippi; the appeal of biblical names evidently diminished with time, as the states west of Ohio acquired their place-names in the nineteenth century.

The square that contains the largest number of biblical names, 20, includes southeastern Pennsylvania and adjoining slivers of Maryland, Delaware, and New Jersey. Some continuity is recognizable between eastern Pennsylvania, by way of northern New Jersey and Long Island, and Connecticut, so that one may speak of a northeastern maximum of biblical names having nuclei in Pennsylvania and Connecticut. In Pennsylvania the names are fairly dense from York County and the Susquehanna River eastward, and in the old Connecticut settlements in the northeastern corner of the state. They are almost wholly absent from central Pennsylvania, but become numerous again in the western part, where settlement was closely related to that in the neighboring part of Ohio.

Density of biblical names decreases southward from Pennsylvania across Maryland and Virginia, and increases again in the Piedmont of the Carolinas and Georgia, where two squares have 11 names each. An apparently distinct cluster of names, which gives a third square 11 dots, straddles the boundary between North and South Carolina on the inner

---

5 A circle having the same area as one of the squares, moved about so as to include the maximum number of dots in various parts of the map, yielded results not greatly different from those to be cited in the text. I cite the following counts of dots within this "floating" unit area for comparison with those obtained from the fixed squares and given later: southeastern Pennsylvania, 20; southeastern Ohio, 19; Carolina Piedmont, 13; inner coastal plain of the Carolinas, 15; north-central Georgia, 15; Connecticut and southeastern New York, 16; southwestern Ohio and adjoining part of Kentucky, 11; northern Arkansas and adjoining part of Missouri, 9; northern Alabama, 7.

coastal plain. From Georgia the density diminishes westward across northern Alabama and Mississippi, with values below five per square, toward the great western region having few or no biblical names. The Gulf coastal plain has few, and the part of peninsular Florida cut off in Figure 1 none in my sample. The Piedmont and inner coastal plain of the southeastern states thus exhibits a second maximum of density of biblical names, containing local clusters as dense as any in Pennsylvania.

The religious character of the original colonists in Pennsylvania and Connecticut adequately accounts for the northeastern maximum of density of biblical names. Settlement of the "Up-Country" of the Carolinas and Georgia was mainly by migration from Pennsylvania by way of the Valley of Virginia and then, east of the Blue Ridge, by old trading trails leading to the country of the Cherokees and Creeks in the southern Piedmont. This migration included "Scotch-Irish" Presbyterians, German Moravians and Baptists, and Quakers. It began in the early eighteenth century and reached a peak after the war for independence, diminishing in the early nineteenth century. Religious groups arriving directly from overseas brought some biblical names: Bethania and Old Salem in North Carolina were founded by Moravians, and Ebenezer, Florence County, South Carolina, by "Salzburgers." The southern maximum of biblical place-names seems to be a transplant from Pennsylvania, separated from its source by Virginia, with its lower density. Inland Virginia east of the Blue Ridge was settled in colonial times by expansion from the Tidewater, where biblical names are few. Even fewer are found on the outer coastal plain of the Carolinas and Georgia, the site of the earliest European settlement in these states. This was the country of great plantations, where the dominant social stratum retained its allegiance to the Anglican church. It would appear that as this plantation society and economy spread westward its bearers continued to give fewer biblical names than were given in the Piedmont: these names fade out across the Mississippi in Louisiana and Arkansas into Texas.

Inland from eastern Pennsylvania and the southeastern Piedmont, the Appalachian mountain belt and parts of the Allegheny and Cumberland plateaus have few biblical names. Where they appear, as in western Pennsylvania, the Kanawha Valley in West Virginia, and in eastern Kentucky, they seem to be associated with coal mining, which gives rise to many small communities, and thus to be later than the original settlement. West of the rougher plateau country the density increases again, especially in Ohio; the square on my working map that contains the second-largest number of names, 19, lies mostly in southeastern

Ohio but includes in addition parts of northern West Virginia and southwestern Pennsylvania. The flow of pioneers into Ohio was approximately contemporaneous with that into the southern Piedmont, but was more massive, including many settlers from the northeastern states as well as from Pennsylvania, Virginia, and Kentucky, and persisting well into the nineteenth century. Both the New Englanders and the Pennsylvanians apparently brought a taste for biblical names, giving Ohio more than any other state has. A conspicuous area having almost no biblical names extends northward in the middle of Ohio from the plateau belt of few such names. This country, most of which was in the Virginia Military District, was settled early, largely by Virginians, in contrast with the New Englanders, New Yorkers, and Pennsylvanians who constituted the majority of the pioneers in other parts of Ohio.

The northwestern corner of Ohio was in the possession of Indians until 1812, and contained much wet land in the valley of the Maumee River; it was consequently settled later than the rest of the state. Delayed settlement, here as in the states farther west, effected a progressive dilution of the traditional stock of place-names, including those from the Bible, brought from the East.[6] The indebtedness of Ohio as a whole to New England is indicated by the fact that eight of the ten most numerous biblical names in the state, Salem, Sharon, Eden, Goshen, Lebanon, Canaan, Bethel, and Bethlehem, are also among the ten most numerous ones in New England. Only six are among the leading ten in Pennsylvania.

West of Ohio, only one square on my working map, in southeastern South Dakota, contains as many as nine biblical names. One square in southeastern Minnesota contains seven, one in northern Kansas and an adjoining strip of Nebraska seven, and one in Arkansas eight. In the far west, cut off in Figure 1, only two squares contain as many as four: one in the Utah oasis and one in the Willamette Valley, Oregon.

The statistical uncertainty that afflicts the occurrence of rare events enjoins caution in interpreting the density of dots in Figure 1 west of Ohio. Some differences that appear on the map are, however, probably significant; for example, that between the wet prairies of eastern Illinois, where full settlement awaited drainage works and the building of the Illinois Central railroad, and the valleys of the upper Wabash and the

---

6 Curiously, Connecticut's Western Reserve in northeastern Ohio has few biblical names in comparison with other parts of the state: 2.1 percent in the 12 counties of the Reserve. Only two, Goshen and Sharon, are from colonial Connecticut. Names in these counties are dominated by those derived from personal, mostly family, names, 32 percent, and secular place-names transferred from New England, 30 percent in my sample.

Illinois rivers to the east and the west, settled early in the nineteenth century, probably is. More detailed investigation, based on a fuller sampling of names and due attention to the history of settlement, would be needed to determine whatever significance there may be in the distribution of dots in the left half of Figure 1.

THE NAMES USED

My 803 namings make use of only 101 names, given with greatly varying frequency. Thirty-three names, almost exactly one-third of the total number, appear only once in my list, and 12 others only twice. At the upper end of the range of frequency, the first 12 names and the number of their occurrences in my sample are Salem 95, Eden 61, Bethel 47, Lebanon 39, Sharon 28, Goshen 33, Jordan 27, Hebron 26, Zion 24, Antioch, Paradise, and Shiloh 19. These 12 account for 466 namings, 58 percent of the total 803. Other names that occur more than ten times in my sample are Beulah 17, Bethlehem and Canaan 16, various names for the Mount of Olives 15, Bethany (with the variant Bethania), Corinth, and Palestine 14, Carmel (including Mount Carmel) and Smyrna 13, Tabor (including Mount Tabor and Taber) 12 times. When the leading 12 names are combined with these ten, the 22 names account for 72 percent of my biblical namings. Two of them, Jordan and Tabor or Taber, are ambiguous, in that they occur as family names and hence as potential place-names.

I have accepted numerous variants of names and counted them with the primary forms. The Old Testament Kidron appears as Cedron in John 18:1; my list includes both forms as well as Kedron, each variant once. The prefixes "New" and names of directions are common: New Canaan was given in Connecticut earlier than simple Canaan; Ohio's 17 Salems include one each of New, South, and West Salem. I have also counted Salemburg (Sampson Co., N.C.) with Salem. In addition to all the simple Edens I find Edena, Edenbower, Edendale, Eden Prairie, Eden Valley, Edenville, Edon, and even Mount Eden. I have not counted Edenton, North Carolina, however, since it was named for a colonial governor, Charles Eden, nor its duplicate in Clermont County, Ohio. Zion appears both as a simplex and as Mount Zion, New Zion, Zion Grove, Zionhill, Zionsville, and Zionville. In addition to three simplexes, Siloam appears twice, in accordance with its original use as the name of one of the pools that supplied water to ancient Jerusalem, as

Siloam Springs, once in Arkansas and once in Missouri. The Mount of Olives appears as Mount Olive six times, as Olivet four times; as Mount Olivet, Olive Hill, and Olivette (St. Louis Co., Mo.) once each. I have, however, excluded Mount Oliver (Allegheny Co., Pa.), though some connection may be suspected. I counted Mount Orab (Brown Co., Ohio) with Mount Horeb (Dane Co., Wis.), and Mariah Hill (Spencer Co., Ind.) with Mount Moriah (Lawrence Co., Ala., and Harrison Co., Mo.); these in addition to two simple Horebs and one simple Moriah. Like Kidron, Zarephath (Somerset Co., N.J.) appears once thus in its Hebrew form from the Old Testament and twice in its Greek form, Sarepta (Calhoun Co., Miss. and Webster Parish, La.) from the New.

There can be little doubt that the primary sources of the custom of giving biblical place-names were colonial New England and Pennsylvania. By the end of the colonial period New England had 21 biblical namings from 12 names, including four Salems and three each of Canaan, Lebanon, and Sharon. The first one given was Salem, Massachusetts, 1630, and the second Rehoboth, also in Massachusetts, 1645. Eight of the 12 names, however, were given first in Connecticut: Lebanon, 1695; Hebron, 1707; New Canaan, 1731; Goshen, 1738; Bethlehem and Sharon, 1739; Bethel, 1759; and Bethany, 1762. I do not have the chronology of Pennsylvania's names, but at the end of the colonial period that colony had all of the New England biblical names except Corinth (Vt., 1764), Jericho (Vt., 1763), and Rehoboth; and in addition Emmaus, Ephrata(h), Nazareth, and Philadelphia. Six of the 12 most numerous biblical names in the whole United States, Salem, Bethel, Lebanon, Sharon, Goshen, and Hebron, were used in colonial New England, and Vermont added Eden in 1781. The remaining five, Jordan, Zion, Antioch, Paradise, and Shiloh, were added later and elsewhere. Colonial New York had Goshen and Salem, colonial New Jersey Bethlehem, Lebanon, Salem, and Sharon. Few were found farther south: both Maryland and Delaware had Rehoboth, North Carolina Bethania and Salem, and South Carolina Ebenezer, the last three given by immigrant religious groups. Both the practice of giving biblical place-names and a selected stock of them that would be replicated all across the continent were best represented in Connecticut and Pennsylvania, but were also well established in Vermont and New Hampshire. Migration from Pennsylvania, seconded by immigration from overseas, apparently transplanted the practice and many names to the upland South.

Westward expansion of settlement, from the late eighteenth century onward, in large part following belts of latitude from the eastern states but with much mingling between migrants from the upland South and those from the northern and middle states of the Atlantic seaboard, established the familiar zonation of English-speaking population in the middle of the continent: a northern belt predominantly from the northeastern states, a southern belt from the southeastern, and a broad belt of mixing that extends west from Ohio to Kansas and Nebraska.

Something of this zonation is reflected in the biblical place-names given in the respective belts. In order to compare North and South—the zone of mixing cannot be separated by states—I have taken a group of northern states west of Pennsylvania and one of southern states south and west of Virginia, in which the number of biblical names in my sample is very nearly equal. The northern group consists of Ohio, Michigan, Indiana, Illinois, Wisconsin, Minnesota, Iowa, and Nebraska, which together contain 225 biblical names; the southern group consists of North and South Carolina, West Virginia, Kentucky, Tennessee, Georgia, Alabama, and Arkansas, and contains 224 names in my sample. The intermediate zone of mixing lies mostly in my northern group.

All of these states together contain 84 of the 101 biblical names in my whole list: the southern states 71 of them, the northern states only 55. As biblical names were appropriated for places, the upland South was evidently more innovative than the North, adding more names to the colonial list than the North did. Names are less concentrated in the high frequencies in the southern than in the northern group. Taking the seven names used most frequently in North and South, these seven account for 84 namings in the South, but for 117 in the North. The seven that head the list from the northern group of states are the first seven in frequency in the country as a whole, though their numerical order is slightly different. Salem, first in the list in both groups, occurs 37 times in the northern group, 19 times in the southern. Only three, Salem, Bethel, and Goshen, all found in colonial New England and Pennsylvania, are among the highest seven in both groups. In the North the remaining four are, in decreasing order, Eden, Lebanon, Sharon, and Jordan, three of which were found in colonial New England and two in colonial Pennsylvania; in the South, Antioch, Zion, Shiloh, and Olivet (with variants), none of which appears in the colonial list. Of the 33 names that occur only once in the whole country, the group of southern states provides 13: Kentucky five, Arkansas, Georgia, and West Virginia two each, North Carolina and Alabama one each. The states in the northern group have only six: two in each of Ohio, Michigan, and Illinois. Four of these names are, moreover, ambiguous, possibly of other origin, though they appear in the Bible: Mesopotamia (Ohio), Assyria, Rhodes (Mich.), and Crete (Ill.). Only one of the singular names in the South, Arabia (Ga.), is questionable on the same grounds. One of the two remaining names in the North (but in southern Illinois, which was strongly affected by immigration from south of the Ohio River) is likely to be unfamiliar to the ordinary reader of the Bible: Ruma (Rumah in II Kings 23:36); the other, Zoar (Ohio), appears several times in the Old Testament. Some of the lone names in the South, Dan, Gethsemane (Ky.), Judea, Patmos (Ark.), are familiar, but others are distinctly less so: Amma (W. Va.; Ammah in II Sam. 2:24), Dothan (Ala.), Ekron, Elam(ton), Ezel (Ky.), Tadmor(e) (Ga.), Tirzah (N.C., preceded by a gratuitous "Mount"), and Zela (W. Va.; Zelah in Josh. 18:28). Ammah, Dothan, Ezel, Tadmor, and Zelah are mentioned only once in the Bible, and so would be known only to diligent searchers of the Scriptures. Since none of them is associated with a memorable event, they can scarcely carry any metaphorical connotation, but seem rather to reflect a desire for distinctiveness, even uniqueness. Northerners were apparently more content to repeat the old names familiar from the northeastern states, as they repeated such secular names as Dover and Springfield. Instances of names that occur only once in the Bible and once in my list are found in other states than those just mentioned—Dor (Kans.), Lehi (Utah), Ono (Calif.), Timnath (Colo,)—but they are most numerous in the South.

Even within the zone of mixing of northern and southern immigrants into the Middle West, the contrast between northern and southern practice in the borrowing of biblical place-names can be recognized, though it is not sharp. Taking Indiana and Illinois together, I divided these states into a northern and a southern belt with as nearly equal numbers of biblical names in each belt as is possible: 36 namings in the northern belt, 35 in the southern. In this small sample, in which, moreover, the difference between the belts in composition of their populations is far from distinct, the greater variety of biblical names found in the southern group of states recurs: in the northern belt 18 different names account for 36 namings, in the southern 26 names for 35 namings. Again in accordance with the sectional data, there are eight Salems in the northern belt, only four in the southern. Nine out of 35 different names are found in both belts, all except three, Carmel, Olivet with variants, and Palestine, from the colonial list. In the northern belt, two names more representative of the South than of the North, Antioch and Zion, appear; the southern belt has four such southern-looking names, Macedonia, Nebo, Shiloh, and Smyrna. Thus a difference between northern and southern Indiana and Illinois, familiar to inhabitants of those states on other grounds, makes a blurred appearance in biblical place-names.

METAPHORS IN THE BIBLICAL NAMES

As is well known, the colonists of early New England, religious groups settling in Pennsylvania, and their descendants who peopled the western territories often saw in themselves a resemblance to the ancient Hebrews seeking and subduing a promised land. (There is a Promised Land in Lawrence Co., Ark., but I have not counted it, since the expression does not appear as a place-name in the Bible.) This metaphor gave rise to Canaan, Gilead, Goshen, Hebron, Palestine, and Sharon as place-names, as well as to Rehoboth (Gen. 26:22: "For now the Lord hath made room for us, and we shall be fruitful in the land"). I find, however, only six Rehoboths in my sample, three of them colonial. Only later (Vt., 1781, N.Y., 1812) did pioneers equate their land with Eden, a name that became extremely popular in the West: there are eight Edens in Iowa and seven in South Dakota alone. Paradise has a distribution resembling that of Eden. Beulah, of later introduction and with one occurrence more than Canaan, belongs in this list, though its use in the Bible (Isa. 62:4), for the Jerusalem to be rebuilt after the Babylonian captivity, has no such reference. Its metaphorical use is obviously taken from Bunyan's *Pilgrim's Progress*, in which Bunyan uses it for the pleasant land in which his pilgrims rested before crossing the River of Death into the Celestial City. The imagery of the popular nineteenth-century religious song "Beulah Land," which must reflect the contemporary perception of the name, is taken directly from Bunyan. I have no doubt that this song was better known to members of rural sectarian congregations than was *Pilgrim's Progress*; it may thus have been in some instances the source of the name. Elim, the name of a welcome oasis found by the Hebrews of the Exodus in the Sinai (Ex. 15:27), appears three times in my list. The metaphor of wanderers finding and settling their promised land accounts for more of our biblical place-names than any other.

The primary metaphor represented by Salem, the first and most widely used biblical name, was the identification of a newly-founded community with the holiest of cities, Jerusalem; the four-syllabled full name was evidently too long for convenient use, and occurs only eight times in my list. The shorter synonym Zion is found three times as often. Closely related is the allusion to a new place of worship. Bethel (Gen.

35:1, 3) is the earliest and by far the most frequent name bearing it, given in Connecticut and Pennsylvania in colonial times and replicated freely afterwards. The next most frequent name of this class is Shiloh (I Sam. 1:3), most examples of which are in the South. Other names bearing a similar allusion are Mizpah (Gen. 31:49, Judg. 11:11) and Ramah (I Sam. 7:17, 8:4 ff.), which occur four and three times respectively.

With the exception of Bethany, Bethlehem, Corinth, and Philadelphia, two from the life of Jesus and two from early Christian missionary activity, the colonial names were all from the Old Testament. In my incomplete chronology, the next addition from the New Testament was Smyrna (N.Y., 1808), like Philadelphia the name of one of the seven churches in Asia to which the book of Revelation was addressed (Rev. 1:11). In later times New Testament names were given more often in the South than in the North; in the groups of northern and southern states I have used as exemplifying the sections I find 68 New Testament namings in the southern, 27 in the northern group. Three associations appear in these names. The largest class consists of names associated with Paul's career, 31 in the southern, 17 in the northern group, the most numerous being Antioch (13 namings in the South, four in the North) and Corinth (six in the South, two in the North). The count of Pauline names includes the two mentioned earlier that occur only once, Crete (Ill.) and Rhodes (Mich.), which may derive from the evanescent fashion of giving classical names. The second most frequent class consists of names associated with the life of Jesus, less numerous than those associated with Paul: 22 in the South, 11 in the North. The two most frequent ones are variants of the name of the Mount of Olives, eight in the South, three in the North, and Bethany, which, though first given in colonial Connecticut, is now most frequent in the South: five occurrences in my southern group of states, two in the northern. The third class of New Testament names consists of the names of three of the seven churches in Asia of the book of Revelation: 13 namings in the South, six in the North. The names are Smyrna (seven and two in the respective groups of states), Sardis (five and one), and Philadelphia, the first biblical name given in Pennsylvania, with three occurrences in each of the two groups.

The associations of these names with the aspirations of those who gave them is not always clear. There can be no doubt, however, that many of the biblical names in the South and some in the North were originally names of sectarian churches founded in rural communities that became known by the names of the churches. While some such churches were given names from the Old Testament (Salem, Shiloh, Zion), and some names associated with the life of Jesus (Bethany, Calvary, Olivet), many names were taken from places associated with Paul's career: places where he left small bands of the faithful among a population of unbelievers (Antioch, Berea, Corinth, Damascus) and scenes of dramatic incidents (Mars Hill, Philippi). The most striking metaphor of the little isolated band of the faithful is Macedonia; five namings in the southern group of states, three in the northern. It must seldom, if at all, commemorate Philip's kingdom—in my total count I excluded Macedon, Wayne Co., N.Y., which probably does—but rather the appeal made to Paul in a vision (Acts 16:9), "Come over into Macedonia and help us," and Paul's response to that appeal. The Pauline names are not names given by united groups of pioneers founding their Canaans, Goshens, and Hebrons in the wilderness, but by little groups of sectarians—Presbyterians, Methodists, Baptists, and their many evangelical offshoots—building and struggling to maintain their little Bethels among unbelievers and competing sectarians. These nontraditional names were bestowed in all of the states, but the custom of giving them seems to have been strongest in the upland South, and to have been carried northward and westward by emigrants from that region. Ohio, in addition to its many biblical names transplanted from New England and Pennsylvania, has one each of Antioch, Berea, Bethesda, Beulah, Macedonia, Sardis, and Shiloh.

Once given and accepted as a familiar name, any name might be carried to a new site and given again without reference to its original metaphorical association, as British place-names were carried west from the original colonies. As is true of place-names of secular origin, the biblical names given in colonial New England and Pennsylvania are the ones used most widely and frequently; but new names, most of them emanating from the upland South, were also widely disseminated, and the Bible was always at hand to provide a never-exhausted store of names not previously given.

Berkeley, California

The Selection of Proper Names in English Dictionaries

CLARENCE L. BARNHART

Dictionaries are the repositories of the vocabulary of the language. As such they attracted the interest and scholarship of Francis Lee Utley, who selected a basic list of the important books in English literature that should be read to provide citations for a college dictionary. Utley also considered the problem of defining proper names in an article, "The Linguistic Component of Onomastics," published in the September, 1963 issue of *Names*. This is a problem that is of obvious practical interest to all dictionary makers.

In varying sizes dictionaries contain selections of the total vocabulary pertaining to a particular segment of the population or to a particular subject or department of knowledge. There are approximately 250,000 words in the working vocabulary of English; college dictionaries, the most common of popular dictionaries, contain from 125,000 to 175,000 terms. Obviously there is a space problem for editors of college dictionaries since the editor must show the facts of spelling, the pronunciation, the inflected forms, the derivatives, the meaning or significance of the word, and the etymology of a little over half of the working vocabulary.

In order to conserve space, facts that may be needed one time out of a thousand by the dictionary user are omitted by the editor—an obsolete or archaic word used only in one context, a technical term used only in advanced study, or a slang term or a dialect term used by comparatively small groups of people for a limited time. Words selected for abridged dictionaries are selected on the basis of frequency, range, and cruciality (e.g., their importance as basic terms in a field of knowledge). Proper names are included in the college dictionaries primarily on the basis of their importance to the prospective user.

Unabridged dictionaries, both historical and descriptive, often contain half a million entries and attempt to be a complete record of the vocabulary for the period covered by the dictionary. Such dictionaries usually do not consider proper names to be a part of the vocabulary to be included. The Preface to Volume I of the *Oxford English Dictionary* (1888 edition, p.vi) states its policy:

. . . it has to be borne in mind, that a Dictionary of the English Language is not a Cyclopaedia: the Cyclopaedia *describes things*; the Dictionary *explains words*, and deals with the description of things only so far as is necessary in order to fix the exact significations and uses of words. . . . We do not look in a Cyclopaedia for the explanation and history of *anon, perhaps*, or *busy*; we do not expect in an English Dictionary, information about *Bookbinding, Photography*, the *Aniline Dyes*, or the *Bridgewater Treatises*, or mention of *Abyssinia, Argynnis, Alopecurus, Adenia*, or *Blennerteritis*.

In discussing the inconsistency of omitting the proper adjective *African* while including the proper adjective *American*, the *OED* Preface says (p.ix):

. . . the inconsistency is only on the surface; *American* is included, not on its own account, but to help to the better explanation of derived words; and, in every analogous case, it will be found that a proper noun, or adjective thence formed, is included, not for its own sake and as a proper noun, etc., but because it has other uses, or has derivatives for the explanation of which it is of importance. Every such word must, in fact, be looked upon as exceptionally included, and not as forming a precedent for the inclusion of other words of the same class.

The great descriptive dictionary, *The Century Dictionary*, contemporaneous with the *OED*, takes the same attitude toward proper names (Preface to 1911 edition, p. xix):

. . . THE CENTURY DICTIONARY covers to a great extent the field of the ordinary encyclopedia, with this principal difference—that the information given is for the most part distributed under the individual words and phrases with which it is connected, instead of being collected under a few general topics. Proper names, both biographical and geographical, are, of course, omitted except as they appear in derivative adjectives, as *Darwinian* from *Darwin*, or *Indian* from *India*.

A similar but stricter policy of exclusion of proper names guided the editors of *W3* (Preface, p. 6a, col.2):

This dictionary . . . confines itself strictly to generic words and their functions, forms, sounds, and meanings as distinguished from proper names that are not generic.

One looks in vain in these three dictionaries for such entries as *Bucephalus* or *Labiche* or *Kansas* or *Elbe*.

Where does the reader turn for information on *Bucephalus* and similar entries? Usually he is referred to an encyclopedia, and if he follows that advice in this case he will have to persist in order to find the name. *Bucephalus* is not an entry in either the 1960 or 1970 edition of *Collier's Encyclopedia*; it is not entered in the index of either edition, nor is it mentioned under the encyclopedia article on Alexander the Great. *The Encyclopaedia Britannica* has a varied history; the first edition (1771) does not contain *Bucephalus*, but the first American edition does. The 1946 edition lists *Bucephalus* in the index and has a short article in volume 4; the 1966 edition, however, omits it in the encyclopedia proper and in the index. *The Encyclopedia Americana* (1954) also lists the term in the index and has a somewhat longer article in volume 4 but without a pronunciation; the 1961 edition contains the word with a pronunciation.

In looking up a specific proper name—even one as well known as *Bucephalus*—the reader has a good chance of not finding it at all or of finding it buried in a long article and available only by use of the index. After finding the entry, moreover, the reader will often be unable to discover its pronunciation. Usually none is given in earlier editions of encyclopedias, although there is a tendency to give pronunciations in the newer encyclopedias as they become more dictionary-like in form. But, in general, linguistic facts about proper names—variant spellings, syllabication of the boldface, and pronunciation of the term—are not normally given in encyclopedias. Moreover, encyclopedias are as a rule much more expensive than dictionaries. They tend to be library books, while dictionaries are usually individually owned. This limits the usefulness of the encyclopedia, as it is all too often not available. Many more people use dictionaries than they do encyclopedias.

Giving the linguistic facts about proper names and identifying them is one of the chief functions of college dictionaries, yet unabridged dictionaries as a matter of policy exclude proper names. What is a proper name? How are the proper names accounted for in the grammar of the language? A number of studies and papers have appeared offering a definition of the term *proper name*. In addition to the article by Professor Utley mentioned above, a monograph by John Algeo, entitled *On Defining the Proper Name* and published in 1973 by the University of Florida's Humanities Series, is essential reading for understanding what a proper name is. There are of course those who take the stand that names are not a part of the language. This Algeo regards as a dodge to avoid accounting for facts about language that cannot be conveniently handled by any available linguistic theory.

Algeo examines in detail various criteria for defining proper names that have been suggested: (1) capitalization of proper names versus lower-case words; (2) the syntactic forms of proper names: no plural forms, use without articles, no restrictive modifiers; (3) the uniqueness of proper names in referring to a single individual, and (4) the fact that proper names have no meaning—no characteristics common to several individuals of a group. These four criteria are rejected by Utley, explicitly or implicitly, as well as by Algeo, who by close reasoning and many examples shows their inadequacy.

Algeo does, however, propose a criterion of his own (p. 71): " . . . a proper name is primarily any word X whose meaning can be expressed as 'entity called X' . . . . " Proper nouns differ from common nouns because their meanings are not parallel: a proper name results from an act of name-giving; a common noun is a name that summarizes essential characteristics of a creature belonging to a class of creatures. Algeo continues, "To know that a creature is appropriately referred to by the word *cat*, it is not necessary to observe anyone calling it 'cat.' But to know that some creature is appropriately called *Pyewacket*, it is necessary to observe some instance of the use of that name with reference to the creature" (p. 71).

In his article, Utley examines the definitions of proper name given by Sir Alan Gardiner, Ernst Pulgram, Otto Jespersen, and Charles F. Hockett, and proceeds to demonstrate how each definition fails *qua* definition by being inductively arrived at or by being wholly dependent on semantic, as against formal, criteria.

Thus Utley rejects the *a priori* criterion of *uniqueness* on the grounds that such a sentence as "Last night there were four Maries here" destroys the uniqueness of *Mary* as a proper name. On the criterion of *determiners* Utley goes only so far as to say that "proper names differ in some fashion from common nouns in their use of the articles *a* and *the* and in their use with adjectives and as adjectives" (p. 168) adding in conclusion, however, that "Pulgram rightly considers the article no final indicator of proper or common noun" (p. 170). Utley also rejects *capitalization* as a criterion, citing many conflicting uses of the capital initial letter. Finally, Utley rejects the criterion that proper names are unlikely to be preceded by adjectives, in view of the use of such common phrases as the *Great* Barnum, the *younger* Dumas, *another* Johnson, a *genuine* Rembrandt, and *amazing* Amsterdam.

If linguistic criteria were adopted as the basis for the exclusion of proper names from a dictionary, dictionary editors would have to exclude the *Cenozoic* (geological age), the *U.N.*, the *Mafia*, the *Devil*, and *earth* (the planet) since they satisfy most if not all grammatical criteria for properness. Such standards are difficult to apply: witness *W3*'s entry of the planet *earth* (def. 5 *often cap*) but its exclusion of the planet *Neptune*. Such entries as *Age of Mammals* (the Cenozoic), *Aircav* (a unit of the U.S. armed forces), *Amtrak* (a system of rail passenger service), BASIC (a computer language), *Big Bang* (a cosmic explosion 10 to 15 billion years ago), *Bennett* (a comet sighted in 1969), and *art deco* (a style of design) would have to be omitted as proper names. On the other hand such capitalized terms as *Uncle Tom, White Paper, Chicano, May Day,* and *Rhodes scholar* would be admitted as common nouns. The truth of the matter is that both types of terms belong in a popular dictionary: they have currency in the literature of the day; most of them would not be entered in any other reference work. Frequency, range, and cruciality are the criteria for including or excluding entries in a dictionary; grammatical criteria do not work.

The inclusion of proper names is also helpful in the explanation of names and adjectives derived from them. The proper names are located in space or time and important linguistic facts such as pronunciation and variant spellings or names are given. The definition of *Ishmael,* the secondary sense of which is "an outcast, a person like Ishmael" can be helped by the definition of the primary term. So can *Shelleyan* be helped by the entry of *Shelley.*

The primary terms are so important that their attempted omission results in outlandish treatment that can only puzzle and discourage the average dictionary user. *W3,* which has been the most consistent dictionary in excluding proper names, often puts a definition of the proper name under the proper adjective, thus playing hide and seek with the user of the dictionary. *Labrador,* the peninsula in Canada, is not entered in the dictionary but is explained in the etymology for *Labrador* (the adjective) as follows: "[fr. *Labrador,* peninsula, Newfoundland and Quebec, provinces in Canada]" and again under *Laboradorean*: "[*Labrador,* peninsula, Canada + *E -an*]." The *OED,* which also had the policy of excluding proper names, enters *Labrador* as a main entry and defines it as "the name of a large peninsula in British North America," including it of course as necessary to the understanding of such collocations as *Labrador blue, Labrador duck,* and so on. *The Century* does not enter *Labrador* and does not identify Labrador in the etymology of *Labradorian*: "[*Labrador* + *-ian*]." Each dictionary has its facts selected and arranged in a different way: the *OED* puts the primary sense first, *W3* puts the primary sense in the etymology, and the *Century* puts *Labrador* in the etymology without explanation. There are justifications for each decision, but most American editors of college dictionaries today would follow the policy of entering and identifying *Labrador* as a more important (frequent) term than *Labradorean.* *Labradorean* indeed may be omitted or treated as a run-on entry. On linguistic grounds this may be the wrong policy, but the fact is that the user of the dictionary is usually seeking information about *Labrador* and not *Labradorean.* If he does seek information about *Labradorean,* his curiosity is gratified by simply connecting *Labradorean* to *Labrador.*

In sum, the function of a popular dictionary is to give desired and reliable linguistic information about specific words—whether or not they are proper names; the function of an encyclopedia is to deal with whole fields of knowledge. A descriptive dictionary that selects entries on linguistic principles may be satisfying to some linguists, but it is bound to be inadequate as a source of the information needed by the educated user of dictionaries today. If strict linguistic criteria were to be adopted in the selection of terms to be included in dictionaries, many current words and terms would have to be omitted on theoretical grounds, and information about many terms, especially those that are used to identify particular or individual objects, would be unavailable.

Bronxville, New York

On the Grammar of Afro-American
Naming Practices

J. L. DILLARD

IT IS WELL KNOWN that names are somehow related to grammar, and it is often suspected that linguistics may somehow be able to furnish the solution to any grammatical problem. Francis Lee Utley has dealt in general terms with the relationship between linguistics and names,[1] with some suggestion of syntactic analysis – limited therein, however, primarily to such formulations as that regarding co-occurrence of articles with naming nouns. The present essay deals with a more specific naming problem, limited to what is regarded for these purposes as one specific community, and with a somewhat broader approach to syntactic analysis.

The community selected may be called a part of the Afro-American (in the Herskovitsian sense) community, although the discussion here is limited almost entirely to the Negro community within the United States. Although I believe that a wider discussion of naming practices within an Afro-American cultural group would be valuable, the paper will center on the names of store-front churches in the Negro community in the U.S. It is the belief here that these naming practices are a peripheral manifestation of the linguistic differences which have motivated Stewart[2] to write of the language of the "culturally disadvantaged Negroes of a lower socio-economic stratum" as a "quasi-foreign language." The differences between these church naming practices and those of standard English speaking communities is obvious to anyone looking over a list of names.[3] Naturally, ghetto naming practices are not characteristic of middle-class Negroes closer to the mainstream of American culture – and

[1] "The Linguistic Component of Onomastics," *Names*, XI (1963), 145–176.

[2] William A. Stewart, *Non-Standard Speech and the Teaching of English*, Center for Applied Linguistics (Washington, D.C., 1964).

[3] Excellent lists have been published by James B. Strong, "Chicago Store Front Churches: 1964," *Names*, XII (1964), 127–128; and R. S. Noreen, "Ghetto Worship: A Study of Chicago Store Front Churches," *Names*, XIII (1965), 19–38.

incidentally, speakers of standard American English. Obviously peripheral linguistic phenomena of Non-standard Negro English (NNE) are the result of orderly historical processes,[4] not of "distortion" of either language or naming practices by any presumptive ecological factors in the urban ghetto. Regrettably, but undeniably, the culturally and linguistically naive members of the mainstream culture tend to view such a list with amusement. Writers such as Octavus Roy Cohen[5] and the creators of the even less accurate Amos n' Andy comedy show[6] have given unfortunate emphases to such tendencies. Although distressing from the point of view of racial relations, there is a core of fact upon which they could build.

It is my belief that there is a causative analogy between the humorous reactions felt toward NNE naming practices and the "Spanglish" naming practices in Puerto Rico.[7] The primary difference is that the isolation and description of the interfering language is a much subtler and more difficult problem where NNE is concerned.

Using the native mainstream speaker's reaction as a kind of linguistic discovery device, we may begin analyzing names on the order of

SACRED HEART SPIRITUAL CHURCH OF JESUS CHRIST, INC.

---

[4] For a perceptive preliminary statement of the historical pattern indicated (creolization of a slave pidgin by field servants of slavery days, the ancestors in most cases of ghetto inhabitants, with subsequent decreolization in most areas except for Gullah territory), see W. A. Stewart, "Sociolinguistic Factors in the History of American Negro Dialects", *Florida FL Reporter*, V: 2 (Spring, 1967).

[5] See Inez Lopez Cohen, (Mrs. Octavus Roy Cohen), *Our Darktown Press* (New York, 1932).

[6] See, however, Marshall and Jean Stearns, "Frontiers of Humor: American Vernacular Dance," *Southern Folklore Quarterly*, XXX (1966), 227–235, an article in which there is more than a suggestion that white "blackface" comedy is based upon a genuine Negro comic tradition. The Kingfish and his wife Sapphire of the Amos n' Andy show seem, on this evidence, to be modeled upon Stringbean and Sweetie May or Butterbeans and Susie. The store front church names under discussion here are superficially similar to the *Mystic Knights of the Sea*, although a really good grammar of NNE naming practice would probably not generate that name. The Amos and Andy taxi cab company, *The Fresh Air Taxicab Company of America* " *Incorpulated*" is an approximately equal mixture of real and phony traditions. (Charles J. Correll and Freeman F. Gosden, *Here They Are . . . Amos 'n' Andy* [New York, 1931], p. 163.)

[7] See my articles in *Names*, XII (1964), 98–102; and XIV (1966), 178–180.

(This is a genuine name – some noted in Appendix A are even longer and more complex.) Length might be the first objective factor to be isolated as "different" in some way. In the more ordinary syntactic terms, there is nothing particularly unusual structurally. A singular noun preceded by modifiers and followed by a prepositional modifier is customary. *Inc.* may mark a somewhat unusual lexical item in this particular context, but it certainly occurs where *Inc.* would occur in any normal firm name, so that only in its occurrence in the church-naming field of discourse is it in any way unusual in English.

However, some of the same reactions are produced by the following names, without *Inc.*:

TRAVELING SOULS SPIRITUAL CHURCH
(Washington, D.C.)
THE TRUE TABERNACLE CHURCH OF THE FIRST
BORN (Washington, D.C.)
THE OLD SAMARITAN BAPTIST CHURCH
(Washington, D.C.)
THE TRUE LEE BAPTIST CHURCH (Dallas, Texas)

In order to cope with this problem in some kind of objective manner, a corpus of ghetto store front church names (Appendix A) from the Washington, D.C. area was selected and compared with 20 names (Appendix B) taken from traditional churches from the Washington metropolitan and surrounding areas, where the congregations are middle class, or mainly so, and mostly white. An attempt was made to study these names through a phrase structure analysis, primarily through the device of *branching*, right or left, with the word *church* (or *temple*, etc.) considered as head. This process involves simply selecting a noun as "head" – or nuclear component – by arbitrary if intuitively reasonable procedures and counting as "branching" structures any components which occur to the left or to the right. Conventionally, a prepositional phrase would be considered as one component, even though composed of three or four words; a one-word adjectival modifier of the head noun would also be considered as one component. It is, of course, possible to write more complicated "generative" formulas; but it hardly seems necessary in the course of this discussion.

For the store front churches, the left branching expansion was far more numerous. It was made of noun forms and other pre-modifiers of mainly the adjectival type, with the occurrence of other form classes not generally part of nominal structure in standard English. Concerning the number of pre-modifiers of the head, it can be seen that, where standard English tends to use not more than one to three pre-modifiers, store front churches generally use from three to five of them, e.g.,

CHESTER GRAHAM RESCUE MISSION
EAST FRIENDSHIP BAPTIST CHURCH
MOUNT SION CHRISTIAN SPIRITUAL CHURCH
MOUNT ZION UNITED HOLY CHURCH
NEW MOUNT NEBO BAPTIST CHURCH
THE OLD SAMARITAN BAPTIST CHURCH
FIRST RISING MOUNT ZION BAPTIST CHURCH

Where right branching is concerned, differences in usage from what is usual in Standard English are often to be found. These discrepancies are mainly of the type where the head of the nominal group is followed by two prepositional phrases, sometimes containing as many as nine words in post-modifiers like these two prepositional phrases. This is clearly observable in the following:

CANNANITE (sic) TEMPLE OF THE CHURCH OF GOD
CHURCH OF GOD OF TRUE HOLINESS
THE CHURCH OF GOD UNIVERSAL HOLINESS NO. 1
THE REFUGE CHURCH OF OUR LORD JESUS CHRIST
OF THE APOSTOLIC FAITH

It will be noted of course, that these examples are not without left branching as well. The most usual case, indeed, is multiple branching, which may be the chief source of the intuition that these practices are different from those of standard English. There are frequent nominal strings which not only offer from three to four pre-modifiers – with the inclusion even of verb forms – but also a post-modifier consisting of two prepositional phrases. Examples are

THE HOLY EVANGELISTIC CHURCH NO. 2 OF
NORTH AMERICA

THE SACRED HEART SPIRITUAL CHURCH OF
JESUS CHRIST, INC.
MOUNT CALVARY HOLINESS CHURCH OF
DELIVERANCE OF THE APOSTOLIC FAITH
BETHLEHEM FIRE BAPTIZE HOLINESS CHURCH
OF GOD OF THE AMERICANS

The "traditional" churches chosen for this comparison do have
much more simplified names (see Appendix B), than those of the
Negro store-front churches. It will be noted, particularly, that
right-branching is an uncommon device; where utilized, it consists
entirely of institutionalized sequences like *of the Latter-day Saints*
and *of Jehovah's Witnesses*. Although the traditional, predominantly
white middle class churches display both right and left-branching,
the former is quite limited. Multiple branching is almost nonexist-
ent, except where there are institutionalized forms on the right.

Noticeable differences are to be found in the number of pre-
modifiers of the head of the nominal group. In opposition to the
four and even five pre-modifiers of Negro store front churches, the
traditional ones do not appear to favor long strings of pre-modifiers.
Three appears to be the maximum in this limited comparative list,
with a frequency of usage of only one or two pre-modifiers being the
most common. Most modifiers tend to be limited to the institutionalized forms.

A facile assumption would be that the store front church naming
practice reflects a kind of exuberance of language – and, elsewhere
popular writers apply such terms as *exuberant*[8] to the Afro-American
dialects. After checking hundreds of city telephone books (including those from certain cities in the South where Baptist churches,
for example, are still listed under *Negro* and *White*), I am inclined
to believe that, insofar as *exuberant* has implications of "spontane-
ous improvisation", the truth may be a more pedestrianly grammatical one. Components like *Bethel (Church of XYZ)* recur very
frequently, modified into *New Bethel XYZ* and *Greater New Bethel
XYZ No. 2*, etc. As is the case with NNE in general, the components
do not differ from those of SE; it is the putting together, the syn-
tax, which differs. (A striking non-onomastic case is NNE *You been*

[8] Noreen, p. 19, writes of the "vitality and imagination expressed in the names
of these churches," compared to which "traditional church names of established,
sophisticated denominations are somber and colorless."

know that.) A few cases of deviational morphology (*Fire Baptize* in
store front names; *he brother* in the NNE of relatively early age
grades,[9]) call attention to themselves rather strikingly, yet their
complete implications are not apparent until they have been placed
in the total context. Admittedly this paper is only a halting first
step in that placing in context for store front church naming
practices. By implication, however, it would extend to other naming
practices.

An additional dimension in grammatical complexity is suggested
by a few names in Noreen's list

> THE LORD IS ABLE HOUSE OF PRAYER
> LOOK AND LIVE COMMUNITY CHURCH
> RISE AND SUN SPIRITUAL CHURCH

where the first, particularly, is grammatically unlike the names of
middle class churches. All three examples are apparently unembedded sentences, the last two being imperatives (not so unusual, admittedly, in Standard English naming practices as is the
first) and the last being perhaps an original *Rising Sun* which was
made to conform to the pattern. The use of the untransformed
sentence as a modifier is the feature which I wish to call attention
to, and hesitantly to compare to naming practices of the same type
in West Africa and in the Caribbean. These are vehicles, and the
head noun which would presumably be modified by the sentence is
usually not overtly expressed. It would be easy to supply *Bus,
Mammy Wagon, Voiture* or some other such name. Bus ("Mammy
Wagon") names from West Africa include

> People Will Talk of You[10]
> Love is Nice
> Life is War
> All Shall Pass[11]
> If It Must It Will[12]
> Rien n'est total dans la vie[13]

---

[9] Noreen, p. 26, cites *State Street Move of God Church*, where *Move* is apparently *mother* — reflecting a well-known and very widespread NNE dialect pronunciation.

[10] Jan Harold Brunvand, "A Note on Names for Cars," *Names*, X (1962), 279–284.

[11] N. T. Keeney, "The Winds of Freedom Stir a Continent," *National Geographic*, Vol. 118, No. 3 (Sept. 1960), 303–359. (Footnotes 12 and 13, see page 236)

even omitting the very frequent use of imperative sentences in such function. Equivalent unembedded sentences used in naming structures, again apparently without head noun, occur in Martiniquan canoe names

> Dieu Seul Sait
> Le Jour est Arrive
> Ç.A.Q.F.CA Ç. D. LAR D
> (Initial name, interpreted by owner as "Ça qui fait ça a cent dollars")[14]

Whether these naming patterns are to be explained as cultural survivals or in some other way, they provide interesting departures from "traditional" (European) naming practices.

APPENDIX A

The Bible Way Church of Our Lord Jesus Christ World Wide, Inc.
Bethel Commandment Church of the Living God
Bethlehem Fire Baptize Holiness Church of God of the Americans
Brookland Union Baptist Church
Brown Memorial AME Church
Cannanite (sic) Temple of the Church of God
Chester Graham Rescue Mission
Church of God of True Holiness
Deliverance Church of God in Son
Emmanuel Church of God in Christ
East Friendship Baptist Church
First Rising Mount Zion Baptist Church
Full Speed Gospel Church
Georgetown Psychic Healing Church
Gospel Union Church of Christ
Gospelite Full Gospel Church
Holy Mount Olives Church of Christ of the Apostolic Faith
International Constitutional Church Organitional
Marantha Gospel Hall
Montell Avenue Baptist Church
Mount Calvary Holiness Church of Deliverance of the Apostolic Faith
Mount Pleasant Baptist Church Inc.

---

[12] Langston Hughes, *An African Treasury* (New York, 1960).

[13] J. L. Dillard, *Afro-American and Other Vehicle Names*, Institute of Caribbean Studies, Special Study No. 1 (March 1965). Several other names of this type, primarily from Haiti, are included.

[14] Richard and Sally Price, "A Note on Canoe Names in Martinique," *Names*, XIV (1966), 160.

Mount Tabor Baptist Church
Mount Zion United Holy Church
New Bethel Baptist Church
New Mount Nebo Baptist Church
Old Way Baptist Church
Peoples Church
Royal Fellowship Center
Second Eureka Baptist Church
The Church of God Universal Holiness No. 1
The Full Gospel Baptist Church
The Holy Evangelistic Church No. 2 of North America
The Old Samaritan Baptist Church
The Refuge Church of Our Lord Jesus Christ of the Apostolic Faith
The Sacred Heart Spiritual Church of Jesus Christ, Inc.
True Baptist Church
United House of Prayer

APPENDIX B*

Foundry Methodist Church
Cathedral of Sts. Peter and Paul
St. Dunstan's Episcopal Church
St. Alban's Episcopal Church
Kingdom Hall of Jehovah's Witnesses
Washington Cathedral
Church of the Epiphany
Walker Methodist Church
St. Dominic's Church
The National Methodist Church
Metropolitan Memorial Methodist Church
Grace Lutheran Church
Epiphany Episcopal Church
St. John's Church
Trinity Episcopal Church
St. Agnes Catholic Church
St. Mary's Church
Immanuel Presbyterian Church
Langley Hill Meeting of the Religious Society of Friends

---

* Appendix B is shorter than Appendix A because of special conditions in the District of Columbia, which make it difficult to find "traditional" churches about which one can be certain that there is no mixture of store-front tradition. A few articles have appeared on names of "traditional" churches; e.g., Charles A. Ferguson, "Saints' Names in American Lutheran Church Dedications," *Names*, Vol. 14, No. 2 (June, 1966), pp. 76–82.

Yeshiva University